THE ULTIMATE GUIDE TO PRACTICAL NUMEROLOGY
Mapping Your Path & Purpose

THE ULTIMATE GUIDE TO PRACTICAL NUMEROLOGY
Mapping Your Path & Purpose

Felicia Bender, PhD

Copyright © 2022 by Felicia Bender - The Practical Numerologist. All rights reserved. Not part of this book may be reproduced by any mechanical, photographic, or electronic process, or in the form of a phonographic recording; or may it be stored in a retrieval system, transmitted, or otherwise be copied for public or private use—other than "fair use" as brief quotations embodied in articles and reviews—without prior written permission the publisher.

FAB Enterprises, Ltd.
Denver, Colorado

ISBN 978-0-9851682-7-8

Library of Congress Control Number: 2022904670

Interior Design: Hammad Khalid

Graphic Design: Latif Ullah

Cover Design: theBookDesigners

Photographer: Andrea Flanagan

1. Numerology 2. Self-help 3. Metaphysics 4. Life Coaching 5. Relationships

CONTENTS

Introduction 9
What Is Numerology, Anyway? 12
How Do I Start? 14
The Life Path Number 21
What If I Don't Identify With My Life Path Number? 23
Calculate The Life Path Number 28
  1 Life Path...33
  2 Life Path 51
  3 Life Path...69
  4 Life Path 90
  5 Life Path...110
  6 Life Path...133
  7 Life Path...151
  8 Life Path...168
  9 Life Path...187
  Master Numbers 207
  Master 11/2..212
  Master 22/4..219
  Master 33/6..226
  Numbers In A Nutshell...231
  The Expression Or Destiny Number.......................................238
  Calculate The Destiny Or Expression Number 240
  Destiny/Expression Calcuation 242
  Destiny/Expression Number Definitions................................245

The Soul Urge 259
Calculate The Soul Urge Number 262
Soul Urge Definitions 264
The Personality Number 284
Personality Number Definitions 288
The Birth Day Number 294
The Birth Day Number Definitions 297
Karmic Debt Numbers 306
Karmic Debt 19/1 310
Karmic Debt 13/4 314
Karmic Debt 14/5 317
Karmic Debt 16/7 320
The Maturity Number 325
Maturity Number Definitions 327
Your Numerology Profile As Your Life Script 334
Through Line Of Action . . . By Number 336
Mapping Your Numerology Life Script 337
Numerology & Cycles Of Time 339
Universal Year Themes 341
The Personal Year Cycle 343
1 Personal Year 347
  1 Personal Year By Life Path 350
2 Personal Year
  2 Personal Year By Life Path 356
11/2 Personal Year
  11/2 Personal Year By Life Path 360
3 Personal Year
  3 Personal Year By Life Path 368

4 Personal Year
    4 Personal Year By Life Path 377
22/4 Personal Year
    22/4 Personal Year By Life Path 380
5 Personal Year
    5 Personal Year By Life Path 389
6 Personal Year
    6 Personal Year By Life Path 398
7 Personal Year
    7 Personal Year By Life Path 407
8 Personal Year
    8 Personal Year By Life Path 416
9 Personal Year
    9 Personal Year By Life Path 425
How Do I Use My Personal Year Cycles? 434
The Pinnacle Cycle 438
Calculating Pinnacles 440
Calculate Your Age During Your Different Pinnacles 443
1 Pinnacle 448
2 Pinnacle 451
3 Pinnacle 455
4 Pinnacle 459
5 Pinnacle 463
6 Pinnacle 467
7 Pinnacle 471
8 Pinnacle 475
9 Pinnacle 479
Putting It Together 482
Challenge Numbers 487

1 Challenge 494

2 Challenge 496

3 Challenge 498

4 Challenge 500

5 Challenge 502

6 Challenge 504

7 Challenge 506

8 Challenge 508

0 Challenge: 511

Numerology & Relationships 513

Relationship Compatibility By Life Path 516

How To Continue To Use Numerology As A Tool In Your Everyday Life 544

3 Keys To Unlock Your Path & Purpose 546

Recommended Resources 552

About The Author 555

INTRODUCTION

Isn't it funny how life is—ultimately—a numbers game? *Do you know yours?* Numbers are everywhere and once you get a taste of how they operate on a vibrational plane, you'll most likely never look at numbers quite the same way again. Numerology is a fantastic tool to add to your self-actualization tool chest.

The art and science of numerology offers you tools to work with your inherent strengths, tendencies, and obstacles. Understanding numerology gives us a clear picture of not only our personality profile, it also provides information about cycles of time we experience and how to understand the lessons, opportunities, and challenges specific periods of time offer us. Rather than "personality profile," I choose to call the core numbers in your numerology chart your "*purpose* profile!"

In this book, I'm taking a practical, contemporary, and user-friendly approach to numerology. My goal is for you to have a comprehensive guide that you can come back to again and again to assist you with your real day-to-day life. This book is structured in a way that you can build on basic numerology knowledge and key concepts—and then have the ability to read, interpret, and understand your own basic numerology profile. With any grace, the way this is organized offers a simple way to see how your core numbers and key cycles of time offer you a rather astonishing amount of detailed information about why you're here and what to do about it!

I've decided to create this guide as just that—a *guide*. A lengthy guide, to be sure, yet a guide nonetheless. Believe me, I have personally scoured and studied every morsel of numerology I could find because that's just how much of a numerology geek I've become! Yet I realize that not everyone wants to become an expert numerologist, even though you might want to really dig into detail about what numerology can offer you across the board.

The point of this guide to practical numerology is to offer a systematic way to begin to look at the core numbers and core cycles in a numerology profile—and learn how to read and interpret it. If you want to dig into the intricacies and complexities numerology offers, please refer to the list of resources at the end of this book. I provide a list of books I have found useful in my study of numerology.

This book is designed to offer an in-depth exploration of the key components of a basic numerology profile. We're *not* going to learn about some elements of a numerology chart that you might delve into if you really want to get into more advanced areas of study. This is what I mean when I say that this book isn't going to teach you every element that the science of numerology offers. For example, this book does not include an explanation of the Planes of Expression, Transits, the Psycho-Matrix, Essence Cycles, or many other aspects of numerology.

My goal with this guide is to make it simple enough to actually use, yet complex enough to give you a depth and breadth of actionable knowledge.

Also know that there are aspects to numerology that can be more esoteric and "woo-woo." There are times where I'll bring in the "woo" and yet over-all my purpose is to offer you a way to build your own basic numerology profile for yourself and for others—and then make some sense out of it. My hope is that this information resonates with the first-time explorer of numerology as well as with the advanced spiritual seeker.

I'm focusing on how to use numerology to understand yourself and others better, to validate aspects of yourself (and others), highlight how to strengthen what you already do really well, and offer some suggestions on how to alter what might not be working for you. Or an even more empowering way to think about it is that the information numerology provides offers us some great pathways from which to embody and experience our purpose. Throughout the book I'll offer ideas, suggestions, and examples in hopes of offering ways to explore key concepts or issues that might show up with certain numbers.

I often get a response from people who are absolutely blown away by their numerology reading and yet then are left with the question: *Now what? What do I do with all this information?* I hope to offer a few "Now what?" suggestions along the way.

At the end of the book, I offer a section devoted to a conversation about numerology and relationships, because this is a topic that occupies a lot of intrigue for those interested in numerology. Understanding the numerology of relationships is key not only to our love lives. It's about *all of our relationships*—friends, family, colleagues, the works! It also holds a key to showing you how to align with a career that aligns with you. Numerology offers important intel that can be applied to identify your strengths and weak links, reveal the "highest-and-best" version of yourself, and define and validate your purpose-driven gifts and talents to serve the world on the highest level.

WHAT IS NUMEROLOGY, ANYWAY?

What *is* numerology?

For clarity, there are different kinds of numerology, just like there are different forms of astrology and different forms of any "olgy." I'm working with Pythagorean numerology and this is the type of numerology you'll learn in this book.

Numerology was developed around 530 b.c.e. by Pythagoras, a Greek mathematician, philosopher, and mystic—remember the Pythagorean Theorem of Geometry? *Same guy.* Pythagoras suggests that each number not only represents a quantity (for instance, one apple, two apples, and so on), it also carries a *vibration and a frequency* that has a particular meaning and influence.

Much like gravity or the mystery of cell phone reception, we don't have to understand how it affects us or even to believe in it for it to operate. It's rather like Morse Code. To the untrained, hearing the random dots and dashes of Morse Code just seems like random or garbled sounds. Yet to those trained in the language of Morse Code, the dots and dashes communicate very specific information. You just have to know the language to understand it.

It's the same with numerology. Once you learn the defining qualities of the numbers 1-9—along with some additional "code"—you can understand the message and information that the numbers carry with them whenever they show up.

I'm not a mathematician. It's a rather cruel cosmic joke that I'm hooked on numerology. The fact is: I despise math. Math has always been my most excruciating subject. I remember sitting on the bed when I was in grade school, my mother whipping multiplication flash cards in my face until I wept. I could never get a grasp on math and particularly couldn't understand any real practical ramifications of higher forms of math like Geometry, Calculus, Algebra, Trigonometry, or any other "ometry."

I mention this so that if you have any hesitancy about numbers or negative experience with math, so did I! For me to gravitate to numerology is quite a leap. Ultimately, I didn't find numerology—numerology found *me*. When I stumbled upon numerology, I was absolutely amazed at the accuracy and deep levels of information the numbers offer. I don't understand *how* it works. All I know is that it does work, every single time.

I have a Doctorate in Theatre and I'm a student of human behavior. I study behavior and emotions and I find that numerology offers a distinct way to explore, understand, and in some way categorize human behavior. Yet the difference between this and, say, psychotherapy, is that *all you need is your name and birthdate*. With this basic information, you can rapidly see what you intended to study and master in your life. You can truly reveal your purpose in life and uncover ways to understand it and *live* it!

And often this clicks with people on a soul level. It's as if the information numerology provides can see into your soul and expose aspects of yourself that are difficult, if not impossible, to discern through other forms of self-help. People turn—*and return*—to numerology for this reason. It feels as though a sacred contract is being revealed to you. You get to either rediscover or validate why you're here and what you signed up for—and see how you're bringing your own individual uniqueness to the mix.

HOW DO I START?

In order to calculate your basic numerology profile, the *original name as it appears on the birth certificate* and your *full date of birth* are used to create your chart.

Unlike astrology, we don't need the location of birth or the time of birth.

Numerologists believe that we come in with a particular numerological matrix that we chose prior to being born into this lifetime.

This book explores the *core components* of the numerology profile:

- Life Path (also called the Birth Path number)
- Expression (also called the Destiny number)
- Soul Urge (also called the Heart's Desire number)
- Birth Day number
- Personality number
- Maturity number

All of these numbers are the foundation for the overall personality profile. *Please know that there are different names for the same numbers.* I mention some of those along the way and yet not all of them. For instance, I have a habit of referring to the Expression or the Destiny number as Expression/Destiny number. This is a quirk I have. The reason I do this is because of all the numbers, this one seems to have a 50/50 way that numerologists refer to it—half call it the Expression number and half call it the Destiny number. Whereas the other numbers, I have chosen what I consider the most known or "popular" way to refer to the number. Again, this is my take on it. Other numerologists have different points of view. I'm simply sharing mine with you.

Then we'll delve into several numerology cycles:

- Universal Year
- Personal Year
- Pinnacles
- Challenges

There are other cycles and transits that can be examined with numerology, yet we'll focus on the cycles that I feel are the most foundational. The great thing about numerology is that it can give really great indicators about cycles of time we experience so that you can understand the themes in a way that offers the opportunity to work much more successfully during that period of time—if that time is now or in the future.

And you can review your past cycles and derive some great information about what you were learning and experiencing during that time. Often this allows for deeper understanding and can also allow for letting go and even forgiveness—of yourself and others—if there were difficulties or traumatic experiences.

Everyone experiences nine-year cycles (the Personal Year Cycle) that immerse us in different energies during different years. By knowing the numbers related to the years in your cycles, you can align more clearly with the energy of your year and also have a specific understanding of the obstacles that are bound to come into play.

Calculating your Pinnacle Cycle and identifying the challenges inherent within those cycles is not so much a predictive tool as a tool that offers support and guidance for decisions and actions. This tool can be used to map out a vision of your past and future and help you clarify the direction you're heading in life. Knowledge of the Pinnacles and Challenges is a platform upon which you can construct your life in a more conscious and meaningful way.

In this *Ultimate Guide to Practical Numerology*, we're going to focus on the basics, yet with some depth—with an effort to delve into the core elements of a numerology chart. *Understand that different numerologists have specific schools of thought about how to (and how not to!) enter into each numerological calculation.* I have attempted to provide the basic options available to you. It's my goal to synthesize disparate trains of thought and give you the opportunity to decide for yourself what you feel is the most accurate way to come up with the numbers.

I also understand that this can feel somewhat confusing, if not overwhelming. Yet this is the way it is with everything in life, right? Every subject has different points of view and different angles to sift through, and we must make personal determinations about how to work with it. While many of you are interested enough in numerology to learn how to do calculations manually, many of you will simply use a numerology calculator or a software program to do it for you. Therefore, this book is a resource mainly for definitions, interpretations, and how you might apply the knowledge to a numerology profile. Yet we'll also go through the calculation process as well.

Understand that there are ways to represent the chart that are quite technical (see Hans Decoz at decoz.com for just one example) and yet my goal is to leave you with a manageable way to use numerology to understand your own basic numerology chart and perhaps give you the tools to create and interpret a simple chart for someone else—without having to spend the time and bandwidth to become a professional numerologist.

In my own practice, I often find that *less is more*. Shoving an avalanche of material and information in front of someone is over-whelming and paralyzing. I want to *empower* you to use numerology—not give you brain-freeze and make you run away screaming. We'll focus on the overall basics that might comprise a chart, depending on your personal style and emphasis. I trust that when you're done with this book, you can have a firm grasp on how to interpret your core numerology profile and will also be jazzed enough about numerology to begin to read the numbers for other people in your world.

I also want to point out that we'll constantly be working with the optimal qualities that the numbers bring with them and then we'll get to see how we might manage the difficulties. Understand that when we talk about possible careers, for example, what I might list here is not a full list of careers that are suitable to you! It's impossible to give every option. Yet my focus is to give you a really good idea about gifts, talents—and most importantly—*the underlying reason and motivation* for a particular career as it pertains to your numerology.

Sometimes you can be a cashier, a garbage collector, or work at any other job or career and be happy and satisfied if the underlying emotional needs are being met either with the job or outside of your job life. I use this as an example so that we can have an understanding at the get-go that you'll get the most out of this book when you can understand the basic components of the numbers and then learn to apply it to each individual situation or circumstance. As you continue to work with the numbers, you'll come up with your own way to apply and interpret a chart—like coming to the dance floor with your own interpretive dance!

I'll also talk about certain things that might push some buttons. For instance, there are times when I'll mention addictions as they show up with certain numbers. To be clear, I feel that we can't be human without having some form of addiction—whether it's drugs and alcohol, or overwork and too much exercise (yes, there is such a thing!). Or even addiction to negative thinking patterns. Yet numbers in numerology have certain leanings or propensities. What I want to stress here is that part of practicing and honing your knowledge and expertise with numerology is being able to *apply* the knowledge to illuminate how it might show up for each individual.

And what I adore about numerology itself is that it's beautifully non-judgmental and non-critical. It simply and—with neutrality—outlines optimal qualities that each number brings to the table and then also highlights the opposing forces that accompany each as well. Because whatever themes or key-words the number brings with it become your *thing*, it'll also mean that it's your *issue!* I figure you'd rather I'd be direct than indirect, and so I'll opt for laying it on the line. Strangely enough, many people actually get more out of knowing the destructive tendencies, challenges, and obstacles in their chart than they get out of knowing the optimal aspects of their numbers.

I would add that I feel that practicing numerology or any other esoteric art is a privilege and what I might consider to be a sacred honor. While there are times when it can be handled almost as a "party game," remember that there is great power here and misusing it isn't to your benefit, *ever*. I've had clients come to me with story after story about a "bad" psychic reading or a numerologist who demolished them with a negative reading. I had a 2 Life Path client who was told by a numerologist that she could never make money because of her numbers. It was devastating to her. And moreover, it's not true! Understand that your words and how you relay the information numerology provides contains a lot of impact, more than you might understand.

As a practitioner of a spiritual message, it's in the best interest of your client (or friend or family member) to present it as positively as possible. We all know that we respond best to positive reinforcement rather than harsh criticism. Keep this in mind if you decide to become a translator or interpreter of the numbers for others.

The key component is to have some fun with it and remain curious and open to your own process of understanding and applying the information. You'll have a unique way of going about looking at how the numbers work together (and how they challenge each other!) in any given chart. Understand also that it doesn't take psychic ability or healing ability to become a highly skilled numerologist. I'll promise you, though, that the more you work with the numbers, the more tapped in and in tune you'll become with your own intuitive language. This can be a huge service to you and to those you might work with as you become more intuitively connected with the best and most effective ways to deliver the information.

I've found myself saying words or phrases to someone that I never say. Yet as it comes out of my mouth, the client will say: "Oh my God! That's exactly what my mother used to say to me when I was feeling overwhelmed." Or whatever the connection might be for them. I've brought up songs, movies, and other cultural references with a client, again having no clue why it came to mind or came out of my mouth. And it always holds a message that I don't need to understand.

When you practice the art and science of numerology, it can become an integral part of how you start viewing the world and the people inhabiting it. It'll expand your perspective about life, about why we're here, and about how to act on your life's purpose. Knowing your own numerology and the numerology of those close to you has the potential to help you step back and see that everyone in your life is living their own life experience. You may be a part of it, but certainly you're not *it*. This alone can be such a relief and offers you an avenue to practice healthy emotional detachment that will benefit both you and those with whom you engage.

And you'll discover pretty quickly that we make things much too hard on ourselves. The purpose of one's life is never that one shining moment. If you think about it, it's not the Oscar you won, the billion-dollar business you started, or how many books you wrote. Certainly, those huge accomplishments are a part of your feelings of satisfaction and of acting on your sense of purpose.

Yet life consists of the small, consistent, everyday things—the responses, the actions, the attitude, the choices. The relationships. My yoga teacher shared a statement that resonates here. He said: "When you're off track, it's supposed to feel bad." Numerology offers an amazing gauge for defining ways that we might be off-track and also holds out even more ways to create alignment and clarity. It'll never be *easy*. Yet the approach can be *simple*.

Life Path

This is your ULTIMATE DESTINATION as you begin to map your PATH & PURPOSE.

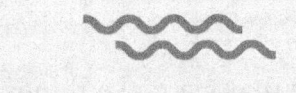

This is what you checked in to learn, master, grow into, and evolve toward.

Focus on the KEY THEMES your Life Path number reveals to you in order to stay on course!

THE LIFE PATH NUMBER

The Life Path number is calculated from your birth date. It's like the sun sign in astrology. In numerology, we work with the numbers 1-9. The zero comes into play at times and yet it's not necessary to work with the zero right now.

The Life Path number is a key to understanding your life's purpose, innate tendencies and talents, and the obstacles you'll face as you continue to master the lessons to be learned.

The Life Path number indicates the primary mission in life—it outlines what you're learning, mastering, and evolving into. While you'll have innate gifts and talents in this particular arena, you'll also have more distinct or heightened obstacles in getting there. As I said before, your *thing* is also always going to simultaneously be your biggest *issue*.

That's why it's called your Life Path—it takes a lifetime to learn and master the purpose you've checked in to live. It's not just a weekend workshop. It takes time, experience, and levels of mastery to get there—and a lot of repetition!

In addition, we'll discuss Master Numbers 11/2, 22/4 and 33/6. I've written an entire book on the Master numbers, so if this is something you want to really dive into with much more depth and detail, take a look at *Master Numbers 11, 22, 33: The Ultimate Guide*. Also understand that having a Master number in your chart isn't better or worse than having a "regular" number. In fact, if your numerology profile includes a Master number, it means you have intensified obstacles—as well as heightened potential—in your life. One number is never *better* than any other.

I often observe that when I teach workshops that some people seem disappointed if they don't have a Master number—and somewhat envious of those who do. Be careful what you wish for, as many times those with Master numbers experience more bumps and bruises along the way.

Keep in mind that numerology offers information about how to establish and maintain some level of harmony between the *constructive* and *destructive* aspects of your number. You could also call these aspects "positive/negative" or "under-active/over-active." Your Life Path number paints a picture of what's possible when you embrace and understand your core mission. And remember that we're also constantly being challenged with the oppositional qualities of the number. You might think of the challenges as *the opposing forces*.

WHAT IF I DON'T IDENTIFY WITH MY LIFE PATH NUMBER?

You might take a look at the description of your Life Path number and question it because you don't feel it describes you accurately. Or perhaps you look at the Life Path number of your ex, your family member, or even your child and have trouble seeing certain traits or attributes that the Life Path number is *supposed to be* about. In fact, you could feel that you're the opposite of what your Life Path number says about you or them.

Let's say, for instance, that yours is a 3 Life Path. A 3 Life Path is all about communication and emotional self-expression. But you're scared to death to speak in front of people and feel rather detached emotionally—not very 3-like. You'll perhaps say that the number can't be right.

I had a woman in a workshop one time (a 3!) who was quite irritated, if not angry. She raised her hand and blurted out: "This doesn't describe me *at all*." I could tell she was upset and ruminating. After a break and toward the end of the workshop, we were all having a discussion about how the numbers resonated with us. When it was her turn, she paused for a while and fought back tears. Then she said: "Wow. I've really been hiding out." I use this example because sometimes we're truly ensconced in the default settings of our Life Path.

I'll often work with 8 Life Path's who argue that they can't possibly be an 8 because they don't care about money—*which is often a symptom of working with the number 8*. Many times 4 Life Path's strongly dislike structure, have a terrible time embracing the need for stability, and are incredibly disorganized. Often a 2 Life Path struggles to find the right relationship and has a very limited amount of patience. These are just a few examples of how to begin to work with the glitches and levels of resistance as they might show up when working with the numbers.

In cases like this, a person is experiencing the flip-side of the Life Path purpose. This indicates that you're probably engaging with the challenging aspects of the Life Path number much more consistently than with the constructive aspects. Remember, whenever a number shows up, we're being presented with both the optimal qualities *and* the oppositional qualities. It's a good idea to set up your thinking at the get-go to look at each number and know what the optimal qualities are and then understand that there will be a strong pull toward the opposite aspects as well.

Because people often experience both the constructive and destructive aspects of their Life Path numbers, we'll focus both on what it looks and feel likes when you're working with the most constructive elements of your number—and then we'll also focus on what you look and feel like when the default mechanisms of the destructive aspects come up.

Also understand this very important concept. Your chart is made up of several numbers. We can learn how to put these numbers together almost like puzzle pieces in a puzzle. Knowing one number by itself—even your Life Path number—only gives you a partial picture of your over-all trajectory from a numerological perspective. It's crucial to know the other key numbers in your chart in order for everything to make sense. That's why I'm setting this up to start with the foundations that each number brings to the table with the Life Path number. Then we'll be building a fuller picture from there by defining and discussing all of your core numbers and investigating how they work together.

For instance, let's say your friend is a 5 Life Path and yet for the life of you, it just doesn't fit her. She's not all that outgoing, she has little streaks of adventure yet nothing consistent, and she's been happily married since she was twenty-two years old. Then you discover by looking at her full chart that her Destiny/Expression number is a 2, her Soul Urge is a 2, and her Birth Day number is a 6—all more home-based vibes. Yet her Life Path—what she's checked in to *learn and embody*—is the sensuous, adventurous, fearless 5.

You can start to learn how to read people's charts as you gain more experience with the numbers. In this case, your friend most likely presents with more number 2 elements and so perceiving her as a freedom-loving 5 Life Path is a reach. Yet when you can then see that while she has more 2 energy in her chart, *she's being prodded to step into her more adventurous 5 Life Path*. And then you realize that she and her family travel to exotic destinations every chance they get and that your friend *does* fit the rather fun, gregarious energy of the 5 Life Path, even though she's very much family oriented. Remember: *The Life Path number is what we're learning, mastering, and evolving into.* It'll have some more substantial challenges and roadblocks along the way.

As you gain more knowledge and practice with numerology, the more you'll be able to see the nuances and intuit how it all comes together. Sometimes a person's chart will flow with numbers that are basically in alignment with each other. Sometimes a person's chart will sputter with incongruent number combinations. Sometimes a person's chart is full of Master numbers and Karmic Debt numbers—sometimes not. It's imperative to learn how it all works together to form a person's overall purpose profile. And then knowing a person's cycles allows you to understand context with much more depth.

I'll also mention this simple truth. Sometimes it's very difficult (if not impossible) to actually see the more challenging or destructive elements we might be personally engaged with. How others observe you and how you observe yourself are often two very different things!

Let's face it, we've spent a lot of time operating a certain way and to see that we actually have options is a difficult stretch for many of us. I'll emphasize this one more time: Always remember that we are often pulled toward the opposite of the optimal quality of the number.

For instance, just a few possible scenarios:

- 1 Life Path—instead of leading, we follow (and hate it)
- 2 Life Path—instead of being cooperative, we're combative (and wonder why we aren't well liked)
- 3 Life Path—instead of enjoying the spotlight, we would rather die than present in front of an audience (and yet we're always being pulled toward that venue)
- 4 Life Path—instead of committing to a stable living situation, we continue to wander from place to place or job to job (and can't grasp why we're frustrated or depressed)
- 5 Life Path—instead of being a fearless adventurer, we are overly fearful (and wish we weren't)
- 6 Life Path—instead of nurturing friends and family, we're highly critical and judgmental about them (and can't understand why that doesn't work)
- 7 Life Path—instead of investigating spirituality, we operate on a superficial realm (and wonder why we feel so empty)
- 8 Life Path—instead of taking charge of our financial life, we blame everyone else for our failures (even though we realize we missed opportunities by not empowering ourselves)
- 9 Life Path—instead of involving ourselves in humanitarian or charitable service of some kind, we separate ourselves from others (and feel lonely and unfulfilled)

These are just a few examples of how the oppositional energies for each number can show up.

While it's a constant challenge and negotiation to harmonize the disparate energies indicated in your numerology chart, you'll be guided toward making the balanced decisions by *keying in to how you feel*. When you feel off, you're making choices that are off. When you feel good, empowered, and on target, you're making choices that are in alignment with your path and purpose. How you feel is the most reliable measure of your state of being at any given time.

Certain elements speak to people at different times in their lives, particularly given our age. If you're in the early stages of your life, you'll experience the information differently than you will in the middle or later stages of your life.

One of the most basic and beautiful benefits you might glean from numerology is the simple fact that everyone doesn't think like you, behave like you, treasure the same values as you do, or even see the world at all the way that you do. When we can really *get* this, we can let go of a lot of frustration, anger, and wasted energy trying to herd everyone over into our own camp. The world not only revolves in spite of all this, it revolves and evolves because of it.

CALCULATE THE LIFE PATH NUMBER

To calculate the Life Path Number, simply add the numbers of your birth date together.

In numerology, we always reduce to a single-digit number.

If there is a double-digit number at the end of your first calculation, it's an intermediate number.

Do another step of calculation that leads you to a single-digit number.

There are a few different ways to determine the Life Path number.

I've been taught that the most accurate way to calculate is by segmenting the month, day, and year of birth and then adding those numbers together.

Example: June 18, 1990

6/18/1990

June = 6 (June is the 6th month of the year)

Day = 18; 1 + 8 = 9

Year = 1990; 1 + 9 + 9 + 0 = 19

Keep adding since we get a 2-digit number here: 19 = 1 + 9 = 10

Keep adding since we get a 2-digit number here: 10 = 1 + 0 = 1

Now add the month, day, and year together like this:

6 + 9 + 1 = 16

Keep adding since we get a 2-digit number here: 16 = 1 + 6 = 7

The person in this example has a 7 Life Path

Other numerologists determine the Life Path number by adding the month/day/year together like one long addition problem.

June 18, 1990

6 + 1 + 8 + 1 + 9 + 9 + 0 = 34

34 = 3 + 4 = 7

You'll see as you get more into numerology that the sequence of numbers you get prior to reducing to a one-digit number makes a difference.

In this example, the first way of adding reveals a Karmic Debt number 16/7—which you'll learn about later in this book.

The second way of adding reveals a different combination of numbers—the 3 and 4. That combination would influence how you might understand this person's 7 Life Path with more depth and specificity (see Dan Millman's *The Life You Were Born To Live*).

For the final number to be accurate, you must use all of the digits from the year of your birth. You can't use 6/18/90, for instance, since that's missing 19 (for the century) and skews the results.

If your Life Path number is a 2, 4, or 6, you'll need to do additional calculations to determine if your Life Path number contains one of the Master numbers: 11, 22, or 33. These are double-digit numbers that show up in the first round of your addition process.

Master Number Example:

Birth Date: December 3, 1960

12/3/1960

Month: 12 = 1 + 2 = 3

Day: 3

Year: 1 + 9 + 6 + 0 = 16; 1 + 6 = 7

3 + 3 + 7 = 13; 1 + 3 = 4 or Karmic Debt 13/4

Another way to do the calculation is by adding all the numbers of the birth date together like one long addition math problem.

1 + 2 + 3 + 1 + 9 + 6 + 0 = 22

22 is a Master number (remember the Master numbers are the repeating double digits 11, 22, 33).

Some numerologists never reduce a Master number to its one-digit sum, while others do reduce it while also indicating that it's a Master number.

2 + 2 = 4

It's often written like this: 22/4

Also note that if you get a 10, 20, 30 you continue to add until you get that 1-digit number (so 10 = 1 + 0 = 1; 20 = 2 + 0 = 2; 30 = 3 + 0 = 3).

The Life Path reference guide that follows describes the defining qualities of the numbers 1 - 9, as well as of the Master numbers 11/2, 22/4, and 33/6.

Please keep this important idea in mind as you begin.

While we're focusing in the beginning on the Life Path number so that we can really hit the ground running, know that when you familiarize yourself with the defining qualities of all the numbers you'll begin to learn how to "plug them in" whenever and where ever they show up. And while it's tempting to only focus on your own number, your whole chart will most likely have other numbers present and so it's important to see what resonates with you and associate yourself with the basic elements of all the numbers.

Even if you don't have a certain number in your chart, you'll experience the influence of every number throughout your life through your Personal Year Cycles, if nothing else.

Also note: As I write each section for the Life Path numbers, I purposefully volley from referring to "you" and then also referring to the number itself or the number as "it." The reason for doing so is to encompass (as much as I possibly can) how the number shows up in various ways. Like I said, as you read for the Life Path numbers, know that the characteristics and key concepts apply whenever this number shows up. I refer to *you* if you're traversing the Life Path, yet also you can read with someone else in mind and also just for the overall themes and energies each number brings to the table. Just know that this is a style of expressing the information that I'm aware of and that has been consciously chosen.

1

How to Calculate Your Life Path Number?

Use your Date of Birth "November 23, 1992" Add Your Month + Day + Year

November = 11
23 = 2 + 3 = 5;
1992 = 1 + 9 + 9 + 2 = 21;
2 + 1 = 3;
11 + 5 + 3 = 19 and 1 + 9 = 10;
1 + 0 = 1
(11 is a master number and isn't reduced)

KEY THEMES

- Creativity / Self Confidence
- Following your "Weird"
- Leadership / Independence
- Individuation
- Risk-Taking Innovation
- Courage

CORE LESSONS AND CHALLENGES

- Can be self-centered
- Lack of self-confidence
- Judgmental and cynical
- Fear of failure
- Can't see others' point of view

YOUR POWER

- Innovation and master problem-solver
- Incredibly independent
- Effective and powerful leader
- Creative and forward-thinking
- Beautifully confident

The 1 Life Path tests your ability to fall down and pick yourself up again! It's the School of Hard Knocks... You can do it!

YOUR MISSION STATEMENT

To develop creativity and self-confidence without becoming too self-focused.

SOME FITTING CAREERS

- Entrepreneur
- Politician
- Lawyer
- Creative
- Artist
- Athlete

RELATIONSHIP COMPATIBILITY

- 1 AND 1 = LEADERSHIP & LEADERSHIP
- 1 AND 2 = LEADERSHIP & HEART
- 1 AND 3 = LEADERSHIP & CREATIVE EXPRESSION
- 1 AND 4 = LEADERSHIP & SECURITY
- 1 AND 5 = LEADERSHIP & FREEDOM-SEEKING
- 1 AND 6 = LEADERSHIP & NURTURING
- 1 AND 7 = LEADERSHIP & SPIRITUALITY
- 1 AND 8 = LEADERSHIP & POWER
- 1 AND 9 = LEADERSHIP & COMPASSION

WELL-KNOWN 1s

- Miley Cyrus (November 23, 1992)
- Lady Gaga (March 28, 1986)
- Steve Jobs (February 24, 1955)
- Bradley Cooper (January 5, 1975)

1 LIFE PATH

THE INNOVATIVE LEADER

Believe in yourself and all that you are. Know that there is something inside of you that is greater than any obstacle.

— Christian D. Larson

OPTIMAL EXPRESSION

A 1 Life Path's optimal expression is boldness, innovation, risk-taking, resilience, and following the inner voice.

Your personal mission is to develop creativity and confidence in every aspect of your life.

Your life purpose is to bring positive creative energy into the world and to achieve independence even as you relate—and are in relationship—with others.

INDEPENDENCE

A born leader and innovator, the 1 is self-motivated, independent, and a diligent worker. If ever there was a born individualist, it's you! You thrive in a competitive environment, although you're also hypersensitive to criticism. The 1 Life Path often has a bit of a thinner skin than they let on, usually offering a more confident or perhaps belligerent "I don't care what anyone thinks about me" façade.

The 1 Life Path engages in three specific stages of development: *dependency, rebellion,* and *actualization*. You're meant to learn healthy independence, therefore often find yourself—particularly early on—in situations where you feel very much *dependent*.

This can be in early family situations where perhaps your family has a certain religious belief that you don't feel fits for you. Or perhaps the family status isn't "you"—meaning your family is wealthy and you question the values inherent in that. Or your family struggles with money and that doesn't fit for you either. These are just a few examples of how this might manifest.

Your sense of dependence can be anything that feels that you're being asked to fit in and be defined by it, and yet down deep you know that it *isn't you*. It can take a while for you to understand and define what it is that's blocking your sense of self and your sense of independence.

The second tier of development is the *rebellion* stage. Once you decide that you want to break free of this dependence, then you revolt. Often this too takes a while to learn a healthy and empowering way to differentiate yourself. This can express with some semblance of self-destruction—"How many piercings do I need to really tell the world I'm *not* a Smith?"—or how many different drugs can I experiment with to opt out of this world that doesn't understand me? Or how long can I avoid taking responsibility for my life by not focusing on something productive or developing a career? What am I gaining by pushing up against everything all the time, just out of obstinance or just to assert my Will? Often the 1 pushes back against anything and everything, yet not to its ultimate benefit.

Or alternately, this is when you *want* to rebel and can't find the courage and so you instead choose to diminish yourself—and that's when the patterns of frustration and anger can begin to find their way into the life of the 1.

The third tier of development shows up after you've *done your work*, as they say. This level comes to you when you've identified where you feel dependent and have extracted yourself from that in a way that is both realistic, healthy, and productive.

I think about the 1 Life Path as either the president of student counsel, captain of the football team, or the lead on the debate team—the one who's *large and in charge* and taking on leadership roles early on. Or alternately (and more likely), the 1 Life Path is the Goth kid who's rebellious, non-conforming, and anti-authority—despite the fact that in order to be a Goth, you have to follow a strict dress and attitude code in order to fit into that group! The 1 Life Path grapples with a strong sense of wanting to belong and to be seen as different, unique, and special—mixed with a heightened need for approval and admiration.

INDIVIDUALIST

As an individualist, you've most likely felt unique in many ways. When you're feeling insecure, you feel you just don't fit in or belong anywhere—as though you're really out of synch with the demands and expectations of the world. When you're being authentic and true to yourself, you're the kindest, most trustworthy, compassionate, and compelling individual.

When you aren't feeling confident or when you feel you're being told what to do, how to act, what to believe, or who to be—then you may tend to be pushy, defensive, aggressive, or angry. Those emotions can be your chosen outlets when you're having self-doubts and when confidence is lacking. It's crucial to work on honing your skill at anything you do, whether your job skills, communication skills, or relationship skills. Reaching a level of expertise instills you with a reliable sense of self-confidence—with self-confidence being on ongoing life-long theme for the 1 Life Path.

As a 1 Life Path, having complete trust in the skills you've learned and mastered will serve as a kind of security blanket when you're feeling insecure or your sense of confidence is under fire. Having the ability to fall back on high-level skills you know from the inside out will stabilize you and get you back in your game.

You need to understand that you're not meant to follow the crowd—on the contrary. You're the one who's the "odd duck." The sooner you can *embrace your weird* the better off you'll be. You'll never fit into the mold. Usually, you'd rather die than become the suit-wearing time-clock puncher. Your gift is to believe in your ideas, galvanize your plans, and take strategic and calculate risks. Understand that your fail-rate will be higher than most, yet that's because you'll be trying more and risking more on a much more consistent basis than most people try in an entire lifetime.

INNOVATOR & ACHIEVER

You're a pioneer, an innovator, and capable of great success and achievement in the world. In fact, it's your birthright to be "the achiever." You need to be in charge and managing in some way. You make a great entrepreneur or inventor. Often the highest and best use of your abilities is when you mastermind a project, get it up and running, make sure management systems are in place, and then you're off to the next venture. You might feel stagnant, bored, or under-utilized if you don't allow yourself to tackle new challenges.

You're full of creative energy, so embrace your creativity and understand that this is your gift. Imagine new things, introduce new concepts, and then delegate the details and either move on with another project or continue developing your enterprise while taking it to the next level of success.

However you define it, you enjoy being on the move and having a variety of things to do. The key comes with confidence, preparation, and focus. The 1 can default into the low-level administrative assistant or be the college drop-out—or you can take yourself seriously enough to train well, educate properly, and expand your horizons. And when I say educate properly, that doesn't necessarily mean through *traditional* education. It means to learn by doing, accept constructive criticism, and to seek out information.

I always share this story to illustrate the illustrious incongruency that often follows the 1 Life Path. A friend of mine was a kid growing up in 1950s Chicago where his father owned a tavern. He told this story of a man who frequented the bar and was quite a character. He asked my friend (who was just a boy at the time): "So, my question is this. When you go to Wrigley Field to watch a baseball game, what do you really want? You've got your beer, you've got your hotdog. It's a hot day, you're sittin' in the sun. Whaddya' want? *Just plain water!*" This man (I know in my heart he was a 1 Life Path!) invested every cent he had in producing bottled water. I think he even named the brand "Just Plain Water." In the 1950s! And guess what? He lost his shirt—and probably also lost his house and his wife. He was 20-years ahead of his time. Bottled water didn't become popular until the 1970s. He was an entrepreneurial visionary, yet in true 1 Life Path form, just too far ahead of his time. My friend said that the man always sat at the bar and would tell the story to anyone who would listen to it (and buy him a drink!).

The 1 Life Path is built to create things—whether it's new ideas, products, or services. You strive to be #1 at all you do and can use your innate competitive spirit to move yourself and your ideas forward into reality. Just know that you'll experience set-backs, missteps, and downright failures along the way.

LEADERSHIP

Anything that calls for tapping into your unique voice, independent action, and decision-making is your forté. You're being asked to develop your sense of risk and embrace a particular level of uncertainty in life. When you're secure in your abilities and have confidence, you're dynamic and let's face it, irresistible!

As you develop your leadership skills, nurture the best in others and understand that creativity flourishes in an atmosphere of inner security and confidence—meaning you must open up, take risks, and step off the beaten path. Your constant challenge is to consistently and consciously develop your sense of being self-assured, self-directed, and centered *while also taking the needs of others into consideration.* When you express your passion from the heart—and not just the head or through your ego—you can achieve great things in the world.

Be careful of succumbing to feelings of superiority, judgment, and criticism. The 1 is most effective when working directly with people and keying into their innate gifts and strengths. You're at your highest and best use when you accept or develop leadership roles, whether at work, family, or with hobbies and other social outlets.

While you may not perform in a leadership role at work, for example, you can move that creative energy into proper use as the President of the YMCA Fundraiser or founder of your own product you sell on-line. You're here to forge a path and use your (metaphorical) machete to clear the path.

SCHOOL OF HARD KNOCKS

The 1 Life Path rivals the 8 Life Path in the School of Hard Knocks. Think about it. If you're meant to be a pioneer, inventor, entrepreneur—or whatever other aspect of life that taps into and uses your creativity and revolutionary ideas—then certainly you will undergo more false starts that most people.

You're not meant to play it safe or color within the lines. So why would you think that you'll be met with open arms, rousing acceptance, and consistent approval? Nope. Impossible. Even though you innately know this, you also have an internal soft spot for acknowledgement, approval, and crave "Rah-Rah's" in life, both in your career and in your personal life.

There's a lot written about "failing forward" and this concept can certainly be your mantra. In an interview, musical artist Pitbull stated: "I don't understand the word *lose*. I only understand the word *learn*. There's no failure, only opportunities. And there are no problems, only solutions. So to me, failure is the mother of all success."

Wise words—and words to live by—when you're traveling the 1 Life Path. When you understand at the get-go that yours isn't necessarily the "easy" route—for instance, say, you're training to be a boxer, not a florist. Your training is more intense, it's physical and psychological, and you'll come home with some blood and broken bones—if not a concussion or two. Your life's work isn't linear or safe. The 1 falls down and gets back up again, taking the lessons gleaned from the fall into the next experience in order to derive successful results.

1 LIFE PATH & RELATIONSHIPS

In relationship, the 1 Life Path wants to be in charge. You're the leader, so you need followers. You're not the best at sharing power and control. You can often mistake the creation of a healthy love relationship when you feel you're giving someone "their share" of power. Yet this is often defined by you and controlled by you.

Often the 1 Life Path attracts partners who are more like students. Yet when the student absorbs all that you have to give, then the relationship disintegrates. While you're a powerful presence, often you choose partners who aren't your equal. Only when you attract and choose someone who's your equal intellectually, financially, and spiritually will you maintain and thrive in relationship. And that takes learning to dig into your self-confidence while keeping ego at bay, learning to modulate power in the relationship, and learning to connect with and understand the needs of someone else. You need a cheerleader in life and yet cheerleading can turn to empty accolades when pushed to its limit.

Since you're here to learn about independence and individuality, often the 1 Life Path struggles with a strong sense of self-centeredness making it hard to understand what a balanced relationship might look or feel like. The 1 Life Path benefits by coming to the table ready, willing, and able to co-create a balanced relationship, forgoing the need for absolute control for the balance of mutual respect, and a modulation of control within the relationship.

If you are—*or are involved with*—a 1 Life Path, they need praise and positive reinforcement. The 1 needs to be allowed plenty of processing and thinking time—just in general, yet also for dealing with relationship matters.

The 1 can have a short fuse and so need to be aware of their need to control impulsive anger. The 1 Life Path is a creative person and needs to be encouraged to follow their own unique pathway. They thrive when supported and yet encouraged to dig in and gain the skill level and stick-to-it-ness to realize their potential. Be aware that the 1 can have a temper and—*in the extreme*—can display narcissistic tendencies. The 1 can have issues with co-dependency.

1 LIFE PATH & CAREER

The key to revealing your best career choice is to answer this question: What are you totally passionate about? With a 1 Life Path, it's not so much what you do, it's how you do it. It's much more about believing in yourself in terms of what you're passionate about—not what other people think you should be doing.

When you've figured this out, dive in with gusto and trust your creativity, innovation, and uniqueness. Your success resides in taking some risks and trusting your unique voice. The 1 Life Path needs to master and develop foundational skills in order to have success, so don't shy away from hard work and honing your skillset. Get out there, take charge, and don't be a slacker.

It's likely that your entrepreneurial skills will develop as you do. You'll have failures so you must learn to fail forward. You're an innovator and a pioneer. You're being called upon to balance your sense of self-confidence while strengthening your knowledge base. When in doubt, always take action rather than hover with indecision.

You're here to act upon your creative ideas and to be a leader, innovator, and courageous pioneer. Any field that you have a personal interest or passion about is perfect. You'll automatically strive to reach the top if you're having fun and feel as though you're in charge.

A few possibilities:

- Business with an emphasis on innovation, invention, and entrepreneurship
- Leading through teaching as a coach, professor, principal or trainer
- Any competitive sport as an athlete, broadcaster, TV announcer
- Medicine as a physician, researcher or in sales
- Entertainment as a musician, actor, promoter, producer, agent, or manager
- Politics as a politician or manager for a campaign
- The law as a judge or attorney
- The fashion industry as a designer
- You thrive with creative endeavors and can do well with off-the-beaten-track careers—like a location scout, industrial psychologist, stunt person, or sommelier
- The Military
- Aviation as a pilot
- Restauranteur as the owner or head chef
- Real Estate as an agent, developer, or designer
- Any business where you develop and market your own concept—whether it's a product, service, or idea
- Sales

1 LIFE PATH
Opposing Forces

LACK OF SELF-CONFIDENCE

One of the major obstacles to achievement for the 1 Life Path is a deep sense of self-doubt and crippling lack of self-esteem. You're often sidetracked by listening to the non-stop voice of criticism in your head, whispering incessantly: "You're not good enough. Who do you think you are? Nobody's ever done that before…blah, blah, blah…"

Since the 1 Life Path is rife with lessons involving failure, it's easy to become beaten down fairly early on in life. Rather than being the kid who has a hundred questions and does extra credit for fun, you end up being the quiet—if not sullen—kid who always sits at the back of the room praying you won't be called on by the teacher.

I've often found that 1 Life Path's can grapple with some roadblocks when it comes to traditional education. It's as though you just don't want to follow the prescribed rules or do what's expected of you. The 1 Life Path can be diagnosed with ADHD, dyslexia, or other "learning disabilities" that place you outside of the traditional educational structure. This is just an example of how it might play out for some 1 Life Path's. Meaning, you get to learn early on how to color outside of the lines, think outside of the box, and make things happen that don't fit the existing structure or don't follow the existing rules.

As a 1 Life Path, this can deplete you *or* inspire you! It's your choice. A 1 Life Path friend of mine loves watching audition shows. Early on, he was an actor and yet never felt he had adequate encouragement along the way, which is his primary reason for not pursuing his acting dream. He regrets having detoured away from his passion. He observed that he's inspired by the people who audition and notices that those who usually do well and move up in the competition are the people who have a large support team cheering them on. He felt that if he'd had that kind of support, he would have had a successful acting career. Often the 1 Life Path feels adrift without the kind of ongoing support and encouragement from others to provide enough confidence to take a risk.

Just know that you're not meant to fit in and the more you embrace and act upon your uniqueness, the better off and more successful you'll be. You know the thing you're most embarrassed about or that you feel is the weirdest thing about you that you've always tried to hide or downplay? This is *the thing* that you're being asked to expose, revel in, and expand upon.

SELF-CENTERED FOCUS

The number 1 is the number of self—of *the self*. It's all about #1 baby! It's no wonder that one of the flip-sides for the 1 Life Path is self-centeredness and ego identification—sometimes to the point of narcissism. What is narcissism? The basic characteristics of narcissistic behavior present as a basic inability to feel empathy for others, an excessive need for admiration, disregard for others' feelings, an inability to handle criticism, and a sense of entitlement.

The 1 Life Path's learning a healthy sense of self and that makes all issues relating to dependence and independence—as well as individuality and achievement—a focal point. You're meant to lead and to exert yourself and yet you're also being challenged with learning how to take others into consideration and how to work with others in an effective way.

Often the 1 Life Path institutes a "my way or the highway" attitude, particularly after you create a certain amount of success. Think about 1 Life Path Steve Jobs and how dynamic he was—and yet also how much he struggled with reining in his bullying demeanor and inability to "work well with others." While one might observe that this was part of his brilliance—which it certainly was—it was also a key aspect to some of his over-all struggles and something he expressed regret about at the end of his life. The 1 is always learning how to be an effective and powerful leader—not a belligerent dictator.

JUDGMENT & CRITICISM

A downside to the energy of the number 1 comes into play when you aren't rising to the challenge in your life—when you find yourself dependent, lacking creative outlets, or even simply as a response to a constant internal sense of inadequateness.

The 1 can default into presenting a wall of judgment. The underlying reason for succumbing to such harsh judgment is so that you aren't held responsible for where you find yourself in your life. It's a deflective mechanism. It's like a bully who concentrates all their energy on bullying others so that they themselves won't be the target of harassment or criticism.

Certainly blaming world leaders, family, spouse, bad luck or anything else is the way to deflect personal responsibility onto someone or something else. Being a victim can feel more palatable than initiating change or simply taking responsibility for yourself. If this is the route you choose to take, you can opt to find the negatives in virtually everything. As you judge those around you, it's also easy to find fault everywhere. People are idiots. The internet is leading to the fall of mankind. The housing market is pointing to Armageddon. Your boss can't do anything right and most certainly doesn't understand or value your brilliance. It's easy to find the bad and the ugly. It's much more challenging to be a problem solver and visionary, which is your birthright. No one said it would be easy! If you don't learn to co-create and to widen your viewfinder to include the wants and needs of others, that's when "1" can be the loneliest number.

BULLYING

As a 1 Life Path, you can exchange robust leadership for petty bullying— rivaling the number 4 in assertiveness and the need to be right. It's a delicate balance with the initiating and achieving energy of the number 1 and it can easily topple over into blunt force, if you know what I mean.

You're much more interested in a winning outcome totally in your favor—not necessarily a "win/win" outcome. Your focus is most often on negotiating a competitive advantage and a winning outcome for yourself, which often comes at the expense of someone or something else. It's the rule of the jungle, after all—the 1 Life Path can be heavy on negotiation and light on mediation.

It can be challenging for you to even care about someone else's point of view. Your eye is on the prize and you know what it takes to get there. No "soft underbelly" for you. And if there is a soft underbelly, you'll make darn sure that it's fully camouflaged and protected.

And remember, the real reason people resort to bullying is to detract from personal weaknesses. Given that you're learning how to wield power and take the lead—and you're often grappling with an underlying lack of self-confidence—it makes sense that you might deflect some of the deeper issues at hand with some assertive bullying.

Every human being needs to stand on their own feet in life. Everyone needs to individuate and develop a healthy ego and a solid sense of self-esteem. Yet as a 1 Life Path, individuation and healthy independence are focal points and aspects for development all your life. Therefore, the themes of independence and self-assertion directly connect with the characteristics of the key people who play certain roles in your life script, whether as intimate partners, family members, teachers, colleagues, or even random meetings.

The themes of the 1 (independence/dependence, balanced ego, creative leadership) direct traffic in terms of the situations you find yourself in, the people who show up, and as the way life lessons come your way.

Biggest Blind Spot: An inability to actually care about or see someone else's point of view.

1 Life Path Superpower: Bringing innovative ideas and concepts into material form. Activate yourself, embody yourself, be yourself!

1 Life Path Mantra: "I march to the beat of a different drummer."

PRACTICAL ADVICE FOR THE 1 LIFE PATH

Don't be so stubborn! I know, I know. You're a force of nature. You're a born rebel. You're learning to exert your Will and learning to be one step ahead of the crowd. Yet you get in your own way when you won't open up and ask for or accept help, advice, or knowledge from others.

When in doubt, return to something you know. Many 1s feel they can fly by the seat of their pants on "good looks" and their salesmanship and creative ideas. Remember, with innovation comes a need for skill (as well as talent). Don't bypass your commitment to study, training, and practicing certain skills that empower you. This can be anything from what you learned about bookkeeping in accounting class to the benefit of working out at the gym.

Play This Game: *What If . . . Our Roles Were Reversed?* A friend of mine was extraordinarily gifted at all things real estate. His go-to negotiating tactic was to use this game or this avenue of thought. He would always ask the other person what they would do if their roles were reversed? *"What would you do if you were me?"* This is something you can practice early and often as a 1 Life Path in order to widen your lens of perception and train yourself to learn to explore other points of view and other emotional reactions. And it works both ways! The trick is to ask what *you* would do *if you were the other person?*

Learn to share . . . play well in the sandbox! Remember that book *All I Really Need To Know I Learned In Kindergarten?* That is a great truth for you, 1 Life Path. Since your life's work is focused on healthy individuation, coming back to the rules of kindergarten are valuable for you. Sharing, saying you're sorry, enjoying running and playing, learning to use your words—and your indoor and outdoor voice! All of these basics are key to your success in life and are concepts worth revisiting again and again.

Erin Weed, a 1 Life Path colleague, posted this missive on social media. This speaks volumes to how the 1 Life Path operates. She writes:

"This is a shoutout to all the biggest Cheerleaders who are behind the boldest Creatives who are putting their work into the world. Creatives include people who are launching a business, writing a book, giving a talk, making the art … it doesn't matter, it all comes from the same inspired place. Cheerleaders have long, exhausting conversations with the Creative as they thrash with self-doubt. Cheerleaders assure the Creative it's not complete shit, even when they want to throw the whole damn thing in the trash can. Cheerleaders remind the Creative to eat and sleep. Sometimes on social media we only see the outcome of the Creative's work, but we'd be nowhere without the Cheerleaders. … To the coaches, consultants, teachers, mentors, partners, friends, assistants, colleagues and significant others who help the Creative shine—I salute you!"

This is spoken by a mindful and conscious 1 Life Path, who sees this necessary dynamic both in her own life as a creative entrepreneur and for those who also choose the path of risk and innovation.

INSPIRATION FOR THE 1 LIFE PATH

A few good reads to inspire, educate, and inform the 1 Life Path. These are simply suggestive of topics that would speak to your 1 Life Path mission on some level.

Any book, class, or tool that offers you ways to think about taking healthy risks, developing confidence and self-esteem, learning leadership and entrepreneurial skills, and the development of negotiating tactics are perfect for you.

Here are just a few suggestions, yet depending on when you read this book—now or 20-years from now (which may be your *now* if that's when you're picking up this book), there will be many new books and resources from which to choose.

I simply encourage you to read biographies and autobiographies of those on the 1 Life Path to find a sense of connection and also as cautionary tales that can save you from making similar missteps.

- *Daring Greatly* by Brene Brown
- *The $100 Start-Up: Reinvent the Way You Make a Living, Do What You Love, and Create a New Future* by Chris Guillebeau
- *The Power of Self Confidence: Become Unstoppable, Irresistible, and Unafraid in Every Area of Your Life* by Brian Tracy
- *Celebrating Failure: The Power of Taking Risks, Making Mistakes and Thinking Big* by Ralph Heath
- *Start: Punch Fear In The Face, Escape Average and Do Work That Matters* by Jon Acuff
- *The Rise: Creativity, the Gift of Failure, and the Search for Mastery* by Sarah Lewis
- *Start With Why* by Simon Sinek
- *Why Now Is The Time To Crush It: Cash In On Your Passion* by Gary Vaynerchuk
- *The Tipping Point* by Malcolm Gladwell
- *Originals: How Non-Conformists Move The World* by Adam Grant

A FEW WELL-KNOWN 1 LIFE PATH'S

Miley Cyrus (November 23, 1992)
Kate Winslet (October 5, 1975)
Gwyneth Paltrow (September 27, 1972)
Lady Gaga (March 28, 1986)
Scarlett Johansson (November 22, 1984)
Khloé Kardashian (June 27, 1984)
Carol Burnett (April 26, 1933)
Lilly Wachowski (December 29, 1967)
Charlize Theron (August 7, 1975)
Sally Field (November 6, 1946)
Chrissy Teigen (November 30, 1985)
Drew Barrymore (February 22, 1975)
Shakira (February 2, 1977)
Steve Jobs (February 24, 1955)
Tom Hanks (July 9, 1956)
Eddie Vedder (December 23, 1964)
George Clooney (May 6, 1961)
Tiger Woods (December 30, 1975)
Nikola Tesla (July 10, 1856)
Martin Luther King, Jr. (January 15, 1929)
Dick Cheney (January 30, 1941)
Tom Cruise (July 3, 1962)
Charlie Chaplin (April 16, 1889)
Prince Harry (September 15, 1984)
Bradley Cooper (January 5, 1975)
James Corden (August 22, 1978)
Hugh Jackman (October 12, 1968)
Will Ferrell (July 16, 1967)
Eddie Vedder (December 23, 1964)
Nicolas Cage (January 7, 1964)

2

How to Calculate Your Life Path Number?

Use your Date of Birth "MARCH 11, 1977"

Add Your Month + Day + Year

MARCH = 3
11 = 11;
1977 = 1 + 9 + 7 + 7 = 24;
2 + 4 = 6;
3 + 11 + 6 = 20 AND 2 + 0 = 2

(11 IS A MASTER NUMBER AND ISN'T REDUCED)

KEY THEMES

- LOVING / PEACEKEEPING
- "POWER BEHIND THE THRONE"
- PATIENCE / CONFLICT AVOIDING
- HIGHLY EMOTIONAL / MEDIATOR
- RELATIONSHIPS / DETAIL-ORIENTED
- SERVING GROUP DYNAMICS

YOUR MISSION STATEMENT

To develop your ability to be patient, fair-minded, service-oriented, and loving while establishing healthy emotional boundaries.

SOME FITTING CAREERS

- NURSE
- ASSISTANT
- ACCOUNTANT
- STYLIST
- FLIGHT ATTENDANT
- MEDIATOR

CORE LESSONS AND CHALLENGES

- GIVING TO THE POINT OF RESENTMENT
- LEARNING TO DEVELOP HEALTHY EMOTIONAL BOUNDARIES
- COMBATIVE AND CHILDISH
- LEARNING NOT TO BE A "DOORMAT"
- SELF-SERVING AND VICTIMIZED

RELATIONSHIP COMPATIBILITY

- 2 AND 1 = HEART & LEADERSHIP
- 2 AND 2 = HEART & HEART
- 2 AND 3 = HEART & CREATIVE EXPRESSION
- 2 AND 4 = HEART & SECURITY
- 2 AND 5 = HEART & FREEDOM-SEEKING
- 2 AND 6 = HEART & NURTURING
- 2 AND 7 = HEART & SPIRITUALITY
- 2 AND 8 = HEART & POWER
- 2 AND 9 = HEART & COMPASSION

YOUR POWER

- DIPLOMATIC AND A GREAT LISTENER
- LOVING AND RELATIONSHIP DRIVEN
- HIGHLY INTUITIVE
- EMOTIONALLY SENSITIVE
- PATIENT AND GIVING

THE 2 LIFE PATH TESTS YOUR ABILITY TO ESTABLISH YOUR SENSE OF YOURSELF WITHOUT NEEDING OUTSIDE APPROVAL OR ACKNOWLEDGMENT. YOU CAN DO IT!

WELL-KNOWN 2s

- JENNIFER LOPEZ (JULY 24, 1969)
- KATE MCKINNON (JANUARY 6, 1984)
- PRINCE WILLIAM (JUNE 21, 1982)
- KANYE WEST (JUNE 8, 1977)

2 LIFE PATH

THE INTUITIVE DIPLOMAT

Love makes your soul crawl out from its hiding place.

— Zora Neale Hurston

Optimal Expression

A 2 Life Path's optimal expression is patience, fair-mindedness, diplomacy, service-oriented, loving, and being lovable.

Your personal mission is to be a loving mediator with clear personal boundaries in every aspect of your life.

Your life's purpose is to clarify the limits of your responsibility and learn to work in cooperation with harmony, balance, and mutual respect.

HARMONY - PEACE - BALANCE

The 2 Life Path is a seeker of harmony and deeply conflict avoidant. You're the peacekeeper of the world and creator of harmonious environments, whether physically, emotionally, or energetically. The 2 Life Path is highly attuned to your surroundings and thrive when you feel protected and nurtured in your own environment. You do your best to offer yourself to others as a safe haven—you're a person people trust with their deepest secrets because they know you'll keep their confidence. You're in your element when you're the creator of a light, clear, buoyant, and harmonious atmosphere.

You rival the 6 as consummate nurturer, harmonizer, and worrier. It's as though you're on high alert at all times, scanning the emotional playing field and mapping out ways to make things nice, loving, and a soft place to land for everyone involved. The 2 is the love-bug of numerology! Relationships are your wheelhouse and emotional sensitivity is your blessing—and sometimes a curse. Intuitive guidance is available to you every day and in every way. It's all about discovering how to understand it, define it, and refine it.

EMOTIONALLY & ENERGETICALLY SENSITIVE

The 2 Life Path is a born empath. The 2 is *very sensitive*, so much so that you get your feelings hurt every day in ways no one but you can understand. *Even you* don't understand the degree to which you're emotionally wounded day in and day out. You're acutely aware of what's going on in everyone else's emotional life and often take on their emotions. Your primary tasks are to realize that you're hypersensitive and that other people don't necessarily see the world and take it in the same way you do—and to construct your own set of psychic armor to protect yourself from the onslaught of emotional energy you take in daily. Only with awareness can you find healthy balance.

Your sensitivity is a gift and yet it can also become one of your most challenging obstacles. The 2 can be one of the most emotionally attuned Life Path numbers, yet it takes some time to take control over it rather than letting it take control over you! The key here is about discernment—understanding who you are from the inside out. Who are you? What are your values? Can you say "no" when you mean no and "yes" when you mean yes? Can you separate yourself from others enough to stand strong and with confidence?

The 2 Life Path doesn't necessarily enjoy the spotlight and has a tendency to get defensive if pushed or threatened. Your trademark is a tendency to do everything for everybody to the point where you feel drained, frustrated, and unacknowledged—and then withdraw with resentment. Oddly, when pushed to this level you default into a black and white mentality, despite your tendency to give people the benefit of the doubt. Even though you're here to serve and love, from the outside people may observe that you give yourself a little too much credit.

The intriguing factor is this: The 2 is all about others and is supportive, feminine energy in numerology. The irony can be that the 2 Life Path wants to please others so much that—*in essence*—the 2 is actually incredibly self-centered. It's all about how you're perceived, how you look to others, how your approval rating is on any given day. Therefore, the 2 is constantly reflecting on itself and has an innate sense of insecurity that demands a rather impossible flow of acknowledgment and support from outside sources. Ironically, the 2's ultra-sensitivity can lead to *insensitivity*.

You aren't meant to receive intense validation from external sources. Why not? Because learning to give yourself your own kudos and support is part of the pathway for the 2 Life Path. Oftentimes you judge yourself on what everyone else says or thinks about you—or what you *think* they think about you. The challenge is to develop your internal compass and turn inward for validation. The strange and beautiful irony here is that as soon as you figure this out and decide that you really don't care what anyone thinks anymore—this is when everything starts flowing to you! As soon as you let go of that insatiable need for acceptance and approval is when it comes to you with effortless ease.

The 2 must be careful not to take on the problems of the people you love, who are more than happy for you to do so. It's best not to place yourself completely at the disposal of others, because soon you'll get angry and resentful for being taken advantage of and unappreciated. When you're clearly on task, you're luminous, content, and satisfied with life. Knowing that you're here to serve, love, and be of use to yourself and to others will keep you focused on the constructive aspects of your 2 Life Path.

This isn't to say you're here to abandon yourself and to only be at the beck and call of others. On the contrary. The biggest leap for the 2 Life Path resides in coming to terms with who you are and what you value from the ground up. When you hold your own under any and all circumstances, you've really begun to master the fine art of the number 2. Often the 2 Life Path is a shape-shifter, mutating to fit the needs and desires of every person and every situation you find yourself involved in.

The trick here is this: You're a pleaser and want others to like you *and* the focus is on how to help and support other people. Yet you'll give and give—without acknowledgment or without much in return—and exist in a cycle of use and emotional abuse *(rinse, repeat, rinse, repeat)*.

The cruelest joke of all is that what you guess other people want is not really what they want or need (usually), making your efforts even more futile and unfulfilling. You want people to read your mind—because certainly you read the minds of other people!—and yet that will never happen.

A client of mine came to me, exasperated and ready to divorce his 2 Life Path wife. He loved her dearly and yet expressed absolute frustration. He was bored with her because he didn't have any idea who she was! She did everything for him, for his business, and was at the ready at all times. Yet she had no life or identity of her own outside of his. He didn't like the pressure this placed on him and he also wanted to be married to a woman with her own dreams, her own goals, and her own aspirations.

The highest and best for the 2 Life Path comes when you establish strong and supple emotional, physical, and energetic boundaries. The whole world opens up to you when you finally stop trying to please everyone and instead get to know yourself, who you are, what you want, and what your values are across the board—and then act on that identity constantly and consistently. *You'll always be a caretaker.* You'll always lead with a loving heart. It's simply a matter of moving yourself out of a perpetual state of insecurity.

The 2 Life Path is being asked to put yourself into the shoes of others in order to mediate conflict, yet the mastery comes in when you can put yourself in someone else's shoes and yet not wear those shoes and take them home with you!

LOVING & RELATIONSHIP-DRIVEN

The energy of the 2 is all about *love* and *relationships*. You're here to love others and be loved in return. Do you know the song "I Want You to Want Me"? That defines you. You crave giving and receiving unconditional love. Since the number 2 is the number of love and relationships, as a 2 Life Path you're *learning about* relationships. Often that means you'll have a few practice runs! You're learning how not to be a doormat for others because of your loving and compassionate nature. That desire—combined with a strong sense of service and emotional sensitivity—brings amazing things into your life, as well as consistent challenges.

To quote George Sand: "The only happiness in life is to love and be loved in return." The trick is not to focus on needing love to the point of desperation or losing yourself and your own identity in the process.

In fact, often it takes the 2 Life Path a while to discern that you're so mutable you lose yourself in the perceived needs, wants and desires of others. Your true mission involves setting healthy emotional boundaries and getting to know yourself in a deep and profound way. Only then will you attract the partnerships into your life that offer the unconditional love, admiration, and support that you crave.

And since you're learning about relationship, you'll have the opportunity to be walked on a few times before you shake it off and start taking control over defining yourself and establishing your own wants and needs. Along with the 6 Life Path, you're built for marriage or a committed partnership and usually desire the stability and security a one-on-one long-term relationship provides.

MEDIATIVE & DIPLOMATIC

It's an understatement to observe that the blessing of the 2 Life Path is also its curse. In order to be an expert meditator, what's needed? That's right—*conflict*. And there's not a lot that gives you an upset stomach more than conflict. Yet it's your calling to be the diplomatic presence in all areas of your life and therefore will attract certain levels of conflict. Rather than curse it or not understand why you continuously draw these people or experiences into your life, perhaps it will resonate with you that you're not meant to avoid conflict.

Your path is to develop your boundaries and emotional resiliency enough to become a master mediator. Yours is the patient path as you master the ability to see all points of view. You're the one who notices and tends to the details—big or small. A friend of mine has a saying that's perfect for the 2 Life Path: "Don't look at me in that tone of voice!" You're the one who takes in body language and can read a person by a gesture or unspoken word. Often you perform this function on various levels—within your family of origin, your own family, your friendship circle, or your work family. You can be counted on to listen and reserve judgment, seeing options and solutions where others can't.

THE 2 LIFE PATH & RELATIONSHIPS

You contain a powerful combination of strength and sensitivity that doesn't always show on the surface. You often serve as a supportive, dependable, caring partner when you're working with your most positive aspects. The 2 Life Path tends to gravitate toward family life. Your ambition as a 2 Life Path is funneled into your relationships. Often, home and family takes priority for the 2 and your relationship circle takes on the most significance in your life.

If you are—*or are involved with*—a 2 Life Path, know that this is someone you can count on! The 2 is all about *love* and so being in a loving relationship is very important to the 2 Life Path. You're super-emotionally sensitive, so be aware that you get your feelings hurt easily.

It's an understatement to say that the 2 Life Path is very much attuned to the emotions of others. Involvement with relationships of all kinds form the nucleus of the life of the 2 Life Path, whether it's intimate partnership, parenting, collegial relationships, business connections, or involvement in community on any level. The 2 has a sixth sense when it comes to relationships.

The 2 Life Path can be a worrier and can lean towards being smothering or co-dependent. The 2 must have an arena to fully express themselves in their relationship with you or they'll shut down. They are givers who love to please. Know that the 2 Life Path is usually conflict-avoidant and yet can also be great mediators and often the 2 knows what you want or need before you know it.

Be aware that the 2 Life Path can be co-dependent and overly-sensitive with their own emotions and the emotional state of others. They also can be a champion micromanager. The 2 can have a tendency to smother their partner—the saying "the urge to merge" was coined for the 2 Life Path! If working with the destructive aspects of their Life Path mission, the 2 can default to being antagonistic, aggressive, and immature.

You'll often find the 2 Life Path apologizing for … well, for virtually anything and everything! Sometimes, the 2 Life Path appears to apologize for taking up any space, any oxygen, or even existing at all. They can merge so much with their environment and the people in the environment that their own identity is lost or blurred. Insecurity can haunt the 2 Life Path and lead you down the path of co-dependent or destructive relationships.

THE 2 LIFE PATH & CAREER

You're happiest when you're being of service to yourself, your family, your group, or when you're excelling in a service-oriented career. Working in a group environment is often the best for you to achieve success and to feel purposeful.

Part of your task as a 2 Life Path is to perfect the art of one-on-one relating. You're the detail person, the one everyone turns to in order to get the job done and get it done right. The 2 thrives in an environment of support and solid direction, so you may not enjoy working for yourself or might not find ultimate success or happiness as an independent contractor. Envision yourself as Oprah's assistant—not Oprah. You're born to be the power behind the throne, so to speak. Yet you don't have much (or any) desire to be the point person or the superstar.

You feel purposeful when you're the one who's in charge of making it all work and ensuring that it all happens as planned. Overall, you thrive when engaging with others, not in isolation. Most 2 Life Path's aren't necessarily driven by career ambition. Of course, there are always exceptions! Yet the 2 Life Path is primarily geared toward placing their relationships into a higher priority than power and career.

The key question to ask yourself is: How can you find a career where you work in a group that you feel in *simpatico*? With a 2 Life Path, it's all about feeling needed, loved, and that your contributions are respected. You have a giving nature and are innately intuitive. You blossom when your talents are being used to serve the greater good of a group or enterprise, so stay away from career choices where you'll be working solo.

You have a big heart, so you need a career where you can be of service to other people in some way, shape, or form. You'll be tested you to step into your sense of yourself without needing constant outside approval. The 2 Life Path is happiest and most satisfied when you're in charge of your segment of the workload, and yet also thrive with clear instruction and well-defined goals and rewards. Since you're a pleaser at heart, you also do well with a social environment and enjoy the connection and camaraderie of working with a team.

Beware of getting your feelings hurt and of getting involved with office politics in a way that isn't healthy. People will always try to pull you into their drama. Or, perhaps you *are* the drama! You love being the one behind the scenes who makes everything tick. You're the heart and soul to any enterprise and offer emotional connection and intuitive insight.

A few possibilities:

- Business support - accountant, administration or HR
- Flight attendant
- Nurse or medical/healthcare
- Interior Designer
- Personal Assistant
- Teacher, caregiver, parent
- Paralegal or court stenographer
- Fashion designer
- Feng Shui consultant
- Real estate agent within a Team
- Restaurant host/hostess, server, bartender
- Leasing agent
- Daycare provider
- Counselor
- Member of a Non-Profit, grant writer, or receptionist
- Hair stylist
- Make-up artist
- Editor
- Proofreader
- Wedding planner or caterer
- Personal or Virtual Assistant

2 LIFE PATH

Opposing Forces

CHILDISH & COMBATIVE

While you usually do whatever you can to avoid conflicts and confrontations, sometimes you take the opposite route and instigate or stimulate conflict. When you're combative and agitated, you can be sure you're responding to situations in a reactive way that happens when you've given too much without getting much back in return. While this may sound like a no-brainer, you often don't realize when you're creeping over to the dark side because you feel as though you've been taking the emotional hits *forever*.

You tend to hold on to the feelings for a long period of time and then when it comes out, it comes as an explosive burst—as an assault—rather than as a point for discussion or actual conversation. Often this also becomes something you beat the drum about for a very long time, allowing the event (person, place or thing) to become an obsessive point of focus.

For instance, you can be miserable at your job and feel your boss is a jerk—*for years*. You can threaten (only to friends or family members who'll listen over and over again) to quit your job for a long period of time and then when you're fired, you're shocked and devastated, despite the fact that you've wanted to quit for a long, long time. The 2 Life Path rivals the number 6 in the way you can withdraw as a punishment to those around you. Yet no one understands why because you've neglected to come to the table and communicate your feelings directly as the infractions occur. You wait until they compound to express and by then it's too late to do anything constructive to remedy the situation. By the time the emotional explosion happens, often it's too late to repair the damage. You're done. Over. *Finito*.

EMOTIONAL WITHDRAWAL

As a 2 Life Path, one of the constant hurdles is to express your thoughts and feelings as they occur—with some thoughtful processing prior—before they become an explosive internal mix. Your tendency it to hang on to what was said and done in the past as though you're submitting the report to the court for review—who said what, when, and with what tone of voice and with what form of body language.

Since you despise a confrontation, you often feel that everyone "should just know" how you feel (because it's so obvious) and not only should they just know how you feel, it should also be a priority for everyone to *care how you feel*—and want to do whatever it takes to make you feel better. And when this doesn't happen (and let's face it—it *never* happens!), you continue to give. And give. And give some more. Hoping, praying, that they'll see the light. Until that one little straw that breaks the proverbial camel's back gets placed on your overburdened back and *boom*—either explosion or withdrawal.

UNDISCIPLINED EMOTIONS

Since you're so emotionally sensitive, your tendency can be to become so identified with your heightened emotional states that you have no idea how much you live in a world designed around this rather extreme emotional enmeshment. As a 2 Life Path, you're learning how to discipline your emotions—how to recognize when you're falling into the abyss and snap yourself out of it before the point of no return. You have trouble understanding how people can operate without delving deeply into the nuances of emotion. And overall, you want everyone to either be really happy and conflict-free (and to thank you for making it all possible) or you have a strong desire to punish those who aren't living up to your expectations.

The 2 Life Path might have a tendency to be overly nice to the point of irritation for others. You can be *sweet* to the point of *saccharin* and place yourself at the service of others at a level that's irritating. A friend of mine went on a retreat and the day the participants arrived at the hotel, one of the women who was also attending the retreat made an intense effort to take people's suitcases to their rooms, open the door for people, and generally place herself in the role of *Sherpa*. My friend found out later that the woman was a 2 Life Path. This is an example of the kind of over-helping and over-giving that makes a 2 Life Path anxious and filled with nervous tension—and somewhat annoying to others who don't need or want the kind of "help" the 2 Life Path bends over backwards to provide.

SABOTAGING RELATIONSHIPS

When you end up living in the destructive aspects of the energy of the 2, no one knows who you are or what you want, including you. You're too preoccupied doing what you think you're supposed to do and are quick to expect others should do the same. The 2 Life Path finds themselves in a chronic state of codependence. Your giving turns to resentment, as you give too much and then you withdraw completely. Only when you realize you're totally free to form your own life through your own sense of internal guidance, while detaching from your skewed sense of what others expect from you, can you truly reach your potential.

Since you're so sensitive and also want to give and get love all the time, you may have a tendency to smother your loved ones or have expectations that can never be met. On the other end of the spectrum, you may back away from wanting love because it hurts too badly. When you can come to an understanding about how to balance your intense need for love, you'll feel secure and supported. The trick for you is to give *yourself* the acknowledgement you need, rather than seeking it from outside sources.

A 2 Life Path friend of mine once said in a fit of despair: "I guess I'm just meant to die alone!" This was after an emotionally unavailable boyfriend dumped her. Rather than reviewing her part in the relationship and taking charge of that, she fell into childish victim mode and also into depression that she refused to dig herself out of. This can be a default for the 2 Life Path when hurt emotionally.

One of the biggest hurdles in creating healthy, loving relationships is the 2 Life Path's tendency to communicate in an indirect and somewhat passive-aggressive manner. Insecurity and self-consciousness set the stage for the 2 Life Path to always be apologizing, justifying, and avoiding. Sometimes it's as though the 2 Life Path is always saying they're sorry just for existing, as though their sheer presence is taking someone else's spot. This can keep the 2 Life Path in a loop of anxiety, disappointment, and with a general sense of being upset as they attempt to navigate the emotional terrain of daily existence.

Every human being needs to be self-determined. Everyone needs to understand the fine art of loving, giving, and being intuitively aware. Yet as a 2 Life Path, emotional and energetic boundaries and healthy attachments are focal points and aspects for development all your life. Therefore, the themes of sensitivity and diplomacy directly connect with the characteristics of the key people who play certain roles in your life script, whether as intimate partners, family members, teachers, colleagues, or even random meetings.

The themes of the 2 (mediation, relationships, patience) direct traffic in terms of the situations you find yourself in, the people who show up, and as the way life lessons come your way.

Biggest Blind Spot: Shape-shifting into what you think other people want you to be—and then resenting it.

2 Life Path Superpower: You're the glue that holds it all together. Your superpower is in your caring and loving energy—and your ability to support, nurture, and deeply understand others.

2 Life Path Mantra: "I want you to want me!"

PRACTICAL ADVICE FOR THE 2 LIFE PATH

DON'T TAKE IT PERSONALLY

Whatever happens around you, don't take it personally ... Nothing other people do is because of you. It is because of themselves. All people live in their own dream, in their own mind; they are in a completely different world from the one we live in. When we take something personally, we make the assumption that they know what is in our world, and we try to impose our world on their world.

Even when a situation seems so personal, even if others insult you directly, it has nothing to do with you. What they say, what they do, and the opinions they give are according to the agreements they have in their own minds...Taking things personally makes you easy prey for these predators, the black magicians. They can hook you easily with one little opinion and feed you whatever poison they want, and because you take it personally, you eat it up....

If you keep this agreement, you can travel around the world with your heart completely open and no one can hurt you. You can say, 'I love you,' without fear of being ridiculed or rejected. You can ask for what you need.

— excerpt from *The Four Agreements* by Don Miguel Ruiz

GET TO KNOW THE DIFFERENCE BETWEEN EMPATHY & CO-DEPENDENCE

One of the biggest lessons for the 2 Life Path is in understanding the difference between being an empath and being co-dependent.

Here are some key comparisons.

Empathic:

- I feel deeply and that extends to my own feelings and to the feelings of others. This is a strength I have that allows me to have deep emotional connections.
- I am okay with allowing others to experience their own pain, discomfort, or any other feeling without feeling the need to step in and "make it better."
- I set limits without guilt or the need for constant justification.
- Key centering thought: *"I can care for myself. You can care for yourself. We are both responsible for ourselves, our reactions, and our behavior."*

Codependent:

- Let me feel your feelings for you. Not only let me feel your feelings for you, let me hold and carry your pain—anger, trauma or any other emotion you don't take personal responsibility for—and allow it to weigh me down and become my personal burden to bear.
- I am unable to witness others in physical or emotional pain and will do anything to fix it or carry it for them.
- I don't know how to establish and maintenance healthy limits between myself and others.
- I always feel as though anything bad or negative that happens is somehow my fault or my responsibility.
- I'm consistently over-extended emotionally and often it shows up physically.
- I'm in a consistent state of worry, guilt, shame, or fear. I feel unworthy.
- Key codependent thought: "Let me be responsible for you and contain your pain, discomfort or unworthiness. If I succeed with it, maybe I'll deserve to have someone help, support, and love me in return. If I keep trying harder, maybe you'll become the person I think you should be and maybe you'll love me."

INSPIRATION FOR THE 2 LIFE PATH

A few good reads to inspire, educate, and inform the 2 Life Path. These are simply suggestive of topics that would speak to your 2 Life Path mission on some level.

Any book, class, or tool that offers you ways to think about relationships, healthy emotional boundaries, mediation skills, and intuitive development are perfect for you.

Here are just a few suggestions, yet depending on when you read this book—now or 20-years from now (which may be your *now* if that's when you're picking up this book), there will be many new books and resources from which to choose.

I simply encourage you to read biographies and autobiographies of those on the 2 Life Path to find a sense of connection and also as cautionary tales that can save you from making similar missteps.

- *The Four Agreements* by Don Ruiz Miguel
- *Loving What Is* by Byron Katie
- *How To Stop Worrying and Start Living* by Dale Carnegie
- Any book by Brené Brown
- *Emotional Intelligence* by Daniel Goleman
- *Set Boundaries, Find Peace: A Guide To Reclaiming Yourself* by Nedra Glover Tawwab
- *The Highly Sensitive Person In Love: Understanding and Managing Relationships When The World Overwhelms You* by Elaine Aron
- *Difficult Conversations: How To Discuss What Matters Most* by Bruce Patton, Douglas Stone and Sheila Heen
- *The Course of Love* by Alain de Botton
- *Conscious Loving: The Journey to Co-Commitment* by Gay and Kathlyn Hendricks, Ph.D.

A FEW WELL-KNOWN 2 LIFE PATH'S

Here's an interesting element about this Life Path number. Rarely does a 2 Life Path end up seeking the limelight! Most 2 Life Path's who are in the public eye have the Master 11/2 Life Path.

Check out the section on the Master 11/2 for a deeper understanding of the Master number and the different ways to calculate it and for more well-known people who share the 2 or 11/2 Life Path.

Kate McKinnon (January 6, 1984)
Meg Ryan (November 19, 1961)
Emma Watson (April 15, 1990)
Julie Andrews (October 1, 1935)
Madonna (August 16, 1958)
Jennifer Aniston (February 11, 1969)
Jackie Kennedy Onassis (July 28, 1929)
Jennifer Lopez (July 24, 1969)
Judi Dench (December 9, 1934)
Tim Burton (August 25, 1958)
Ryan Reynolds (October 23, 1976)
Kanye West (June 8, 1977)
Barack Obama (August 4, 1961)
Jared Leto (December 26, 1971)
Bill Clinton (August 19, 1946)
Rush Limbaugh (January 12, 1951)
Woody Harrelson (July 23, 1961)
Prince Charles (November 14, 1948)
Prince William (June 21, 1982)

3

How to Calculate Your Life Path Number?

Use your Date of Birth "February 21, 1987"

Add Your Month + Day + Year

February = 2
21 = 2 + 1 = 3;
1987 = 1 + 9 + 8 + 7 = 25;
2 + 5 = 7;
2 + 3 + 7 = 12 AND 1 + 2 = 3

Key Themes

- Optimism / Joy
- Emotional self-expression
- Creativity / Communication
- Inspiration / Artistic
- Buoyant / Fun
- Speaking your truth

Your Mission Statement

To develop your ability to be emotionally attuned, highly creative, and a master of impeccable communication while infusing joy and optimism into everything you do.

Core Lessons and Challenges

- Debilitating self-doubt
- Emotional highs and lows
- Fearful of criticism
- Cynical and critical
- Depressive and scattered

Relationship Compatibility

- 3 AND 1 = Creative Expression & Leadership
- 3 AND 2 = Creative Expression & Heart
- 3 AND 3 = Creative Expression & Creative Expression
- 3 AND 4 = Creative Expression & Security
- 3 AND 5 = Creative Expression & Freedom-Seeking
- 3 AND 6 = Creative Expression & Nurturing
- 3 AND 7 = Creative Expression & Spirituality
- 3 AND 8 = Creative Expression & Power
- 3 AND 9 = Creative Expression & Compassion

Your Power

- Creative and intelligent
- Communicative
- Emotionally expressive
- Joyful and optimistic
- Witty and inspiring

Some Fitting Careers

- Presenter/Speaker
- Entertainer/Performer
- Counselor
- Writer
- Salesperson
- Hospitality

The 3 Life Path tests your ability to shine your light into the darkness that life often presents. Acknowledge the problems yet focus on solutions. You can do it!

Well-Known 3s

- Kate Middleton (January 9, 1982)
- Anne Frank (June 12, 1929)
- David Bowie (January 8, 1947)
- Jon Stewart (November 28, 1962)

3 LIFE PATH

THE CREATIVE COMMUNICATOR

Doubt kills more dreams than failure ever will.

— Unknown

Optimal Expression

A 3 Life Path's optimal expression is dynamic, self-assured, joyful, emotionally balanced, expressive, performative, and inspiring.

Your personal mission is to use creative expression and develop healthy, emotional connection in every aspect of your life.

Your life's purpose is to use your emotional sensitivity and creative talents to heal and express yourself while you uplift and inspire others.

PERFORMANCE & EXPRESSION

The 3 Life Path was born to perform and take center stage, however you personally define this. You're wired for creativity, communication, and connecting with people. The optimal 3 communicates brilliantly and clearly, consolidating information easily. The 3 Life Path embraces brimming creative impulses with gusto and follow-through. You're a master at intuitively knowing how to rework existing information into new, vibrant ideas.

Overall, you can be the life of the party—clever, witty, entertaining, and good company. You make a great host or hostess and people feel nurtured and comfortable around you. You make it all look so easy. Often the 3 Life Path has many creative skills and talents in select areas, including anything related to media, dance, cooking, music, design, speaking, writing, coaching, and self-help. You're naturally inclined to the arts and other forms of expression that offer a conduit for your effervescent energy and unbridled creativity.

COMMUNICATION

Since your life's work is all about communication, you're being asked to hone and perfect your communication skills every day and in every way. Your mission in life is to develop and practice impeccable communication on all levels. If there's anyone who innately knows that words have tremendous power, it's the 3 Life Path. You're usually direct and compassionate, yet if you're still developing these skills, your tendency might be to become domineering and to state your thoughts and feelings bluntly, which is hard on those around you. You may end up regretting things you say, so contemplating what you want to communicate and how you want to say it—hopefully in a supportive way, with a little cushion underneath it—will be in your best interest.

You can also work long and hard to even identify that you *have* feelings or opinions. If this is the case, your communication is rudimentary at best or non-existent at worst. Sometimes the 3 Life Path experiences a lack of emotional bandwidth or a rudimentary understanding of the way that emotions actually can be felt, owned, and expressed. Either way, *communication* is a theme you work with all your life. Part of your life's work is to come to the point where you *feel* your emotions rather than just *think* about them.

Oftentimes, the 3 can default into sarcasm and inappropriate humor. This is the person who's talking all the time and saying absolutely nothing. Or this is the person who makes everyone in the room grimace with off-color and inappropriate jokes. On the other end of the spectrum, this can be the person who never communicates anything at all. They clam up and never express thoughts, opinions, or emotions and then wonder why they never experience emotionally satisfying relationships or are highly misunderstood by others. Just know that the 3 sometimes goes through periods of stunted or blocked communication where they can, for instance, be great communicating on the job and yet in family and personal relationships, they're in their infancy.

POSITIVE & OPTIMISTIC ATTITUDE

The 3 is truly the energy of *joie de vivre* (the joy of life). Part of your function is to appreciate and express the simple joy of living. Sounds easy, right? This is one of the many ironies of the 3 Life Path, because often the 3 struggles with finding lightness within all of the heavy emotional energy you're here to experience, process, and express.

Many numerologists maintain that the 3 Life Path is the "easiest" of all the Life Path numbers in numerology. Yes, the 3 often can put a shine and a good spin on virtually anything. Yet it goes much deeper than that. The 3 is learning how to choose to have a positive experience in life, even when it's hard to do so.

One of the major goals for the 3 Life Path is to see and engage with the lighter elements of life and bring joy and optimism into your interactions. Ultimately, you're here to inspire and uplift others—and yet you achieve this by tapping into deep core emotional elements in your own life and in the lives of other people.

The power of the 3 resides in your ability to bridge for yourself (and for others) the gap between fully experiencing all of your emotions—the good, bad and the ugly—and come through on the other side with pearls of wisdom gained through delving deeply into the emotional crevices. And add to that, you must come out the other side with humor, good grace, and healthy discernment.

You're here to learn to speak your truth, find your joy, and be creative. As you do this, your effect on others has rather glorious ramifications.

As you move through life, you serve as an example to others of how to move through adversity and come out smiling—not in a saccharin or fake sort of way—in a real and profound way. The mantra for the 3 Life Path: When you're laughing, you're learning!

EMOTION OCEAN

If you're working the constructive aspects of the number 3, you're connected with your emotions—and you have a lot of them. Many 3s spend years learning to gauge that they even *have* emotions and then they spend more years learning how to express them in a constructive and healthy way.

Most 3 Life Path's take years to come to terms with your emotional life and the way in which you have hardwired your coping mechanisms for emotional (dis)engagement. You're intensely emotionally attuned to others (you rival the number 2 in this particular arena) and often don't realize to what extent you pick up the emotional flotsam and jetsam from those around you—and you carry it in your overloaded backpack (metaphorically speaking) forever.

Or at least until you can get a handle around what's *yours* and what's *everyone else's*. You're like tofu—you take on the flavors of whatever you're soaking in. There are 3 Life Path's who choose the stoic route, not acknowledging emotions in any way, shape, or form. Yet often this won't last long until there is a major health issue or other crisis that breaks the emotional center wide open.

Then there are 3 Life Path's who spiral out of control as they exaggerate and accentuate every fragment of their emotional engagement to the point of exasperation—so much drama! The goal for the 3 Life Path is to embrace emotions, experience them, and move through them fully and completely. The endgame is about expressing emotions through the creative outlet of your choice, balancing and harmonizing emotions, and using your own emotional acuity as a bridge connecting you to hold space for others to express themselves.

QUICK WIT & INTELLECT

The energy of the 3 is vital, curious, and quick. Your mind moves so quickly that when someone is slow thinking, you easily get frustrated. Your brain moves a mile a minute and while that's a gift it can also be part of your challenge.

One of the components of the 3 is the energy of creation—the 3 is the number of the Trinity, after all. It's your birthright as a 3 Life Path to experience, dabble, and study a wide variety of things during your life. Yet you're also being asked to ultimately take all of that information and experience and create something unique with it. Your highest and best use is when you can settle on something—or a focused combination of things—and bring it into practical reality.

Often a 3 Life Path will get into their 40s or beyond and experience defeat and frustration because you feel you have nothing to show for yourself. You can easily become the jack-of-all-trades and master of none. Often this happens because you feel that you'll disappoint other people if you do what you're really called to do. It's your task to step into yourself and take your talents seriously—and enjoy doing it! In fact, one of the pressures of the 3 Life Path is that you're so good at everything you do you have a difficult time choosing what to focus on. Often you feel that "everyone can do that!" even when very few actually can—you have a tendency to downplay your talents.

Sometimes you have difficulties following through on plans, projects, or ideas. You may observe that you just can't decide how to direct your energy and become scattered and ultimately depressed and ineffective at completing whatever you set out to do. *So many ideas, so little time.* The 3 is always working on a commitment to follow-through. You can talk yourself out of virtually anything and you can also become distracted or easily bored. You can find the tiniest fault with your big idea that stops you from proceeding past the fun part. You like fun and immediacy. Although you have a great amount of reserve and tenacity, you often spend it on other people and not on yourself.

THE 3 LIFE PATH & RELATIONSHIPS

The 3 Life Path is passionate, energetic, and fun. You're a giver at heart and therefore you must be careful about with whom you spend your time because you'll attract takers if you aren't careful. You must learn to walk away from relationships unbalanced in this specific way.

You're most often physically and emotionally passionate and crave relationships that are based in a deep emotional and physical connection. You want and need a partner who's emotionally available. One of the most basic needs for the 3 Life Path is a *need to be heard*. You need to have a partner who'll encourage your emotional expression—someone who will consistently listen and support you as you go through your process. *Your* job within this partnership is to discipline your emotions and not drown in your emotional life—taking your partner down with you in the process!

You can be romantic and fiercely loyal. You're a natural counselor who sees potential in others, so you might choose a partner who is almost like a patient you think you can save or fix, either consciously or unconsciously. Some 3 Life Path's can also find relationships—*overall*—too confining for their passionate spirit.

Sometimes a 3 is more married to their creative projects than they are to another person. Or alternately, the 3 gives up their independence in relationships and squelches their creativity—or dumbs it down so substantially that they feel they aren't living up to their purpose in life. This is when depression becomes a regular force in the life of the 3 Life Path.

If you are—*or are involved with*—a 3 Life Path, know that they are quite passionate, full of humor, emotionally expressive, and can be great fun to have by your side. The 3 is joyful and caring. They can be somewhat dramatic. Since the 3 Life Path is driven by the need for intense and deep emotional connection, they usually want to share every feeling, every emotion, and every experience with their partner or the relationship feels empty.

The 3 thrives with someone who can support them emotionally and reveal their creative strengths to them. The 3 Life Path thrives with a sense of playfulness in their relationships and needs encouragement along the way.

Be aware that the shadow side of the 3 Life Path in relationships can show up as an inability to commit to or be satisfied with a relationship partner for the longer term. Sometimes the 3 is the ultimate introverted extrovert, needing solitude and uninterrupted time and space for their creative projects—and then tapping into the extroverted part of themselves when they need to present that creative project to the outside world.

The 3 Life Path is often known as the *pleasant path* in numerology—happy, care-free, lucky, attractive, and always landing on their feet, no matter what. Yet what I find is vital for the 3 Life Path to understand is in the realm of *trauma*. Often, the level of emotional trauma you endure is substantial and always becomes the foundation you need to attend to as you traverse and embody your 3 Life Path purpose of emotional and creative self-expression. In reality, this is your true blessing and your curse. Emotional trauma is your most important teacher and also can be your most terrifying foe.

The 3 Life Path can be the best "actor" in the world—winning the Academy Award for masking and downplaying the trauma you've experienced. For instance, I've had many 3 Life Path clients observe that their ex-spouses saw them as consummate actors within the marriage, playing the role of the dutiful partner until the 3 Life Path walked out the door.

Many times, the 3 Life Path will express themselves in a way that their partner doesn't recognize as urgent or a drop-dead dealbreaker until it's too late. Since authentic expression is a key for the 3, it's also one of the hardest for the 3 to master. The 3 Life Path invariably works through significant blockages with communication and expression. Especially given that the 3 Life Path often grows up in an environment where it's more-or-less forbidden to express emotions, particularly anger or hurt feelings. In the process, the 3 Life Path often contains a visceral element of sadness or melancholy that takes great effort—and personal expense—to camouflage.

Another caveat for the 3 is that they demand a heightened level of emotional connection and communication from a partner, yet often they're actually incapable of providing that *for* their partner. They're learning how to express and so there can be rough patches in regards to the 3's ability to relay and express their emotions effectively in real time. Interestingly, I have worked with 3 Life Path's who have undeniable blockages with communication—by stuttering or having speech impediments.

The 3 Life Path might struggle with depression and if this is the case, this is a huge deterrent in building a happy and healthy relationship. Some of the other pathways the 3 Life Path can traverse is where they are always scattered, only concerned with superficialities, and ultimately end up being rather frustrated, unproductive, and frivolous. When challenged, the 3 can experience huge blocks in expression, can be emotionally detached, and extremely self-absorbed.

THE 3 LIFE PATH & CAREER

It's not surprising to find many 3 Life Paths in entertainment, politics, speaking, broadcasting, writing or any other industry that requires expert communication skills, intellect, adaptability, and a good sense of humor. Any profession where you can present your ideas to an audience is right up your alley.

The key for you is to understand that you're spending a lifetime developing and honing your communication skills. Therefore, you'll have opportunity after opportunity to practice and perfect this in both your personal and professional realms. You aren't necessarily a nine-to-five job person—you don't necessarily work well under the supervision of others or within a rigid structure.

The 3 Life Path is the ultimate up-cycler. You learn about so many different topics, you experience so many different things—then you sit down and take everything you're really good at and that you really love and put it all together and create something new and relevant that you can then give out to the world. This can be an idea, product, service—or just way of viewing and engaging with the world.

Remember, at the end of the day you're here to inspire and uplift both yourself and others—and that can take on many different qualities and manifestations. I don't know one 3 Life Path who's had a linear resumé. The 3 usually has various degrees (or trainings/certifications) and if they don't, their life experience makes up for it. At the end of the day, the 3 Life Path often has different jobs, various certifications, and many career paths.

The key question to ask yourself is: Can you move through self-doubt and commit yourself to developing your amazing creative talents? With a 3 Life Path, you might feel that everyone can do what you do because you find it to be oh-so-easy. But not everyone can drink from the fountain of creativity as readily as you!

The trick is to develop the verve so that you can make a living with it and to side-step the naysayers or those who wish you'd choose a more practical path. You must realize that it's beneficial to explore outside of your circle (if you are already in the arts, for instance), as you'll gain valuable perspective about your skills and talents in a way that gets muffled when you only engage with others in creative fields.

The 3 Life Path can be a professional amateur, so the key is to step up and dig past a surface-level knowledge of something and devote yourself to perfecting more of an expertise with a depth of knowledge that digs well below the surface. You can be scattered and lacking follow-through, so it's up to you to not flit through and be a novice at everything you do. It's your challenge to dig in and develop a deep level of expertise. Strive to become an expert, not a dilettante.

Understand also that *creativity* transfers to different careers in different ways. You can be a creative problem-solver, artist, or actor—or depending on the other elements in your chart, you can be a creative business-minded person as well. One of the keys for you is to tap into what really brings you joy and feels fun and engaging.

The 3 Life Path is here to act upon your creative genius and develop your emotional connection and expression. Communication is your focus, whether it's through the arts or in other areas such as counseling, writing, training, or presenting. You thrive in environments that allow and encourage innovation and creative solutions to problems.

A few possibilities:

- Actor
- Director
- Playwright, screenwriter or author
- Therapist
- Entertainment as a musician, actor, promoter, producer, agent, or manager
- Broadcaster
- Videographer
- Social Media Manager
- Chef or cook
- Musician or singer
- Energy worker
- Herbalist
- Artist
- Political activist
- Food stylist
- Interior designer or stager
- DJ
- Bartender
- Social worker
- Nurse or play therapist for kids
- Consultant
- Coach
- Song lyricist

3 LIFE PATH

Opposing Forces

SELF-DOUBT & FEAR OF CRITICISM

One of the biggest road blocks for the 3 Life Path is intense self-doubt. Feelings of insecurity can stop you in your tracks and literally stun you into submission. While everyone experiences self-doubt at certain times in life, this is a ruling factor when you're on the 3 Life Path.

Fear of criticism hits a 3 Life Path very hard—particularly in the younger years—so much so that a 3 will often abandon or sublimate their creative track because of not-so-supportive experiences. Especially in the early years, the fear of criticism can be overwhelming. I've worked with 3 Life Path's who were told by drunk Uncle Charlie when they were twelve years old that being an actor was ridiculous. And despite the fact that being an actor was the only thing they ever wanted to do, they didn't pursue it because of the criticism or lack of support they received early in their lives—as illustrated by drunk Uncle Charlie's negative remark.

A 3 Life Path client I once worked with applied to a school to become a film editor. When she wasn't accepted into their program, rather than applying again or applying to a different school, she abandoned her film-editing dream and got a job as a barista in a coffee shop. She woke up one morning with partial facial paralysis and an inability to physically speak—she was otherwise healthy and in her 20s. This is a physical example of how emotions manifest in different aspects of the life of a 3 Life Path—and how depressing your creativity can manifest physically and emotionally.

Avoid getting stuck overanalyzing or over thinking every single thing. You'll mud wrestle with analysis paralysis over and over again. When you resort to that, you'll drive yourself (and everyone else) crazy. When you experience these feelings, your best action is to *take action*, even when you feel paralyzed. Just moving through the doubt by taking one step beyond it will move your energy forward and allow you to feel out and act upon a creative solution.

DEPRESSION

3 Life Paths make the best manic-depressives, experiencing extreme highs and lows. If you're not using your talents, you'll experience mood swings. When you realize that your journey is an emotional one, you can learn how to manage the ups and downs more effectively. I don't know a 3 Life Path who hasn't experienced some level of depression in their lives. Often you can go from "awesome!" to "despair" in a moment (and back again). This doesn't have to be a constant. When 3's learn to identify when they are literally and energetically *depressing* their emotions, their creativity, and their authenticity—then they can bridge over into their true and joyful number 3 energy.

The flip-side for the 3 Life Path comes into play when you hold down (*depress*) your emotions and your creativity. The result is often a lingering depression that begins to define you. Alcohol can become the depressant of choice, complicating the ability to lean into complex and sometimes painful emotions.

While many numerologists observe that the energy of the number 3 is the "pleasant path," I don't know one 3 Life Path who hasn't endured substantial emotional trauma. Your job is to blaze through it, find your joy and optimism, and model this for other people. Otherwise, the 3 can become a negative vortex—the depressive cynic or the person who lives only on a superficial or emotionally volatile realm.

The 3 Life Path often lives with a certain sense of melancholy—underneath the buoyancy and humor can be a persistent sense of inexplicable sadness. I think of the song "Someone That I Used To Know" by Goyte, where the lyrics say: "…You can be addicted to a certain kind of sadness. Like resignation to the end, always the end." More than most Life Path's, the 3 can find that sadness and underlying depression can be a default setting for how you experience life.

SUPERFICIALITY

When a 3 Life Path is off track, one of the defaults is superficiality. The 3 can just skim the surface of life, stirring up emotional drama and trauma, feeling victimized, and placing all their energy into the surface elements of life. This might show up as becoming slightly obsessed with appearance, focusing on wardrobe, beauty products and procedures, and other aspects of outward appearance to the point of distraction or obsession.

The 3 can be extremely impressionable. While this is part of the attraction of the 3—enthusiasm, curiosity, and openness—this can also become problematic when not held in check. The 3 can be the one who's always on the new diet, taking the new supplement, buying the latest whatever-it-is, or ordering that piece of equipment they saw on the infomercial. While this isn't innately bad, the 3 can often become so impressionable that they focus the lion's share of their energy and resources on these sorts of things, much to the detriment of their over-all success or innate sense of self. It comes down to being a tool of avoidance.

The 3 can also default to negative communication. I once heard this observation: There are three levels of communication people can engage in. The highest form of communication revolves around ideas and problem solving. The second form of communication revolves around events. The lowest form of communication revolves around talking about other people. The 3 can resort to the lowest form of communication as a way of diverting from digging deeper within yourself.

EMOTIONAL VOLATILITY

When you want your partner to support you as you wallow in unhealthy emotional expression, it won't work. Often this is a way in which relationships disintegrate with a 3 Life Path—when you expect your partner to become an emotional garbage pail as you wallow in negative emotions. In this scenario, you're unwilling to work on positive solutions.

Yet you expect your partner (or anyone else) to listen and verify every fragment of your emotional rollercoaster.

The 3 can have a tendency not to let go of past relationships. You mull them around in your head again and again, picking apart things said and done, what could've been and what wasn't. You level blame on yourself and on others. The 3 Life Path tends to obsess over the smallest emotional hooks that bog you in a pool of cynicism or emotional defeat. You often find yourself grinding over an issue and shredding it into a pile of goo on the floor (so to speak). When this happens, your best solution is just to leave it alone. Just stop. If it's really vital and needing your input, it'll come back into play for you when it's less emotionally charged.

Relationships can falter if depression becomes part of your daily existence. It's also fair to say that the 3 Life Path—similar to the 5 Life Path—can also display addictive behaviors that serve as a way to numb, avoid or deny personal responsibility for doing the healing work needed to align yourself with your pathway to creative self-expression.

THE GLASS IS HALF-EMPTY

The off-target 3 Life Path is the anti-3. Instead of finding joy in life, you find despair. Instead of engaging with optimism, you're the ultimate pessimist. Instead of seeking fun, you think everything and everyone is stupid. When a 3 is way off, the glass isn't just half empty, the waiter never even came to the table with the water glass to begin with—and it's everyone else's fault that the waiter ignored you.

A 3 Life Path who presents in this manner hasn't been able to muster the courage or resolve to move through emotional blockages and extreme self-doubt. You can become the ultimate procrastinator when feeling stuck or over-whelmed. There's really nothing more grating than a 3 Life Path who refuses to embrace their birthright as a joyful, supportive, and emotionally engaged and communicative person.

Every human being needs to express their creativity and learn how to manage emotions in life. Everyone needs to communicate effectively and develop an optimistic attitude. Yet as a 3 Life Path, communication and expression are focal points and aspects for development all your life. Therefore, the themes of impeccable communication and creative expression directly connect with the characteristics of the key people who play certain roles in your life script, whether as intimate partners, family members, teachers, colleagues, or even random meetings.

The themes of the 3 (emotional sensitivity, communication, positive expression) direct traffic in terms of the situations you find yourself in, the people who show up, and as the way life lessons come your way.

Biggest Blindspot: Being unaware of how emotionally vulnerable you can be, ignoring the need to work to heal trauma, and weak emotional boundaries.

3 Life Path Superpower: Ability to connect with people with a deep level of emotional intelligence. When you're laughing, you're learning!

Your Mantra can be borrowed by *The Who*: "See me, feel me, touch me, heal me."

PRACTICAL ADVICE FOR THE 3 LIFE PATH

Here's my take on the complexities of the 3 Life Path. Many numerologists will assert that the pathway for the 3 is paved with luck, charm, and ease. Yet in my practice, I have never met a 3 Life Path who didn't have a heap of emotional trauma. Period.

This makes sense, after all, considering that the 3 is all about shining light into the darker crevices of the world and transforming those darker places with hope, love, and emotional connection. Yet the 3 must traverse a dark path in order to pick up the tools of the trade, so to speak, so that they can practice what they preach.

With that said, I don't know a 3 Life Path on the planet who hasn't grappled with a deep sense of melancholy, if not outright depression. Often the 3 puts a good face on it and genuinely feels this vivacious sense of creative drive and prefers to express the positives in life.

Yet let's use a few 3 Life Path's as examples of what I'm referring to here. Look at incredible 3 Life Path Nina Simone, soulful singer and musician, who battled anger, depression, and other issues as she brought her other-worldly musical talent to the world. A musical powerhouse and civil rights activist, Simone was a 3 Life Path who embodied many of the attributes of the multi-talented and multi-leveled 3. Yet her underlying rage and discontent couldn't be camouflaged.

Elizabeth Smart endured unspeakable atrocities at the hands of kidnappers. Smart has become an advocate and speaker for crime victims, using her 3 Life Path gifts of emotional connectivity and communication to inspire and help others.

Anne Frank (3 Life Path) left her legacy in the way the 3 is naturally gifted—in writing—with her diary where she says: "It's difficult in times like these: ideals, dreams and cherished hopes rise within us, only to be crushed by grim reality. It's a wonder I haven't abandoned all my ideals, they seem so absurd and impractical. Yet I cling to them because I still believe, in spite of everything, that people are truly good at heart."

Frida Kahlo epitomizes the extremity of the 3 Life Path with her art that found its way to manifestation from unfathomable physical and emotional pain. This quote from Kahlo encapsulates a sentiment I often hear from the 3 Life Path: "I hope the exit is joyful. And I hope never to return." Despite an undertone of sadness or emotional heaviness, the 3 is the one who takes despair and channels it into art that has the power to move people and to incite emotional response and connection. The 3's gift is to use emotional—and sometimes physical—pain as a conduit and tool for creative expression.

If we look at the general personality of other 3 Life Paths, there's humor, intelligence, and a sense of emotional fragility—for example, Daniel Radcliffe, Ed Sheeran, Jon Stewart, Hozier, and David Bowie. Or even Cameron Diaz, Katy Perry, Katie Couric, Brooke Shields, and Ellen Page. Their power resides in the depth and breadth of emotional feeling and expression, yet it must always be expressed through emotional experience and emotional depth or it loses traction and becomes superficial or frivolous.

At the end of the day, the 3 Life Path is learning how to dig into whatever creative or expressive tool they choose and become an expert rather than a dilettante.

The practical advice is this: The 3 Life Path is here to dig into the emotional terrain, yet the tendency is to want to avoid it altogether, resulting in one of two things: Denying emotions and covering it up with toxic positivity—or being so self-indulgent with expressing emotions that it's exasperating to those around you. Or getting so mired down in emotions that the weight of it brings you into a perpetual state of hopelessness—two forms of denial, two different pathways to handle the denial.

The delicate balance with the 3 Life Path is to experience all of it fully and completely, without judging it or yourself, and allowing it to move through you like a wave going back out to sea. When you bottle the emotion up, it becomes an internal tsunami seeking expression either by imploding inside of you (depression and self-loathing) or outwardly (self-centered and abusive to others).

The best practical advice for the 3 Life Path is to get therapy and/or emotional support early in life and stick with it! This can be traditional talk therapy, energy work, somatic therapy or any other therapy that allows you to dig into your emotions and unearth your traumatic experiences—and then devote yourself to consciously heal yourself so that you can extend that to others. This coupled with giving yourself lifelong permission to use your creative energy through art, performance, and communication of any kind is recipe for alignment with your path and purpose.

INSPIRATION FOR THE 3 LIFE PATH

A few good reads to inspire, educate, and inform the 3 Life Path. These are simply suggestive of topics that would speak to your 3 Life Path mission on some level.

Any book, class, or tool that offers you ways to think about relationship communication (with an emphasis on co-dependence and narcissistic relationship partners and patterns), expression (writing, speaking, any method for expression), trauma work, and intuitive development are perfect for you.

Here are just a few suggestions, yet depending on when you read this book—now or 20-years from now (which may be your *now* if that's when you're picking up this book), there will be many new books and resources from which to choose.

I simply encourage you to read biographies and autobiographies of those on the 3 Life Path to find a sense of connection and also as cautionary tales that can save you from making similar missteps.

- *The Big Leap: Conquer Your Hidden Fear And Take Life To The Next Level* by Gay Hendricks

- *Steering by Starlight and Finding Your Own North Star* by Martha Beck
- *On Writing* by Stephen King
- *Unglued: Making Wise Choices in the Midst of Raw Emotions* by Lysa TerKeurst
- *The Obstacle Is The Way* by David Wilcox
- *The Artist's Way* by Julia Cameron
- *Emotional Agility* by Susan David, Ph.D.
- *The Emotionally Intelligent Manager* by David R. Caruso and Peter Salovey
- *Permission To Feel: The Power of Emotional Intelligence to Achieve Well-Being and Success* by March Brackett, Ph.D.
- *My Life In Art* by Konstantin Stanislavski

A FEW WELL-KNOWN 3 LIFE PATH'S

Katy Perry (October 25, 1984)
Mary J. Blige (January 11, 1971)
Celine Dion (March 30, 1968)
Christina Aguilera (December 18, 1980)
Nina Simone (February 21, 1933)
Elizabeth Smart (November 3, 1987)
Hillary Clinton (October 26, 1947)
Frida Kahlo (July 6, 1907)
Ellen Page (February 21, 1987)
Cameron Diaz (August 30, 1972)
Lana Wachowski (June 21, 1965)
Kate Middleton (January 9, 1982)
Reese Witherspoon (March 22, 1976)
Katie Couric (January 7, 1957)
Winona Ryder (October 29, 1971)
Anne Frank (June 12, 1929)
Simon Sinek (October 9, 1973)
Bill Cosby (July 12, 1937)
Jon Stewart (November 28, 1962)
Snoop Dogg (October 20, 1971)
Daniel Radcliffe (July 23, 1989)
Kevin Hart (July 6, 1979)
David Bowie (January 8, 1947)
Alec Baldwin (April 3, 1958)
John Lithgow (October 19, 1945)
Mahershala Ali (February 16, 1974)
Hozier (March 17, 1990)
Channing Tatum (April 26, 1980)
Jamie Foxx (December 13, 1967)
John Travolta (February 18, 1954)

How to Calculate Your Life Path Number?

Use your Date of Birth
"August 22, 1871"
Add Your
Month + Day + Year

August = 8
22 = 22;
1981 = 1 + 9 + 8 + 1 = 19;
1 + 9 = 10 and 1 + 0 = 1;
8 + 22 + 1 = 31 and 3 + 1 = 4
(22 is a master number and isn't reduced)

Key Themes

- Honesty / Process
- Healing Family Issues
- Step-By-Step / Hardworking
- Builder of Systems / Stability
- Security / Knowledge

Your Mission Statement

To develop your ability to develop a systematic approach to life — to be practical and hardworking while establishing a personal sense of security.

Some Fitting Careers

- Educator
- Real Estate
- Architect
- Manager
- Healthcare
- Athlete

Core Lessons and Challenges

- Self-limiting and self-sabotaging
- Working through and around limitations
- Bossy and opinionated
- Repeats mistakes
- A martyr about work and responsibility

Relationship Compatibility

- 4 and 1 = Security & Leadership
- 4 and 2 = Security & Heart
- 4 and 3 = Security & Creative Expression
- 4 and 4 = Security & Security
- 4 and 5 = Security & Freedom-Seeking
- 4 and 6 = Security & Nurturing
- 4 and 7 = Security & Spirituality
- 4 and 8 = Security & Power
- 4 and 9 = Security & Compassion

Your Power

- Solid and Steady
- Methodical and Systematic
- Hard Working
- Seeker of Knowledge
- Honest and Loyal

The 4 Life Path tests your ability to achieve stability and security by patiently following a gradual process toward clearly defined goals — even in the face of limitations. You can do it!

Well-Known 4s

- Octavia Spencer (May 25, 1972)
- Nicole Kidman (June 20, 1967)
- Jimmy Fallon (September 19, 1974)
- Brad Pitt (December 18, 1963)

4 LIFE PATH

THE TEACHER & SYSTEMS BULDER

It's hard to beat a person who never gives up.

— Babe Ruth

Optimal Qualities

A 4 Life Path's optimal expression is being practical and detail oriented, sharing knowledge, working to establish a sense of security, and to understand and implement the power of productive process.

Your personal mission is to create stability and security in every aspect of life while accomplishing something of lasting value.

Your life's purpose is to achieve stability and security by patiently following a gradual process toward your goals. Healing family wounding takes place organically as you create your family of choice which provides the security the 4 Life Path craves so strongly.

PROCESS & STABILITY

A 4 Life Path is all about developing stability through process—to understand and implement the power of process. The 4 Life Path usually presents with a rather serious character and demeanor. Overall, the 4 is cerebral, intelligent, and a seeker and cultivator of knowledge. If you were to audition for the cast of *Winnie the Pooh*, you would land the role of Owl—really smart, if not slightly bossy.

You know how to build solid foundations—or you'll learn it, eventually! The 4 Life Path is often placed in charge of developing operating systems and is expected to look after the details.

The 4 Life Path is the workhorse, worker-bee, and master builder of the world. You devour information so that when you find a topic or subject that interests you, there's no end to the depth of your knowledge about it and your ability to impart that knowledge to others. You're a born teacher. You may not become a teacher in the traditional sense, yet you demonstrate an undeniable depth of knowledge and just can't help sharing what you know with others.

Your mission in life is to learn the advantages of using system and order. You're learning and mastering how to use systematic ways of thinking and organizing. *The 4 brings order to chaos.* You'll be tempted to skip steps on the way—yet when you do, you'll have to go "back to go"—for Monopoly fans: "Don't pass go, don't collect $200." You'll always pay the price of wanting to jump ahead. The 4 Life Path must understand how to take the proper practical steps to achieve the end goal.

Like it or not, you're becoming a master of step-by-step processes. You manifest great things when you articulate a goal and then map out all the steps it will take to get there. Even more than that, you manage to meet goals and manifest something tangible and lasting. The 4 Life Path isn't here to create momentary gain or disposable objects.

Someone wrote this comment about the 4 Life Path on my YouTube channel: "4 is boring!" I would argue with that on so many levels. I bring this up because the 4 often gets a bad rap as mundane and humorless. I would personally disagree with that! Jimmy Fallon has a 4 Life Path—Chelsea Chandler, Brad Pitt, and others (see the extended list of well-known 4's at the end of this section) are on the 4 Life Path and I don't find these folks boring. *Au contraire!* The 4 is learning to be methodical, reliable, and success comes when you commit to your goals, whatever they may be.

HARD WORK

The 4 is the number of hard work and concerted effort. The 4 is foundations energy and is often referred to as the architect number. As a 4 Life Path, lucky breaks are few and far between. Whatever you do requires effort, fortitude, and tenacity. It's rare that you'll find yourself in the midst of something that doesn't require that you put in the hours (overtime, anyone?) to get it done. While others are frolicking at the coffee shop behind their computer screens or out clubbing the night away, more than likely you're on your feet behind the counter, out in the field, or any number of other more down-to-earth activities.

It's funny about the 4 Life Path, because sometimes you'll find yourself—in your younger years—considerably less directed. You can squeak by in school without much effort (you're a smartie, after all!), be totally uncertain about a career or college major, take odd physical jobs or low-paying jobs, sit around smoking pot on the couch, and whatever other diversions you can concoct. Yet as time wears on, you'll feel this gnawing sense of unrealized purpose and potential that will keep hounding you until you make the leap and decide to focus on something, step it up, get some systems and routines in order, show up to the table, and make an effort. It's all about taking responsibility for your life—and when you turn this corner, it starts to feel really gratifying.

Yet more often than not, you're that 4 Life Path who grows up in the trenches, working at an early age and taking on more adult responsibilities for your own (and sometimes others') well-being than a "normal" child. You can be the one who works his or her way through school while forgoing the traditional college partying and socializing. You must be serious about your finances—because they're sparse and you receive little-to-no support otherwise—and so you miss out on the lighter or more fun elements of life out of this financial necessity.

In this way, you become a *realist* fairly early in life. You can also *choose* to do more serious endeavors as opposed to engaging in the more frivolous aspects of life when growing up—or even in adult life. It's as though you don't have time, energy or desire to engage in activities that aren't designed to *get you somewhere*. You tend to be immensely pragmatic and logical. You're all about accomplishment and results, plain and simple.

Either way, *hard work* is a consistent theme for you and you're learning—while you will always exert more than the lion's share of work—how to modulate it by either not being a work martyr or a slacker. The 4 Life Path often finds themselves feeling tapped out, burned out, and exhausted. You'll learn how to pace yourself, how to find outlets for true relaxation, and how to lighten up or you'll feel constantly stressed and burned out.

SYSTEMS & FOUNDATIONS

The 4 Life Path feels most comfortable when you're moving slowly and deliberately. You work out your plan and want life to be orderly. Underneath all that planning is a fear of chaos and a real dislike of appearing stupid or naïve in any situation. You'd rather opt out of trying something new than to stumble and fall. Overall, you're eminently practical, hardworking, and determined. No matter what the odds or obstacles, you'll get it done. No doubt about it, you are the rock! Think about the how the number 4 looks when drawn on a piece of paper. If you turn the 4 upside-down it resembles a chair or even a box (if you use your visual imagination!)—a sturdy surface planted solidly on the ground.

Certainly, the energy of the 4 is known as operating *inside the box*. I always suggest to the 4 Life Path to use this visualization as a point of reference: Visualize yourself curled up inside of a box. Then find the side-door that opens the box. Move yourself outside of the box and climb up and stand on top of the box instead! This way, the box serves as your foundation and root-system, yet you can solidly stand on it and get a multi-dimensional birds-eye view from the top.

As a 4 Life Path you're meant to contribute the foundational ideas, products, services, or systems of management to the world. *You bring matter into material form.* You're earth energy and thrive when connected with the earth in a variety of ways—whether literally in the garden with your hands and feet in the dirt—or more broadly through your gifts having to do with planning and making sure foundations are securely set. You can literally be a contractor or architect—digging, designing, and building actual foundations for people's lives.

BEARER OF KNOWLEDGE

As a 4 Life Path, you're always absorbing information and seeking out knowledge. For instance, if a family member is diagnosed with cancer, you immediately research everything there is to know about that particular form of cancer, consolidate the information, share it with other family members, and wonder why everyone else doesn't actively do the same.

You're always reading something, watching videos, keeping up with news outlets or podcasts you follow, and lean toward media and entertainment that's more informational rather than escapist entertainment. Not that you don't have your moments! Yet overall, you're constantly learning, learning, learning.

Animals often play an important role in your life, either as pets/family members or—in the wider sense—a 4 Life Path can often be found in the position of President of the Audubon Society, Humane Society, or other animal-related organization or cause. You're someone who learns all about animal behavior and makes sure you're providing the best possible environment for your fur baby.

And while you have a reservoir of creative talent, often it displays in more technical ways—photography, calligraphy, pottery, musical instruments—anything that calls for technical skill rather than flamboyant creativity. Think Ansel Adams, not Jackson Pollack. The 4 Life Path is often more of an artisan rather than a vortex of messy creative impulses.

Overall, the 4 Life Path is the bookworm and the one who pays for the documentary channel. You're the one who'll learn everything there is to know about a particular country or city if you're planning to travel there. You're the one who actually balances your checkbook, has money in your savings account, and enjoys a few interesting hobbies—like cheese-making, car renovation or throwing pottery.

SLOW & STEADY

Because of a potentially volatile upbringing, you have a desire to protect—yourself, things, and the people around you. You often take on the role of protector. You like things that are tangible, solid, and can be rationally explained. Honesty and loyalty are crucial to you. You have an overarching drive to earn respect from others and how you're perceptive by others is important. You're honest and above-board in all things and prefer to be known as someone who can be counted on.

The 4 Life Path takes in everything and can experience a lot of sensory over-load—meaning, you're best when doing one thing at a time, not multitasking. You process information with a slower and steadier pace. Anytime you feel pressed to think more quickly or juggle several tasks at once can lead to feelings of overwhelm. Because you absorb and process information with great depth, you need to take plenty of time for yourself and cultivate peace and quiet in your environment. This is imperative for your mental and physical health.

Overall (with some exceptions, of course!), the 4 Life Path has a sensible, traditional, well-behaved demeanor and aren't into people who are otherwise. You don't understand people who are big risk takers, don't follow the rules, or don't thrive in a more structured work or family environment. The 4 sometimes has a loner quality—you usually have no issues with taking time alone, away from the barrage of responsibilities from which you often feel burdened.

Remember that nature's beauty has a calming effect on you, so use that as one of your outlets for relaxation. You're a natural gardener or dabbler with outdoor activities. Getting your hands and feet in the dirt is a natural mind-release for you. Flexibility is a key theme for the energy of the number 4. Often the 4 can become quite rigid and inflexible—both mentally and physically. Any exercise promoting and establishing flexibility (yoga, Pilates—and kind of agility training) works wonders for your ability to adapt in a more expansive way with your body and with your mind.

THE 4 LIFE PATH & CAREER

Since *hard work* is a theme for the energy of the number 4 you might find yourself in one of two camps—either you have always taken on much more responsibility than most people *or* you avoid taking on responsibility and putting down roots. Sometimes this can show up as an odd back-and-forth.

I've known 4 Life Path's who feel that they take on a massive amount of responsibly, yet in the over-all scheme of things, it's a self-imposed perception. For instance, some 4's feel an overweening responsibility for siblings when their parent's divorce and feel as though they become the parent. Yet it's often an emotional response rather than an actuality—an internal feeling that they are taking on direct responsibilities when in reality, they're simply dealing with the issues related to having divorced parents that all of the children are saddled with, not just the 4 Life Path alone.

Which is to say, while the 4 Life Path most often comes to this lifetime with difficult family dynamics, many times the 4 adds to that dysfunction by feeling that they're taking on responsibility that isn't theirs, yet they take it on out of a martyrish sense of responsibility that simply adds to the difficulties. The 4 is learning how to step aside and go live their own life without carrying around a cart of family-related wounds with them. Ask any 4 Life Path—this is easier said than done.

This is one of my favorite quotes from a 4 Life Path: "That's why it's called *work*. It's not *supposed* to be *fun*." And since *work* is a constant theme, many 4s have some difficulty connecting with the job or career that truly lights them up. It often takes a while for a 4 to get clear on what they want to do given that *work* ultimately defines how you truly identify yourself in the world.

The identity of the 4 Life Path resides very directly in a sense of accomplishment. A 4 Life Path who doesn't settle on a favorable career or a home-base ultimately feels like a soul lost at sea. More than most of the Life Path numbers, the 4 needs to plant roots and build a solid and secure life from early on.

The 4 is the architect number and you often thrive in the construction industry. Anything requiring effort and endurance works well for you, including being an athlete, any construction trade, landscaping, law enforcement, and the military. Of course, teaching in any capacity is a great fit for the 4 Life Path. You do well in management positions and thrive with prescribed rules and regulations—and you prefer a fair and equitable salary with clear rewards and benefit program. You would forgo a little more money (and more volatility) for less money (and more consistency and predictability).

The key question to ask yourself: Can you decide upon a field in which you'll allow yourself permission to pursue success with passion? Also, know that following your true passion is all-important for you and yet this is also a challenge. Many times the 4 Life Path struggles with defaulting to the more mundane or practical path rather than doing what they truly love. Often a 4 finds themselves working in jobs in order to survive during certain times in your life—rather than focusing on what speaks to your soul.

If this describes you, it's a challenge to see the ways to advance yourself on levels that don't always place you in this more practical and work-related role. For instance, if you're in college and you want to go abroad for a semester or take a gap year, find a way to do it! Don't say you can't because of limiting circumstances. There's help and support for you if you seek it out, yet the 4 Life Path often feels that they have to go it alone because you haven't had a supportive environment growing up.

Shouldering it all on your own is your default setting and it can come back to haunt you. Learning to seek personal support and ask for help and guidance is not a natural response for the 4 Life Path.

You're here to act upon your ability to create great management systems and relay information and knowledge in a direct and no-nonsense way. You thrive in environments that offer clear rules of engagement. You're a natural manager and are often put into positions where your organizational skills and hard work ethic are required.

A few possibilities:

- Construction
- Real Estate agent
- Architect
- Athlete
- Accountant
- Police officer
- Stock broker or banking
- Pet sitter or veterinarian
- Photographer
- Firefighter
- Business franchise owner
- IT for a company or non-profit
- Website developer
- Coach
- Teacher
- Professor
- Principal
- Security professional
- Patent or trademark attorney

- Nutritionist or dietitian
- Personal trainer
- Massage therapist
- Acupuncturist
- Human Resources specialist

THE 4 LIFE PATH & RELATIONSHIPS

In relationship, you're solid, steady, and no-nonsense. If you're a woman, you may be strong to the point of being perceived as more masculine because of your *take charge* energy—you take care of everything and are super responsible. Many 4 Life Path women are drawn into intimate relationships with a partner whom they end up financially supporting.

If you're a 4 Life Path man, you don't want drama—you want a partner who appreciates your ability to provide a secure and safe haven. You're not one to embrace a lot of change or volatility in relationship. A 4 Life Path friend of mine always said that he loved his quiet, drama-free life, and he turned away a lot of relationship possibilities that didn't immediately fit into his box. It was impossible for him to imagine altering his routine in any substantial way in order to invite a new intimate partner into his world. Yet as he aged, he felt a deep regret that he didn't open up to other possibilities and find a way to be in a relationship.

And as a 4 Life Path, the first cut is the deepest (as Rod Stewart would say) and you can often carry-over your emotional wound from the first divorce (or first rejection) in a way that rivals no other. It becomes the baseline for your reaction and engagement in other relationships, often to your detriment. At the risk of looking gullible or wrong, you can either trip from similar relationship to similar relationship or opt for staying on the fence. Self-sabotage is a default for the 4 Life Path with relationships when you're feeling too vulnerable or feel you're being forced to alter your personal routines or ways of doing things.

Either way, opening yourself to a certain level of vulnerability can prove to be a challenge. The 4 can often put on the front that you've "gotten over" all of it (your alcoholic ex, your abusive father, your absent mother) and intellectually, that may be true. Yet on a core emotional and cellular level, working through these difficult and complex family and relationship issues is key to your life's work and also key to forming a life with someone with whom you can feel safe and secure. And doing this isn't something that truly has a finish point—it's an ongoing and life long process.

4 LIFE PATH
Opposing Forces

IT'S JUST NOT FUNNY

While the 4 Life Path can certainly have a sense of humor and moments of lightheartedness, you tip the scales toward seriousness, brainy activity, and rational thought. Sometimes the opinions and assertions of the 4 Life Path have a tendency to land like a sledgehammer. You may come off as cynical or abrasive when you offer advice, yet what you're really trying to do is offer information you think will help a person or a situation. Some might observe that you can have a certain smug or even combative quality.

There's a seriousness to the 4 Life Path that can show up as wanting to dominate a situation through *rational discourse*. You're the first to say you don't want to argue, and yet you most often end up in arguments because you tend to be opinionated about things you feel you know a lot about. You need a lot of positive affirmation and are uncomfortable with, or even afraid of, criticism. If you can't do something perfectly according to your standards, you often don't do it at all. As a result, sometimes you wonder why you feel so stuck or why nothing ever works out for you. You can make the same mistake over and over (and over) again—the irony being that your primary goal is *not* to make any mistakes.

LIMITATION

The number 4 is about *limitation*. You're here to learn how to identify how you limit yourself and also how to move through (around or over) the limitations presented to you. Given that this is a theme for the vibe of the 4, you'll get more than your share of limitation in your life.

The energy of the 4 invites you to either stand strongly and firmly *on top of the box* or it pulls you toward placing yourself *inside of the box*. It's up to you to navigate which direction you want to take. Yet, the 4 Life Path is known for being more of an *inside the box* thinker. You benefit from allowing yourself to rise above the water line—so to speak—and see that there are other ways of thinking and operating.

Often the 4 is the ultimate micromanager and only when you step out of your own way can you truly have success. So, while your knowledge-based and systematic thinking is a gift you're developing, it's also what you're working with softening and massaging into flexibility. As a 4 Life Path, you crave structure and security—yet as in all things, this needs balance and modulation.

FAMILY WOUNDS OR ISSUES

Home is important to you. You crave a sense of security that *home* exemplifies. One of the primary issues faced by the 4 Life Path is the necessity to work through issues with family of origin. While all of us have family history to deal with, the 4 Life Path rides a particularly rough or intense road with family that's at the core of the healing and learning you've come here to do. Many 4 Life Paths have family histories that include literal or figurative abandonment, abusive parents, drug or alcohol abuse by one or both parents, an early death of a loved one, and other forms of trauma.

Some 4's experience issues that are perhaps more subliminal, yet still make a mark on you in a core way that effects how you engage with the world. In order to work optimally with the gifts of the 4, you benefit when you take a look at your wounded or problematic relationships and work through the feelings of lack and pain they've brought to you. Often this comes when you create a secure environment for yourself in whatever way works for you, either in the creation of the family you wish you'd had or mindfully choosing your family of choice with friends, pets, and others.

Often a 4 Life Path will staunchly assert that they're *over* their family issues and yet they still occupy a lot of emotional energy. It's a matter of truly coming to terms with it and letting it go in a deep way. Of course, all human beings benefit from healing their personal trauma. *It's just that this is a foundational theme for you and is often a contributor to your intense need for a sense of security.*

For instance, I know a 4 Life Path young woman who's an only child and her parents divorced when she was three years old. She went back and forth between her mother and father's houses as a child—sometimes a three-hour drive one way. She moved to different towns and attended different schools with her mother's job changes. While she's adaptable, she craves the stability that she didn't have as a child.

This sense of insecurity and over-whelm guides her choices as she's faced with decisions about college and projecting what she wants for her future. She's a bright and intelligent young woman and yet doesn't really see the world as her oyster—rather she wants to create a world that she feels is less chaotic and unpredictable. That can become a coping mechanism for the 4 Life Path and yet ends up creating a more limited reality.

RIGIDITY

There's a definitive tendency for the 4 Life Path to develop somewhat rigid black-and-white rules for life that you feel everyone should adhere to, respect, and act upon. Let's face it—you're baffled at people who can't make a plan, who don't follow the rules, and who live more in the emotional realm. These people just need to get real, get with the program, and get a life, right?

For you, rigid thinking begets a rigid physical body. You're challenged with devoting effort to keeping your mind and body flexible. The 4 is the number of *health* in numerology. The 4 Life Path benefits when you have friends or a partner who push you just a little bit out of your comfort zone and encourage you to take a little risk.

Part of the result of rigidity comes out as blunt communication. And while there is something to be said for honesty, I remember hearing actress Kristen Bell in an interview where she quoted her therapist who said: "Honesty without tact is cruelty." The 4 Life Path benefits with the cultivation of tact and diplomacy.

Every human being needs to overcome limiting circumstances and learn how to take stable and systematic steps to accomplish things in life. Everyone needs to take responsibility and learn how to work hard to accomplish their goals. Yet as a 4 Life Path, hard work and limitation are focal points and aspects for development all your life. Therefore, the themes of rooting yourself and taking the longer-range view directly connects with the characteristics of the key people who play certain roles in your life script, whether as intimate partners, family members, teachers, colleagues, or even random meetings.

The themes of the 4 (seeking out knowledge, working hard, being practical, taking responsibility) direct traffic in terms of the situations you find yourself in, the people who show up, and as the way life lessons come your way.

Biggest Blind Spot: Self-limiting behaviors that stem from blaming others or circumstances. The 4 Life Path will fight a duel to the death insisting that life must be hard, punishing, and grueling.

4 Life Path Superpower: If there's anyone who can get the job done, no matter what the job is, it's the 4 Life Path. Focus, tenacity, and endurance are your superpower.

4 Life Path Mantra: "Slow and steady wins the race."

PRACTICAL ADVICE FOR THE 4 LIFE PATH

Practical advice for the most practical and pragmatic of the Life Path's! The breakthrough for the 4 resides in coming to terms with—and finding ways to let go of—stubborn resistance to change and limiting belief patterns. How to absolve yourself from self-sabotaging behaviors while also fulfilling the nature of your stability and security-seeking 4 Life Path?

First and foremost, it's about *awareness*. Like most things, awareness is the first step. Seeking information and developing it into knowledge is second. And then it's about committing to the quest of consciously getting out of your own way! I'll be brutally honest. Can you surrender your need to be right about everything—and be flexible enough to lighten up and open to other perspectives and possibilities?

Many 4's find it impossible to step away from whatever dogmatic position they find themselves devoted to, even if it would lead to better health, happiness, and well-being. There's an underlying element of fear just underneath the surface that drives this tendency to *white knuckle* it—to hold on so hard and so tightly, even when what's being held onto isn't even what you want. Why? Because, well, *it's what you know*. Familiarity breeds content—or contentment with discontent.

Find ways to lighten up! Life is heavy enough, no need to add to the heap by taking everything so seriously. The "To-Do" List won't ever go away, so make sure you put *yourself* on your list. Seriously, you must get *less serious*. Step away from it all for a moment and devote yourself to healthy routines that include proper exercise, nutrition, and relaxation. Remember, the 4 is the number of health, therefore you must prioritize proper care and maintenance. This isn't just a once-a-year affair! We're talking about a lifestyle choice. Make this a life-long priority.

Elevate your emotional intelligence. According to Daniel Goleman, author of *Emotional Intelligence: Why It Can Matter More Than IQ*, the five key elements to emotional intelligence (EI) are: self-awareness, self-regulation, motivation, empathy, and social skills. The 4 is always learning how to engage your emotional connection with people (and with yourself) rather than relegating people and experiences into pragmatic chunks of data that are devoid of emotional nuance. You reach your highest potential as a 4 Life Path when you merge your intellect, organizational and managerial skills, and systems-building skills with emotional intelligence.

Pursue information and therapeutic tools for healing trauma. While one would agree that this is practical advice for every Life Path number, it's the ultimate conduit for the growth and highest expression of the 4 Life Path. This is where the pot of gold is buried. When the 4 can identify and come to terms with the locus of why you feel so responsible for everyone—and so beleaguered and tired because of the effort it takes to do things without foundational support—this is when life can become more effortless and flow with more ease. This is when the 4 can give yourself permission to flow *with* life rather than continuous struggle *against it* as you try to control it.

INSPIRATION FOR THE 4 LIFE PATH

A few good reads to inspire, educate, and inform the 4 Life Path. These are simply suggestive of topics that would speak to your 4 Life Path mission on some level.

Any book, class, or tool that offers you ways to think about creative problem solving, healing trauma and family dysfunction, learning about how to develop systems, and how to disengage from limiting beliefs are perfect for you.

Here are just a few suggestions, yet depending on when you read this book—now or 20-years from now (which may be your *now* if that's when you're picking up this book), there will be many new books and resources from which to choose.

I simply encourage you to read biographies and autobiographies of those on the 4 Life Path to find a sense of connection and also as cautionary tales that can save you from making similar missteps.

- *Buddha's Brain: The Practical Neuroscience of Happiness, Love and Wisdom* by Rick Hanson and Richard Mencius
- *Taking a Risk* by Caroline Easton
- *Healing from Trauma: A Survivor's Guide to Understanding Your Symptoms and Reclaiming Your Life* by Jasmin Lee Cori and Robert Scaer
- *Broken Open: How Difficult Times Can Help Us Grow* by Elizabeth Lesser
- *Unspoken Legacy: Addressing the Impact of Trauma and Addiction within the Family* by Claudia Black, PhD
- *Emotional Intelligence: Why It Can Matter More Than IQ* by Daniel Goleman
- *Thinking in Systems* by Donelia H. Meadows
- *Systems Thinking for Social Change* by David Peter Stroh
- *Emotional Agility: Get Unstuck Embrace Change and Thrive in Work and Life* by Susan David
- *Inside the Box: A Proven System of Creativity for Breakthrough Results* by Drew Boyd

A FEW WELL-KNOWN 4 LIFE PATH'S

4 Life Paths
Chelsea Handler (February 25, 1975)
Téa Leoni (February 25, 1966)
Adam Sandler (September 9, 1966)

4 or 13/4 Life Paths
Nicole Kidman (June 20, 1967)
Oprah Winfrey (January 29, 1965)
Grace VanderWaal (January 15, 2004)
Kate Hudson (April 19, 1979)
Kim Kardashian (October 21, 1980)
Octavia Spencer (May 25, 1972)
Meghan Markle (August 4, 1981)
Nicki Minaj (December 8, 1982)
Drake (October 24, 1986)
Jimmy Fallon (September 19, 1974)
Brad Pitt (December 18, 1963)
Benedict Cumberbatch (July 19, 1976)
Usher (October 14, 1978)
Bill Gates (October 28, 1955)
Elton John (March 25, 1947)
Jake Gyllenhaal (December 19, 1980)
Keanu Reeves (September 2, 1964)
Jordan Peele (February 21, 1979)

4 or 22/4 Life Paths
Viola Davis (August 11, 1965)
Tina Fey (May 18, 1970)
Will Smith (September 25, 1968)
Clint Eastwood (May 31, 1930)
Matthew McConaughey (November 4, 1969)
Charles Manson (November 12, 1934)
Leonardo DaVinci (April 15, 1452)
14th Dali Lama (July 6, 1935)
Richard Branson (July 18, 1950)

5

How to Calculate Your Life Path Number?

Use your date of birth
"June 4, 1975"
Add your
Month + Day + Year

June = 4
4 = 4;
1974 = 1 + 9 + 7 + 5 = 22;
6 + 4 + 22 = 32 and 3 + 2 = 5
(22 is a master number and isn't reduced)

Key Themes

- Freedom / Fearlessness
- "Depth of Experience"
- Adventure / Focused Change
- Versatility / Fun
- Sensual / Travel
- Self-Discipline

Your Mission Statement

To develop your ability to develop your sense of fearlessness, adventurousness, and to show others how to face their fears — you're meant to develop the constructive use of freedom.

Some Fitting Careers

- Sales
- Travel Related Careers
- Web Development and Design
- Restaurant Service
- Performer
- Social Media Manager

Core Lessons and Challenges

- Self-indulgence and excess
- Addictive tendencies
- Lacking focus and initiative
- Fearful and restricted
- Drama and procrastination

Relationship Compatibility

- 5 and 1 = Freedom-seeking & Leadership
- 5 and 2 = Freedom-seeking & Heart
- 5 and 3 = Freedom-seeking & Creative Expression
- 5 and 4 = Freedom-seeking & Security
- 5 and 5 = Freedom-seeking & Freedom-seeking
- 5 and 6 = Freedom-seeking & Nurturing
- 5 and 7 = Freedom-seeking & Spirituality
- 5 and 8 = Freedom-seeking & Power
- 5 and 9 = Freedom-seeking & Compassion

Your Power

- High energy and fun
- Fearless and adventurous
- Agent of change and freedom-seeking
- Progressive thought and action
- Sensual and tactile

Well-Known 5s

- Angelina Jolie (June 4, 1975)
- Russell Brand (June 4, 1975)
- Jay-Z (December 4, 1969)
- Alexandria Ocasio-Cortez (October 13, 1989)

The 5 Life Path tests your ability to find inner freedom through discipline, focus, and committing to depth of experience. Even when you're challenged with reigning it in. You can do it!

5 LIFE PATH

THE SENSUOUS FREEDOM SEEKER

For to be free is not merely to cast off one's chains, but to live in a way that respects and enhances the freedom of others.

— Nelson Mandela

Optimal Qualities

A 5 Life Path's optimal expression is fearlessness, adventurousness, self-discipline, and the ability to show others how to live their lives fearlessly.

Your personal mission is to develop the constructive use of freedom and use self-discipline to experience all life has to offer.

Your life's purpose is to find inner freedom through discipline, focus, and depth of experience.

FREEDOM

The 5 Life Path is all about the expression of freedom through self-discipline—the constructive use of freedom. You're always working toward creating multi-levels of freedom in your life. To find physical freedom, one must exercise, pay attention to what you eat, moderate stress, and generally be mindful about the proper care and maintenance of the physical body.

To build financial freedom, one is required to decide on your financial wants and needs, determine the best job or career to meet those needs, do what it takes to secure that job, invest wisely, and enjoy the expansive freedom that having financial resources offers.

To create spiritual freedom, one must explore the depths and self-evaluate along the way, mutating all experiences into spiritual growth and evolution. Emotional freedom is linked to spiritual seeking and often goes hand in hand with the potential journey of the 5 Life Path. At the end of the day, the 5 Life Path is learning engage the ultimate freedom—freedom of mind, body, and spirit.

Yet the pathway to create this freedom certainly can occupy a lifetime! It's all about the *experience*, after all, and the 5 Life Path's mission has everything to do with traversing this lifetime as an intrepid traveler. Of course, the issue resides with a cultivation of balance and focus. As Janis Joplin sings in "Me and Bobby McGee," is freedom just another word for nothing left to lose (nothin' ain't worth nothin' cause it's free)? Or is freedom more than that? Or is it something else entirely? *Freedom* is a key and central theme for the 5 Life Path and you get to work with how you define and act upon your sense of freedom throughout your life.

The 5 *feels* everything intensely! It's all about how things look, how it feels, how it tastes, and how it smells. The 5 is meant to enjoy all the sensuous experience life has to offer—sex, delicious food, the fragrance of a flower (perfume, or cookies baking in the oven) and the feeling of beautiful fabric against the skin. Sometimes freedom is confused with self-indulgence.

Since it's all about the experience, all about the *high*, all about "what's next?"—the 5 Life Path can grapple with pushing their freedoms a bit over the edge. How? With addictive behaviors, with self-focus, and with a certain level of irresponsibility. Somehow, the 5 Life Path feels this perpetual gnawing sense that something's *missing*—what exactly that might be is often elusive.

The 5 Life Path lives an unfiltered life. What you need to know is that you basically operate *without a filter*. You experience everything in a big way and in what I call "ADHD time." By this I mean that you have all sorts of information swirling around you all of the time and you find it difficult to choose a focal point or to filter information out by priority. You feel you must experience little tidbits of *all* of it.

I think of it this way. It's as though you experience life as though you've walked into a bar on a Saturday night. It's packed. Music is blaring, there are six TV's strategically placed around the room (all playing different channels), the bartenders are clinking glasses and filling drink orders, people are laughing and talking at high volumes, and you keep hearing fragments of different conversations wafting in and out of your perception. You walk into the room and find it absolutely impossible to filter all the stimulus—your eyes dart to the TV's, your attention distracted by the heated conversation going on between two people at the bar, and you already downed a second cocktail just to get an immediate buzz so that you can cope with it all.

That's how I envision the 5 Life Path experiencing basic day-to-day life. Does that ring true for you, 5 Life Path?

Or put differently, you might tend to get overwhelmed easily because you lack the ability to filter and prioritize information and experiences. It's like you're a little kid who won't go to sleep at night when your parents have company over for the evening, because you're afraid you'll miss out on something.

Your job is to develop self-discipline and some routine in your life so that you have a container for your boundless energy and for the information you're attempting to process. If you don't establish discipline, light routine, and a focused sense of purpose, life will be entirely too chaotic and out of control.

A funny yet relevant example: A friend of mine (a 5 Life Path with other 5's in her chart) keeps a list taped to her wall by her bed. It goes something like this: "1. Get up before 11 a.m. 2. Drink 6 glasses of water 3. Take at least a 20-minute walk . . ." Where a "normal" person might scoff and think that her list was pretty much "no-duh" in terms of what activities comprise any given day, this 5 Life Path needs to remind herself and hold herself accountable for what others might consider obvious basics.

For a 5, often life is so freewheeling that you skip over the basics and then wonder why everything is spinning out of control. A 5 Life Path needs supportive reminders to eat consistently, to hydrate, and to do some of the other essentials that might come easily and without conscious consideration for other people.

The theme to your party as a 5 Life Path is the *constructive use of freedom*. That means that you must first determine what freedom actually means or represents to you. What degrees of freedom are vital to you? The trick is to have enough discipline to produce a positive or lasting result. It's easy for a person to do anything they want to (whenever they want to) and label it *freedom*. And yet, is the person who can't hold down a job really free? Is the person who eats and drinks whatever they think they want really free? There's a distinct difference between true freedom and mere self-indulgence or rebelliousness. The ultimate expression of the 5 is all about having something to show for your efforts—and to sprinkle in some fun along the way.

SENSUAL EXPERIENCE

The 5 Life Path is extremely passionate and here to experience the raw physicality of life on earth in every way, shape, and form you can muster. The world is your oyster (if not your brothel)! Your desire for experience manifests itself in many different ways—through all the sensual and tactile experiences you can embrace. Your life is all about the senses. You long to experience everything in its fullest degree. Things must taste right, smell good, look pretty, and feel pleasing or you're just not happy. And yes, you're a little OCD about some of these things.

The 5 can lean toward extremely self-oriented needs regarding how things look, feel, and taste. Many 5s make quite a show of choosing their wine or liquor at a restaurant, deciding on clothing, or getting your food *just right*—it all must be the highest and best quality (or at least to your standards, whatever those standards may be!). You like to look attractive and so you invest time and money in your appearance. You relish sensual and earthy pleasures.

Yet if you become enmeshed in seeking constant stimulation, you could find yourself struggling with addictions. Be aware that your desire for fun, adventure, sensual pleasure, and escape will draw you into seeking highs—whether you gain peak experiences through sex, food, drugs, alcohol, travel, or overwork. Any addictive behavior that initially feels comforting will *most likely* become problematic down the road.

This can show up in various ways. There are 5's who have weight issues due to over-indulgence in food and 5's who are anorexic or bulimic. Many 5's can have a monogamous sex life and yet excesses might show up with gambling, drinking, or workaholism. I know a 5 Life Path who isn't interested in sex at all, yet he loves to drink wine—and a lot of it. The same 5 barely gets out of the house and isn't altogether social, yet he's committed to traveling to different places to hunt during hunting season. It's his way of expressing his freedom—he says he never feels more of a sense of freedom than when he's by himself in the wild. My point is that *freedom* is a pejorative term and can express in myriad ways.

What I want to stress is that every human can struggle with additions. This isn't reserved only for the 5 Life Path! While addictive tendencies tend to be a central theme or issue for the 5, this is also part of the pathway to living and expressing the 5 Life Path purpose. It's all about how serious or destructive the addictions you choose become for you and how long it takes you before you've *been there, done that* and use that experience to make your life better and to inform your personal growth.

I'll use 5 Life Path Russell Brand as an example. If you know anything about comedian Russell Brand, to me he is a poster child for the 5 Life Path—*in neon!* Russell's story revolves around his rather outrageous and compulsive personality. Early on, he worked as a comedian and actor. Talk about living without a filter! He'll tell you he was seriously addicted to sex, alcohol, and drugs to the point where he was laying on the floor after shooting heroin and realized if he didn't get help, he would die sooner rather than later.

He got help through spirituality—with transcendental meditation and other modalities. He got clean and sober, is compulsive about attending support groups to keep him on track, got remarried, has children, and now focuses his efforts on getting the word out about personal growth with a podcast and other outlets. By the time you read this book, who knows what he'll be doing!

Brand was once asked how he remains clean and sober—if he ever feels the impulse to use again. He answered by saying that it's a choice he and every addicted person must make every single day. He said that the three things that keep him on track are his wife and kids, the support groups he attends, and that he has instituted *structure, order, and routine into his life.* This is the ultimate expression of the 5 Life Path—freedom by drawing boundaries, instituting productive routines, and establishing a structure from which to stabilize yourself. There are no boundaries as long as there's stability.

THE CATALYST

The 5 Life Path insists on variety and gets bored easily. In fact, you need and seek constant stimulation. One of the attributes of the 5 Life Path is progressive thought and action. You're never the one longing for what was "back in the day." *Change is freedom and freedom is change.* When you're around, you're always a reminder that life should be lived, relished, and devoured. The term *carpe diem* was coined for the 5 Life Path—live for the day! What's the point otherwise, right? *Come on, people! Live a little!*

You're a magnet attracting people who could be considered off the beaten path and opt for the quirky and forward thinking in all aspects of life. You're a rebel and will stand for what you believe in. The energy of the 5 is all about pushing the envelope. The 5 Life Path walks into the room and shakes things up. How? With your vivacious energy. With your ability to query, have a real conversation, and ask real questions—while wanting to know the real answers! You have an uncanny and unusual ability to be, well, *unusual!* You're all about the exploration and with it, you change people's perspectives and offer new ways of seeing life.

FEARLESSNESS & ADVENTURE

Freedom is won by coming face-to-face with fear. And since this is your life's mission, you'll be met with many things in life that will elicit fear in you—from the minor internal forces to the larger and more extreme outer forces. You're being trained to risk, to dive in, to embrace a little bit of danger, to extend yourself into situations where you must engage with the immediacy of the situation and trust your reflexes—and your gut!

There's a difference between throwing yourself into the abyss and forging a fearless path. You're learning the difference between getting the "Darwin Award" and mastering a healthy sense of risk and fearlessness in all aspects of life—when skydiving or when engaging in a hard conversation.

At the end of the day, your life's purpose centers on showing other people *through your example* (not by jabbering about it!) how to live an adventurous and fearless existence—and how to embrace and thrive with change and transition.

There's an adventurous quality to you and you thrive when you listen to the urge to travel and experience different aspects of the world. Part of your mission as a 5 Life Path is to embrace *the other* and to experience (or accept and acknowledge) different cultures, different racial backgrounds, different sexual preferences, different economic status, and different political and religious beliefs. I'm not saying you have to *be* on the outskirts. I'm suggesting that you're always drawn to learning more and experiencing things (people, environments, experiences) that are outside of the box, outside of your home town, outside of the social mores with which you were brought up. Often the 5 Life Path is the family member who continues to cause eye-rolling and is asked at family gatherings: "*So, when are you going to settle down?*" The 5 Life Path often gets cast in the role of the black sheep of the family.

CHANGE & TRANSFORMATION

Author Kevin Quinn Avery has this to say about the 5 Life Path:

> . . . Those born under this sign will live a life of constant change. If they accept and seek this change, they will find success, and everything else that anyone could ever dream of. If they reject this change, they are going to have more misery than a dozen others put together. Theirs is a life of adventure, romance, travel, attainment, and sex. They are quick witted, outgoing, and usually well liked in an instant by others. They are magnetic; they will live more in their life span than a score of others. . . . On the positive side this is quite possibility the greatest happiness that one can find in life; one the negative side it is abject misery. The 'Five,' often classified as the rolling stone, is misunderstood by those that would like to see him stay put. But to 'stay put' is not his life; let others stay in their ruts, for the 'Five' is the path of freedom and all that goes with it. The 'Five' must be more careful in his life than others that he does not cause hurt or unhappiness on his way. The 'Five' should above all numbers understand his path well, so that he may plan his life in regards to marriage, business. The 'Five' is found to be the most faithful of husbands or wives, once married. (*The Numbers of Life*, 11-12)

This is a lifetime where you're developing and embracing resilience and a sense of trust in the unknown. Not only are you being challenged to invite and allow substantial change, you're being asked to invite it, trust it, embrace it, and cultivate it—and to act on it with a certain sense of fun, curiosity, and trust.

The magic ingredients are healthy discernment and focus. It's easy to get distracted by the bright and shiny objects along the way. And sometimes those detours add to the satisfaction of your over-all journey. Yet when you can determine a healthy saturation point and then level a degree of focus on making things happen, this is when you're at your highest and best.

THE 5 LIFE PATH & RELATIONSHIPS

Since the 5 Life Path is meant to experience the sensual nature of life, you might decide against marrying young—yet if you do, chances are you'll get married more than once (join that club, right?). The crucial element resides in how you perceive your freedom within the relationship. The 5 can't stand a clingy partner. "Don't control me" and "Don't fence me in!" are your touch-tones.

You need a lot of space and freedom, especially early in your sexual life. You often feel restless to the point of second-guessing the person you're with, finding faults based on skewed expectations or boredom, and often ending it when you find that the grass is greener in someone else's bedroom.

There is a sense of restlessness to you that's undeniable. Since you're all about sensual pleasures, you can be quick to jump in and out of relationships and can be lured away from a current relationship by the promise of more passion, sex, and excitement elsewhere. Deep down you're probably not interested in commitment—or at least not until you have burned through some years of high intensity and sensual exploration. *Space* and *freedom* mutate in meaning as you mature, yet early on, the 5 Life Path often experiences a revolving door of relationship partners.

After you've *been there, done that*, the 5 Life Path can be the most committed marriage partner. When you make up your mind it's what you want *and you won't be missing out on anything*, this is when a committed long-term relationship becomes a priority. Yet you still need to maintain a certain level of autonomy and be with a partner who understands your sometimes quirky need for space.

A dear 5 Life Path friend of mine jokingly (*not jokingly?*) says that his M.O. in his relationship life has been to be constantly in the revolving-door, feeling like he's in a loop where he keeps missing the exit and has to keep navigating his way around and around in the loop until he can finally make it out. He observes that as soon as he enters into a relationship (and he's virtually always in a relationship), he instantly experiences a feeling that comes with an image that he's an animal caught in a trap and he has an internal impulse to start chewing his own arm off so that he can escape!

The 5 Life Path usually displays a certain degree of self-absorption and inability to understand the needs of a partner. When you and your *other* communicate about wants and needs effectively, you can be a loving and committed partner. Until then, you're usually experimenting, trying things out, and feeling your way through without landing anywhere—at least not for long. Understand that this isn't usually a diabolical plan that you've concocted to *love 'em and leave 'em.* You live in the moment and dive into a relationship with intensity. It's just that it can lose its luster sooner rather than later and the 5 is more prone to seek satisfaction elsewhere rather than to move through the more mundane demands that a day-to-day partnership requires.

Or alternately, the 5 Life Path hangs on and hangs in with a relationship far past the time to exit, wishing for their freedom and feeling miserable about how constrained and pinned-down they feel.

THE 5 LIFE PATH & CAREER

As a 5 Life Path, you're a natural salesperson when you believe in what you're selling. To use the cliché, you can sell ice to Eskimos. You're likely to be entrepreneurial and would rather not be subject to someone else's authority. This can show up as being a salesperson, consultant, or other career where you work for another entity—the stability and structure you need—yet you have more freedom of movement and control over what you do. *Don't fence me in* applies to your work-life as well as to your personal life.

You're a natural forensic scientist, as you love a mystery. Exploring, probing, and questioning are second-nature to you. The 5 is often drawn to the metaphysical world and can excel in many healing arts modalities. Like a 3 Life Path, you're versatile, curious, creative, and high-energy.

Often, you'll have more than one career designation in your lifetime and often they'll be highly different. Construction manager turned massage therapist. Computer programmer turned food entrepreneur. Actor turned clothing designer. Travel guide turned real estate investor. The sky's the limit for you and yet the bottom line resides in your ability to focus and follow-through—and also to know when to say *good-bye* to something and when to stick with it.

Can you embrace the fact that you're meant for travel, adventure, and will experience a lot of changing circumstances in your life? With a 5 Life Path, it's all about experiencing the world in its full glory. You're at your best when you can tap into a fearless sense of adventure, use your versatility in a focused and dynamic way, and see the world as your big adventurous playground. Usually being a bank teller or any 9-to-5'er just won't cut it for you—at least not for the long-haul. Anything where you can act on your adventurous spirit is perfect.

Usually, you won't do one thing for an extended period of time or if you do, it's because it has built-in variety. The 5 is all about the experience and so you're more apt to follow your impulses and you need to experience different forms of stimulation.

Your biggest nemesis is feeling confined and tethered. Work on not abandoning something before you even begin. Or alternately, not hanging on to something long after its expiration date! You're here to act upon your amazing versatility and dynamic forward-thinking energies. You're an agent of change and are meant to push boundaries and show others how to tame fears and enjoy life. You're a catalyst for change. You thrive in environments offering freedom and variety.

A 5 Life Path's optimal expression is fearlessness, adventurousness, and the ability to show others how to live their lives fearlessly—by living your own life as an epic adventure.

A few possibilities:

- Web developer
- IT
- Travel guide
- Bodyworker
- Actor or musician
- Forensic scientist
- Environmental activist
- Ski instructor
- Travel writer
- Skydiving instructor
- Pilot
- Mechanic
- Motivational speaker
- Parole officer
- Bartender
- Drug/addiction counselor
- Comedian
- Consultant
- Traveling salesperson

5 LIFE PATH
Opposing Forces

EXCESS

The number 5 is the number of excess, plain and simple. And while excess usually shows up in the ways you'd expect it to—with drugs, alcohol, and that sort of thing—you may choose a more retracted form of excess by way of excessive control over yourself and situations, excessive fear around pretty much anything, or excessive reclusiveness. Excessive sensitivity. Meeting things in life *excessively*. This can also show up less in addictive tendencies than in, say, excessive travel. You get the drift.

And again, this is something you rarely recognize because it's simply how you live in the world. Doesn't everyone experience the world in full techno-color? Not really. Not in the way you do.

Yet, getting back to your primary mission and cosmic classroom—on every level you're learning about freedom. What it is, what it isn't, and how to cultivate it. The 5 Life Path sometimes has trouble with healthy routine, keeping a calendar or planning ahead of time. You can start something with vigor and quickly the enthusiasm dissipates and soon the diet is out the window, the exercise class is skipped, or the resolve to change something reverts back to where it started. *There's a difference between being spontaneous and being indecisive, procrastinating or irresponsible.*

Sometimes the 5 leans toward self-absorbed indecisiveness rather than spunky spontaneity. You can be the one who'll arrive late because you just weren't paying attention to the time. Or you can be the one who won't commit to a plan until you feel darn good and ready—without taking other people's schedules or feelings into consideration. Sometimes you must be careful to not make it all about *you* all the time.

Since you tend to run on all cylinders, special care needs to be taken with your adrenals and with cortisol levels. Since your tendency is to produce a bit of drama, your normal stress levels are fairly high. Understand this: When I suggest that you produce a bit of drama, realize that this may not even be outward drama—this can be *internal drama*. The 5 Life Path's constantly responding in heightened ways to daily occurrences.

For instance, sometimes a 5 Life Path finds eating on a regular basis a challenge. They'll forget to eat or be too busy to eat. Then they'll binge. Or finally eat after a day of not eating and wonder why they can't think properly or why their blood sugar has crashed or any number of other conditions that relate to not eating consistently. Sometimes a 5 Life Path has a lot of dietary restrictions and the sheer act of eating becomes a major issue. I'm using food as just one example of how health might be impacted by the frenetic day-to-day engagement you have with daily functions and routines.

A tendency you might have as a 5 Life Path has to do with an over-focus on how you personally feel—*all the time*. There are 5's who won't get out of bed unless they *feel like it*. Or they'll cancel appointments because they feel a headache coming on. Or they won't exercise because they don't like being sore the next day—or, or, or. It's an *over-engagement* with how you feel at any given moment. There's an exaggerated emphasis on your own feelings.

As a counterpoint, a 4 Life Path will slap you on the back and tell you to get over yourself and get to work, because they're the ones who muscle through adversity and stick to a commitment no matter how they might personally feel at that moment.

And even as I discuss this, I know that often the 5 Life Path might say: "What? No, not me!" without having an overarching understanding about the ways in which they linger over every little thing happening to them and around them. There's no point of reference for understanding that not everyone experiences life without a filter in this manner, dear 5 Life Path! It's your blessing—and it also can prove to be a stumbling block to your ability to execute the kind of results you would like to receive in life.

ESCAPE

Escape can be the name of your game. Understand that escape can also present itself as *running away* or *avoiding responsibility*. If you aren't making use of your high energy and drive, life can easily turn into a soap opera. The 5 can thrive on drama and emotional turmoil, finding escape hatches in TV, movies, books, or other diversions—video games, crossword puzzles, podcasts or meddling in other people's business.

Most 5s tend to need constant stimulus, until they want to be left alone! Your mind works overtime and so it's no wonder you need a way to relax and clear your head. The trick will always be in the balance and in the choice of relaxant. Read a book or smoke a bong? Go for a jog or keep playing video poker? No one can say that crossword puzzles are bad for you—unless you're working on them at the expense of your involvement in other key aspects of your life.

As a general rule, the 5 Life Path opts for an easier or more *fun* route whenever possible. There's nothing wrong with the easier route—yet for you, that often comes with some detours around personal responsibility.

Detours can look like sabotaging intimate relationships (to escape commitment), habitually turning to drugs or other substances (to numb or lessen emotional intake and escape "reality"), or retracting from life (to protect yourself from fearful experiences). You can also escape by retreating, which sounds antithetical for the sensual and gregarious 5 Life Path.

FEAR

Since the 5 is all about stepping full-throttle into all life has to offer with a fearless spirit, the downside to your *go all-in or go home* agenda might be that you turn into the anti-adventurer and the anti-freedom seeker. We're always dealing with the oppositional elements that our Life Path purpose puts in front of us.

The mandate of the 5 Life Path includes becoming fearless, inviting heighten levels of fear to be faced. Expansion, fearlessness, and change are your key values. When you shut down those aspects of yourself, you start to retract and life becomes smaller and smaller.

A few possible scenarios: If you begin working from home, you might become reclusive and have difficulty garnering the courage or energy even to step out of the house to run errands or buy groceries. There are 5 Life Path's who hyperventilate at the thought of packing their suitcase, have no desire to go out and interact with people socially, and who have many phobias.

I've known several 5 Life Path's who experience issues related to being confined. The fears can show up as being unable to use an elevator, drive a car over a bridge, or get an MRI because of severe claustrophobia. As a 5 Life Path, you can experience more than your share of fears that might not have any rational explanation, yet the way they affect your life is very real.

RESTRICTION

Issues that the 5 Life Path experiences in the *fear realm* often connect very directly with *restriction*—fears that are based in having your freedoms limited or taken away. The 5 often feels this deep sense of FOMO (Fear Of Missing Out) and yet it's much deeper than that. The fear of being confined, tethered, and boxed in can keep you in a perpetual state of *one foot in and one foot out*, whether it's with a career choice or a relationship.

This results in several things—the first being that you surprise and upset people who feel you're *all in* when you're really not. When you flee the scene, so to speak, you leave collateral damage along the way. Other people can see the 5 as lacking integrity—or having a tough time taking responsibility for yourself, your emotions, and your actions.

In fact, a 5 Life Path will always deal with more than their share of restriction. Sometimes, rather than throwing yourself into the sensual nature of the world, you choose to cut yourself off from it. More than others, you may gravitate toward restrictive or controlling relationships, restrictive or confining aspects to your job, or have health restrictions, just to name a few examples.

There's truth to the fact that often your biggest fears are placed in your path in order for you to live your 5 Life Path purpose. As Joseph Campbell suggests: "The cave you fear to enter holds the treasure you seek." Overcoming and befriending your biggest, most debilitating fears is the name of the game as you evolve and master your freedom-loving 5 Life Path.

EMOTIONAL PARALYSIS

Since you experience the world without a filter, the 5 Life Path has a tendency to experience a somewhat perpetual sense of overwhelm. You can be hit by emotional paralysis on various levels. This can come into play when you meet up with an obstacle that requires some recalibration of thought and action—rather than moving through it in your usual (somewhat) lucky and breezy way. The slightest frustration can send you over the top.

In relationship, this can become erosive because—while you expect your partner to meet your needs and express their feelings with clarity—chances are that these are areas where you're personally somewhat weak. You might expect from others what you don't even know you're not extending to them. Are you asking *them* how they feel and *respecting it?* Perhaps not.

In your work life, you need freedom and a certain sense of self-regulation—yet most of the time you don't see how this impacts others on your team or with whom you interact with in the work environment. Sometimes you have difficulty meeting an issue head-on and will instead choose the side-door and then wonder why you aren't getting what you want.

The 5 Life Path has a tendency to either abandon something before it has a chance to get going, or in this case, the 5 hangs on to something far after the shelf-life has expired.

Every human being needs to face fears and learn how to enjoy life's pleasures. Everyone needs to be adventurous and learn how to create their desired levels of freedom. Yet as a 5 Life Path, freedom through self-discipline and sensual experience are focal points and aspects for development all your life. Therefore, the themes of facing and managing fear—and experiencing life to the fullest—directly connect with the characteristics of the key people who play certain roles in your life script, whether as intimate partners, family members, teachers, colleagues, or even random meetings.

The themes of the 5 (constructive use of freedom, fearless adventure, instigator of change, excessive behaviors) direct traffic in terms of the situations you find yourself in, the people who show up, and as the way life lessons come your way.

Biggest Blind Spot: Being unaware how self-focused on *how you feel* all the time and how it affects you and those around you.

5 Life Path Superpower: You're a sparkling ray of life-giving energy and offer different perspectives, different directions, and alternative avenues to inspire others to get the most out of life.

5 Life Path Mantra: "Don't fence me in! (*and don't tell me what to do…*)."

PRACTICAL ADVICE FOR THE 5 LIFE PATH

A 5 Life Path acquaintance of mine made this comment: "*Recommitment* is the fuel that keeps me going when something I committed to doing all-of- a-sudden gets challenging. And, I'm realizing that this is the real fuel. *Commitment* gets me shiny object syndrome. 'This is cool! Let me play with *this*...' *Recommitment* gets me to the finish line even after the 'play' might start feeling a bit like a 'chore.'"

This is crucial to the mindset for the 5 Life Path. Most often, the 5 meets a snag and takes the first exit outta' there. Or you slog away, feeling detached, trapped, and longing for the excitement of *the next thing*—but stuck in your current quagmire.

Either way, the concept of *commitment* as the lure—the spark, the idea that draws you into something in the beginning as something that's worth nurturing and tending to with focused intent—can be a true game-changer. *It's through recommitment to the initial spark that can reignite your focus and follow-through.*

Or you can truly determine that the initial bright and shiny object was just that—a blip, a flight of fancy, an impulsive moment, a happy idea that ignited for a moment and fizzled out like a bottle rocket. Yet, taking the step to recommit offers the 5 Life Path an opportunity to follow through with something that just doesn't feel like true fun anymore.

It's like when you realize that a long-term relationship can't feel like the first months—or even first year—when everything's new, you're having sex all the time, and the thrill and excitement literally changes your hormonal and biological responses. After a while, it's *meant to level out*. If all of life were like the first months of a new relationship, nothing would ever get accomplished!

The 5 Life Path can have an over-arching tendency to feel a sense of discontent when there isn't the whirl of excitement happening a good portion of the time. It's the primary addiction or compulsion the 5 needs to modulate and master. The "how" is the biggest question, right?

On the highest end of the spectrum, the 5 Life Path can come to terms with impulsiveness and the need for constant stimulation by devoting to mind/body practices that help develop quieting of the mind. Meditation, conscious breathing techniques, and other tools used for spiritual growth are key. What is the ultimate freedom, after all? Enlightenment. Freedom of mind, body and spirit—finding expansion and contentment even under confining circumstances.

On the *just getting started* level, learning basic formulas and practices that teach you how to institute productive routines and organizational patterns into your life are crucial. Time management techniques, tools that teach focus and follow-through, and stress management are foundational to grounding your energy so that you can accomplish something for the longer-haul. Master Numerologist Hans Decoz observes that—for the 5 Life Path—*moderation is wisdom.*

INSPIRATION FOR THE 5 LIFE PATH

A few good reads to inspire, educate, and inform the 5 Life Path. These are simply suggestive of topics that would speak to your 5 Life Path mission on some level.

Any book, class, or tool that offers you ways to think about creating healthy routines, learning how to quiet the mind, exploring different cultures (languages and travel), and how to move through fear are perfect for you.

Here are just a few suggestions, yet depending on when you read this book—now or 20-years from now (which may be your *now* if that's when you're picking up this book), there will be many new books and resources from which to choose.

I simply encourage you to read biographies and autobiographies of those on the 5 Life Path to find a sense of connection and also as cautionary tales that can save you from making similar missteps.

- *Eat, Love, Pray* by Elizabeth Gilbert
- *Uncertainty: Turning Fear and Doubt into Fuel For Brilliance* by Jonathan Fields
- *Energetic Boundaries: How To Stay Protected and Connected in Work, Love, and Life* by Cyndi Dale
- *Fear: Essential Wisdom For Getting Through The Storm* by Thich Nhat Han
- *The Science of Self-Discipline* by Peter Hollins
- *The Practicing Mind: Developing Focus and Discipline in Your Life* by Thomas M. Sterner
- *The Alchemist* by Paulo Coelho
- *Recovery: Freedom from Our Addictions* by Russell Brand
- *Brain Lock: Free Yourself from Obsessive-Compulsive Behavior* by Jeffrey M. Schwartz, MD with Beverly Beyette
- *Carry On, Warrior: The Power of Embracing Your Messy, Beautiful Life* by Glennon Doyle

A FEW WELL-KNOWN 5 LIFE PATH'S

Angelina Jolie (June 4, 1975)
Ellen Degeneres (January 26, 1958)
Beyoncé (September 4, 1981)
Elizabeth Gilbert (July 18, 1969)
Brené Brown (November 18, 1965)
Monica Lewinsky (July 23, 1973)
Lily Tomlin (September 1, 1939)
J.K. Rowling (July 31, 1965)
Betty White (January 17, 1922)
Kristen Wiig (August 22, 1973)
Marianne Williamson (July 8, 1952)
Georgia O'Keefe (November 15, 1887)
Gillian Anderson (August 9, 1968)
Tina Turner (November 26, 1939)
Helen Keller (June 27, 1880)
Denzel Washington (December 28, 1954)
Mick Jagger (July 26, 1943)
Michael J. Fox (June 9, 1961)
Desi Arnaz (March 2, 1917)
Marlon Brando (April 3, 1924)
Russell Brand (June 4, 1975)
Steve Martin (August 14, 1945)
Steven Spielberg (December 18, 1946)
Adolf Hitler (April 20, 1889)
Abraham Lincoln (March 4, 1861)
Malcolm X (May 19, 1925)
Jay-Z (December 4, 1969)
David Hasselhoff (July 17, 1952)
Andy Kaufman (January 17, 1949)
Ron Howard (March 1, 1954)

6

How to Calculate Your Life Path Number?

USE YOUR DATE OF BIRTH
"SEPTEMBER 25, 1952"
ADD YOUR
MONTH + DAY + YEAR

SEPTEMBER = 9
25 = 2 + 5 = 7;
1952 = 1 + 9 + 5 + 2 = 17;
1 + 7 = 8;
9 + 7 + 8 = 24 AND 2 + 4 = 6

KEY THEMES

- LOVE / DUTY
- "AESTHETIC BEAUTY"
- SERVICE / RESPONSIBILITY
- VISIONARY / CREATIVE
- ARTISTIC / WORRY
- MAGNETISM

YOUR MISSION STATEMENT

THE 6 LIFE PATH IS THE "DOMESTIC" PATH — LOVING, NURTURING AND DRIVEN TO SERVE.

SOME FITTING CAREERS

- COUNSELING
- HOME-BASED BUSINESS
- LEGAL PROFESSIONS
- DESIGN
- BEAUTY INDUSTRY
- MUSICIAN

CORE LESSONS AND CHALLENGES

- STRIDENT PERFECTIONISM
- CONTROL FREAK
- SELF-RIGHTEOUS AND OVERBEARING
- MEDDLING AND DEMEANING
- OVERLY HIGH EXPECTATIONS

RELATIONSHIP COMPATIBILITY

- 6 AND 1 = NURTURING & LEADERSHIP
- 6 AND 2 = NURTURING & HEART
- 6 AND 3 = NURTURING & CREATIVE EXPRESSION
- 6 AND 4 = NURTURING & SECURITY
- 6 AND 5 = NURTURING & FREEDOM-SEEKING
- 6 AND 6 = NURTURING & NURTURING
- 6 AND 7 = NURTURING & SPIRITUALITY
- 6 AND 8 = NURTURING & POWER
- 6 AND 9 = NURTURING & COMPASSION

YOUR POWER

- CARING AND NURTURING
- SERVICE-CENTERED AND RESPONSIBLE
- VISIONARY AND CREATIVE
- JUSTICE MINDED AND FAIR
- HOME AND FAMILY FOCUSED

THE 6 LIFE PATH TESTS YOUR ABILITY TO BALANCE YOUR SENSE OF RESPONSBILITY — TO HELP WHERE YOU CAN AND YET LIVE AND LET LIVE. YOU CAN DO IT!

WELL-KNOWN 6s

- JENNIFER LAWRENCE (AUGUST 15, 1990)
- JESSICA CHASTAIN (MARCH 24, 1977)
- JUSTIN TIMBERLAKE (JANUARY 31, 1981)
- WARREN BUFFETT (AUGUST 30, 1930)

6 LIFE PATH

THE NURTURING VISIONARY

People take different roads seeking fulfillment and happiness. Just because they're not on your road doesn't mean they've gotten lost.

— The 14th Dalai Lama

Optimal Elements

A 6 Life Path's optimal expression resides in taking responsibility—while also allowing others their own lives without judging and criticizing their choices and actions. You allow for personal imperfections while being a nurturing presence. You're a visionary who trusts—and is inspired by—your ability to see the big picture in front of you.

Your personal mission is to modulate responsibility, develop and hone your visionary abilities, and to learn acceptance in every aspect of your life.

Your life's purpose is to reconcile your high ideals with practical reality and to accept yourself, the world, and the present moment by embracing the perfection of all the apparent imperfection—and to add your loving touch to everything you do.

RESPONSIBILITY

Overall, the 6 Life Path is the cosmic parent and your nurturing presence is felt every day and in every way. Understand that your primary task is to *modulate and balance your sense of responsibility*. Meaning—not being overly responsible nor irresponsible. Ah-ha! *Gotcha'!* Yes, this is a lesson to be mastered throughout your life and I was going to say that it sounds easy enough, yet really, it doesn't even *sound* easy. From childhood, you're the one who has more than your fair share of responsibility thrust upon you. You learn at the get-go how to take responsibility for yourself—and for others on top of that.

As you mature, you attract people and situations where you're the primary responsible party. Have you ever noticed that people are drawn to you, almost as if you're a magnet? Do people come to you with their problems and ask for your help? Do people place you in positions of responsibility even though you don't ask for it? Are you always relegated to the role of *designated driver*, so to speak? These are all aspects of your Life Path that you need to get used to and embrace. If you dislike being *the responsible one*, you'll live a life of frustration and resentment. Down deep, you get the greatest sense of gratification from helping and supporting others.

Knowing that more responsibility will be thrown your way allows you to utilize your innate skills and talents in these areas with a compassionate heart. The trick is to derive satisfaction through the responsibilities you accept—and not to accept responsibilities where you feel used, abused, and under-appreciated.

A key feature to your life's work as a 6 Life Path—*in neon*—is learning how to care for and about yourself as much as you do for others. It sounds corny, like a self-care cliché (*cue visual image with rose petals sprinkled, candles lighting the way to the luxurious bathroom with the bubble-bath waiting for you, complete with soft music and a fluted glass of champagne . . .*). While I don't discourage this spa-related form of self-care, certainly the nurturance I'm suggesting has more to do with establishing healthy boundaries and allowing others to figure a few things out on their own, without you doing all the emotional heavy-lifting for them.

HOME & FAMILY

As a 6 Life Path, you're a natural nurturer. You lean toward love and marriage like the proverbial horse and carriage. If you choose not to be a parent in the traditional sense, you'll parent in other ways—with pets, co-workers, and friends. There's a distinct nurturing quality to you. The number 6 even looks like a pregnant belly! You're pregnant with love and nurturing. Many numerologists call you The Cosmic Parent and there's a good reason for that! Your energetic antenna is always perked up and scanning your environment. Is everyone fed? Does anyone need anything? How's everyone's day been? What's the general energy in the room—what's the overall mood? How can you meet someone's needs before they even know they need something?

The 6 is learning all about the domestic realm—home and family is a primary focus. In numerology, the 6 is known as "marriage and divorce" energy. You're always working on and perfecting the fine and intimate art of relationship.

As a 6 Life Path, you're most likely seeking a one-on-one intimate partnership and the security of home. You crave a happy, serene, and beautiful nest as your home base. Like the number 2, you often seek partnership, yet also might struggle with it! The 6 feels more complete and on purpose when in relationship and when you're involved in positively serving some sort of family dynamic.

Overall, the home is your castle and you don't thrive in the outer world until you've happily established a satisfying home life, no matter what that looks like for you. Please understand this about the number 6 and about the meaning of *home and family*. I know many 6's who choose not to marry, have children, or go a more traditional home and family route. This doesn't mean they aren't fulfilling their power and purpose as a 6 Life Path! If this is the case, the 6 Life Path often creates a den-mother environment with friends, family of choice, and colleagues. Perhaps the 6 comes across more directly with the career of choice—as a realtor or interior designer. Or perhaps as a counselor or family law attorney. The list can go on and on, yet the 6 Life Path offers wise counsel and a nurturing and caring environment no matter where it shows up.

LOVE, DUTY & SERVICE

The 6 Life Path is a life of service. There's a note of self-sacrifice in the personality of the 6 that can unfold as sensing the wants and needs of others before they do. The 6's always paying attention to the details, making every environment a comfy and inviting place to be, and just making everyone feel seen, heard, and loved.

You feel a sense of duty—to family, country, community—duty is just something that's an innate pull for you on a grand scale. You're a natural teacher and counselor. Surely you comprehend that you have an intuitive sense with people—and you can also simply step outside of the fray and see the whole picture in ways that most people can't. In this way, people come to you for advice and you're more than happy to give it to them—and to offer answers and shortcuts to solve their problems.

The issue is: Do they take your advice? Heck no! People generally only learn their lessons by experiencing it themselves—not by being told what to do, or what to stop doing, or what to avoid. Experience isn't the best teacher, it's the *only* teacher. Yet you're consistently being asked to chime in and get involved in other people's drama, issues, and conflicts. You're the voice of reason, the rock of Gibraltar, and the one who can cut through the crapola.

This really is your life's work as a 6 Life Path. How to be there for people—to support, love, nurture, cajole, and pick people up when they fall. This is a delicate balance to be sure. The 6 can lean toward meddling and controlling rather than offering advice and moving on—without an attachment to the outcome or to whether or not your advice has been heeded. "Live and let live" could be your tattoo of choice, as you need to be reminded of this truism on a daily basis.

You live a life of compassion—helping and supporting others. Yet you can tend to sacrifice too much in the name of love, duty, and service. Ultimately, the lesson of the 6 is to care for and nurture *yourself* as much as you care for and nurture *others*.

VISONARY

You're a creative person who sees the world in an ideal sense. You have a gift of seeing how things *could* and *should* be and can't understand why others can't. The 6 can get derailed or easily frustrated when the world doesn't meet your expectations. Your internal dialogue: "Why can't everyone just see that it can work *this* way? It's so *obvious*!" And yet when no one can see it, you would love to throttle them until they do—because everything would be so much easier and so much better if they could *just get it*.

The 6 Life Path sees solutions where people don't even see there's a problem. This is where you have a gifted intuitive sense—you can envision grandeur where others can't see anything existing at all. A key to your success and sanity is to understand that you'll need to adjust your course early and often.

Understand that you'll have the most success when you can troubleshoot and see the point of view of others. Even when you don't agree with another point of view, you can see it and—in some way—integrate it into the final product, whether that's a family dynamic or a work-related issue.

Your visionary gift has the potential to make the world a better place on both the microcosmic and macrocosmic levels. You have a visual style for your home and surroundings, making the energy of your home feel like a resting place, a nest, and a soft place to land. Out in the world, you bring a rich tapestry of creativity and often lead with the heart, with an overall focus on nurturing, supporting, and caretaking.

Many 6 Life Paths use their talents in creative fields where their visionary capabilities can be tapped and used to their fullest. Warren Buffet is a 6 Life Path who uses his talents to see into the future and into trends in financial markets. Justin Timberlake's a 6 Life Path who's multi-gifted with dance, singing, and playing multiple instruments in different musical genres—and is a husband and father. Stephen King's superlative writing abilities span genres in a way that can only be described as genius. Albert Einstein understood the field of quantum physics before we had a name for it. The 6 Life Path brings imagination, creativity, and love into whatever they do.

BEAUTY & AESTHETICS

Often a 6 Life Path is physically attractive and so you present a sense of beauty to the world and expect a certain sense of decorum and sophistication. As a 6, you're intrinsically artistically creative and must find ways to use your creativity constructively. Otherwise, you'll default to frustration and that usually comes out as over-involvement in the lives of those in your intimate circle and work life.

You have a natural propensity to cultivate harmonious environments. The beauty and balance of your own home is imperative for you. An extension of your talents often bleeds over into other realms—you appreciate texture, color, placement, and the richness that proper design brings to your immediate world. In fact, you feel a sense of agitation when you find yourself having to deal with people or places you find ugly, off balance, or out of synch. The 6 Life Path has a particular sense of style and how you look is important to you—and the appearance of others also holds weight for you and makes a difference in your over-all contentment and sense of ease with your daily life.

THE 6 LIFE PATH & RELATIONSHIPS

While the natural habitat for the 6 Life Path is marriage and parenthood, know also that not every 6 chooses marriage—and often a 6 might need to do a few go-arounds in the marriage department before getting their feet on *terra firma* in terms of idealistic expectations about a partner.

You feel most at home when you're literally *at home*. If happily coupled, you'd rather spend time with your spouse than with others. These tendencies with partners show up with those who are gay, straight, or any other dynamic. If you're single, you'll establish family dynamics in whatever you do. If you're a 6 Life Path woman you might tend to attract partners who have Peter Pan Syndrome (never grow up!). The 6 has a tendency to throw yourself into the lives of your children and can have difficulty seeing them as grown-ups or as individuals.

If you're a 6 Life Path male, the tendency is to attract partners who are damsels in distress and then you wonder why you're again the responsible party in the relationship. In any event, domestic tranquility is actually the goal for you, no matter how you go about it.

You have a tendency to put people—particularly a significant other—on a pedestal and then feel betrayed or disappointed when you discover that they're only human after all. In your optimal, you're a flowing source of love and support whose ultimate satisfaction comes when you engage with everything in your world with a nurturing hand.

THE 6 LIFE PATH & CAREER

Oh, 6 Life Path, you're not one to take orders from others! So, often you'll prefer to manage or own your own business. Or if that's not quite in your wheelhouse, you'll need some control and autonomy within your job or career. You also have trouble taking advice or instruction from others. Sound familiar? Often, you'll work for others just long enough to learn the ropes and create your own business. And if it's a home-based business, better and better!

Money flows easily to you when you're engaging in something you feel is a service to others. Success and money come somewhat fluidly when perfectionism is tamed and the focus is on manifesting creative and visionary goals. You have a better chance at making money easily than, say, the 8 Life Path. Why? With the 8 Life Path, money is a central theme and so money can show up as a struggle or as an issue. For the 6, money can flow as an extension of your focused service or as an outcropping of your superb creative or performative abilities.

When you center yourself on giving, service, and using your creativity, money flows to you almost effortlessly. Often a 6 Life Path is highly artistically creative, particularly in the field of music—singing or playing an instrument. Any career having to do with creating beautiful things is in line for you—including the beauty industry (hair, make-up, clothing), design, and art.

You also excel in any justice related field, including police work, firefighting—or within the court system. The 6 is a natural with any home-based business where you can create something, sell it (or offer your service), and be your own boss. Anything having to do with healing or counseling is right up your alley, especially if it has to do with children, the elderly, family, or relationships.

A primary question you might ask yourself is: Is there a way for me to be creative and also give back? You're here to act upon your visionary capabilities and to nurture the best in yourself and in others. Yours is a path of service, duty, and high levels of responsibility. You thrive in environments where you can be in charge and where you can provide a service that's supportive to other people, while also expressing yourself creatively. Your mantra to remember: Start before you're ready.

A few possibilities:

- Any home-based business
- Counselor—therapist or school counselor
- Justice-related fields—police officer, lawyer, bailiff, corrections officer
- Work with the elderly—at retirement centers or with social services
- Musician, singer or music agent

- Actor
- Artist
- Make-up artist
- Interior Design
- Landscape Design
- Entrepreneur
- Child care
- Stay-at-home parent
- Real Estate agent or developer
- Fashion model
- Hair stylist
- Set Design

6 LIFE PATH

Opposing Forces

PERFECTIONISM & CONTROL

With the 6 Life Path, it's all about learning to appreciate the perfection of the imperfection of everyone and everything—including yourself. And yet, if you haven't noticed, you're a control freak. You set the bar so high that it's impossible for most people to meet your expectations—and certainly those around you can't read your mind, despite the fact that you feel they should already know what they're doing wrong. *It's. So. Obvious.*

And let's be clear: Your perfectionist tendencies start with *yourself*. You expect the moon and back from yourself, every day, no matter what. Remember—part of your mission in life is to learn how to give yourself the love and nurturing that you give to others. You're always seeking balance and harmony. Yet often it takes years to even fully comprehend how high your standards actually are and why you feel so agitated or anxious most of the time.

Julia Cameron has this to say about perfectionism: "Perfectionism is not a quest for the best. It's a pursuit of the worst in ourselves, the part that tells us that nothing we do will ever be good enough—that we should try again." This is food for thought as you traverse your balance-beam of perfectionism and explore ways to let go of controlling tendencies.

If you're not happy, ain't no one happy! The 6 Life Path can walk into a room and silently punish those who aren't pleasing to you. It's admirable that you've got it together and set the royal standard all around, yet you'll achieve more balance and relaxed satisfaction when you give yourself and others a break once in a while.

You might use the fourth agreement (of Miguel Ruiz's *The Four Agreements*) as your tagline: "Always do your best." And yet the continuing message with this agreement is that your best fluctuates and isn't constant. Your best one day might be just being able to roll out of bed. Your best another day might be showing up and accepting your Grammy. It's all your best on any given day.

SELF-RIGHTEOUSNESS

When you're feeling unappreciated, undervalued, or overwhelmed your tendency is to feel self-righteous, lofty, and superior to everyone else. You wonder why everyone can't be like you and feel everyone else is wrong—or at least sub-standard—because they don't believe the same things you do or behave in the same manner as you.

When you turn into Judgey McJudgerson, you're not at your highest and best. Whether you realize it or not, you can exert a crushing sense of criticism and judgment on those around you. One of your greatest talents is your ability to make others feel guilty or unworthy. The irony here is that deep down you feel this way yourself, being your own worst critic. When you're feeling down or agitated, you can put up a wall that is cold and punishing.

The 6 Life Path is an "If you want something done right you just have to do it yourself" kind of person. You want to feel indispensable and then resent being indispensable, even though you're the one who set it up that way.

The bottom line is that you're working optimally when you're seeing the perfection in everyone and everything at whatever juncture they're in with their own process. That includes you. When you let go of the *should* and instead rely on your wonderful sense of nurturing, compassion, and service, you'll be the most content. Stop "shoulding" on yourself and others.

LOSS OF IDENTITY

I find a loss of identity to be an epidemic with 6 Life Path women. It can happen with men as well. Yet 6 Life Path women tend to submerge themselves fully and completely into the lives of their significant other, family, community, and children. You're so busy nurturing everyone, making the house a home, knowing who's allergic to what, what everyone's favorite food is, and what their favorite TV show is that you have no clue who you are and what your own preferences might be.

You're always serving others. Often this comes as a crisis when you hit your 40s and beyond. Who am I? What am I doing? What do I want? *When's it my turn?* And the cruel reality is that *only you can give yourself a turn.* No one else will do it for you—and if they did, you would refuse it!

Brené Brown digs into the underlaying meaning of perfectionism when she observes: "Many people think of perfectionism as striving to be your best, but it's not about self-improvement; it's about earning approval and acceptance" (see Brené Brown's *The Gifts of Imperfection*). Remember: If you do something out of duty, it'll deplete you. If you do something out of love, it'll energize you.

Every human being needs to learn how to nurture their relationships and step into responsibility in life. Everyone needs to love and be loved, and learn how to modulate expectations. Yet as a 6 Life Path, family life and acceptance are focal points and aspects for development all your life. Therefore, the themes of balanced relationships and letting go of controlling perfectionism directly connect with the characteristics of the key people who play certain roles in your life script, whether as intimate partners, family members, teachers, colleagues, or even random meetings.

The themes of the 6 (nurturing, fair play, service) direct traffic in terms of the situations you find yourself in, the people who show up, and as the way life lessons come your way.

Biggest blind Spot: The inability to relax into life and go with the flow. The 6 Life Path doesn't understand their high anxiety levels stemming from unattainable expectations.

6 Life Path Superpower: When you're in your game, you're the most loving, accepting, supportive, and nurturing being on the planet. You're the healer, the artist, and the person who instinctively understands how to hold space for others.

6 Life Path Mantra: "The world is perfect in its imperfection."

PRACTICAL ADVICE FOR THE 6 LIFE PATH

An article titled "Are You A Drama Mama?" by Martha Beck could have been written for you, the 6 Life Path. She asks: "If you're chronically overextended, under-appreciated, and very very angry, there's a simple solution: Stop playing the martyr."

She goes on to say that "often martyrs create and rehearse their parts in a dysfunctional pattern of interaction called the Karpman drama triangle . . . the triangle involves three possible roles: victim, rescuer, and persecutor."

She goes on to observe that the simple yet-not-easy solution to this pervasive condition is to set boundaries and to tell the truth.

Often the 6 Life Path creates these dynamics (victim, rescuer, and persecutor) unconsciously. Remember this simple and almost cruel fact: *We train people how to treat us.* Moreover, we actively agree to participate in this triangulated system and choose to play the role that we play.

The only way to break free of this pattern is first by understanding that this is your responsibly: *Your* words, behavior, actions, efforts, mistakes, ideas and the consequences of your actions. This is *not* your responsibility: *Other people's* words, behavior, actions, efforts, mistakes, ideas and the consequences of their actions.

It's all about understanding and acting upon your authenticity. For all humans this is an ongoing exercise—and for a 6 Life Path, the added weight here resides in your over-reaching sense of responsibility, duty, and self-sacrificing service. The big issue here resides in having a grounded, individuated sense of yourself outside of your identity within family or relationship dynamics.

Astrologer Henry Seltzer makes this observation that's perfect for the 6 Life Path: "The savior in you brings out the victim in another."

The best practical advice for the 6 Life Path has to do with educating yourself about healthy detachment and supportive yet firm emotional boundaries. You'll pursue this as a life-long endeavor! You can find your way through concepts, practices, and modalities that speak to you as an individual. Perhaps through traditional talk therapy, somatic practices or any other avenue that reveals the ways you wish to control, fix, or perfect yourself and those around you.

Often the 6 Life Path wants to project an image of perfection to the outside world—like the most filtered social media account. Yet the pressure here is enormous and the benefits almost zero. It's coming to the realization that perfection isn't only highly over-rated, it's virtually impossible. The sooner you can develop a "who really cares what they think?" attitude, the higher you'll soar.

I worked with a 6 Life Path client once who was the poster child for the 6—artist and interior designer, wife, mother, grandmother, expert cook, hostess, and all around giving and generous soul. She was getting ready to undergo back surgery and was panicked that her family's world would collapse without her availability to fill her daily role. Worse than that, she couldn't bear the thought of being a burden to anyone—to need any help or support herself. I asked her what she thought would happen if she cared for herself as lovingly and intently as she cared for others. She literally gasped and said: "I could never do that!" When I asked why not, she replied: "Because it would be *selfish*."

This story illustrates some deep-seated issues that the 6 Life Path is here to conquer. Any avenues to get to know yourself and to balance your deep sense of responsibility toward others is key to your path and purpose as a 6 Life Path.

INSPIRATION FOR THE 6 LIFE PATH

A few good reads to inspire, educate, and inform the 6 Life Path. These are simply suggestive of topics that would speak to your 6 Life Path mission on some level.

Any book, class, or tool that offers you ways to think about creating healthy boundaries, to educate yourself on the difference between support and enabling, on developing your creative passions, and on creating healthy and loving relationships are perfect for you.

Here are just a few suggestions, yet depending on when you read this book—now or 20-years from now (which may be your *now* if that's when you're picking up this book), there will be many new books and resources from which to choose.

I simply encourage you to read biographies and autobiographies of those on the 6 Life Path to find a sense of connection and also as cautionary tales that can save you from making similar missteps.

- *Radical Acceptance* by Tara Brach
- *Loving What Is* by Byron Katie
- *Leading An Inspired Life* by Jim Rohn
- *Present Perfect: A Mindfulness Approach to Letting Go of Perfectionism and the Need for Control* by Pavel Somov
- *The Gifts of Imperfection: Let Go of Who You Think You're Supposed to Be and Embrace Who You Are* by Brené Brown
- *Passionate Marriage: Keeping Love & Intimacy Alive in Committed Relationships* by David Schnarch, Ph.D.
- *The Relationship Cure: A 5 Step Guide to Strengthening Your Marriage, Family, and Friendships* by John Gottman
- *Getting The Love You Want* by Harville Hendrix, Ph.D.
- *The Joy Of Being Selfish: Why you need boundaries and how to set them!* By Michelle Elman
- *The Set Boundaries Workbook: Practical Exercises for Understanding your Needs and Setting Healthy Limits* by Nedra Glover Tawwab

A FEW WELL-KINOWN 6 LIFE PATH'S

Jennifer Lawrence (August 15, 1990)
Frances McDormand (June 23, 1957)
Britney Spears (December 2, 1981)
Goldie Hawn (November 21, 1945)
Victoria Beckham (April 17, 1974)
Meryl Streep (June 22, 1949)
Melissa McCarthy (August 26, 1970)
Rosie O'Donnell (March 21, 1962)
Ted Turner (November 19, 1938)
Stephen King (September 21, 1947)
Ben Affleck (August 15, 1972)
Richard Nixon (January 9, 1913)
Bruce Willis (March 19, 1955)
Eddie Murphy (April 3, 1961)
John Oliver (April 23, 1977)
Christopher Reeve (September 25, 1952)
Justin Timberlake (January 31, 1981)
John Denver (December 31, 1943)
Michael Jackson (August 29, 1958)
John Lennon (October 9, 1940)
Christian Slater (August 18, 1969)
Warren Buffett (August 30, 1930)
Michael Caine (March 14, 1933)
Steve Carell (August 16, 1962)
Albert Einstein (March 14, 1879)
George W. Bush (July 6, 1946)
Seth Meyers (December 28, 1973)
Bruce Willis (March 19, 1955)
Eddie Murphy (April 3, 1961)
Robert DeNiro (August 17, 1943)

7

How to Calculate Your Life Path Number?

Use your date of birth
"January 31, 1977"
Add your
Month + Day + Year

January = 1
31 = 3 + 1 = 4;
1973 = 1 + 9 + 7 + 3 = 20;
2 + 0 = 2;
1 + 4 + = 7

Key Themes

- Trust / Openness
- "Inner Development"
- Wisdom / Analysis
- Reflection / Processing
- Isolation / Misunderstood
- Self-Exploration

Your Mission Statement

The 7 Life Path is on a deeply "internal" journey and is data-driven, intuitive, and on a different wavelength.

Some Fitting Careers

- Researcher
- Programming
- Spiritual teacher
- Professor
- Writer
- Analyst

Core Lessons and Challenges

- Trust and vulnerability
- Emotional connection
- Aloof and "in your head"
- Superficial and depressive
- Blunt communication

Relationship Compatibility

- 7 and 1 = Spirituality & Leadership
- 7 and 2 = Spirituality & Heart
- 7 and 3 = Spirituality & Creative Expression
- 7 and 4 = Spirituality & Security
- 7 and 5 = Spirituality & Freedom-Seeking
- 7 and 6 = Spirituality & Nurturing
- 7 and 7 = Spirituality & Spirituality
- 7 and 8 = Spirituality & Power
- 7 and 9 = Spirituality & Compassion

Your Power

- Spirituality
- Intuition (let's face it, you're psychic)
- Faith and trust
- Solitude and inner growth
- Intellectual refinement

The 7 Life Path tests your ability to balance your need to spend time contemplating and processing — while still engaging in the what the world tosses your way. You can do it!

Well-Known 7s

- Taylor Swift (December 13, 1989)
- Lady Diana (July 1, 1961)
- Freddie Mercury (September 5, 1946)
- Stephen Hawking (January 8, 1942)

7 LIFE PATH

THE ANALYST (AND SOMETIMES RELUCTANT) SPIRITUAL SEEKER

You see, you closed your eyes. That was the difference. Sometimes you cannot believe what you see, you have to believe what you feel. And if you are ever going to have other people trust you, you must feel that you can trust them, too—even when you're in the dark. Even when you're falling.

— Mitch Albom

Optimal Elements

A 7 Life Path's optimal expression is being attuned equally to intuition and intellect, to gather and offer wisdom, to be at peace with yourself, and not being afraid of opening up emotionally to yourself and others.

Your personal mission is to develop trust the flow of life—and to ask and open up to deep personal and spiritual growth and awareness.

Your life's purpose is to trust yourself and trust in the process of your life so that you can feel safe enough to open up and share your inner wisdom with the world. You're meant to ask and seek out the answers to life's most profound and important questions. Yours is a lifetime of spiritual growth measured by you and by you alone.

TRUTH SEEKER

The number 7 is the number of faith and spirituality. You were born to learn to have faith in yourself and in others, yet—like all the Life Path numbers—you get some higher climbing walls in order to get there! The 7 Life Path needs a strong spiritual base, yet this takes years to develop.

Often 7's come into the world into a family without solid or consistent religious values or alternately, come into a family with rigid religious views that must be experienced and dissected before you can act upon your own sense of spirituality.

Do you feel as though you're out of place in the world? Many 7 Life Paths feel as though they're old souls who are here exploring the material world ("*What am I doing here again?*"). You're bright, intelligent, and intense. The 7 is a natural with technical problems, data analysis, and in discovering and uncovering things.

Do you feel psychic? The 7 has a natural intuitive ability that's at odds with your highly analytical mind. This can be a point of confusion for you. On one hand, you're all about data, knowledge and research—and you need accepted systems of thought to operate in this realm. On the other hand, you're constantly receiving intuitive data that you can't qualify or quantify and it may scare or baffle you. Either you block and suppress your intuition—which could lead to dissatisfaction and ill health—or you learn to respect and balance both aspects of your highly calibrated mind and soul.

Perhaps you experience the opposite: You fully embrace your psychic awareness and refuse to use your grounded, analytical abilities. Either way, inviting both aspects of your cognition (analysis and intuition) to co-exist and co-create will have a profoundly positive impact on your life.

Many 7 Life Paths experience certain psychic abilities as children—often through clairvoyance, precognition, mediumship or other forms of intuitive and psychic ability. Yet the 7 will often disown or denounce their abilities because you realize it's not "normal." Many 7's take a long time to circle back around to accept and develop their intuitive gifts.

PERFECTIONSIM

Ultimately, you're a perfectionist. While the number 6 has perfectionist tendencies, those tendencies reside more fully with controlling human behavior. The 7 Life Path's perfectionism resides more directly in the way you gather and analyze data and information. There's a built-in skepticism guiding how the 7 navigates life.

You're at your highest and best when you make a decision to specialize in something—*you're a specialist*. Yet you must find the thing that intrigues you enough to hold your interest for a lifetime of inquiry and practice.

You can find ultimate satisfaction researching a topic or doing lab research. You can perfect your skills with data analysis, financial analysis or find intrigue with the medical field. Philosophy or research of any kind is your natural habitat.

You're a natural psychic and can spend a lifetime specializing in aspects of the spiritual world—the world of healing, energy or any course of metaphysics or esoteric study. You have a way about you that is always asking, tweaking, probing, and perfecting.

TRUST & BEING TRUSTWORTHY

You have an air of secrecy about you and enjoy a sense of mystery, even if you don't really see yourself this way. You need space and privacy and don't allow others into your personal life unless you invite them in. You may appear aloof to others, yet you are simply observing the world and processing it in your own way.

One of your biggest issues is that you're misread by other people—over and over again. Often you give off the impression of being stuck-up or haughty even though that's the last thing you are or how you see yourself. You're mostly just processing on overtime and overdrive—giving the appearance of detachment.

You're an introvert. If you don't operate with the higher-level vibration the 7 Life Path number brings with it, then you're probably exhausting to be around because you'll focus on petty things and can appear to be somewhat shallow. Since you're learning about trust, you'll experience more than your share of what you consider to be betrayal. Yet you're being asked to move past the betrayal, forgive in whatever way you can, and move forward with a healthy openness and a healthy level of vulnerability.

Part of your mission in life is to learn to explore and express your deepest feelings. Yet feelings and emotions can feel oddly foreign to you. I had a 7 Life Path client who once lamented that emotions were *useless*. Certainly you have a reservoir of emotions, yet as a 7 you feel more comfortable when you can deal more directly with hard data—not subjective and mutable emotions. The mantra for the 7 Life Path: "Oh all right, if we're all having a spiritual experience in a human body, *prove it*. Show me the data."

THE 7 LIFE PATH & RELATIONSHIP

In healthy, loving relationships you lean toward being honest, loyal, and direct. You tend to get stuck in your head, overanalyzing everything and every situation. You're also not always the best at understanding people's wants and needs. Often people are more like spreadsheets to you rather than emotionally driven beings. And the crux of the issue with you and relationships is this: You kind of want to be involved in a relationship and on the other hand, you maybe-kinda'-sorta' don't. The 7 Life Path's destiny is to spend certain amounts of time alone—*not as a punishment, but rather as a choice and a preference.*

The 7 prefers and needs solo time—to process, to dig into your internal contemplation, and to unplug from the static of the world. I have a 7 Life Path friend who has experienced a few key relationships in her life. She rejected the idea of marriage for herself and would usually leave a relationship because she felt that the cost was too high—that she had to give up too much of herself to blend in or to play the role her partner wanted her to play within the relationship.

Overall, you're here to learn to engage with and then express your deepest feelings and share your most critical findings. In terms of communication, you can have a sharp tongue, so you need to think about your style of relating and the goals you have for communicating. The 7 can feel as though they're telling it like it is, yet this can feel assaultive, uncaring or somewhat robotic to those on the receiving end. You can also come off as somewhat eccentric and difficult to understand. Mostly, you want relationships with depth and character, whether it's an intimate relationship or a friendship.

THE 7 LIFE PATH & CAREER

Since the 7 Life Path is a spiritual seeker, you might excel as a philosopher, analyst or researcher because you're always seeking truth, knowledge, and you love delving into life's mysteries. You tend to devour information and excel when you're able to consolidate meaning out of a stack of data and then share your findings with people. Your brain *is* the analytics department!

You are at your highest and best when you find something to become an expert in. The 7 Life Path thrives as a specialist in something, whether it's yoga, a certain kind of nutritional practice, a computer program or any other product, service or even some kind of intellectual theory. The 7 Life Path enjoys working with others and yet finds optimal balance and satisfaction when working alone, at least part of the time.

Oddly enough, most often (not always!) work and career really isn't a top priority for the 7 Life Path. The 7 can often find solace and satisfaction doing almost anything to make a living. The real point of satisfaction comes with your soul searching and ability to have the time and income to *know thyself* in the deepest, most consistent way possible.

Like all the Life Path numbers, the 7 benefits greatly when you know your Expression/Destiny number. This number gives you a strong indication of what career or work would be most fitting for you. More than other Life Path numbers, the 7 can glean guidance with your career by knowing the Expression/Destiny number since the 7 is a more diffuse and mutable energy in terms of work and career.

Understand that you can be incredibly successful in the material world—think of 7 Life Path's Elon Musk, John F. Kennedy or Melinda Gates. Sometimes 7's feel defeated or frustrated believing they can't make it in the real world. This just isn't so. You'll simply bring a depth to whatever you do and take it as it comes, enjoy the flow, and trust the process. Your power of intention can't be under-estimated.

You're here to act upon your highly refined intellect while also developing your intuitive connection. You're working on moving through the superficial and into the deeper crevices of cosmic knowledge—not to be too dramatic about it! *You're a truth seeker.* When you tap into both your analytical mind and your intuitive energy, you're at your most powerful.

A few possibilities:

- Business with an emphasis on analysis
- Spiritual guide or psychic
- Massage therapist, bodyworker, energy worker
- Past-life regression therapist or hypnotherapist
- Wildlife Manager
- Marine biologist
- Research analyst
- Financial analyst
- Marketing

- Personal Assistant
- Yoga instructor or retreat leader
- Philosopher
- Professor, trainer or teacher
- Natural food industry
- Clothing designer or model
- Writer or technical writer
- Therapist
- Animal psychic or trainer
- Scuba instructor

7 LIFE PATH
Opposing Forces

SUPERFICIALTY

You're here to peel your own human and cosmic onion. This doesn't have a conclusion—it's your ongoing journey. You're learning to uncover some of your darkest corners and also bolster your brightest light. It takes courage, effort, and desire to continue on the path to spiritual opening and enlightenment. Its rewards are often intangible and deeply personal. Therefore, you might have a tendency to veer away from the more meaningful path and instead travel along the path of superficiality or the mundane. Skimming the surface of life can feel less threatening and opens you to less vulnerability.

In the extreme, the 7 can become a high-strung social media personality or the file-clerk working the graveyard shift. Either way, the pathway of the 7 leads to self-awareness and spiritual evolution, yet avoidance of that pathway can come in many shades and many colors.

Remember that one of your major lessons resides with the development of trust and faith. The 7 Life Path can spend some time—usually in younger years—hovering on the surface of life. You might picture a group of off-track 7's as *The Real Housewives (or Husbands) of Fill-In-The-Blank*—wine glass (or shot glass) in one hand and designer handbag in another. Cat fighting, hyper-drama, and stirring the pot. You get the picture. Not a deeper or "spiritual" thought to be pondered when life is already overflowing with made-up issues designed to detour or distract from a more soul-centered experience.

This can also show up as opting out—punching the time clock and just trying to get through the demands of earthly existence. Many times, the 7 Life Path is terrified of spending any extended time alone because you're actually being asked quiet the noise and delve inward.

FRUSTRATION

The 7 Life Path is a journey of cultivated wisdom. No wonder you can experience heightened levels of frustration throughout your life, even with the smallest of events, experiences or day occurrences. When feeling overwhelmed or rudderless, you're the one who's always tired, exasperated, and done-in by living this petty life on planet earth. You can be the one who can't tolerate the driver who cuts you off in traffic, the customer who said something stupid or the family member who's an ongoing jerk. Where others might overlook these infractions, you grind about them until you weep.

You often feel intense frustration when you're feeling stuck or without the sense of purpose you know is your birthright. Yet it's up to you to embrace your mystical, magical engagement with life and understand that you truly reside on a different wavelength than most people. Frustration manifests when there is an innate lack of trust, when you're pushing against something without even knowing why. Frustration yields to contentment when you align with inner guidance and give up the need to control the uncontrollable. Trusting the flow of life and all its uncertainty is key.

INTROVERSION

A healthy amount of alone time is beneficial for the 7 Life Path. Yet sometimes that can trip over into extraction from—or avoidance of—life. You can become reclusive and self-focused. Again, your path is all about digging deep and knowing yourself on all levels. Yet—like all the Life Path numbers—there can be a tendency to take it too far. Given you find it challenging to express your feelings, there can come a time where you simply don't set yourself up in living arrangements or in relationships that demand this sort of one-on-one engagement.

Since you feel a bit out of place most of the time, it's no wonder you prefer activities where you don't to have manage yourself in large groups—or if you gravitate toward group activities it's so that you can "disappear" and not have to engage on anyone else's terms. Since trust is an issue, you're infinitely a *private* person.

I know 7s who feel very strongly about what personal details are shared or talked about. Other people often think you're secretive or slightly paranoid—sometimes to the extreme. For instance, the 7 can be the person who finds cocktail talk about sex or other private matters unacceptable—or takes offense when topics you feel are off-limits are pushed upon you for open discussion.

Ultimately, you can present as detached and otherwise distracted with your own thoughts. You thrive with a certain level of solitude, yet you can traverse into an unhealthy retraction from life rather than a balance between your spiritual quest and engagement with your human world.

Some numerologists suggest that the 7 Life Path will experience feelings of loneliness at different times in their lives. You require downtime and unplugged time, yet this can push you into being a hermit.

I often say that the 7 Life Path is like a character on *The Big Bang Theory*! I love this quote from the television show *Young Sheldon*. In a voice-over, Young Sheldon says: "My mother never understood that I actually enjoyed being alone. Solitude allowed me to think about important things, like the effect of gravitational forces as you approach an event horizon. As opposed to less important things, like how many grapes my brother could fit in his mouth." This about says it all in terms of how the 7 Life Path often engages with life.

DEPRESSION

The vibe of the number 7 is introspective and somewhat lower energy. And by lower energy, I mean high *spiritual* energy—lower *physical* energy. Meaning, as a 7 Life Path you experience the constant pull to ponder, investigate, and percolate. You're mostly living in your head and have some issues connecting with your physical body. I know lots of 7 Life Path's who are high-energy and active people. The point here is that there's a lot of internal processing going on and so the 7 often feels this need to extract from more tumultuous engagement with people. You often need more rest and time to process.

Everything the 7 does needs slow, gradual, and in-depth processing time. You're ultimately extremely energetically sensitive, which is one of the ironies! You're *so* sensitive that you appear desensitized to those around you.

The 7 is the ultimate thinker—and over-thinker. Talk about a busy mind! If you haven't figured out how to calm or clear your mind through meditation, exercise or other relaxation techniques, you can tend toward depression. Many 7 Life Path's have trouble sleeping, sometimes to the point of insomnia.

There can be some addictive tendencies coming into play. Drugs, alcohol, cigarettes—substances that allow you to zone out or numb out can be enticing. Meditation is imperative. Nature is rejuvenating. You flourish and relax when you connect with the natural environment in some way. You need consistent exercise to move your energy around as well.

Self-care is necessary for you to have a balanced life. The 7 Life Path often experiences certain physical issues—food allergies, TMJ, digestive problems, a mystery illness or reoccurring issue—and this is actually designed to keep you *in your body*. Meaning—you're so heady and brain-driven that you can abandon your body most of the time. Have you ever heard the saying "She's just not in her body"? This is often the case with the 7. So, if your body offers you a few reasons to notice it and nurture it by having a few issues, then you can actually enjoy a more balanced existence.

Some 7's have an intrinsic instinct about when you need a cleanse—or how to keep your body purified or detoxified. Often 7's are super-clumsy, despite your over-all dignity and refinement. In some ways, it's as if you're visiting the planet because you really don't feel as though you're from here—like you're wearing an awkward costume that is your human form.

You have profound gifts to share with the world. Powerful intuition, refinement, science, and philosophy are your strengths in a lifetime optimally devoted to study and inner reflection.

Every human being needs to evolve spiritually and learn how to properly process data and information. Everyone needs to develop their intuition and learn how to go with the universal flow. Yet as a 7 Life Path, spiritual development and research are focal points and aspects for development all your life.

Therefore, the themes of specialization—and having faith and trust in yourself and others—directly connects with the characteristics of the key people who play certain roles in your life script, whether as intimate partners, family members, teachers, colleagues, or even random meetings.

The themes of the 7 (trust, openness, spiritual growth, and intuitive development) direct traffic in terms of the situations you find yourself in, the people who show up, and as the way life lessons come your way.

Biggest Blind Spot: Resistance to exploring the more "woo-woo" aspects of life mixed with fear and skepticism about your intuitive abilities.

7 Life Path Superpower: To be centered, secure, and at ease with life as it unfolds for you and all around you. You bring knowledge and a depth of wisdom and truth to all of your interactions, both large and small.

7 Life Path Mantra: "If we're spiritual beings going through a human experience—prove it!"

PRACTICAL ADVICE FOR THE 7 LIFE PATH

Be mindful of what you put into your body. The 7 Life Path is particularly sensitive to food, medicine, drugs, alcohol, and other substances. *I'm not a physician, therefore do not consider this medical advice.* In my practice, I have found a common theme with 7's that revolve around this sensitivity. The sooner you understand this, the better off you'll be! My personal understanding of the reason this happens consistently for the 7 is this: Since you're literally operating on another wavelength and are mostly in your head or out in the etheric realms, the body is here to remind you that you opted in for this ongoing moment in human form and therefore you're reminded to pay attention to it. Otherwise, the 7 would be "out there" all the time. When you have some kind of physical issue that keeps calling for your attention, care, and maintenance, this keeps your feet on the earth in a way that grounds you in a manner that you wouldn't commit to otherwise. I have also found that this can serve as the opening to a pathway for the 7 Life Path to become a healer for others—by needing to go through healing themselves.

Get out and into nature. The 7 Life Path begins to atrophy if you aren't allowed to recharge and reconnect with yourself through the energetic presence nature provides. Often this is through hiking, swimming, gardening, camping (or Glamping!), running or any other outdoor activity that brings you into the natural world. This is used as meditation—as a time to clear mind, body, and spirit. Water is a huge healing resource for the 7, including baths, steaming, boating, and any other connection with water.

Get curious about intuitive development. Let's face it, you're living a lifetime that's a very personal internal journey of spiritual growth, soul's growth, and personal evolution. The sooner you open your mind, body, and soul to the metaphysical world, the faster you come to terms with your Life Path purpose. There's no right way to do this. Could it be that you have some mysterious health concern that drives you to pursue outside-of-the-box ways to heal yourself? As a child, did you have experiences that scared you to such an extent that you shut down that psychic part of your being? Perhaps you could see energy (clairvoyance), saw dead people (mediumship), heard messages (clairaudience), had dreams or visions that came true (precognition) or perhaps you just know things that defy the norm (clairsentience). Maybe you experience a deeply life-changing event that makes you question purpose, meaning, and existence that drags you into finding out more about different kinds of spiritual practices. However this shows up for you, the 7 Life Path is meant for a slow, gradual, and deep exploration of life from the inside out.

INSPIRATION FOR THE 7 LIFE PATH

A few good reads to inspire, educate, and inform the 7 Life Path. These are simply suggestive of topics that would speak to your 7 Life Path mission on some level.

Any book, class, or tool that offers you ways to think about quieting the mind, learning tools for analysis and data collection, developing intuition, and digging into life's more profound questions are perfect for you.

Here are just a few suggestions, yet depending on when you read this book—now or 20-years from now (which may be your *now* if that's when you're picking up this book), there will be many new books and resources from which to choose.

I simply encourage you to read biographies and autobiographies of those on the 7 Life Path to find a sense of connection and also as cautionary tales that can save you from making similar missteps.

- *E2: Nine Do-It-Yourself Energy Experiments That Prove Your Thoughts Create Your Reality* by Pam Grout
- *Loving What Is* by Byron Katie

- *Daring To Trust: Opening Ourselves To Real Love And Intimacy* by David Richo
- *Awakening Intuition* by Dr. Mona Lisa Schulz
- *Breaking The Habit of Being Yourself* by Joe Dispenza
- *The Untethered Soul* by Michael A. Singer
- *The Gifts of Imperfection* by Brené Brown
- *The Art of Happiness* by The 14th Dalai Lama
- *What On Earth Am I Here For?* By Rick Warren
- *The Theory of Everything* by Stephen W. Hawking

A FEW WELL-KNOWN 7 LIFE PATH'S

Elle Macpherson (March 29, 1964)
Jessica Chastain (March 24, 1977)
Portia deRossi (January 31, 1973)
Kristen Bell (July 18, 1980)
Marilyn Monroe (June 1, 1926)
Taylor Swift (December 13, 1989)
Lady Diana (July 1, 1961)
Melinda Gates (August 15, 1964)
Natalie Portman (June 9, 1981)
Julia Roberts (October 28, 1967)
Helen Mirren (July 26, 1945)
Emma Stone (November 6, 1988)
Amy Poehler (September 16, 1971)
Katherine Hepburn (May 12, 1907)
Dax Shepard (January 2, 1975)
Heath Ledger (April 4, 1979)
Leonardo DiCaprio (November 11, 1974)
Antonio Banderas (August 10, 1960)
Johnny Depp (June 9, 1963)
Stephen Hawking (January 8, 1942)
John F. Kennedy (May 29, 1917)
Freddie Mercury (September 5, 1946)
Elon Musk (June 28, 1971)
Dr. Phil McGraw (September 1, 1950)
Al Pacino (April 25, 1940)
Heath Ledger (April 4, 1979)
Christian Bale (January 30, 1974)
Ethan Hawke (November 6, 1970)
Jack Black (August 28, 1969)
Mark Manson (March 9, 1984)

How to Calculate Your Life Path Number?

USE YOUR DATE OF BIRTH
"JULY 27, 1972"
ADD YOUR
MONTH + DAY + YEAR

JULY = 7
27 = 2 + 7 = 9;
1972 = 1 + 9 + 7 + 2 = 19;
1 + 9 = 10 AND 1 + 0 = 1;
7 + 9 + 1 = 17 AND 1 + 7 = 8

KEY THEMES

- MONEY / CONTROL
- "POWER AND EMPOWERMENT"
- AUTHORITY / MANAGEMENT
- ORGANIZATION / ETHICAL
- DYNAMIC / SUCCESSFUL
- INFLUENTIAL

YOUR MISSION STATEMENT

TO STEP UP (OR GET STEPPED ON!) WHILE USING YOUR MONEY, AUTHORITY, AND INFLUENCE TO POSITIVELY INFLUENCE YOUR OWN LIFE AND THE WORLD.

SOME FITTING CAREERS

- BANKING
- PHILANTHROPIST
- ENTERTAINMENT
- REAL ESTATE AGENT/INVESTOR
- CEO
- LEGAL FIELDS

CORE LESSONS AND CHALLENGES

- OVER FOCUS ON MONEY
- CONTROLLING AND OVERLY OPINIONATED
- DISEMPOWERED AND VICTIMIZED
- CHALLENGED WITH BEING ETHICAL
- LOVE/HATE RELATIONSHIP WITH MONEY

RELATIONSHIP COMPATIBILITY

- 8 AND 1 = POWER AND LEADERSHIP
- 8 AND 2 = POWER AND HEART
- 8 AND 3 = POWER AND CREATIVE EXPRESSION
- 8 AND 4 = POWER AND SECURITY
- 8 AND 5 = POWER AND FREEDOM-SEEKING
- 8 AND 6 = POWER AND NURTURING
- 8 AND 7 = POWER AND SPIRITUALITY
- 8 AND 8 = FINANCIAL FOCUS & POWER
- 8 AND 9 = POWER AND COMPASSION

YOUR POWER

- ABILITY TO MASTER THE WORLD OF FINANCES
- POWERFUL PRESENCE EVERYWHERE YOU GO
- MADE FOR SUCCESS AND ACHIEVEMENT
- POSITIVE INFLUENCE TO MAKE THE WORLD A BETTER PLACE
- AUTHORITATIVE AND COMMANDING

WELL-KNOWN 8s

- AMY SCHUMER (JUNE 1, 1981)
- TREVOR NOAH (FEBRUARY 20, 1984)
- CATE BLANCHETT (MAY 14, 1969)
- CHRIS PRATT (JUNE 26, 1956)

THE 8 LIFE PATH IS INTENSE! IT TAKES EFFORT, FOCUS AND TENACITY TO EMPOWER YOURSELF AND BECOME THE FINANCIAL POWERHOUSE YOU WERE BORN TO BE. YOU CAN DO IT!

8 LIFE PATH

THE EMPOWERED MANIFESTOR

Money is only a tool. It will take you wherever you wish, but it will not replace you as the driver.

—- Ayn Rand

Optimal Elements

An 8 Life Path's optimal expression is being at ease with financial abundance, using power and authority wisely and for the good of others, not dwelling in the negative or becoming a victim to circumstances—and being abundantly giving of time, money, and influence to make the world a better place.

Your personal mission is to create material abundance and be personally empowered in every aspect of your life.

Your life's purpose is to use your financial influence and power to make a mark in the world and to help other people.

MONEY & FINANCES

The mission of the 8 Life Path is in mastering how to manage your personal relationship with all aspects of the material world, including—but not limited to—money and power. Where the 7 Life Path is about the mastery of the internal spiritual world, the 8 Life Path is about the mastery of the earthly and material plane of existence.

Understand that the number 8 is the number of infinity and it's also an amplifier. When an 8 shows up, it amps up everything—it's an intensifier. No wonder your life isn't for the faint of heart! If you have an 8 Life Path, know from the get-go that yours is an intense pathway and often this starts right out of the chute in childhood. The ultimate mission is focused on establishing and building financial and material wealth and security. You seek the freedom that comes from being financially successful.

From early on, your drive centers on money, one way or another. While you can say that all of us have issues with money, the difference is that—for the 8 Life Path—money is a *central theme*. Whether there's plenty of money, never enough money—or anything in between—the focus is on how much is located in your bank account or portfolio. More than most people, 8's have a distinct love/hate relationship with money.

A little example: An 8 Life Path I know always comes back from a vacation and describes his experience through his 8-tinted glasses. Rather than focusing on the scenery or an activity that was memorable, he frames his telling of the trip by how much money everything costs. Rather than "I had the most sensational meal in Venice!" he will frame it this way: "When we were in Venice, I ordered the most expensive meal I've ever eaten in my life!" An 8 Life Path often sees things in dollar signs, one way or the other. The 8 desires the finer things in life and strives toward the status and respect money and success can bring with it.

POWER & EMPOWERMENT

Life for an 8 is often rife with opportunities to step up or be stepped on. The first tier of mastery on the 8 Life Path is that of personal power—of stepping into a strong sense of yourself and your power in the world at large. Many 8 Life Path's have trouble making it past this level on the testing field and become victims of life rather than the captain of their own ship.

I get this all the time as a numerologist: "I can't be an 8 because I hate money! I don't care about success. I can't stand people who are wealthy. I have it really hard and never catch a break, anyway. There's no way I'm an 8 Life Path." Sorry—*yes, you are an 8.*

This is often a scenario for the challenges on an 8 Life Path journey. It's all about stepping into your power and not yielding to disempowerment. You're being called upon to make friends with money and pursue something business-related. You're being asked to seek and act upon a balance of power—power versus force. The first rung of the ladder to aligning with your 8 Life Path purpose has to do with *empowerment*. If you can't get a handle around your personal power, nothing else can follow.

Yours is the journey of money, power, and authority—and while that may sound fabulous, this path demands a great deal of discipline, wisdom, ethics, and fortitude. The 8 Life Path isn't particularly easy sailing given that you're meant to make a positive difference in the material world using the highest ethics and—*ultimately*—give generously to others. Once you accept that yours is a life meant for success and achievement, the real work begins.

The 8 usually has excellent executive and management skills, yet of course your innate abilities need to be educated and developed. A key for you is to think big and find the right processes and people to support you in your enterprises.

Like the 4 Life Path, the 8 Life Path is rife with family issues. Understand that you've endured some profound experiences in your life and either you can be ground up and spit out by them or you can choose to see them as your best teachers—they were hard on you, giving you the opportunity to learn about yourself, and about how to exert your Will in the world. Combining ambition with your special gift of a powerful commanding presence is something you're working on developing lifelong.

CONTROL & SELF-CONTROL

One of the biggest life lessons for the 8 Life Path has to do with control. Since the 8 is learning how to work effectively with power, issues related to control are an integral part of who you are and how you show up in the world. As an 8 Life Path, you want absolute control over your life—your situation in life, and your ability to gain prestige and respect. It's a high priority to be able to exert control over your financial life as well. One of the tricks here is to garner a balance between healthy control and destructive levels of control.

The 8 Life Path is on the fast-track to learning about control. You're met with the demand that you control specific areas of your life and with that, you'll attract circumstances and people who will make it their business to control you, tell you what do to and what not to do—and attempt to place you into circumstances where you're under the dominion of someone or something outside of your immediate command. More than most of the Life Path's, the 8 butts up against people and situations again and again that challenge your ability to control your environment, while also navigating the controlling agendas of others.

It's up to you to chisel your pathway by mastering the fine art of self-control. The 8 Life Path is often the belligerent employee, rebellious student or the one who simply wants the world to revolve around its self-perception as the boss or the one who's in charge—whether that's in career, relationship or in any other venue.

Often the 8 feels an unbridled need to thrash around and exert themselves *against*—just against the way the world is set up or against what they feel they're being forced to do against their Will. I have an 8 Life Path friend who will tell you that every difficulty she's had in life—and there were many—were what she has labeled *self-imposed*. She chose to drop out of school, to marry an abuser, to take jobs with unrelenting bosses, to push back against her normal yet alcohol-laden family. Eventually, she turned to meditation, Alcoholics Anonymous, and became one of the most sought-after mediators in the legal field. Quite an example of the potential arch of an 8 Life Path!

AUTHORITY

I've never met an 8 Life Path who doesn't have authority issues out the wazoo! This ranges from being overly acquiescing to those who are in charge to being outwardly defiant against authority. The reason the 8 is handed these hard and rigorous lessons starting early in life is because you've signed up to actually *be an authority*. Therefore, once again you find yourself on the fast track to learning how to be a great mentor, boss, and authority figure.

On rare occasions, you can be the lucky 8 who's gifted with strong and positive authority figures from whom you model yourself. Yet mostly, the 8 Life Path is confronted with difficult authority figures who are placed in your path in order to show you in real-time what *not* to do! Have you ever found yourself saying: "I can be a better boss than *that!*" The point is: Yes, you can! Get out there and *do it!*

Once again, the key is with balance. I knew an 8 Life Path who was a successful real estate investor. Overall, this 8 was generous to a fault to those who were deferential to him, showered him with respect, and welcomed his domineering personality. He donated a substantial amount of money to charitable organizations, delighted in over-tipping at restaurants, and only felt he could be himself when he consumed a lot of alcohol. Yet, when he was able to "be himself" with alcohol, he also became belligerent, dominating, and incredibly aggressive.

The 8 Life Path is challenged with managing a reservoir of highly-charged energy that is often directed (or misdirected) into a heightened need to dominate and control. You're a force of nature, oh-8 Life Path! Just know that you—and everyone around you—benefits when you have an awareness about how forceful you actually are and do your best to soften your demeaner. Little do you know, you're still the most powerful, commanding presence in the room, even when you take down the "volume" by about fifty percent.

ETHICS

The 8 Life Path is fairly unforgiving. You don't get away with much. If you're driving five miles over the speed limit surrounded by ten other cars doing the same thing, you're the one who'll get a ticket. It may not seem fair, but that's the way it is.

Martha Stewart (born August 3, 1941) is on an 8 Life Path and her story provides a perfect example. How many other people engaged in the same type of insider trading as Martha Stewart? Yet she's the one who was arrested, tried, convicted, and went to prison. Right or wrong, the 8 Life Path must act with uncompromising ethics at all times. Martha Stewart bounced right back. How many people can come out of prison and re-tool their brand, partner with Snoop Dogg, and expand their empire to soar above where it was before?

Resilience is another 8 Life Path trait, so take note of it. Yet the message is clear: Your ethics will be tested. It's not random chance that you find yourself in the trenches over and over again. The tough stuff is the core of this calling, making the ultimate rewards you get for your efforts even sweeter and resonate even deeper.

Let's go back to Martha Stewart to illustrate the resilient qualities of the 8 Life Path. You're positioned to bounce back from adversity when you stay positive and keep your ethics clean. Or, in Martha's case, do your time and come back swinging. How many people could go from being America's cooking and homemaking expert to convict and back again without much tarnish? Lesser folks would have slunk away from the spotlight with their tails between their legs. Not 8 Life Path Martha Stewart.

Another observation relevant to the energy of the 8 has to do with the legal system. The 8 often finds itself engaged in legal issues or dealing with time in court, on one side of the fence or the other. If you think about it, this is the utmost platform for the expression of the serious consequences of wielding authority, power, and control in a material and financially-driven world.

THE 8 LIFE PATH & RELATIONSHIPS

You're often a *time is money* kind-of person and you think in business-like terms, even in your relationship life. You look for a partner who fulfills the role of the *other half* of your power couple and the 8 often appreciates someone who's physically attractive and who looks good on your arm. You're often much more focused on work and career, so much so that your significant other can tend to feel neglected and overlooked, even though you're simply attempting to be a stellar provider. You have a need to control and that extends to relationships. Work and career often serves as a main point of identity. Also know that some 8 Life Path's marry a powerful partner and live out their 8 Life Path experience as a key player in the partnership.

The 8 Life Path can be generous, although you might tend to feel that money or status can be used as a substitute for one-on-one engagement. Emotional availability can be a challenge for you. One thing you have trouble getting past in your personal life is infidelity—any kind of personal betrayal is unacceptable. This also goes for betrayal in business. You have zero tolerance for anyone who crosses you, either in love or in business.

Overall, you have a strong desire to be the pillar of the community and to be someone in-the-know. You seek a relationship that can support and help you fulfill your goals in life.

THE 8 LIFE PATH & CAREER

The energy of the 8 is hard driving and as an 8 Life Path, you do best when you take charge of an existing enterprise or when you build your enterprise from an existing template—like a real estate investment partnership or a financial group. You excel in corporations and or even franchise situations where you walk into a structured enterprise and become the CEO, team leader or manager. As opposed to the 1, who's best at creating something new and innovative, the 8 is gifted with management and organization—not necessarily in being the entrepreneur. The boss, yes. The creator of the business?—maybe not.

In numerology, the 8 is also the number associated with real estate. Often, you find great success in real estate as an agent or owner of income property. Anything having to do with real estate is enhanced by the energy of the number 8. You're designed to be in the world of business and finance, where ethics and integrity are rare commodities.

Can you embrace the fact that you're meant to think big and be a financial success? With an 8 Life Path, you're destined to make a big splash in the world of movers-and-shakers. Yet it won't be an easy dash to get there. You need to key into your sense of personal power—and that will be tested from very early on in your life. Once you get a handle around that, then it's off to the races! Yet you must recognize that you have authority issues you need to balance. Understand that it's up, down and all around for you—yours isn't a linear path to riches. You must be resilient, ethical, hardworking, and above-board at all times.

Understand that an 8 Life Path often has more of a love/hate relationship with money than most. It takes coming to terms with the negative conditioning around making money to commit yourself to your life's work. You're here to act upon your gifts of endurance, healthy assertion, and making your mark in the world. Financial success is your birthright, yet it won't necessarily come easily nor be the simplest to hold onto.

You're learning to take yourself seriously—*but not too seriously!*—and step into your power. Concerted effort, focus, management, and organization are key elements for success.

A few possibilities:

- Any business field where you can act as a manager or CEO, COO or CFO
- Entertainment as an actor, producer, director, camera operator or other lead positions in the industry
- Restaurant industry—manager, head chef, sommelier, or owner

- Real estate development and investment
- Fashion designer
- Record or music producer
- Influencer on social media
- Judge
- Litigator/Attorney
- Upper-level positions in the military
- Franchise owner
- Surgeon, physician, sales of medical devices or pharmaceuticals
- Philanthropist
- Publisher, agent, PR
- University President or Chancellor

8 LIFE PATH
Opposing Forces

OPINIONATED

You're easily misinterpreted by others, so must learn to be tactful in your communication. The 8 can see things in a black-and-white manner with little room for gray—other than your own gray area that's reserved only for you. You have strong and often immovable ideas and ideals. To say you're stubborn and opinionated is most likely an understatement. You compete with the 4 Life Path in your need to be right, coupled with a forceful and directive nature. The 8 Life Path usually doesn't understand the effect that your abrupt or aggressive manner can have on others.

While you need a lot of strength and a certain amount of ego to get the job done as an 8 Life Path, chances are you might have to work at understanding the importance of maintaining a certain balance and reserve. You tend to be direct, to the point, and quite business-like in all your dealings, whether professional or personal.

OVER-FOCUSED OR UNDER-FOCUSED ON MONEY

You may be the classic workaholic, which partly comes from wanting to be a great provider and be a respected member of your community. Interestingly, being on the 8 Life Path—with its emphasis on money and power—is no guarantee that you'll live a charmed financial life. An 8 is just as likely to be drawn toward scarcity. You could end up destitute at worst and just making ends meet at best. If you can, however, embrace the idea that making money is all right—and for you, not only all right, but imperative to your life purpose—you'll discover it doesn't take much to launch into success.

The 8 provides the energy with which to achieve financial abundance through concerted effort, ethical conduct, and attention to your higher purpose. I know many 8 Life Paths who have struggled with a load of issues from childhood who have either succumbed to addiction and victimization or blazed through their fear and anger over their circumstances to rise from the ashes like the Phoenix. That's how dramatic the 8 Life Path can be. I know many 8 Life Paths who've been like the poster child for "The Rise and Fall and Rise of [insert your name here]." They're destitute, addicted, irresponsible, and then—through some strange turn of events—clean and sober, passionate about *something,* and a millionaire within a short period of time. No kidding.

DISEMPOWERED

Since you're on the hard road to personal empowerment, the flip-side can be that you don't step into your power and instead lead a life of limited means. The 8 Life Path can be a rudderless addict or the person who struggles daily to make enough to pay the rent—or anything in between. Understand that while the 8 is the "money number," it's primarily a *power* number. If you don't empower yourself, the money rarely follows.

Also know that the highest level of the number 8 consciousness resides in understanding and acting upon the spiritual freedom money provides. Sometimes this can present itself as a choice to opt out of high finance and create a comfortable existence for yourself and others based not in high levels of material gain, but in spiritual and material philanthropy or service.

I have a friend who is a 7 Life Path with an 8 Destiny/Expression. She's a healer and energy worker who works as a healer and spiritual guide. Her early years were spent in the fashion industry and then as a massage therapist in a resort town. She knows all about the finer things in life (definitely the influence of the 8 Expression) and while she's not wealthy, her finances cover the way she wants to live. She's an empowered woman who's found her place between the material and the spiritual realms.

This is just an example of how the energy of the 8 can show up for you. Just because you're not a millionaire doesn't mean you're not successfully living your 8 Life Path purpose. The key is in the choices you make around what you value and what you want to create and then being empowered and tenacious enough to manifest it.

CONTROLLING & DOMINEERING

As an 8 Life Path, you can struggle to balance your desire to control everything and everyone around you. It's as though you always feel you have to prove yourself—over and over again. You're here to master the art of control. Therefore, others can see that you have little patience or desire to suffer fools gladly.

A friend of mine recounted a story about her 8 Life Path relative—that every time this little 8 Life Path girl would come to visit, the 8 would be the one who insisted on leading all the other kids, bullied them and told them what to do, and demanded that all the other children play what she wanted to play (and to play *how* she wanted them to play it!). Even as a child, this 8 Life Path grappled with issues related to power and control much more than other kids.

Often the 8 Life Path feels as though the world and the people inhabiting the world should part like the Red Sea when you walk into a room or into a situation. Even if you don't consciously know this, there is an underlying need to be the royal sitting on the throne. This driving need is part of your gift, yet like the infinity symbol the number 8 exemplifies, a constant flow of energy and power is the secret to the proper expression of the powerhouse 8 Life Path.

One of the attractions of the 8 is your ability to take charge and take control of situations. People gravitate to your charming persona and often see you as the one who has it all together. Depending on the type of 8 Life Path you are, it's always about holding steady and strong. It's about the balance. The most significant lesson to be mastered by the 8 Life Path is the consistent practice of *self-control*.

A friend's father-in-law is a wealthy 8 Life Path who—while charming on many levels—insists on grabbing her arm and placing her in the seat he wants to her sit in when they go to a restaurant for a family dinner. Whenever he feels out of control, he can change like Dr. Jekyll and Mr. Hyde—yelling, demeaning others verbally, and pounding on tables with his fists. You might find that the challenged 8 Life Path has little to no tolerance for those who don't do as they say. Hopefully it doesn't come out so explosively, yet there is a tendency for high intensity with the 8 Life Path.

On the other end of the spectrum, I have a friend whose brother is an 8 Life Path and also has an 8 Birth Day number. He has struggled from day one. He was the baby of three children. Their parents divorced when he was three years old and he got the brunt of that transition. His mother was promiscuous and frequently left him alone as a child—and they lived with very limited means after the divorce. He started being rebellious, quit school and began a long and arduous road of addition with drugs, alcohol, and sex. He couldn't hold down a job, was homeless for a while, and now lives within very limited circumstances. Again, the 8 Life Path demands that you step into yourself in a powerful and self-determined way.

Every human being needs to deal with money and learn how to empower themselves in life. Everyone needs to master finances and learn how to take ourselves seriously. Yet as an 8 Life Path, self-mastery and financial abundance are focal points and aspects for development all your life.

Therefore, the themes of power and financial success directly connect with the characteristics of the key people who play certain roles in your life script, whether as intimate partners, family members, teachers, colleagues, or even random meetings.

The themes of the 8 (money, power, control) direct traffic in terms of the situations you find yourself in, the people who show up, and as the way life lessons come your way.

Biggest Blind Spot: The overpowering way you relate to others lends to aggression and a tendency to dominate and intimidate others.

8 Life Path Superpower: You're the most dynamic force to be reckoned with when you're in your most empowered and altruistic state of mind. You have a natural gift for knowing how to manifest anything you want—and affect long-reaching influence and positive change in the world.

8 Life Path Mantra: "Money equals freedom."

PRACTICAL ADVICE FOR THE 8 LIFE PATH

Practical advice for the 8 Life Path resides most directly in coming to terms with the requirement to deal with money and finances. As an 8 Life Path, you'll often over-focus or under-focus on money. Yet the necessity to learn about money and how to handle and take charge of your material needs is foundational.

If you're a parent and have an 8 Life Path child, it's imperative that you talk with them about money and that you offer the 8 Life Path child a consistent financially-based boot-camp from the ground up. Starting with chores and allowance—along with your child tithing or holding back a certain percentage for charitable giving—will do wonders for them.

The 8 Life Path child also gets to learn about power and empowerment, right? Therefore, offering them a distinct system of responsibilities and rewards also sets them up for success as an 8. Praise and reinforcement for standing up for themselves and also for caring for others is a good focal point for the 8 Life Path child. Helping them save their money and then allowing them to decide how to spend it (even if they make a mistake with what they buy!) is crucial. The hard part as a parent of an 8 is holding your ground and letting them bear the burden of the consequences—one way or the other.

What about the 8 Life Path adult? If you didn't have someone show you the financial ropes—which is most likely the case—it's up to you to get yourself up to speed. This means you have to decide that learning about money, finances, and the nuts-and-bolts of your material world remains the cornerstone and foundation for your pathway as an 8. How to do this? Read books. Take courses. Seek out relationships with people who are successful and you admire who can be friends and mentors. As soon as you focus your energy and efforts to move with the flow of the material world, that's when the 8 Life Path begins to feel as though you're finally in your element.

The practical advice extends to empowerment—taking charge of yourself and your life. Many 8's deflect and detour around your calling by rejecting your own power. The faster you can learn to step up and hold yourself accountable for everything that happens to you—even when it's *not your fault*—the better off you'll be.

Also have an awareness around the shadow-side of the 8, which can show up through addictions and stubborn resistance to accepting help and support. Think about 8 Life Path Amy Winehouse, who left us far too soon. Her song "Rehab" can be seen as a siren-song for shadow elements with the intensity of the 8 Life Path: "They tried to make me go to rehab, but I said no, no, no …"

The best practical advice:

- Learn about how money works by understanding stocks, real estate, and investments of all kinds.
- The 8 is the number of the divine feminine—learn to harness the power of your feminine (whether you're male or female).
- The key to the flow of abundance resides in the constant flow—learn how to trust the flow by giving to others.
- Understand that you operate most effectively when you create order, institute proper systems of management, and organize properly. Don't reinvent the wheel—learn from those who've already done it and use their systems.

INSPIRATION FOR THE 8 LIFE PATH

A few good reads to inspire, educate, and inform the 8 Life Path. These are simply suggestive of topics that would speak to your 8 Life Path mission on some level.

Any book, class, or tool that offers you ways to think about understanding money and finance, development of self-awareness as it pertains to empowerment, tools for management and organization, and on spiritual growth are perfect for you.

Here are just a few suggestions, yet depending on when you read this book—now or 20-years from now (which may be your *now* if that's when you're picking up this book), there will be many new books and resources from which to choose.

I simply encourage you to read biographies and autobiographies of those on the 8 Life Path to find a sense of connection and also as cautionary tales that can save you from making similar missteps.

- *Blink: The Power Of Thinking Without Thinking* (or any other book by Malcolm Gladwell) by Malcolm Gladwell
- *Traction: Get A Grip On Your Business* by Gino Wickman
- *Drive: The Surprising Truth About What Motivates Us* by Daniel H. Pink
- *The 4-Hour Work Week* by Timothy Ferris
- *Dare To Lead* by Brené Brown
- *Start With Why* by Simon Sinek
- *How To Win Friends and Influence People* by Dale Carnegie
- *Give & Take* by Adam Grant
- *13 Things Mentally Strong People Don't Do* by Amy Morin
- *Cleaning Up Your Mental Mess: 5 Simple, Scientifically Proven Steps to Reduce Anxiety, Stress, and Toxic Thinking* by Dr. Caroline Leaf

A FEW WELL-KNOWN 8 LIFE PATH'S

Sandra Bullock (July 26, 1964)
Amy Winehouse (September 14, 1983)
Elizabeth Taylor (February 27, 1932)
Maya Rudolph (July 27, 1972)
Penélope Cruz (April 28, 1974)
Cate Blanchett (May 14, 1969)
Halle Berry (August 14, 1966)
Martha Stewart (August 3, 1941)
Amy Schumer (June 1, 1981)
Olivia Wilde (March 10, 1984)
Jane Fonda (December 21, 1937)
Jessica Simpson (July 10, 1980)
Lucille Ball (August 6, 1911)
Hedy Lamar (November 9, 1914)
Trevor Noah (February 20, 1984)
Paul Rudd (April 6, 1969)
Chris Pratt (June 21, 1979)
Lin-Manuel Miranda (January 16, 1980)
Paul Newman (January 26, 1925)
Chris Isaak (June 26, 1956)
Philip Seymour Hoffman (July 23, 1967)
50 Cent (July 6, 1975)
Edgar Cayce (March 18, 1877)
Dan Millman (February 22, 1946)
Dwayne Johnson (May 2, 1972)
Pablo Picasso (October 25, 1881)
Matt Damon (October 8, 1970)
Ben Stiller (November 30, 1965)
RuPaul (November 17, 1960)
Bob Dylan (May 24, 1941)

9

How to Calculate Your Life Path Number?

USE YOUR DATE OF BIRTH
"JULY 12, 1997"
ADD YOUR
MONTH + DAY + YEAR

JULY = 7
12 = 1 + 2 = 3;
1997 = 1 + 9 + 9 + 7 = 26;
2 + 6 = 8;
7 + 3 + 8 = 18 AND 1 + 8 = 9

KEY THEMES

- CONCLUSION / COMPASSION
- "HUMANITARIANISM"
- ROMANCE / FORGIVENESS
- CREATIVITY / ARTISTRY
- LETTING GO / ALTRUISM
- LIMITED REWARDS

CORE LESSONS AND CHALLENGES

- BITTERNESS AND LIVING IN THE PAST
- ISOLATED AND EMOTIONALLY DISCONNECTED
- CONTROLLING AND NARCISSISTIC
- ENABLER AND FAMILY ENMESHMENT
- WON'T ACCEPT HELP OR SUPPORT

YOUR POWER

- QUIRKY AND CREATIVE
- CHARISMATIC AND INNOVATIVE
- GIVING AND COMPASSIONATE
- CHAMPION OF THE UNDERDOG
- WISDOM AND INTEGRITY

THE 9 LIFE PATH TESTS YOUR ABILITY TO EMBRACE A LIFE OF SELFLESS SERVICE IN SOME WAY, SHAPE, OR FORM — WHILE ALSO OPENING YOURSELF TO RECEIVING AS WELL AS GIVING. YOU CAN DO IT!

YOUR MISSION STATEMENT

THE 9 LIFE PATH IS QUIRKY, GIVING, AND COMPASSIONATE.

SOME FITTING CAREERS

- PERFORMER
- ARTIST
- MEDICINE
- ENTREPRENEUR
- BUSINESS
- SPIRITUAL LEADER

RELATIONSHIP COMPATIBILITY

- 9 AND 1 = COMPASSION & LEADERSHIP
- 9 AND 2 = COMPASSION & HEART
- 9 AND 3 = COMPASSION & CREATIVE EXPRESSION
- 9 AND 4 = COMPASSION & SECURITY
- 9 AND 5 = COMPASSION & FREEDOM-SEEKING
- 9 AND 6 = COMPASSION & NURTURING
- 9 AND 7 = COMPASSION & SPIRITUALITY
- 9 AND 8 = LEADERSHIP & POWER
- 9 AND 9 = COMPASSION & COMPASSION

WELL-KNOWN 9s

- MOTHER TERESA (AUGUST 26, 1910)
- ADELE (MAY 5, 1988)
- MORGAN FREEMAN (JUNE 1, 1937)
- JIM CARREY (JANUARY 17, 1962)

9 LIFE PATH

THE COMPASSIONATE HUMANITARIAN

The purpose of any charity is simply to turn people's mirrors into windows. An outward view of the world's needs are vast in comparison to an inward one.

— Shannon L. Alder

Optimal Elements

A 9 Life Path's optimal expression resides in extending yourself in the service of something greater than yourself, learning to detach from dysfunctional or enmeshed family dynamics, becoming an empathetic listener, and being open to new experiences every day.

Your personal mission is to act with integrity while pursuing a creative and giving path.

Your life's purpose is to live in with the highest integrity, to align your life's purpose with your heart's intuitive wisdom, and to inspire others by your example.

HUMANITARIAN & ALTRUISTIC

The 9 Life Path is the most evolved in numerology because it contains the qualities of all the other numbers. Some forms of numerology don't use the 9 in certain calculations because the number 9 is considered *sacred*. If your belief system supports the idea of reincarnation, you might be relieved to know that the 9 is that of a wise old soul, returning once again armed with a reservoir of past-life knowledge and wisdom. If you don't believe in reincarnation, know that your life is meant to be expansive, creative, and spiritually challenging.

The number 9 is the number of endings—of completions, surrender, and letting go. These are key themes to your life. I think of the 9 Life Path as the ultimate training ground for the primary teachings of Buddhism. It's all about the practice of experiencing the present moment, letting go of the past without bitterness and regret, and moving into the future with curiosity and an open heart.

Sounds super easy, right? (*not so much*) Yours is truly a lifetime to focus fully and completely on letting go and *letting it flow*. It's all about surrendering and on gaining and acting upon higher spiritual principals, however you define them. You have a strong inclination to follow something you believe in, and you'll pursue this with great ambition and drive. You have an authentic regard for humanity, so your goals usually involve serving others in some way. The 9 is often regarded as a servant to the Brotherhood of Man, yet I would say that the optimal 9 Life Path is the personification of Universal Wisdom.

What does *that* mean? If we put a few well-known 9 Life Path's energies into a blender and see what we get, let's use these: Mother Teresa (no pressure!), Mahatma Gandhi, Greta Thunberg, Jim Carrey, Elvis Presley, Prince, Robin Williams, and Adele. Put it all together and what do you have? A line-up of pure badassery. They're quirky, creative powerhouses and in many ways, other-worldly. The 9 marches not only to the beat of their own drum, they're the drum major to their own marching band!

I conceptualize the 9 Life Path this way. It's as though you're a piece of canvas and you stretch that canvas on a frame of your choosing. The canvas is created out of pure, unconditional love. Then you decide how large or small the frame is and what medium you'll use to create your masterful piece of artwork that is your life. Is it in black and white?

Oil or watercolor paints? Mixed media? Pencil or chalk? Perhaps it's a landscape, still life, self-portrait, or an eclectic expressionistic piece. The common denominator is the underlying energy that the canvas of unconditional love brings to your masterpiece. The way you create it is up to you.

CHAMPION OF THE MARGINALIZED & THE DISENFRANCHISED

Yours is a path of compassionate service and yet that pathway must be learned through experience. In childhood, you can find yourself the odd one out, feeling distinctly out of place in the world. It's almost like when you watch a video and the sound isn't quite in synch with the person talking. There's a weird delay—the mouth moves and the words follow a half-beat behind. You can feel a sense of displacement that might feel somewhat like you do when you watch that video. Then you wonder if everyone is seeing this sound delay with the video or is it just you who notices?

You can be the champion of the underdog early on, identifying and protecting those who are disabled or who're just a little *off* according to traditional standards. You gravitate toward helping those on the fringes or who are disenfranchised. Or alternately, the 9 can be the bully—until you have a dramatic experience that shifts your perspective.

I remember watching an audition for *America's Got Talent* and felt that this young man must have been a 9 Life Path. He auditioned as a comedian. When he opened his mouth, he could barely speak a full sentence without stuttering, and his stuttering was the foundation for the comedy in his act.

The judges loved him. Then he told his story: He was a popular kid in school—an athlete. During a baseball game, he was hit in the throat with a baseball. It damaged his voice box irreparably, giving him a severe stutter. As he told the story, his eyes filled with tears as he asserted that when he was in school, he would have never befriended or even spoken to anyone like him. Before his accident, he made fun of other kids and in some ways bullied them for being different or insignificant. *And now he's one of them.* It was a powerful statement that speaks to the life lessons of the 9 Life Path.

Sometimes you must learn the difficult way how to care for people in the broadest and most compassionate sense. Sometimes you're there right out of the gate—the child who gravitates toward nursing sick animals, befriending children or adults who are perhaps defined by some kind of disability, or the one in the family who cushions difficult family dynamics. And then sometimes you learn how to care about other people the hard way.

A TORNADO OF CREATIVITY

The 9 Life Path is enigmatic and incredibly charismatic. Your creativity has no limits. You're gifted in many areas—it's your job to cultivate what makes your heart sing. For some of you it's music, acting, or stand-up comedy. For others, you're a creative genius with business and entrepreneurship. You can find and act upon your creative gifts on various levels, through creating financial abundance to use to help yourself and others or being an expert creative problem solver.

You can use your creativity as a healer, architect, or writer. The world is your stage and your oyster—remember that you have inner resources that you can't even fathom. Your mantra might be: "Fake it 'til you make it!" You have a soulful connection with people and an inexplicable depth of expression when you choose to step into it. Using your creative expression is key to your sanity and to bringing your higher energetic frequencies into their highest and best use.

Often the 9 Life Path will traverse life and engage with several different tributaries with their creative souls. Anthony Hopkins is a 9 Life Path—actor, painter, and composer of classical music. Jim Carry started as a stand-up comedian, performed in sketch-comedy on television, acted in movies (both comedic and non-comic), is a painter and cartoon artist, and also sings.

David Byrne of *The Talking Heads* is a musician, singer, song-writer, author, photographer, director, installation artist and performance artist. Eddie Izzard is dyslexic, creator of stand-up one-man shows who performs in at least six different languages, actor, political activist, marathon runner, and transvestite (as of 2022, s/he leans more toward transgender).

The 9 Life Path often is a volcanic explosion of artistic and creative genius. Yet, even as we look at this list of 9 Life Path's, it's clear that there's nothing *easy* about their personalities!

LOSS & LIMITED REWARDS

Your amazing potential reminds me of the 2008 film *The Curious Case of Benjamin Button*, a story in which Benjamin is born an old man in an infant's body. As he matures, he meets himself in the middle of his life and then begins to become younger as time passes. He eventually dies of old age as an infant again.

The key element to take away from Benjamin Button's story is that he flows through his life with awe and appreciation, with a healthy sense of detachment, soaking in all of his experiences in the moment, observing other people, engaging in love, and not clinging to any single part of his multilayered life journey.

You can use his story as a primer for creating your own life. You're certainly at your best when you're moving with the flow rather than ensconced in old stories about the past and replaying old hurtful experiences. It's all a matter of perspective.

The 9 is learning how to let go, forgive, and not to live in the past or cling to the past. The 9 often chews on past experiences and stories without swallowing, digesting, and then expelling them! Move forward as you gently release yesterday, live today, and embrace tomorrow.

There are also some 9s who—instead of hanging on to the past with bitterness or regret—instead look at everything through rose-colored glasses and opt for the denial of the painful or difficult experiences in their lives. Toxic positivity, anyone? You're learning to open your heart to all life experience and all of the emotions that come with each experience. One of your primary life lessons is to learn to both give *and* receive.

THE 9 LIFE PATH & RELATIONSHIPS

The 9 Life Path is an idealist and a romantic at heart. In relationship, you want to please and also would love to be adored by your partner. The key is to extract yourself from co-dependent relationships. It'll take a lot of strength and courage, because it'll take a while for you to realize that your family-of-origin dynamics aren't serving you. If you marry and have your own family, you want nothing less than to be the perfect parent or partner. When it comes to the family, you can't handle interference—which is often made even more difficult because of the enmeshed family-of-origin dynamics.

If you have trouble with your partner, you don't want anyone to get involved. You feel capable of resolving the issue. You most likely want to handle everything behind closed doors. You do such a great job at taking care of everybody's business that when you're in trouble or need support, people don't even notice. You must let your guard down and ask for support or a sounding board when you're struggling with something. Your needs aren't easily read by others—you have to ask for help. You're the type of person who can literally be drowning in quicksand and yet when there's a person passing by who notices you're in a precarious position and asks if you need help, you're the first one to wave them off and assert that *everything's fine*. Again, you're here to learn how to both give *and* receive. This is hard one for you and a life-long endeavor.

THE 9 LIFE PATH & CAREER

Your higher purpose is to inspire others with your compassion for humanity. I know that sounds really lofty, so let's bring it down to earth for a moment. As a 9 Life Path, you have all kinds of skills at your disposal. Like the 7 Life Path, it's even more imperative for you to investigate your Destiny/Expression number to get a good idea about the work and career that would satisfy your deepest longings.

Say your Destiny/Expression is a 4. Perhaps you excel in architecture or some kind of systems building—and you wrap that up with a humanitarian bow. Or maybe you have a 3 Destiny/Expression. Chances are your career would be in the arts as an actor, musician, or some other performative and creative realm—all wrapped up in a humanitarian or service-oriented bow.

You're in your element when you're inspiring others by your example, not by what you say. You have incredible charisma and can choose to use that in either positive or negative ways—*where you lead, they will follow.* Many 9 Life Path's care deeply about the state of the world and find that it's their self-imposed place to instruct others in exactly how do what needs to be done in order to make the world a better place. Yet the 9 often stews about it, having little patience for the collective consciousness playing out before them.

For example, often the 9 can have strident political views that are immutable and can actually be intolerant of other points of view. The 9 has a load of charm and can finesse any situation, yet when it comes to the 9 and career, there can sometimes be a rather delicate balance that needs to transpire between the outspoken 9 Life Path and those in their work environment.

Again, 9's can be and do just about anything—from marketing to owning their own company to being a janitor. The key resides in where your heart and soul leads. You would make an amazing teacher, counselor or therapist. You're often good with children or the elderly. You also would do well in any creative field. The 9 Life Path makes a wildly successful entrepreneur or businessperson if it's something you feel wholeheartedly passionate about. *You must choose work that has meaning for you or you'll feel lost or empty.* When you're optimizing your energy, you're a powerful force for positive change.

I've found that many 9 Life Paths have an incredible capacity for success with anything they set out to do. Remember: You hold the constructive elements of all of the other numbers in numerology and you hold all of the destructive elements as well. Sound like a big responsibility? It actually is. This responsibility lies deeply within you and in your ability to understand the vastness of your playing field if you come to embrace it. Yours is ultimately the higher path of gratitude and service.

A key question you might ask yourself is: How can you go with the flow of your creative and humanitarian impulses? With a 9 Life Path, you're versatile and unusual. It's through creativity and helping others that you find your groove. Understand that you're challenged with asking for support or help, so the sooner you can learn to ask, the better. While at the same time you can have a mild obsession with getting your own way, no matter what.

Know that you might have a propensity to devour information focused on spirituality or psychology. Business can call you as well as any career in the arts—from music or acting to architecture or painting.

Overall, you're working on learning how to express and understand your own feelings and to bridge that into serving the greater good. The 9 is the path of selfless-service and there are many rewards along the way. Tap into your creativity and into something that you feel gives back to others and you'll be living your dream.

Sometimes (not always!) a 9 can have a few issues with traditional education—whether it's with some kind of learning "disorder" (ADHD or dyslexia, as an example) or whether it's simply a rebellious attitude about having to fit all the round pegs into square holes.

You're here to act upon your gifts of insight, creativity, and heart-felt service. The 9 is the ultimate path of selfless-service, and yet that can manifest in many different ways. You have myriad abilities and talents, it's just a matter of directing your focus to what feeds your soul.

A few possibilities:

- Spiritual leader, minister, priest, or anything with religion as its focus
- Teacher
- Entertainment—actor, comedian, filmmaker, musician
- Medicine—doctors without borders, peach corps, or public health
- Business person with emphasis in service industry
- Politician
- Lawyer or judge
- Arts—painting, composer, choreographer
- International and foreign affairs
- Travel guide
- Language translator
- Sales and marketing
- Innovator for products & services serving those with special needs
- Caregiver for elderly, children or those who are ill
- Life Coach
- Writer, speaker, presenter
- Innovator and inventor of products & services to clean up the environment
- Natural foods industry
- Natural cosmetics industry
- FBI, CIA or other government work

9 Life Path

Opposing Forces

CODEPENDENCY OR ENABLING

One of the characteristics of the 9 Life Path is that you often have issues with your original family. You may have felt unloved or abandoned as a child or perhaps felt an overweening responsibility for your parents or siblings. In any event, your attachment to your original family is up for investigation during your life. Unlike the 4 Life Path or the 8 Life Path, your family issues reside more distinctly in enmeshment and co-dependence.

Often the 9 Life Path has a good deal of family enmeshment that feels more like the old television show *Dallas* or *Falcon Crest*—or you can think of it as "The Kardashian Complex." The Kardashian Family had their own reality television show chronicling their business and personal entanglements with each other. To me, this is an example or metaphor for the origin of the 9 Life Path. This sometimes shows up as being born into a family business, where family dynamics are interwoven with personal lives and financial lives that all interconnect—whether you like it or not. It takes a long time to even realize that other people don't have to deal with these kinds of inner workings.

Also know that there are some 9 Life Path's that don't fit directly into this mold, yet finding a way to extrapolate yourself and forge your own quirky pathway is embedded into the 9 Life Path lifetime.

Sometimes you luck out as a 9 Life Path and don't feel you have the kind of enmeshed family dynamics I'm talking about here. If that's the case, congratulations! Even so, family and family expectations will still be a star player in your life's script. You must find a way to maintain healthy personal boundaries with your family and find the courage to leave unhealthy dynamics behind. The trick for you is to detach and establish your sense of yourself without the enmeshment with your family without totally rejecting or abandoning them.

If you're a parent (or a parent to your parent, sibling, spouse, or other family member), your life-long task is to extract yourself from participating in an enabler/enablee situation. Often you create situations where you enable those around you either emotionally or financially. Then you look at the monsters you've created and wonder how the heck to get out of this mess! Or perhaps you're the enablee—where you've allowed yourself to be controlled and disempowered (either emotionally or financially—or both) by another person in your life.

A friend of mine is a 9 Life Path. He grew up as the distant-second to his older brother, who was the golden child in the family. My 9 Life Path friend had undiagnosed dyslexia and always fell behind in school. His grandparents owned several major businesses in the small town they lived in and his father resigned himself to taking on many aspects of the family businesses, despite the father's strong desire to leave the small town and strike out on his own. This 9 Life Path's father suffered with drug and alcohol addiction and died when the 9 Life Path was a young adult. In the meantime, the older brother was given royal status by the patriarch of the family (also a philandering alcoholic) and the 9 Life Path struggled to find his place in the family dynasty.

Due to a dysfunctional turn of events, the 9 Life Path was disinherited by the grandfather and relegated to a management role in one of the family businesses that he wasn't qualified for and that he hated, a sure recipe for the grandfather to prove the unworthiness of the 9 Life Path. Finally, the 9 Life Path submitted his resignation to his grandfather, secured a different job within an entirely different industry, sold his house, and moved he and his wife to another town.

The sheer strength and courage it took to extract himself from the only world he'd ever known was monumental. After several years, he was able to integrate into family gatherings for holidays or other celebrations, without getting sucked into the vortex and toxicity of feeling "less-than" and unworthy. This is just one example of the intricacies that a 9 Life Path might experience as you create a life free of toxic or negative attachments.

FEELING UNWORTHY

When you're in a room, everyone assumes you're in charge. You're a leader in many ways, yet you place a lot of pressure on yourself. Often a 9 Life Path feels a deep sense of unworthiness on some indescribable level. This is predicated by the fact that you don't really feel you belong on the planet, if you know what I mean. You rival the 1 and 7 Life Paths with feelings of not quite belonging.

Yet you can have an intimidating quality—even though putting others at ease is actually one of your gifts if you cultivate it. You're a pleaser and yet when pushed to your limit, you can crush people with criticism and an inability to give positive reinforcement. Belligerence, thy name is 9 Life Path! Given your underlying sense of unworthiness, you can project onto others a heightened level of expectation for superior behavior that can never be fulfilled. Underneath it all, you're running as fast as you can to prove that you're okay, which can come off as intolerance or belligerence.

BITTERNESS & REGRET

Since yours is the path of loss and surrender, there are many opportunities to succumb to feelings of bitterness, regret, and agitation. You'll experience a good deal of loss in life. Even though everyone experiences loss, yours holds a magnified intensity and depth. It's testing you to step into your higher purpose as a servant to humanity. Just saying it like that feels so deep and lofty. Yet it's true. Yours is a high calling. Spirituality is *true self-awareness*. The 9 Life Path is traversing the highest pathway of spiritual practice and self-awareness.

Therefore, as a 9 Life Path you can feel defeated and tired of surrendering and letting go—over and over again. You can resist the Universe's demand that you accept the limited rewards of your undertakings. Yet I want to be extremely clear about how I define "limited rewards." With the 9, it's all about doing what you're doing *because you can't not do it.* This is the path of limited rewards insofar as you would actually pay to do it or do it for free (whatever *it* is!). When you direct your heart and soul into what you're doing, everything follows. The caveat is if the impetus for your actions is only for self-gain, that is when it all falls apart. When the purpose for what you do resides fully in the passion you have for serving something larger than yourself, that's when the 9 is in alignment with your purpose.

You might find yourself looking in the rearview mirror most of the time, reviewing and reassessing the past and clinging to the shards of memory or experiences that offer you mental solace. You can harbor and hold blame, anger, dismay or sorrow, and allow it to mold the way you engage with your present life.

In the extreme, the 9 Life Path can become reclusive and bitter, living in a self-imposed world of regret, anger, and lack of forgiveness. A key element for you is the realization that to forgive is not to condone. You can forgive someone—*even yourself*—without condoning the infraction. Yet in your act of forgiveness, you can release the power that the person or experience wields over your life.

Some 9's can do the opposite and select their memory file to delete all the difficult or painful memories and instead hype-up the positive in the rose-colored glasses realm. Again—it's simple, not easy. And the 9 Life Path is prodding you to perfect all elements of all the numbers. You signed on for the Doctorate program in your life!

REBEL WITH OR WITHOUT A CAUSE

You're sometimes accused of being patronizing because you have a tendency to preach rather than being an active listener. One of your life lessons is to learn to actually listen and engage with others rather than blaze forward with your own directives. It's interesting because you can often be a rebel with or without a cause, pushing up against anything and everything just . . . *because*. Your life revolves around loss of all kinds, so it can be confusing and disheartening unless you surrender yourself and allow what's next to come into your life with open arms rather than with bitterness and anger. Your story of loss and pain is sometimes overwhelming and can drag you into apathy or resentment.

You might not even know why you resist this thing or that—it's this internal combustion or edginess that must find its way to the surface somehow. As a 9 Life Path, you're learning how to step into your emotions and experience them in a way that serves you and those around you. It's not that you don't have emotions—on the contrary. You have such a reservoir of emotions that it can be too overwhelming, and so you opt to distance yourself from the emotions that feel too dangerous or make you feel too vulnerable. There can be a palpable underlying fear of abandonment and rejection that hides under the surface for the 9 Life Path.

Mother Teresa was a 9 Life Path. A servant to humanity, surely—and a rebel in her own way. The compassionate humanitarian who also defied people and institutions to do the work she was called upon to do. You don't have to be Mother Teresa—yet you effect people in small and more expansive ways when you're in alignment with your higher calling.

I find that 9 Life Path's are passionate and compassionate weirdos in the most spectacular sense. The 9 is meant to follow their own meandering pathway, explore their quirky and impressive artistic creativity, and lead with a giving heart.

A word of caution: *We must be careful not to put anyone on a pedestal.* Even Mother Teresa, Gandhi, and others lived a human existence and have shadow-sides to their personalities. No one is perfect and if we believe that human beings are souls living in human form, then no human is exempt from making the mistakes and learning the lessons necessary for soul growth and also to balance karma.

All the Life Path's have the potential to express the dark and the light—and a combination of the two.

Every human being needs to learn compassion and how to engage in selfless-service in some way, shape or form. Everyone needs to develop their ability to let go and learn how to surrender to higher forces. Yet as a 9 Life Path, focusing on giving and acting with integrity are focal points and aspects for development all your life.

Therefore, the themes of unconditional love and selfless service directly connects with the characteristics of the key people who play certain roles in your life script, whether as intimate partners, family members, teachers, colleagues, or even random meetings.

The themes of the 9 (limited rewards, completions, creativity) direct traffic in terms of the situations you find yourself in, the people who show up, and as the way life lessons come your way.

Biggest Blindspot: An inability to see how much you want your own way at all cost. Your compassion is a blessing and a curse—over-caring or under-caring is your kryptonite.

9 Life Path Superpower: The 9 Life Path is the most deeply caring and compassionate person to the point where you are weighted down with the inhumanity of the world. You bring the highest level of wise and caring energy into every interaction.

9 Life Path Mantra (thanks to John Lennon): "You may say I'm a dreamer, but I'm not the only one. I hope someday you'll join us—and the world will live as one."

PRACTICAL ADVICE FOR THE 9 LIFE PATH

You don't make it easy to provide a platform of practical advice, oh-sage 9 Life Path. You're an enigma, to be sure. If I had to choose one point of focus for the 9, it would be with taming or softening your sermonizing demeanor.

The 9 has a tendency to stress and stew over the injustices and inadequacies of the world—and of other people. The 9 isn't without resolute opinions about, well, about everything! From politics to the environment, technology to capitalism, religion to spirituality, the 9 Life Path usually doesn't waiver in their beliefs and values.

Like the 6 Life Path, part of the pathway for the 9 resides in learning how to allow others their own experiences. This is a fine line and a delicate balance to be sure, given the 9 Life Path is the keeper of wisdom and the compassionate humanitarian.

The best practical advice comes in the form of learning to let go and in seeing the beauty of impermanence. *It's as though you're softening into your strength.*

I have a beautiful French 9 Life Path friend who epitomizes the pathway of the 9. She loves travel and is fluent in several languages. Her career has been varied, mostly in the hospitality industry with an emphasis on wine and French cuisine, of which she's an expert. She loves people, loves learning about people's lives, and has a light touch when it comes to her cheerful disposition. She exudes a masterful level of wisdom, depth of spirit, and compassionate understanding for everyone. She literally sees life as a moveable feast and her true nature is that of putting her heart and soul into everything she experiences, yet with the deep knowledge that all of it is truly a temporary thing—with every moment to be savored and appreciated.

Use your imagination and your dreams to give yourself inner and outer peace. In this turbulent world, the 9 Life Path is the keeper of the gates of imagination and mystical creation. Use these devises as a way to calm your over-active nervous system instead of reeving it up. Enjoy your creative impulses and use them as a meditation rather than as an avenue to prove your point of view to someone else. Chances are whatever you're doing will reach who it's meant to reach—and shift consciousness in ways you can't even conceptualize. Sometimes the 9 feels that they need to *make people change* and spend a lot of time and energy fretting about just that. Just use your high-vibe to offer forgiveness, unconditional love, and your jolt of creative genius. The less you force it, the more effective it will be.

Practice gratitude. This is something every human being benefits from doing, yet for the 9 Life Path, living with a full-out attitude of gratitude directly fulfills your passionate purpose. It's said that you can't hold the thought and energy of gratitude and simultaneously feel anger, sadness, or any other negative feeling. Gratitude overpowers the propensity to dwell in the past, in negativity, or in self-pity.

The Butterfly Effect. The evolved 9 Life Path sees the human experience from a totally different lens. You see that this human matrix is merely transitory. You engage with life with the utmost excitement, knowing full-well that this is just one more blip on your soul's radar. You've been here before and with that innate knowledge, you dive in and enjoy every second of this wild, wacky, frustrating, crazy world. The 9 intimately feels that this is just a fragment of a second in the scope of your soul-scape. The key is in accepting that you can't single-handedly bring all earthlings into the kind, compassionate, perfect Utopia you so long for and can see so clearly in your mind's eye.

Often the 9 Life Path feels an unyielding sense of responsibility to put on their super-hero cape and save the planet. As you let go of that underlying pressure, the true gift you have to give as a 9 Life Path emerges. Instead of feeling you must change the course of history and of the planet by your sheer force of nature and Will, surrender instead to the power of the butterfly effect. The definition of the butterfly effect is: *(in chaos theory) the phenomenon whereby a mixture localized change in a complex system can have large effects elsewhere.*

How to achieve this nearly impossible feat? Develop and practice the tools that help guide you and align you with your innate wisdom and spiritual calling. Meditation, volunteering, charitable giving, physical activity, and consuming nutritious food are all mainstays for the 9 Life Path to walk the walk and talk the talk. When in doubt, opt for a warm hug rather than a stern lecture. Make room for conversations where you hold space for the other person without forcing your own agenda. Listen twice, speak once. When feeling low, clear your energy with body-work, massage, dance, and taking a tech-detox.

INSPIRATION FOR THE 9 LIFE PATH

A few good reads to inspire, educate, and inform the 9 Life Path. These are simply suggestive of topics that would speak to your 9 Life Path mission on some level.

Any book, class, or tool that offers you ways to think about creating healthy personal boundaries, to educate yourself on the difference between support and enabling, on spiritual development, and on understanding the power of forgiveness are perfect for you.

Here are just a few suggestions, yet depending on when you read this book—now or 20-years from now (which may be your *now* if that's when you're picking up this book), there will be many new books and resources from which to choose.

I simply encourage you to read biographies and autobiographies of those on the 9 Life Path to find a sense of connection and also as cautionary tales that can save you from making similar missteps.

- *Getting The Love You Want: A Guide For Couples* by Harville Hendrix, Ph.D.
- *Loving What Is* by Byron Katie

- *Leading An Inspired Life* by Jim Rohn
- *Broken Open: How Difficult Times Can Help Us Grow* by Elizabeth Lesser
- *I Thought It was Just Me (but it isn't): Making The Journey From 'What Will People Think?' to 'I Am Enough'* by Brene Brown
- *The Curious Case of Benjamin Button* (with Brad Pitt and Cate Blanchett), originally a book by F. Scott Fitzgerald
- *Radical Compassion* by Tara Brach
- *Start Where You Are* by Pema Chödrön
- *Flow* by Mihaly Csikszentmihalyi
- *Wired to Create: Unraveling the Mysteries of the Creative Mind* by Carolyn Gregoire and Scott Barry Kaufman

A FEW WELL-KNOWN 9 LIFE PATH'S

Adele (May 5, 1988)
Mother Teresa (August 26, 1910)
Cher (May 20, 1946)
Malala Yousafzai (July 12, 1997)
Yoko Ono (February 18, 1933)
Sharon Stone (March 10, 1958)
Louise Hay (October 8, 1926)
Whitney Houston (August 9, 1963)
Allison Janney (November 19, 1959)
Kris Kardashian (November 5, 1955)
Eddie Izzard (February 7, 1962)
Jim Carrey (January 17, 1962)
Justin Bieber (March 1, 1994)
Kurt Russell (March 17, 1951)
Michael Richards (July 24, 1949)
Bill Murray (September 21, 1950)
Harrison Ford (July 13, 1942)
Morgan Freeman (June 1, 1937)
Prince (June 7, 1958)
Elvis Presley (January 8, 1935)
Mahatma Gandhi (October 2, 1869)
Robert Redford (August 18, 1936)
Kurt Cobain (February 20, 1967)
Bob Marley (February 6, 1945)
Paramahansa Yogananda (January 5, 1893)
Joseph Stalin (December 18, 1878)
Robin Williams (July 21, 1951)
Rowan Atkinson (January 6, 1955)
Spike Lee (March 20, 1957)
Harrison Ford (July 13, 1942)

MASTER NUMBERS

Master numbers hold infinite fascination to those who resonate with numerology. Most people actually *want* to have Master numbers (or a Master number) in their numerology chart. I find that many people want to feel special and identifying a Master number somehow satisfies this desire.

On a practical level, how do we successfully understand and optimize what the Master numbers bring to the table? How do we come to understand how the Master numbers actually behave in our lives on a real and practical level? How do we learn to navigate the demands that a Master number brings when it shows up in our numerology chart—whether it is part of our personality profile or whether it shows up in one of our cycles?

What are Master Numbers?

In numerology, double-digit numbers that repeat the same number, such as 11, 22, 33 and so on, are considered Master numbers. Many numerologists observe only the 11 and the 22 when they work with your core numbers in your chart. Some also work with the 33 and rarely the 44. All the repeating numbers are considered Master numbers—it's just that the ones that show up in a chart are the 11, 22, 33.

Also know that many numerologists never digit a Master number down into its one-digit number—so an 11 is always 11, the 22 is always 22, and the 33 is always 33. Many numerologists indicate the Master number by writing it this way: 11/2, 22/4, and 33/6. It's up to you to feel out what works best and what feels right to you. I usually indicate the Master numbers as 11/2, 22/4, and 33/6.

What does this mean?

To start, if you calculate your Life Path number and get an 11, 22, or 33 before you reduce to the 2, 4, or 6, you show a Master Number as your Life Path number. You can also experience Master numbers in other areas in your chart, including the Destiny/Expression, Soul Urge, Maturity, Personality, and so on. Not to mention that you can also experience Master numbers during your Personal Year Cycles, Pinnacles, and during other cycles. If you find Master numbers anywhere in your chart, you'll benefit from learning more about what it means.

Here's an example of a calculation for a Life Path Master number.

Birth date: February 2, 1987

February = 2

Day = 2

Year = 1987; 1 + 9 + 8 + 7 = 25; keep adding 2 + 5 = 7

Add the Month/ Day/ Year: 2 + 2 + 7 = 11

11 is a Master Number.

It's sometimes written this way: 11/2

Let's use this same birthdate and show another way to add.

You can add the entire birthdate together like one long addition problem:

2 + 2 + 1 + 9 + 8 + 7 = 29

Keep adding: 2 + 9 = 11

To get technical about it, when the Master number *doesn't* show up with the first way of adding (month + day + year), you should add it using the other calculation. If it shows up in only one of the calculations, the energy of the Master number can be viewed as optional. You could make the determination to instead work with the energy related to the single number. While you'll continue to feel some internal *burn* related to the Master number, you can opt for the lower octave and be just fine.

Some numerologists feel this way about the Master numbers overall—that someone can always opt for the vibration of the single-digit number if the demands of the Master number are too overwhelming.

Just realize that the Master number brings with it an intensity that's undeniable. It's generally observed that the Master numbers bring a higher spiritual purpose, no matter how you might define that. In practical terms, this means that you're going to feel high-strung mixed with a certain level of anxiety when you're working with a Master number—particularly when it shows up as your Life Path or another of your core numbers. You're going to feel a constant push and pull to *be* more and *do* better, often to the point of distraction.

You might work with health issues related to this kind of internal combustion—like adrenal burnout, weight issues, headaches, thyroid, intestinal distress, mental health issues or mystery illnesses. You might also notice that you have higher expectations for yourself, even when others can't see that those feelings are going on inside of you. Or should we say, *especially* when others can't see that you experience these internal anxieties.

What does that mean on a practical level? It means that you're here to *master* your life and master the elements presented to you within the themes of the Master number. It means that you have some significant strengths and some more intense challenges.

The bottom line: It's not easy! The Master numbers gestate and ripen with maturity. When we cultivate and tend to the mission the Master number brings to our lives—like a fine wine—we ripen and enrich with age and experience. Many people don't even begin to open to their Master purpose until later in life—in the 40s (or 50s) and beyond.

Master numbers not only demand that you step up and take the lead in life, they also make conflicting demands on you. *The Master numbers are actually in conflict with themselves.* Let me explain. Let's look at the Master number 11/2 as an example.

The 11 is a double 1—all about the self, creativity, initiation, independence, innovation, and self-confidence. Yet, the foundational energy for the 11 is the 2, which is all about others, partnership, group dynamics, is ultra-intuitive and sensitive, and is driven to be supportive and behind the scenes. Can you see how—if you're on an 11/2 Life Path—you might feel conflicted and anxious much of the time?

You're being asked to embody and act upon the most positive elements of two opposing energies. When you understand the demands the Master numbers exert you can begin to work with yourself in more effective ways that can potentially harness all that amazingness you have to offer without crashing and burning in the process. And crash-and-burn or consistent frustration are reoccurring themes when engaged with the intensity of the Master numbers.

Just because you have a Master number doesn't mean you're superior. In actuality, you've enrolled in cosmic boot camp. For life. Yes. For. Life. Period. And remember one of the key components of any boot camp experience—it's meant to *level the ego* and train you to *endure severe circumstances*. It's also training you to take the lead while also being the ultimate team player.

Once you understand how the Master numbers operate you can optimize the beauty and power of this energy to fulfill a greater purpose and function in life. Just understand that it's not meant to happen overnight and rarely comes to you without some darker moments along the road to getting there. You must also learn to pace yourself and give yourself some breaks along the way.

The primary advice for anyone experiencing Master numbers is this: *Working with Master numbers is a marathon, not a sprint.* You must train, be flexible, pace yourself, and invest in the right equipment. Otherwise, you'll either burn too bright too quickly or you'll deaden the flame and always feel as though you were meant for more yet will never find the courage or strength to take risks and move yourself and your enterprises to the next and higher level.

11

How to Calculate Your Life Path Number?

USE YOUR DATE OF BIRTH
"MAY 13, 1964"
ADD YOUR
MONTH + DAY + YEAR

MAY = 5
13 = 1 + 3 = 4;
1964 = 1 + 9 + 6 + 4 = 20;
2 + 0 = 2;
5 + 4 + 2 = 11
(IF YOU HAVE AN 11/2 LIFE PATH, LOOK AT BOTH LIFE PATH 1 AND 2. YOU'RE ONE-PART 2 AND TWO-PARTS 11)

KEY THEMES

- INSPIRATIONAL / LEADERSHIP
- LOVING - WITH AN EDGE
- CREATIVITY / HIGH-STRUNG
- PATIENCE / RELATIONSHIPS
- INNOVATOR / MEDITATOR
- SERVING GROUP DYNAMICS

YOUR MISSION STATEMENT

TO RECOGNIZE AND USE YOUR CREATIVITY, INTUITION, AND HEALING ABILITIES FOR THE BENEFIT OF HUMANITY.

SOME FITTING CAREERS

- NURSE
- DIPLOMAT
- CREATIVE ARTIST
- SPIRITUAL HEALER
- ENTERTAINER
- INTERIOR DESIGNER

CORE LESSONS AND CHALLENGES

- GIVING TO THE POINT OF RESENTMENT
- DEVELOPING HEALTHY EMOTIONAL BOUNDARIES
- LEARNING TO CURB SELF-CENTEREDNESS
- LACKING SELF-ESTEEM
- BULLYING AND CRITICAL

RELATIONSHIP COMPATIBILITY

- 11/2 AND 1 = SPIRITUAL ILLUMINATION & LEADERSHIP
- 11/2 AND 2 = SPIRITUAL ILLUMINATION & HEART
- 11/2 AND 3 = SPIRITUAL ILLUMINATION & CREATIVE EXPRESSION
- 11/2 AND 4 = SPIRITUAL ILLUMINATION & SECURITY
- 11/2 AND 5 = SPIRITUAL ILLUMINATION & FREEDOM-SEEKING
- 11/2 AND 6 = SPIRITUAL ILLUMINATION & NURTURING
- 11/2 AND 7 = SPIRITUAL ILLUMINATION & SPIRITUALITY
- 11/2 AND 8 = SPIRITUAL ILLUMINATION & POWER
- 11/2 AND 9 = SPIRITUAL ILLUMINATION & COMPASSION

YOUR POWER

- DIPLOMACY AND LEADERSHIP
- INDEPENDENT AND LOVING
- HIGHLY INTUITIVE
- EMOTIONALLY SENSITIVE
- DRIVEN TO SUCCEED
- CREATIVE AND INSPIRING

THE 11/2 LIFE PATH TESTS YOUR ABILITY TO TAP INTO THE DOUBLE 1—WHICH IS ALL ABOUT LEADERSHIP, INDEPENDENCE, AND CONFIDENCE—AND YET ALSO EMBODY THE 2—ALL ABOUT DIPLOMACY, PATIENCE, AND LOVE. YOU CAN DO IT!

WELL-KNOWN 11s

- CHRISSY METZ (SEPTEMBER 29, 1980)
- MICHELLE OBAMA (JANUARY 17, 1964)
- DAVID BECKHAM (MAY 2, 1975)
- ROBERT DOWNEY, JR. (APRIL 4, 1965)

MASTER 11/2

THE SPIRITUAL ILLUMINATOR

If you have the Master Number 11/2 anywhere in your chart, on top of the basic characteristics of the number 2, you have added strengths and also more intense challenges. You need to be aware of the attributes of the number 2, which provides you with the foundational energy at work when you show an 11/2 as your Life Path number or whenever it shows up in any other location in your profile.

I advise you to study the defining qualities of the number 1 (and double it!) and also the 2, which is the foundation of the 11/2.

Your special mission—on top of the mission outlined by the number 2—is to recognize and use your creativity, intuition, and healing abilities for the benefit of humanity as a whole. You can achieve this in a multitude of ways—eliciting an emotional response through dance, music, film or art. Working one-on-one or in groups with various healing modalities. You can write, entertain or teach. You might turn to politics and find yourself working as a diplomat. You may be an inventor or motivational speaker. You can engage in any other activity, service or interaction where you touch the lives of people on a grand—if not somewhat subliminal—scale.

Remember, you're a double 1—which is all about leadership and confidence—and yet also a 2, which is all about harmony and love. You come with some special challenges to fulfill your mission. Unlike the Master

22/4, which you'll learn is more practical in its application, the 11/2 is artistic, creative, and inspiring in a rather intangible way.

I like to observe that the 11/2 is like a satellite dish! It's as though you're a walking receptacle for ideas, energies, and other forces to find their way to you and then to be expressed through you. Many inventors, performers, healers, and diplomats have the 11/2 in their numerology profile.

Understand that you are here to share your gifts through helping and healing—or artistic creativity—in whatever form you choose. Yet your contributions can often elude you because your creations change people's lives, yet often not in a measurable way. It's like when you go to an exhibit and simply take in the piece of art and by engaging in that experience, the viewer is altered in some way. It's not tangible—people can't put their finger on it. Yet they'll go away from experiencing your work of art changed in some unspeakable way. That's the energy of the 11. It involves more of a feeling or an indefinable experience rather than a practical, tangible *thing*.

The Master 11/2 offers more of an etheric experience for both you and those around you. You offer people healing energies just by your sheer presence—you honestly don't have to *do* anything when you're aligned with your master presence. The energy of the 11 is a high frequency energy. Do people ever tell you that they feel better after talking with you? That they feel calmer just sitting in the same room with you? When you're feeling like you're not doing whatever it is you think you should be doing on a grander scale (and you'll feel this way a lot!), just remember that your *being-ness* is more than enough to raise the vibration of your little corner of the planet.

Many numerologists say that you're a dreamer rather than a doer. You must work at getting your head out of the clouds and operating on *terra firma*. This is the most challenging aspect for the 11/2 and where most 11/2's find the most dismay or frustration. *You must find a way to keep your feet on the ground.*

Many inventors have the 11/2 in their profile and yet the trick is to harness the ideas and then have the capability to bring those ideas into material form. Often the 11/2 is a fountain of unrealized ideas and has trouble developing the follow-through it requires to bring something into form.

A 2 Life Path will go out of their way to avoid being in the spotlight. A 2 is at peace and most satisfied when they're taking the reins behind the scenes and just the thought of getting out in front of people can make the 2 extremely nervous and anxious. The Master 11/2 (with the double 1's) pushes you into the spotlight and this will have some disconcerting effects on you.

All Master numbers demand that you take a leadership role in whatever capacity you are drawn toward. Keep in mind you're extremely sensitive to criticism and putting yourself out there will always bring criticism from outside forces—and that makes you very uncomfortable. You of all people really need to learn the art of psychic self-protection and of not taking things personally. The 11/2 has a nervous energy that you just can't control. You'll lean toward impatience and criticism—both toward yourself and others—and you're going to arm-wrestle with self-doubt.

The Master 11/2 sets you up for doing battle with a fairly hefty ego (think Madonna, Tony Robbins, and the late Dr. Wayne Dyer as just a few examples of the 11/2 Life Path), which is ironic because you volley from feeling totally inferior to loftily superior—back and forth. The 11/2 often comes off as loving and caring—with an edge.

I encourage you to study the defining elements of the 2, which is the foundational energy of the Master 11/2. Then look at the qualities of the number 1, and *double it*. That's the mixture that defines the pathway for this Master number.

This Master number sets you up for inspired leadership and achievement, yet you'll most likely feel as though you're jumping through perpetual rings of fire to get there. You might even think of yourself as The Wounded Healer because your life provides you with plenty of obstacles to get your footing, embrace your high level of spirituality and intuition, and then act upon your gifts in a way that will bring your message to the world.

With an 11/2, you're at your best when you embrace and act upon your phenomenal artistic creativity. You're super intuitive and have a healing energy whether you're directly working in the healing circuit or offering your energy to others through artistic work. You're at your best when you're healing and transforming others through selfless-service and artistic creativity.

You're meant to do great things, yet you can be conflicted. There is an internal dissonance that comes with the Master 11/2 experience. You have a tendency to question your work, feeling as though you need to do more, something different or something more important. Develop the internal guidance of your intuition and you'll have less difficulty discovering and acting on your true passion.

The 11/2 can trip into magical thinking, which in itself is one of your gifts. Yet magical thinking can also express as feeling you deserve things to happen magically—without following through on the practicalities that are necessary.

On the flip-side, you're working with the intensity of the double 1's, which can bring challenges in not getting too carried away with your own self-importance. Often the 11/2 feels as though they deserve the red-carpet treatment no matter what the circumstances. I have a beautiful 11/2 Life Path client who laughingly told me that her therapist had the perfect description of her, observing that she demonstrated an incredible polarity and duality (*hint, hint—11/2!*) that she described as sometimes showing up as a Damsel in Distress and then at the next moment, turning into the Tyrannical Queen! Two sides of the same coin—the yin/yang of the Master 11/2.

For more details about the Master 11/2, see my book *Master Numbers 11, 22, 33: The Ultimate Guide.*

A FEW WELL-KNOWN 11/2 LIFE PATH'S

Chrissy Metz
September 29, 1980
9 + 11 + 9 = 29
2 + 9 = 11
Alternate way to add:
9 + 2 + 9 + 1 + 9 + 8 + 0 = 38
3 + 8 = 11/2

Michelle Obama
January 17, 1964
1 + 8 + 2 = 11
Alternate way to add:
1 + 1 + 7 + 1 + 9 + 6 + 4 = 29
2 + 9 = 11/2

Jennifer Aniston
February 11, 1969
2 + 11 + 7 = 20
Alternate way to add:
2 + 1 + 1 + 1 + 9 + 6 + 9 = 29
2 + 9 = 11/2

Robert Downey, Jr.
April 4, 1965
4 + 4 + 3 = 11/2
Alternate way to add:
4 + 4 + 1 + 9 + 6 + 5 = 29
2 + 9 = 11/2

Stephen Colbert
May 13, 1964
5 + 4 + 2 = 11/2
Alternate way to add:
5 + 1 + 3 + 1 + 9 + 6 + 4 = 29
2 + 9 = 11/2

David Beckham
May 2, 1975
5 + 2 + 22 = 29; 2 + 9 = 11/2
Alternate way to add:
5 + 2 + 1 + 9 + 7 + 5 = 29
2 + 9 = 11/2

Daniel Craig
March 2, 1968
3 + 2 + 6 = 11/2
Alternate way to add:
3 + 2 + 1 + 9 + 6 + 8 = 29
2 + 9 = 11/2

Ronan Farrow
December 19, 1987
3 + 1 + 7 = 11/2
Alternate way to add:
1 + 2 + 1 + 9 + 1 + 9 + 8 + 7 = 38/11/2

22

How to Calculate Your Life Path Number?

Use your date of birth
"May 18, 1970"
Add your
Month + Day + Year

MAY = 5
$18 = 1 + 9 = 9$;
$1970 = 1 + 9 + 7 + 0 = 17$;
$1 + 7 = 8$;
$5 + 9 + 8 = 22$

Key Themes

- Master Teacher / Honesty
- Healing Family Issues
- Process / Hardworking
- Builder of Systems
- Step by Step
- Security / Knowledge

Your Mission Statement

The 22/4 Life Path is a highly intense vibe demanding the integration and actualization of the loving and emotional 2 with a double dose of the hard-working and pragmatic 4

Core Lessons and Challenges

- Self-limiting and self-sabotaging
- Working through and around limitations
- Bossy and opinionated
- Anxious and overly-sensitive
- A martyr about work and responsibility

Some Fitting Careers

- Educator
- Real Estate
- Writer - Presenter
- Manager
- Healthcare
- Spiritual Leader

Relationship Compatibility

- 22/4 AND 1 = MASTER BUILDER & LEADERSHIP
- 22/4 AND 2 = MASTER BUILDER & HEART
- 22/4 AND 3 = MASTER BUILDER & CREATIVE EXPRESSION
- 22/4 AND 4 = MASTER BUILDER & SECURITY
- 22/4 AND 5 = MASTER BUILDER & FREEDOM-SEEKING
- 22/4 AND 6 = MASTER BUILDER & NURTURING
- 22/4 AND 7 = MASTER BUILDER & SPIRITUALITY
- 22/4 AND 8 = MASTER BUILDER & POWER
- 22/4 AND 9 = MASTER BUILDER & COMPASSION

Your Power

- Solid and steady
- Methodical and systematic
- Hard working and knowledgeable
- Emotionally sensitive and intuitive
- Diplomatic and relationship-oriented

Well-Known 22s

- Tina Fey (May 18, 1970)
- Viola Davis (August 11, 1965)
- Chris Hemsworth (August 11, 1983)
- The 14th Dalai Lama (July 6, 1935)

The 22/4 Life Path tests your ability to refine high-levels of emotional sensitivity and your strict sense of diplomacy. The 22/4 Life Path is focused on bringing inspired ideas into fruition. You can do it!

MASTER 22/4

THE MASTER BUILDER & MASTER TEACHER

If you have a Master 22/4 in your numerology profile, on top of the basic characteristics of the number 4, you have added strengths and also more intense challenges. Your special mission is to execute and build projects that will benefit a wide arena of humankind. You're a master teacher and a systems builder.

I encourage looking at the defining elements of the 4, which is the foundational energy of the Master 22/4. Then look at the qualities of the number 2, and *double it*. That's the mixture that defines the pathway for this Master number.

This is a spiritual path—like all Master numbers—that prods you to step out of the slow, steady security of the number 4 and kick it up substantially. This will be uncomfortable for you until you get the hang of it, because it's contrary to the pull you have with the rule-following, more predictable energy of the 4.

Remember, you're a double 2—which is all about harmony, emotional sensitivity, and relationships—and yet also a 4—all about process, stability, and effort. The 2 is *emotional* and less personally ambitious and the 4 is more *rational* and accomplishment-driven. You come with some special challenges to fulfill your mission.

You'll use all the hardworking, step-by-step qualities of the 4 while tapping into a higher level of purpose and action. You'll learn to take risks and look toward setting higher stakes with your enterprises. You're the Master Builder extraordinaire, so look toward building solid foundations to your enterprises with the big picture in front of you at all times. You can institute systems and manifest things in the material realm that can rock the world. This can show up as teaching, building a business, or managing an enterprise.

Yours is a spiritual path, yet even that basic idea can take years of trial-and-error to embrace and then act upon. You'll find that you'll have even higher hurdles to jump and more complicated roadblocks to work around, over, and through.

I love Brené Brown's definition of spirituality. She asserts that: "…spirituality is recognizing and celebrating that we are all inextricably connected to one another by a power greater than all of us, and that our connection to that power and to one another is grounded in love and belonging. Practicing spirituality brings a sense of perspective, meaning, and purpose to our lives." (see *Rising Strong*). This is a cornerstone to the pathway of the Master 22/4.

You'll most likely be challenged with not feeling up to the task or even entitled to do something that might take you into a bigger enterprise or fame and fortune. You might even cringe at the idea of making a lot of money given the energy of the 4 is more about feeling a sense of security, not necessarily manifesting abundance. It sounds like a small detail, yet mentally this can drag you down.

Avoid your stubborn streak and a tendency to be a know-it-all. Gather your supporters around you, set up the systems to make it work, and hand over some of the responsibilities to others. If you find yourself doing it all *yourself*, you aren't living up to your 22/4 Life Path potential.

With a Master number 22/4, you're at your best when you embrace and act upon your practical wisdom and higher sense of purpose. You're a master teacher and meant to be a teacher of teachers. You have a gift for manifesting things that are meant to change the practical, day-to-day lives for people. You're at your best when manifesting practical ideas into tangible form. Ask yourself: "What am I most passionate about?" And then pursue something in that arena and reach for the stars!

The 22/4 is destined for material and financial success when you focus your energy on making a significant, inspired contribution to the way we think and lead our *everyday lives*. You can do this in any way you desire—through business, politics, art, the humanities or science.

I often call the 22/4 the Oprah number (even though Oprah Winfrey is a 13/4, not a 22/4). It's the most powerful vibe in numerology and it's the workhorse and its mission is to bring practical ideas (products or services) to people on large scale—helping people live a more evolved existence on a day-to-day basis. If you ask Oprah, she'll maintain that she's always known that, more than anything else, she's a *teacher*. The 4 is a teacher—and the 22/4 is a spiritual teacher. You're here to leave something of lasting value to help others and often this transpires through your cultivation of knowledge, providing proven systems, and/or teaching others in whatever way that might manifest for you.

Hard work and endurance reside at the core of the Master 22/4, so don't shrink from your duty. Your challenge is to locate your passion so you can move forward in manifesting your dreams with confidence. If you're working more in the 4 energy (rather than the 22), you'll be exhausted rather than energized. The number 4 is the number of *limitation* and so there can be a tendency to think small rather than big, micromanage rather than delegate—and stop yourself from succeeding through rigid or dogmatic thinking. What this means is that you need to be more inspired and connect to higher ideas. This is a challenge for the 4, which is all about being practical and detail-oriented.

To engage fully in the 22/4, you must pull your focus out of the details and into the big picture. The key is to have others provide the support you need to expand your enterprise. The irony here is that the 2 is more of the supportive, emotion-and-relationship centered energy and needs a supportive push to get out there and pursue something with a strong sense of self-determination. The double 2 energy of the 22/4 offers added intuitive abilities and also a double-dose of emotional sensitivity—with a dash of insecurity!

You're constantly seeking order and have a tendency to let stubbornness get the better of you. You've an innate tendency to act on what you know is right (or *think* is right) without concern for those around you. Surrendering your staff position for the CEO's job can bring about a huge adjustment in the ways you think and traditionally operate. You'll be challenged to find the courage to let go of micromanaging the details and move your project, career or enterprise into the big leagues, where it belongs.

For more details about the Master 22/4, see *Master Numbers 11, 22, 33: The Ultimate Guide.*

A FEW WELL-KNOWN 22/4 LIFE PATH'S

Tina Fey
May 18, 1970
$5 + 9 + 8 = 22/4$
Alternate way to add:
$5 + 1 + 8 + 1 + 9 + 7 + 0 = 31/4$

Caroline Myss
December 2, 1952
$3 + 2 + 8 = 13/4$
Alternate way to add:
$1 + 2 + 2 + 1 + 9 + 5 + 2 = 22/4$

Richard Branson
July 18, 1950
$7 + 9 + 6 = 22/4$
Alternate way to add:
$7 + 1 + 8 + 1 + 9 + 5 + 0 = 31/4$

The 14th Dalai Lama
July 6, 1935
$7 + 6 + 9 = 22/4$
Alternate way to add:
$7 + 6 + 1 + 9 + 3 + 5 = 31/4$

Sam Rockwell
November 5, 1968
$11 + 5 + 6 = 22/4$
Alternate way to add:
$1 + 1 + 5 + 1 + 9 + 6 + 8 = 31/4$

David Duchovny
August 7, 1960
8 + 7 + 7 = 22/4
Alternate way to add:
8 + 7 + 1 + 9 + 6 + 0 = 31/4

Chris Hemsworth
August 11, 1983
8 + 11 + 3 = 22/4
Alternate way to add:
8 + 1 + 1 + 1 + 9 + 8 + 3 = 31/4

J.D. Salinger
January 1, 1919
1 + 1 + 2 = 4
Alternate way to add:
1 + 1 + 1 + 9 + 1 + 9 = 22/4

33

How to Calculate Your Life Path Number?

USE YOUR DATE OF BIRTH
"JUNE 22, 1949"
ADD YOUR
MONTH + DAY + YEAR

JUNE = 6
22 = 22;
1949 = 1 + 9 + 4 + 9 = 23;
2 + 3 = 5;
6 + 22 + 5 = 33
(22 IS A MASTER NUMBER AND ISN'T REDUCED)

KEY THEMES

- LOVE / OPTIMISM
- AESTHETIC BEAUTY
- SERVICE / RESPONSIBILITY
- VISIONARY / CREATIVITY
- ARTISTIC / JOY
- COMMUNICATION

YOUR MISSION STATEMENT

THE 33/6 LIFE PATH IS A HIGHLY INTENSE VIBE DEMANDING THAT YOU INTEGRATE AND ACTUALIZE BOTH THE VISIONARY AND LOVING 6 WITH A DOUBLE DOSE OF THE OPTIMISTIC AND COMMUNICATIVE 3

SOME FITTING CAREERS

- COUNSELING
- HOME-BASED BUSINESS
- BEAUTY INDUSTRY
- MUSIC & ENTERTAINMENT
- DESIGN
- SPIRITUAL LEADER

CORE LESSONS AND CHALLENGES

- EMOTIONALLY VOLATILE AND DEPRESSIVE
- CONTROLLING AND PERFECTIONISTIC
- SELF-RIGHTEOUS AND OVERBEARING
- MEDDLING AND CYNICAL
- OVERLY HIGH EXPECTATIONS

RELATIONSHIP COMPATIBILITY

- 3/6 AND 1 = UNCONDITIONAL LOVE & LEADERSHIP
- 33/6 AND 2 = UNCONDITIONAL LOVE & HEART
- 33/6 AND 3 = UNCONDITIONAL LOVE & CREATIVE EXPRESSION
- 33/6 AND 4 = UNCONDITIONAL LOVE & SECURITY
- 33/6 AND 5 = UNCONDITIONAL LOVE & FREEDOM-SEEKING
- 33/6 AND 6 = UNCONDITIONAL LOVE & NURTURING
- 33/6 AND 7 = UNCONDITIONAL LOVE & SPIRITUALITY
- 33/6 AND 8 = UNCONDITIONAL LOVE & POWER
- 33/6 AND 9 = UNCONDITIONAL LOVE & COMPASSION

YOUR POWER

- NURTURING AND COMMUNICATIVE
- SERVICE-CENTERED AND OPTIMISTIC
- VISIONARY AND CREATIVE
- JUSTICE MINDED AND MULTI TALENTED
- HOME AND FAMILY FOCUSED

WELL-KNOWN 33s

- MELISSA MCCARTHY (AUGUST 26, 1970)
- MERYL STREEP (JUNE 22, 1949)
- STEPHEN KING (SEPTEMBER 21, 1947)
- ROBERT DENIRO (AUGUST 17, 1943)

THE 33 LIFE PATH TESTS YOUR ABILITY TO BE A MASTERFUL HEALER AND AN INSPIRED VISIONARY. YOU CAN DO IT!

MASTER 33/6

THE TEACHER OF UNCONDITIONAL LOVE

With the Master 33/6, on top of the basic characteristics of the number 6, you have added strengths and also more intense challenges. Your special mission is to be a masterful healer and an inspired visionary. This is a spiritual path—like all Master numbers—that prods you toward tapping into your creativity, expressing your emotions, and acting with a nurturing and healing presence. The Master 33/6 is the teacher of unconditional love. Nothing daunting about that, right?

Remember, you're a double 3—which is all about creative expression and emotional sensitivity—and yet also a 6—all about nurturing, acceptance, and vision. You come with some special challenges to fulfill your life's purpose.

I encourage looking at the defining elements of the 6, which is the foundational energy of the Master 33/6. Then look at the qualities of the number 3 and *double it*. That's the mixture that defines the pathway for this Master number.

If you find yourself with a Master 33/6, your mission—should you choose to accept it!—is to become a Master Healer and to bring forward a higher form of love to the world. Sounds a bit lofty, doesn't it? The number 33 is known as the Christ Number. Understand that your purpose falls into the helping, healing, joyful, and creative realms. The 33/6 is the teacher of unconditional love.

Since you have the double 3's, you're called to engage with joy, fun, and heart-felt communication and expression. There are 33/6's who are police officers, wives, mothers, doctors or work behind the scenes at their church. There are many 33/6's in the entertainment industry, as it's a highly artistically creative energy—actor Meryl Streep is a 33/6 who in my opinion embodies many of the higher-level energies of this Master number.

Also understand that the implication of the Master numbers are that they're developed and refined over time. The 33/6 is especially set up where you must—*first and foremost*—heal *yourself*. With that in mind, understand that you'll be put into situations that require that you deal with *responsibility*—with taking responsibility for yourself and your actions while not unduly taking on the responsibilities of others and becoming a martyr, enabler, controller, meddler or crushingly judgmental. Just know from the onset that this master energy isn't easy to modulate.

The Master 33/6 can manifest its power under all kinds of conditions. The calling is to teach and show—*by example*—the power of love. You're meant to serve as a conduit to healing on whatever level you feel most compelled to engage. The Master number presupposes that you'll take on leadership positions and the 33/6 encompasses expression, expert communication—and creativity with a responsible, nurturing, and giving heart.

I think about you as someone who can fulfill your Life Path mission by visiting retirement homes, hospice organizations, and other agencies and offering yourself to those in need of solace. You can be the wealthy philanthropist who opens the new wing at the Cancer Center and offers holistic services not offered before. Entertainment, music, and other artistically creative fields also call your name. You're the couple's counselor, the lawyer who mediates family law, and you can be the dutiful spouse who cares for everyone with a healing touch and light spirit. There are countless ways that you will act upon your Master energies.

Being in alignment with the 33/6 means that you're focused on *giving* and *caretaking*. If you're not focused on *balanced giving*, you're not in alignment with your ultimate purpose. You'll wrestle with feeling over-burdened. Your tendency will be to be emotionally raw, taking in the wounds of the world. Even so, you're still on the path of helping and healing in whatever form you choose.

Your mission (and challenge) is to cultivate your natural, high-minded vision for humanity and support others to reach their own potential. You're here to learn to use your expressive creative energy in the most constructive and uplifting ways. You're in your element when you're working for justice and truth in constructive ways. To succeed, you need to get a grip on your ideals, reign in and focus on a goal, stay practical and realistic—and remain positive, especially in the face of obstacles and in the inevitable heaviness of the world. Remember, you're a visionary and an idealist at heart. Keep those values in tact even when it seems impossible.

On the flip-side, the demands of the 33/6 are quite challenging and you can veer off track fairly easily. Roll the challenging aspects of the 3 (self-doubt, depression, hopelessness, and over-whelm) with the challenging elements of the 6 (controlling, perfectionistic, judgmental, and meddling) and you've got some spontaneous combustion with collisions of overweening self-doubt, hyper-emotionalism, blocked communication, self-righteousness, and superficiality. You can become the anti-6—self-absorbed, struggling with addictions, and unable to channel your masterful energies in a constructive way. The 33/6 can struggle with self-destructive tendencies.

On the other side of the spectrum, there are 33/6's who are so self-sacrificing that they give themselves up for someone or something else. I've known 33/6's who end up caretaking an ill spouse, child, sibling, or parent for years or who are so involved in a cause or a community that they give everything they have for that purpose. This can be devotion to a charitable cause, a church organization, drug rehabilitation center or any other cause that can engulf your time, energy, and passion if you're not careful to balance it with you own personal needs.

For more details about the Master 33/6, *Master Numbers 11, 22, 33: The Ultimate Guide.*

A FEW WELL-KNOWN 33/6 LIFE PATH'S

Melissa McCarthy
August 26, 1970
8 + 8 + 8 = 24/6
Alternate way to add:
8 + 2 + 6 + 1 + 9 + 7 + 0 = 33/6

Meryl Streep
June 22, 1949
6 + 22 + 5 = 33/6
Alternate way to add:
6 + 2 + 2 + 1 + 9 + 4 + 9 = 33/6

Frances McDormand
June 23, 1957
6 + 5 + 22 = 33/6
Alternate way to add:
6 + 2 + 3 + 1 + 9 + 5 + 7 = 33/6

Lindsay Lohan
July 2, 1986
7 + 2 + 6 = 15/6
Alternate way to add:
7 + 2 + 1 + 9 + 8 + 6 = 33/6

Peter Dinklage
June 11, 1969
6 + 11 + 7 = 24/6
Alternate way to add:
6 + 1 + 1 + 1 + 9 + 6 + 9 = 33/6

Robert DeNiro
August 17, 1943
8 + 8 + 8 = 24/6
Alternate way to add:
8 + 1 + 7 + 1 + 9 + 4 + 3 = 33/6

Stephen King
September 21, 1947
9 + 3 + 3 = 15/6
Alternate way to add:
9 + 2 + 1 + 1 + 9 + 4 + 7 = 33/6

Mickey Rourke
September 16, 1952
9 + 7 + 8 = 24/6
Alternate way to add:
9 + 1 + 6 + 1 + 9 + 5 + 2 = 33/6

NUMBERS IN A NUTSHELL

NUMBER 1: *Creativity, Confidence & Leadership*

The 1 is connected with: new opportunity, inspiration, new starts, initiation, standing alone, originality, courage, concentration, determination, and leadership

Optimal: energetic, bold, forward looking, persistent, initiating, confident, ambitious, self-reliant, optimistic, self-determined, and creative

Overactive: impatient, self-important, intolerant, unyielding, defiant, headstrong, arrogant, greedy, possessive, dictatorial, addicted, and domineering

Under-active: dependent, insecure, helpless, victimized, passive, weak-willed, lacking self-respect, wishy-washy, and cowardly

NUMBER 2: *Cooperation, Diplomacy & Relationship Harmony*

The 2 is connected with: sensitivity, teamwork, cooperation, receptivity, tolerance, partnerships, details, friendships, harmony, and right timing

Optimal: flexible, helpful, receptive, courteous, intuitive, supportive, warm, insightful, peacemaking, diplomatic, loving, and emotionally available

Overactive: manipulative, fault-finding, resentful, resisting, devious, disapproving, condescending, interfering, self-serving, and passive-aggressive

Under-active: self-deprecating, indecisive, uncaring, apologetic, dependent, inactive, overly sensitive, gullible, and unresponsive

MASTER 11/2: *Spiritual Messenger & Inspired Artistic Creativity*

The 11/2 is connected with: altruism, spiritual insight, new beginnings, peacekeeping, visionary pursuits, inspiration, harmony, and inspired leadership

Optimal: flexible, helpful, receptive, courteous, intuitive, supportive, warm, insightful, diplomatic, loving, and giving

Overactive: manipulative, fault-finding, resentful, resistant, ego-driven, disapproving, condescending, edgy, self-serving, and anxious

Under-active: self-deprecating, indecisive, uncaring, lacking boundaries, dependent, unambitious, overly sensitive, and immature

NUMBER 3: *Creative Self-Expression, Optimism & Communication*

The 3 is connected with: pleasure, self-improvement, laughter, sexual expression, artistic creativity, communication, writing, quick recoveries, easy financial flow, instability, scattered focus, and dramatic emotional ups and downs

Optimal: literary or media talent, sophisticated, amusing, witty, well-liked, magnetic, optimistic, inspiring, authentic, inventive, imaginative, artistic, emotionally mature, and intelligent

Overactive: scattered, inflated sense of confidence, gossipy, superficial, exaggerating, lacking concentration, difficulty with follow through, emotionally volatile, superficial, overly-dramatic, and irresponsible

Under-active: depressive, jealous, self-doubting, inarticulate, indecisive, bored, petty, temperamental, insincere, unenthusiastic, procrastinating, cynical, hopeless, and fearful

NUMBER 4: *Process, Stability & Systematic Thinking*

The 4 is connected with: material interests, structure, managing finances, creating lasting foundations, hard work, stable finances, solid management, organization, efficiency, physical endurance, and limitation

Optimal: dependable, reliable, frugal, methodical, honest, productive, solid, cautious, disciplined, sensible, loyal, trustworthy, goal-driven, hardworking, and persevering

Overactive: rigid, narrow-minded, brooding, inflexible, dreary, emotionally unavailable, uncompromising, judgmental, shallow, blunt, and lost in detail

Under-active: disorganized, apathetic, sarcastic, impractical, careless, inefficient, distracted, thoughtless, idle, blaming, self-pitying, and neglectful

MASTER 22/4: *Master Teacher & Inspired Practical Ideas*

The 22/4 is connected with: altruism, spiritual insight, intuition, accomplishment, results, knowledge, practicality, harmony, structure, and inspired leadership

Optimal: dependable, methodical, stable, loving, intuitive, supportive, emotionally attuned, insightful, disciplined, diplomatic, loving, and emotionally available

Overactive: manipulative, hyper-sensitive, resentful, self-sabotaging, jealous, emotionally over-wrought, condescending, self-limiting, self-serving, and narrow minded

Under-active: self-deprecating, indecisive, victimized, self-centered, unstable, impractical, overly sensitive, and impulsive

NUMBER 5: *Freedom, Self-Discipline & Sensuous Experience*

The 5 is connected with: promotion, sensuality, sales, sex, freedom, travel, communication, changes, fluctuation, flexibility, excitement, versatility, and adventure

Optimal: reliable, innovative, daring, charming, sets healthy boundaries, forward thinking, high-energy, curious, adaptable, independent, clever, and resourceful

Overactive: indulgent, reckless, abandons relationships too soon, impatient, thrill-seeking, erratic, extremely independent, insatiable, restless, easily overwhelmed, irresponsible, addicted, and highly emotional

Under-active: fearful of change, stagnant, dependent, conforming, fearful of freedom, dull, ineffective, procrastinating, emotionally volatile, and depressive

NUMBER 6: *Nurturing, Responsibility & Acceptance*

The 6 is connected with: home, family, relationships, marriage, divorce, romance, responsibility, friendships, emotions, deliberation, harmony, teaching, community, and justice

Balanced: home-loving, advisory, friendly, tolerant, supportive, responsible, appreciative, peacemaking, protective, devoted, loving, stable, and sensible

Overactive: distortedly idealistic, critical, interfering, opinionated, possessive, stubborn, sacrificing, martyred, unreasonable, obstinate, unforgiving, disheartened, slavish, and self-righteous

Under-active: uncaring, uncooperative, biased, unconcerned, indulgent, lacking energy, unwelcoming, and non-committal

MASTER 33/6: *Teacher of Unconditional Love & Joyful Communicator*

The 33/6 is connected with: altruism, nurturing, communication, lightness, responsibility, visionary pursuits, justice, emotional expression, and joyful optimism

Optimal: unconditionally loving, balanced, responsible, fun, creative, supportive, emotionally expressive, supportive, caretaker, accepting, witty, and artistically creative

Overactive: emotionally volatile, scattered, lacking focus, overly dramatic, petty, superficial, self-centered, uncaring, irresponsible, and lacking integrity

Under-active: depressive, addictive, procrastinating, self-sabotaging, cruel, mean, passive, and communicates negatively

NUMBER 7: *Spiritual Seeking, Data Analysis & Trust*

The 7 is connected to: mysticism, intuition, inner growth, examination, study, analysis, reflection, mental acuity, planning, unsolicited help, specialization, philosophy, solitude, self-awareness, and refinement

Balanced: tolerant, thorough, diligent, intellectual, intuitive, analytical, perceptive, scientific, exact, meditative, mystical, expert, bookish, poised, telepathic, instinctive, truth-seeking, studious, and wise

Overactive: fearful, nervous, critical, obsessive, paranoid, indecisive, secretive, emotionally repressed, distrustful, guarded, intimidating, evasive, self-conscious, perfectionist, and pessimistic

Under-active: superficial, naïve, ignorant, overly trusting, introverted, empty headed, superficial, faithless, undeveloped, uninformed, and unsure

NUMBER 8: *Money, Power & Influence*

The 8 is connected to: influence, money, action, business success, business failure, control, material objects, status, loss, gain, executive administration, management, ego, leadership, and personal power

Balanced: prosperous, entrepreneurial, realistic, planner, commanding, self-confident, persuasive, ambitious, businesslike, clear-headed, disciplined, honorable, ethical, and enterprising

Overactive: abusive of power, egotistical, scheming, aggressive, materialistic, corrupt, demanding, domineering, preoccupied with power and money, unsympathetic, overly ambitious, confrontational, greedy, too forceful, and rebellious

Under-active: passive, vulnerable, fearful, insecure, avoiding of power and money, poor judgment, powerless, and shortsighted

NUMBER 9: *Humanitarianism, Compassion & Creativity*

The 9 is connected to: unconditional love, humanitarianism, reward, leadership by example, dramatic endings, emotional love, emotional crisis, the finer things in life, conclusions, deep love, compassion, magnetism, travel, idealism, charity, artistry, creativity, spirituality, romance, and forgiveness

Balanced: artistic, philanthropic, affectionate, creative, forgiving, passionate, benevolent, warm, tolerant, sentimental, loving, generous, idealistic, romantic, open-minded, enthusiastic, trustworthy, hospitable, and humane

Overactive: deceiving, self-centered, lacking integrity, overly emotional, prejudiced, resentful, presenting a bad example, irresolute, vindictive, hateful, intolerant, belligerent, and hostile

Under-active: close minded, impersonal, arrogant, aloof, distant, unemotional, elusive, submissive, drifting, faint-hearted, victimized, lost, misdirected, and lazy

Destiny - Expression

This indicates HOW YOU'LL GO ABOUT fulfilling your Life Path purpose.

This is the MANNER that you express yourself.

This is the highest level of expression that you're integrating into your Life Path. It reveals your point of destiny!

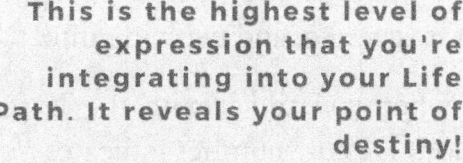

THE EXPRESSION OR DESTINY NUMBER

Now we're getting into a number that's derived from your name rather than from your birth date. Most numerologists would concur that numbers derived from your date of birth indicate what you're here to *learn*. The numbers that come from your name are more indicative of what you're here to *teach*. Of course, before you can *teach* something, you must *learn* it.

Another name for the Life Path is the Birth Path. The Soul Urge is also known as the Heart's Desire. The Maturity number can be called the number of Attainment, and so on. Your Expression number can be known as the Destiny Number.

For some reason, this is a number that I personally refer to using both names because it's been my experience that it's rather a 50/50 gambit as to how people recognize it. The Destiny/Expression number is a vital component or compliment to your Life Path number. The Life Path number indicates your primary purpose in life—it's what you're learning about, mastering, and evolving into.

Yet when you add it with the Expression/Destiny number, the Expression/Destiny number indicates *the manner in which you'll go about achieving your purpose*, as indicated by your Life Path number. For those of you who are astrologically inclined, this a similar to the ascendent or the rising sign, while the Life Path number is synonymous with the sun sign.

Knowing your Expression/Destiny number tells you:

- The flavor and manner of living that you must cultivate and act upon in your life

- Your opportunities for success and your stumbling blocks to achieving your full potential
- At the "end of the day," this is how you're destined to achieve and express your life purpose
- Offers you an idea of how you can make the most out of your life experience
- The kind of work or career that would be a natural complement and expression of your life purpose as defined by your Life Path

When you place your Destiny/Expression number underneath your Life Path number, you get the *way in which* you go about achieving your Life Path purpose. Sometimes a person will present more in alignment with their Destiny/Expression number (*how they go about doing their life's purpose*) than with the Life Path number itself.

For instance, perhaps you're a 2 Life Path with a 6 Destiny or Expression. Chances are you gravitate toward family life. How about a 3 Life Path with a 4 Destiny or Expression? These energies are quite oppositional—the 3 is all about creative self-expression, while the 4 is the systems builder and workhorse. Together they might present as an actor who really works hard at what they do. Or this person could be an architect who has a creative flair for design and an advanced way to communicate their ideas to clients. The combinations are limitless.

Either way, knowing both your Life Path *and* your Destiny/Expression numbers can allow you to put some of the puzzle pieces together in a way you might not have been able to before. Now that you know the basic qualities of your Life Path number, it's time to start building your numerology profile. Then you can take the others numbers in your chart that we're starting to learn about now—the Destiny/Expression, Soul Urge, Birth Day, and Personality—and see how they connect, enhance, or detract from your Life Path purpose.

CALCULATE THE DESTINY OR EXPRESSION NUMBER

Write down the name you were given at birth—*just as it's written on your birth certificate*. Use the chart (below) and apply a number to each letter of your name: *first, middle, last*. If you have more than one middle name, please use all of the names as they appear on your birth certificate. If you're a Jr., Second or Third, please *leave that out of the equation*.

Understand that you must use the name *as it appears on your birth certificate*, even if it's spelled incorrectly or even if you spell your name differently than it appears on the birth certificate.

To be clear: Use the name as it appears on the birth certificate, even if there is what you would consider to be a mistake, like a misspelling or if your name were changed hours, days or years later.

If you're adopted and know the original name as it appeared on your original birth certificate, this is the name to use for this calculation—even if it's "Baby Girl Anderson" or something of that nature. Of course, you'll also calculate for your adopted name, yet the first full name given on the birth certificate—even if your name was changed a few hours or a few days after birth—still provides the information for your foundational numerology profile.

Personally and professionally, I find that people who have significant name changes—through adoption or other circumstances—have additional layers of complexity in their lives in terms of *identity*.

This number is the core of your Expression/Destiny and, while this name changes with a name change, *the original name at birth will always be the foundational energy and mission you opted into this lifetime*. You can calculate the Minor Expression/Destiny number that's based on your current first and last name, yet this is more of an "overlay" to your foundational birth name. In numerology, when something is labeled "minor," it indicates that it's derived from the *current* first and last name, not on the full name as it appears on the birth certificate.

The current name offers an overlay of energy. It's like placing a teabag in water—the longer it soaks, the stronger the tea. While the current name or a name change has bearing on your numerology profile, the original name is always going to indicate your ultimate purpose and pathway in this lifetime.

DESTINY/EXPRESSION CALCUATION

Let's use George (Timothy) Clooney as an example. You calculate this much in the same way you calculate your Life Path number. It's a simple addition problem once you assign a number value to the letter in the name (as indicated by the chart below).

Like always, *you must reduce to a one-digit number for each part of the calculation.* There are different schools of thought as to how this is accomplished. Yet for our purposes, we'll use this method.

1	2	3	4	5	6	7	8	9
A	B	C	D	E	F	G	H	I
J	K	L	M	N	O	P	Q	R
S	T	U	V	W	X	Y	Z	

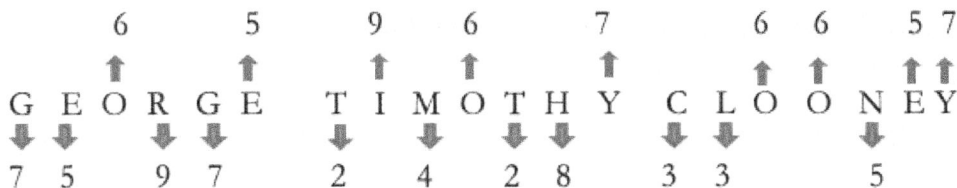

GEORGE
7 + 5 + 6 + 9 + 7 + 5 = 39
3 + 9 = 12
1 + 2 = 3

TIMOTHY
2 + 9 + 4 + 6 + 2 + 8 + 7 = 38
3 + 8 = 11 (11 is a Master number and isn't reduced)

CLOONEY
3 + 3 + 6 + 6 + 5 + 5 + 7 = 35
3 + 5 = 8

Now add each of the name numbers together:
3 + 11 + 8 = 22
22 is a Master number.

George Clooney has a Master 22/4 Destiny/Expression Number

As a sidebar: This gets interesting when you use different software programs to calculate a numerology profile. I have several different programs I use and each of them has their quirks or their specific way of calculating. When you first begin using software programs or Apps, you'll be compelled to do a bit of "Sherlocking" when you get different numbers for the same profile!

For instance, I use a program that doesn't calculate the letters in the alphabet in the repeating pattern of 1 – 9 (as we provide for you in this book). Instead, it runs it this way:

A (1), B (2), C (3), D (4), E (5), F (6), G (7), H (8), I (9), J (1), **K (11)**, L (3), M (4), N (5), O (6), P (7), Q (8), R (9), S (1), T (2), U (3), **V (22)**, W (5), X (6), Y (7), Z (8)

With this school of thought, the K (11) and the V (22) are valued as Master numbers within a calculation involving the name.

I bring this up as you get more involved with numerology, because you'll constantly be offered different avenues of thought about how the numbers show up. It's interesting (if not confounding) to get different calculations using different software programs or Apps.

DESTINY/EXPRESSION NUMBER DEFINITIONS

1 Destiny/Expression: *Your destiny is to become #1 at all you do. You express yourself fully when you tap into your individualistic nature and take the lead.*

How do you go about expressing your Life Path purpose? You express your purpose when you develop your true, authentic self and become a leader in whatever field you're most passionate and skilled—which is defined by the themes inherent in your Life Path. You express your Life Path purpose with determination and aren't satisfied unless you're achieving something you've created. You expect high standards of performance from yourself and, in turn, also expect the same from others.

Your mission is to take the lead and take initiative—the 1 Destiny/Expression number isn't lack-luster or low-key! You're meant to have courage, act independently on your unique and original ideas, be innovative, and take charge.

A 1 Destiny/Expression sets you up for a lifetime of development of your sense of self, leaning into your willpower, and setting out with determination without allowing the naysayers or glitches along the road to weigh you down or demolish your vision. You work hard and play hard.

Even if you grapple with an inconsistent sense of self-confidence or hold yourself back, you're lined up for a destiny that demands that you embrace leadership and innovation. The 1 Destiny/Expression demands that you take yourself from dependence to independence, individuate yourself, and achieve something in the world. Entrepreneurship is favored, creative endeavors are encouraged, and independence is a must.

2 Destiny/Expression: *Your destiny is to bring people together in an atmosphere of harmony and love. You express yourself with diplomacy and kindness.*

How do you go about expressing your Life Path purpose? You express your purpose when you create harmony, balance, and love wherever you go and in whatever you do. Emotional sensitivity and creating loving connections are the cornerstones to the way you perform your Life Path purpose. You're here to learn how to develop your sense of relationship—how to successfully understand and relate to yourself and others. Your path includes developing patience and diplomacy, and in doing so, you're placed into many situations requiring that you mediate conflict.

The 2 Destiny/Expression encourages you to seek to be of service to the larger cause—whether that's your family, your company or any other cause or group you feel strongly about. Your destiny is to develop adaptability, open-hearted caring, and to focus on the higher good of all.

Understand that you need to get out and socialize because when you isolate yourself, you suffer from pessimism, depression, and inaction. You thrive when you're involved with other people and contributing to group dynamics, whether it's with friends, work, family or a community group.

You'll be tested with being overly sensitive and can resort to becoming confrontational rather than a harmonizer. Beware of needing incessant reinforcement from everyone around you, because you're not likely to get it.

Even if you find that you're challenged with being passive or aggressive—indecisive or lacking focus—your calling is to become a peacemaker and harmonizing influence on whatever you touch. Supportive relationships are favored and emotional boundaries are encouraged.

Master 11/2 Destiny/Expression: *Your destiny is to heal and transform others through selfless-service and artistic creativity. You express yourself through loving leadership.*

How do you go about expressing your Life Path purpose? You express your purpose when you recognize and use your creativity, intuition, and healing abilities for the benefit of humanity as a whole. When you express your Life Path purpose through the 11/2 Destiny/Expression, you can achieve this in a multitude of ways—eliciting an emotional response through dance, music or art. You can work one-on-one or in groups with various healing modalities. Or you can write, entertain or teach.

Remember, you're a double 1 (leadership, confidence) and yet also a 2 (harmony, love). You come with some special challenges to fulfill your destiny. A 2 will go out of their way to avoid being in the spotlight. A 2 is most at peace and satisfied when they're taking the reins behind the scenes while the 11 pushes you into the spotlight.

The Master 11/2 Destiny/Expression brings a consistent level of nervous tension to the mix. You'll feel as though nothing you do is ever quite enough. You might lean toward impatience and criticism—toward yourself and others—and arm-wrestle with insecurity. If you're to embrace this destiny, you'll be required to come to terms with a fairly delicate ego.

This number sets you up for inspired leadership and achievement, yet you'll most likely feel as though you're jumping through rings of fire to get there. Your life provides you with plenty of obstacles to get your footing, embrace your high level of spirituality and intuition, and then act upon your gifts in a solid and down-to-earth way that bring your message to the masses. Yours is the destiny of spiritual illumination, however that speaks to you.

The 11/2 is the dreamer rather than the doer, therefore this Destiny/Expression number requires that you plant your feet firmly on the ground. You benefit when you build and use your emotional psychic shield daily (meaning, a development of healthy emotional boundaries).

Creative or healing work is favored and spiritual development is mandatory.

3 Destiny/Expression: *Your destiny is to inspire, motivate, and uplift people. You express yourself with a sense of humor, impeccable communication, and emotional connection.*

How do you go about expressing your Life Path purpose? You express your purpose when you bring a sense of playfulness, lightness, and fun into the mix. You're being called to inspire, heal, uplift, and energize others—which often expresses itself through performance or communication of some kind.

Your ultimate purpose comes through when you're operating with a core sense of optimism, enthusiasm, compassion, and joy. You'll infuse your Life Path purpose with fun and wit—mixed with possible eccentricity, a dash of excitement, and perhaps fame or notoriety. When you've tapped into your authentic sense of emotional expression—and then inspire others to use and express their emotions—you're fulfilling your destiny.

Often the 3 brings so many talents and ideas with it that it's difficult to focus on just one, making procrastination or scattered focus a hurdle. You'll be challenged with learning to identify and embrace your own emotional life. You'll be most effective in helping yourself help others through your gift of words (both verbal and written), through your amazing sense of wit and humor, and by being lighthearted. The mantra for the 3 is *when you're laughing, you're learning!* Being a good communicator and listener is mandatory.

You might find challenges in the areas of emotional ups and downs, depression, or being judgmental and critical. Don't resist your feelings—they offer you profound wisdom. Yet the key is to discipline your emotions and not allow them to be unruly and run the show! The energy of the 3 can play out like a spoiled little child, wanting every whim and personal hurt to be the center of attention.

It's your destiny to express yourself with joy, optimism, and with clear communication. Your 3 Destiny/Expression number calls you to express yourself and help others do the same in the most positive, funny, joyful way possible. Impeccable communication is favored and creative endeavors are encouraged.

4 Destiny/Expression: *Your destiny is to leave something of value that people can find beneficial in their day-to-day lives. You express yourself by methodically accomplishing your goals.*

How do you go about expressing your Life Path purpose? You express your purpose through building something of lasting value—whether that's a family of your own, a business or other enterprise. You bring a sense of stability and security to your Life Path purpose. You're in your game when you create and use actionable processes. With the 4 Destiny/Expression, you achieve through working hard and by working through (around and over) limitations. You're honest, tried-and-true, and eminently reliable. You have the potential to be a stellar marriage or business partner.

The way you express your Life Path purpose is by being practical and hardworking. You're the systems-builder—the keeper of order and thrive on creating a stable environment and security is always something you strive toward. You might lean toward rigidity or stubbornness, yet you're learning how to create solid foundations in order to create greater levels of freedom. You're driven by the need to produce results and you value your accomplishments. Alternately, you could avoid putting down roots, shy away from hard work, and avoid creating a family of your own.

The biggest roadblock for the 4 Destiny/Expression is a fear of appearing dumb (or let's say under informed) and a fear of taking risks. A person with a 4 Destiny/Expression number can wake up one day and realize that none of their dreams have been realized because of their inability to step outside their own self-imposed box.

Even so, your 4 Destiny/Expression number puts you on the path of managing, organizing, and creating a foundation from which to build your life or enterprise. You express yourself optimally when you climb on top of the box rather than place yourself inside of it. Creating your family of choice is always part of this destiny number. Slow and steady processes are favored and finding ways to take healthy breaks are encouraged.

Master 22/4 Destiny/Expression: *Your destiny is to bring forth masterful teaching and inspired practical ideas. You express yourself by building something of lasting value that carries heart and soul.*

How do you go about expressing your Life Path purpose? You express your purpose by executing and building projects that will benefit a wide arena of humankind. This is a spiritual path—like all Master numbers—prodding you to step out of the slow, steady security of the number 4 and kick it up substantially. This will be uncomfortable until you get the hang of it, because it's contrary to the pull you have with the rule-following energy of the 4.

You'll use all the hardworking, step-by-step qualities of the 4 while tapping into a higher level of purpose and action. Yet you also express with a double 2—with emotional sensitivity, diplomacy, and a "behind the scenes" attitude. There is certainly a push-and-pull with this Destiny/Expression. On the one hand, you need to be in charge. On the other hand, the relationship-oriented and emotionally sensitive 2 invites you to second-guess your ability to take charge.

With the 22/4 Destiny/Expression, you'll learn to take risks and look toward setting higher stakes with your enterprises. You're the master builder extraordinaire, so look toward building solid foundations to your enterprise with the bigger picture in front of you at all times. You might be challenged with not feeling up to the task or even entitled to do something that might take you into the spotlight. You might even cringe at the idea of doing well financially given the energy of the 4 is more about feeling a sense of security, not necessarily manifesting abundance.

Numerologists consider the Master number 22/4 to be the most powerful energy in numerology. You're being pushed toward bringing spiritual practices down to the material, day-to-day world. Avoid a stubborn streak and a tendency to be a know-it-all. If you find yourself doing it all yourself, you aren't living up to your 22/4 Destiny/Expression. Slow and steady processes are favored and stepping out of your own way is encouraged.

5 Destiny/Expression: *Your destiny is to effect change and show people how to live life to the maximum. You express yourself by being the wild card—you refuse to let others define you or hold you down.*

How do you go about expressing your Life Path purpose? You express your purpose by engaging your Life Path through adaptability, versatility, and embracing the adventure of life. Freedom is the guiding force and you thrive on hands-on experience. You imbue your Life Path purpose with vivacious energy, an adventurous spirit, and an over-all sense of fun. Your somewhat daunting task is to develop the *constructive* use of freedom—to be responsible, focused, and practice self-discipline while remaining your freewheeling self.

Your purpose is to embrace your sense of fearlessness and follow your curiosity to explore the world and offer your magnetic presence to those around you. Most often the 5 Destiny/Expression is intelligent, philosophical, and can be spiritually minded. You're a natural salesperson when you're dealing with something you believe in. This Destiny/Expression leads you on a roller coaster, where life can feel as though it's coming at you without a filter. Your destiny is one of liberation and freedom, no matter how you slice it.

If you find yourself on the opposite end of the spectrum, you'll do battle with self-absorption, fearfulness, or emotional paralysis. You can move through intimate relationships like you're changing your socks. Your heightened self-centered emotionalism might strain friendships and intimate relationships. You can swerve over into the high maintenance category with great ease, making your love relationships, family interactions, and friendships potentially exasperating to those on the other end of your relationship-pole.

Your destiny is to move forward, recalibrate yourself, reframe your direction, and embrace positive change. Ultimately, your gift is showing others how to live fearlessly through your example. The key to your 5 Destiny/Expression is to learn how to focus and follow-through, prioritize responsibility, and create liberating structure for yourself or life could be chaotic and out of control. Versatility is favored and anchoring yourself by taking responsibility is encouraged.

6 Destiny/Expression: *Your destiny is to provide a nurturing safe nest for yourself and your loved ones. You express yourself by caring for yourself as intently as you care for others.*

How do you go about expressing your Life Path purpose? You express your purpose through nurturing, being the responsible party, and through service to others. Whether it's your family and loved ones or your business or community, you're a master at creating beautiful and harmonious environments. You infuse a sense of fairness, love, nurturing, and self-sacrifice into your Life Path purpose. Love with acceptance is key for you with a 6 Destiny/Expression number.

You express yourself with a polished presentation and denote an air of authority. One of your specialties is damage control, so when things are moving along without trauma or drama, you have a tendency to either sweat it (while you wait for the other shoe to drop) or you stir things up in order to have a problem to focus your energies on. You may find yourself in positions of responsibility early on in your life and that sense of responsibility continues as you mature.

You can express yourself as a people pleaser, sometimes to your detriment. Often your superpower is that you know what everyone wants and needs, even before they do—and you do your best to fulfill those needs, no matter the cost to you personally. You need to feel indispensable to others and yet resent the fact that others rely on you too much. Ultimately, you seek balance with relationships and with the responsibilities you choose to take on.

Remember that part of your mission is to balance and modulate your sense of responsibility—not overly responsible (meddling, self-righteous, perfectionist) and not overly irresponsible (self-centered, judgmental, controlling). You express your life's purpose through loving service, yet the trick is to balance this overweening sense of responsibility.

While you may tend toward self-righteousness and codependency, your true calling is in healthy nurturing, compassionate detachment, acceptance of others (get past that perfectionism!) and adding beauty and your beautiful vision to the world. A focus on family and relationships are favored and modulating an over-the-top sense of responsibility is encouraged.

Master 33/6 Destiny/Expression: *Your destiny is masterful healing and inspired vision. You express yourself through unconditional love, caring, creative expression, and communication.*

How do you go about expressing your Life Path purpose? You express your purpose through by bringing forth a higher form of love to the world. Nothing daunting about that, right? Since you have the double 3's, you also have to do this with joy, fun, and heart-felt communication and expression. Your calling is to teach and show by example the power of love. You're meant to serve as a conduit to healing on whatever level you feel most compelled to engage.

The Master number presupposes that you'll take on leadership positions and the 33/6 encompasses visionary goals, truth and beauty, and a nurturing and giving heart. You'll infuse your Life Path purpose with positive expression, loving inspiration, duty, and service. You might wrestle with feeling over-burdened. The tendency will be to feel emotionally raw, taking in the wounds of the world.

Even so, you're still on the path of helping and healing in whatever form you choose. You'll express your Life Path purpose through love, compassion, and serving the greater good in some capacity. Often you excel with artistic creativity, counseling, teaching, or any other service where you offer love and support to others. Creative pursuits are favored and finding ways to nourish yourself is encouraged.

7 Destiny/Expression: *Your destiny is to develop trust and faith and find your own answer to the meaning of life. You express yourself analytically and also intuitively.*

How do you go about expressing your Life Path purpose? You express your purpose by seeking out information, analyzing it, and coming to determinations based on the culmination of research. You're all about gathering knowledge, yet there is a spiritual connection that's undeniable, even if it takes a while to put two-and-two together! You dig deep and contemplate heavily.

The 7 is the perfect researcher and everything always comes back to informing your own sense of inner wisdom. You bring intuition, spiritual seeking, and analytical thought processes to your Life Path purpose.

Your life-long task is to get to know the true you, inside and out. You need a good deal of private alone time as you traverse the depths of your probing experience of life on earth. Your life is instructed by a powerful collision between practical, tangible data and the analysis of it—with the unspeakable, the unseeable, and the metaphysical. Your gift—and your task—is to integrate the two (your intellect and your intuition) into a harmonious dance team.

The highest and best use of your extraordinary talents are cultivating knowledge, processing it into new ideas or practical usage, and applying your advanced spiritual wisdom to the data. You're a person other people never really truly know because you're most often attempting to figure that out yourself!

The 7 brings exquisite observation skills and when you have a strong sense of spirituality (however that manifests for you), you're at your best. Otherwise, you can fall into superficiality, skepticism, cynicism or depression. You're a gentle soul and your destiny is to share your hard-won wisdom with the world. Your ultimate expression is to specialize in something that assists you in manifesting your Life Path purpose. Spiritual practice is favored and developing your intellect is encouraged.

8 Destiny/Expression: *Your destiny is to manifest financial security that allows you freedom to make a difference in the world. You express yourself by using your influence and power to make positive changes in the world.*

How do you go about expressing your Life Path purpose? You express your purpose as you gain self-mastery. You infuse your Life Path purpose with a financial focus. You're built for achievement and success with business and finances. The only way to get there is by conquering the material world. How? By gaining a strong and balanced sense of personal empowerment. This is gained by learning how to be in control, yet not be controlling nor controlled by others.

Part of your mission includes coming to terms with authority—by not rebelliously thrashing against authority. Rather, by becoming an authority in its strongest and healthiest manifestation. And to top it all off, you must move through life by adhering to and acting with the utmost ethics and integrity along the way. No easy task when you're involved in the unethical world of business and power.

The 8 is a relentless taskmaster and demands that you understand and employ all your abilities to achieve financial abundance and also to give to others generously. When you realize that you're here to harness power and be a source of abundance, your destiny will be fulfilled.

The first item of business that'll open the gate for you to achieve your 8 Destiny/Expression is to dig deep and tap into your sense of personal empowerment. And believe me, you'll be handed a treasure-trove of opportunities to *step up* or be *stepped on*.

Be mindful of expressing your 8 Destiny/Expression with an over-focus on money. Steer clear of greed, ruthlessness, or being overly opinionated, over-bearing, or domineering. Remember that as you give, you receive. This is the natural law of the 8, which is the number of Infinity. Just know that the number 8 signifies a constant flow of energy—its loop is continuous and in order to express fully, you must allow the flow of money and energy rather than hang on to it and block its flow.

It's your task to learn to be a confident and charismatic person without becoming corrupted or hardened by power and money. You're a masterful leader—a powerhouse made for material success. When you're thriving financially and giving generously from your heart, you're doing what you were born to do.

Your flip-side is that you find yourself in the opposite situation—a victim of scarcity, constantly struggling with money, and disempowering yourself in the world. Yet money and power are a consistent theme in your life, one way or another. You often have a heightened love/hate relationship with money.

If you struggle with money, start with establishing and acting on your personal boundaries and take full and complete responsibility for yourself, rather than blaming others for your situation. The energy of the 8 isn't an easy walk in the park. It demands that you dig into your power and move through obstacles—and there will be many obstacles. A businesslike demeanor is favored and learning how to use power wisely and well is encouraged.

9 Destiny/Expression: *Your destiny is to achieve a higher state of consciousness and teach others how to achieve theirs. You express yourself in an off-beat, quirky, and creative way.*

How do you go about expressing your Life Path purpose? You express your purpose by reaching out to help and support people. Your destiny is a humanitarian one. The 9 infuses your Life Path purpose with compassion, charisma, and multi-levels of creativity. Yours is a spiritual path and you're here to love unconditionally, however that may manifest in your life.

You're often a hopeless romantic at heart and can set yourself up for disappointment when people don't measure up to your ideals—and people rarely measure up. The 9 has a tendency to want to make the world a better place, yet overall not overly fond of *people* as a general rule. The

9 brings a caring and an angst about humanity that's so deep and so profound, yet it often can play out as long-term disappointment in the world and in people as a whole.

You're at your optimal when you're expressing yourself creativity, sensitivity, and selflessly. This Destiny/Expression number is a powerful one demanding that you learn to transform and heal—both yourself and others—while letting go of the past freely and without bitterness. With this Destiny/Expression, you can do anything with your strange and unique flare as long as it speaks to your heart. Your pathway is to do what you're doing because you can't *not* do it.

You may find yourself tripping over into the arena of resentment, intolerance or gullibility. You may have to deal with enmeshment with your family of origin throughout your life. Your task is to let go of family issues fully and completely without totally rejecting them, yet also by healthy extraction and detachment. You often feel either resentment toward the family or feel overly responsible for them. You need to be aware that people respond much more favorably to you when you connect through being a compassionate active listener rather than a preacher, lecturer or proselytizer. Understand that you can have an intimidating or belligerent quality to you, despite your big heart.

Often the 9 Destiny/Expression can come off as arrogant or unapproachable. Know that yours is a powerful journey that offers you multifaceted opportunities to touch the lives of others and heal some of your own deepest wounds. You're learning how to both give *and* receive. Spiritual awareness is mandatory and learning to let go is highly encouraged.

Soul Urge

This indicates WHAT YOU NEED DOWN DEEP in order to feel satisfied & gratified.

This is the pathway for your soul's most expansive growth.

This is the UNDERLYING DRIVER for everything you do!

THE SOUL URGE

As you continue to learn about numerology, you'll see that—*like every other "ology"*—there are different ways to go about it. Not only are definitions a matter of interpretation, there are always more than one way in which numbers are calculated.

Reminder: The type of numerology discussed in this book is Pythagorean.

Your Soul Urge number—also called your Heart's Desire—indicates what motivates you down deep into your core. This is the number that reveals to you what drives you from a soul-level. How do you follow your heart? Knowing this number is crucial to define what you'll want and need in order to feel a deep sense of satisfaction and gratification.

This is a great number to know and understand because it might explain some of those irrational thoughts and feelings you come up against—those feelings you just can't explain, yet you feel with great intensity. How surprising they are to you will depend on how in alignment your Soul Urge number is with the rest of your core numbers.

This is also a good number to know for understanding yourself in intimate relationships. Choosing a partner with a Soul Urge number that's compatible with yours often points to a more successful and satisfying relationship. I also find the Soul Urge number to indicate your soul's greatest point of learning and development in this lifetime.

Here's the complicating factor. *Numerologists don't necessarily agree on how to arrive at this number.* Of all the core numbers, this is the number that is the most perplexing—if not frustrating—to determine. The calculation is based on adding together the *vowels* in your full name.

Vowels are A, E, I, O, U—and here's where it gets sticky—and sometimes Y. And sometimes W. Different numerologists believe different things.

Dr. Juno Jordan (and others) will tell you that the "y" *never* enters into the calculation (Dr. Juno Jordan, *Numerology: The Romance In Your Name*). Lynn Buess (and others) contends that the "y" is *always* used in calculating the Soul Urge number (Lynn Buess, *The Heart of Numerology*).

Hans Decoz (and others) will show you that the calculation rests on the "y" being considered a vowel by the way it *sounds*. The energy of the "y" is vacillating. Numerology, after all, is really all about vibration and frequency, so discerning the *sound* that the vowel brings to the name is key to this formulation.

When using the "y" to calculate the Soul Urge, understand that the "y" is considered a vowel when it's the only vowel sound in the syllable. Hans Decoz states:

"When the letter serves as a vowel, and in fact sounds like one, it is a vowel. ... Examples of both of these cases are such names as Lynn, Yvonne, Mary, Betty, Ely, and Bryan. However, if the Y does not provide a separate vowel sound, as when it is coupled with another vowel, it is considered a consonant. In names such as Maloney or Murray, the Y is a consonant, because the vowel sound depends upon the long E in Maloney and the long A in Murray. In general, the Y is a consonant when the syllable already has a vowel. Also, the Y is considered a consonant when it is used in the place of the soft J sound, as in the name Yolanda or Yoda."

A numerology software program I use makes this statement when it asks if a "y" is a consonant or a vowel: "This Y is a vowel if it follows A, E, I, O or U and sounds as one sound (as in Hayes) or there is no other vowel in the syllable (as in Ken-ne-dy) or it is pronounced as a vowel (as in Yves). Otherwise, it is a consonant."

What's a person to do? *All you can do is choose a way of calculation that feels right to you*. Sorry to say it, yet it's true. I've grappled with this personally and I don't know another numerologist who hasn't had to wrestle this alligator. You must choose what resonates with you and the only way to do that is to experiment. Try out both ways and see what feels right. As you gain experience, you'll come to terms with the way you feel is the correct way to manage the "y."

And if you're getting your calculations through a numerology calculator that's a computerized software program or App, then you definitely must choose whether or not the "y" is or is not included in your calculation. This is chosen in the "settings" for the software program. Otherwise, you must do it manually each time. Doing it by hand is fine if that's what you want to do. Yet it won't help you if you're printing out a computerized numerology report. Sometimes an App or program will ask you what your choice is each time a potential vowel shows up so that you can make the determination manually each time the software program or App makes a calculation.

The obvious point to make here is that the whole "y" issue isn't an issue when calculating everyone's Soul Urge number—it's only an issue when a person has the letter "y" in their name. That kind of falls into the "no duh" category, yet I'll mention it anyway. Having to make a decision about how to categorize a potential vowel isn't always an issue. It's only an issue when the name contains one or more "y's."

I find that if you're on the fence about how the "y" should be calculated, do it both ways (calculating the "y" as a vowel and then as a consonant) and then feel into it and see what resonates most directly with you.

Moreover, most numerologists I have studied don't consider the "w" to be a vowel, yet on rare occasions, I have seen it placed as a vowel. Again, this is up to you and yet my purpose is to provide you with a basic overview of general numerology practices. I have never personally considered the "w" a vowel under any circumstances. I also find it intriguing that the letter "y" translates into the number 7—a number that's intrinsically internal, spiritual, and probing.

CALCULATE THE SOUL URGE NUMBER

Write down the name you were given at birth, just as it is written on your birth certificate. Use the chart (below) and apply a number to each letter of your name: *first, middle, last.* If you have more than one middle name, please use all of the names as they appear on your birth certificate. If you're a Jr., Second or Third, please leave that out of the equation.

Let's use Tina Fey as an example.

You calculate this much in the same way you calculate your Expression/Destiny number. It's a simple addition problem once you assign a number value to the letter in the name (as indicated by the chart below). As always, *you must reduce to a one-digit number for each part of the calculation*:

1	2	3	4	5	6	7	8	9
A	B	C	D	E	F	G	H	I
J	K	L	M	N	O	P	Q	R
S	T	U	V	W	X	Y	Z	

```
5  9  1  5              1  1  9  1    5 7
↑  ↑  ↑  ↑              ↑  ↑  ↑  ↑    ↑ ↑
E L I Z A B E T H    S T A M A T I N A  F E Y
```

ELIZABETH (vowels e, i, a, e)
5 + 9 + 1 + 5 = 20
2 + 0 = 2

STAMATINA (vowels a, i)
1 + 1 + 9 + 1 = 12
1 + 2 = 3

FEY (vowels e, y)
5 + 7 = 12
1 + 3 = 3

Then add each name together:

2 + 3 + 3 = 8

Using the "y" as a vowel, Tina Fey has an 8 Soul Urge.

If you don't use the "y" as a vowel in Fey and instead consider it a consonant:

2 + 3 + 5 = 10
1 + 0 = 1

If the "y" in "Fey" is considered a consonant, it's a 1 Soul Urge.

While only Tina would know, what number do you feel would be more fitting for her Soul Urge? The 8 or the 1? Also consider that both the 1 and the 8 have somewhat similar qualities—they're both power numbers.

SOUL URGE DEFINITIONS

1 Soul Urge: *You have a deep need to become #1 at everything you do in your life.*

When you look deep into your soul, you have an underlying and pressing need to be independent, exert your individuality, and achieve with whatever you set your mind toward.

Down deep, your task is to make a unique mark in the world and to become a leader in whatever field you're the most passionate and skilled. You have an underlying need to be the best at everything you do.

Your heart's desire is to take the lead and take initiative—the 1 Soul Urge isn't destined to sit in the backseat. You're meant to have courage, act independently on your unique and original ideas, be innovative, and take charge. You have amazing insights and are highly creative and forward-thinking. Underneath it all, you long to be the trailblazer, the pioneer, the original thinker, and the one who pushes the envelope.

A 1 Soul Urge sets you up for the development of your sense of self, harnessing willpower, and setting out with courage and determination without allowing the naysayers or glitches along the road to derail you. Some of your internal struggles might include a battle with low self-esteem or lack of self-confidence. Beware of defaulting into defeat and staying there. That's when you resort to self-absorption, cynicism, bullying, and possibly battle with addiction.

Your ultimate desire revolves around marching to the beat of your own weird and innovative drummer. Understand that you're learning how to be a leader and innovator—and you're learning how to stand on your own two feet and act with an independent flair. You're also learning how to actually engage with other people and value their thoughts and feelings.

You'll experience many lessons where you'll learn the delicate balance between taking the reins and blazing forward without answering to anyone—and cultivating input from others. You might walk a fine line being overly assertive or passive—yet your inner longing is to be a leader and to achieve whatever you set your mind toward.

Know that you'll be challenged with the opposite of your internal calling—meaning, you can have trouble taking the lead, be overly sensitive to criticism, or have trouble seeing outside of your own wants and needs. Or alternately, you may wear the mask of criticism and judgment while thinking only of yourself. It ultimately depends on the other numbers in your chart and how those energies mix and match with your initiating 1 Soul Urge.

2 Soul Urge: *You have a deep need to love, be loved, and bring harmony to discordant situations.*

When you look deep into your soul, you have an underlying and pressing need to create harmony, balance, cooperation, and create loving dynamics with whatever you do. Love, emotional acuity, and peace-keeping are the cornerstones of your heart's desire.

Down deep, you know you're meant to be in a one-on-one relationship that satisfies your loving spirit. You're here to learn how to develop your ability to co-create healthy and loving relationships. Your innermost desire is focused on being involved in relationships that feed your soul. You're a giver, supporter, and peace-keeper.

The 2 Soul Urge encourages you to seek to be of service to the larger cause—whether that's your family, employer, or any other cause or group you feel strongly about. Understand that you need to get out and socialize, because if you isolate yourself you suffer from pessimism, depression, and inaction. You feel deeply satisfied when you're involved with other people and contributing to the group dynamics—whether it's with friends, work, family or a community group.

You'll be tested with being overly sensitive and can resort to becoming confrontational or reactive rather than harmonizing and diplomatic.

Some of your internal struggles might include an incessant need for acknowledgment from everyone around you—just be aware that you're not likely to get it. Insecurity and over-giving are hallmarks of the 2 Soul Urge.

Understand that you're learning how to be in the middle of conflicting situations—something you actually despise—and be at the helm in finding common ground and winning situations. You're also learning how to actually engage in groups and bring in your harmonizing presence without taking on everyone's psychic garbage and emotional baggage. You'll experience many lessons teaching you how to grow out of being a doormat for other to wipe their feet upon. The 2 Soul Urge is learning how to stand in someone else's shoes—without wearing the shoes home!

You might walk a fine line with being passive or aggressive—indecisive or lacking personal ambition—yet your inner longing is to become a peacemaker and harmonizing influence with whatever you touch. Know that you'll be challenged with the opposite of your calling—meaning, you can have trouble with relationships, be overly sensitive, and have trouble with compromise.

Or alternately, you may wear your heart on your sleeve and show this more tender side of yourself more often than not, yet with mutating boundaries and a lack of a core sense of who you are and what you value. It ultimately depends on the other numbers in your chart and how those energies mix and match with your harmonizing number 2 Soul Urge.

Master 11/2 Soul Urge: *You have a deep need to heal and transform others through spiritual service and artistic creativity.*

When you look deep into your soul, you have an underlying and pressing need to form meaningful relationships—while having the spotlight shine on you! The foundation of your deep desire resides with the energy of the number 2.

Underneath it all you're a lover, not a fighter. You're amazingly emotionally sensitive and working on trusting timing through patient process. Yet then you must add on the self-focused calling of the double 1.

It's as though you're a Siamese twin and your twin is the Yang to your Yin. The 1 is all about *you* while the 2 is all about *the group*. The 1 contains the energy of drive, initiation, leadership, innovation, independence, and is often the quirky individualist. The 1 seeks to take the lead while the 2 seeks to be the supportive power behind the throne. Can you see how there might be a few issues along the way?

It's a constant push/pull between wanting to tell others what to do while also wanting others to define tasks and have others tell *you* what to do. It's a mix of being pushed into the spotlight—while there's nothing that scares you more than that. It's a constant wrestle with leveling your delicate ego to manageable and productive realms. You're perpetually riding the teeter-totter of me/us, diplomacy/leadership, and independence/interdependence.

The 11/2 is the spiritual messenger. You bring a heightened and refined energy to whatever you do and yet here is the inherent frustration: What you bring to the mix is somewhat intangible. Therefore, it's difficult to trust that you're on task or having any significant impact because what you do best is primarily etheric and energetic—it's not quantifiable. The 11 is the number of spiritual illumination. It's a doorway to higher consciousness and yet it's not something you can catalogue, define or check off the punch-list.

Know that you have gifts in the realm of artistic creativity, however that shows up for you individually. You're at your optimal when acting upon healthy emotional and energetic boundaries, serving the needs of a group dynamic and developing your relationship with yourself, with others, and with the spiritual realm.

This Soul Urge number is a powerful one demanding that you learn how to level your ego, trust your intuition, and serve as a conduit for spiritual energy to move and speak through you.

Some of your internal struggles might include being more of a dreamer than a doer. You might find that you have trouble bringing forth any of your ideas into form in the material world—meaning, you're full of dreams and ideas—yet find it impossible to bring those dreams into reality. Since you're learning all about the intricacies of relationships, you can struggle with establishing and maintaining healthy relationships.

Know that your 11/2 Soul Urge is a profound journey that offers you multifaceted opportunities to create loving environments, dig deep into relationships, and bring an evolved and spiritually heightened energy to all of your interactions. At your core, you're a spiritual messenger who is highly intuitive and creative.

With the 11/2 as your Soul Urge, this might be something only you can see or feel. Or alternately, you may tap into your loving diplomacy, heightened creativity, and super-charged spirituality in a substantial way. It ultimately depends on the other numbers in your chart and how those energies mix and match with your inspired and spiritually focused 11/2 Soul Urge.

3 Soul Urge: *You have a deep need to create, perform, and communicate in order to inspire, motivate, heal, and uplift people.*

When you look deep into your soul, you have an underlying and pressing need to communicate in order to inspire, heal, uplift, and energize others. You have a deep longing to be in the spotlight. Your soul longs to take the stage and use your creative impulses. Your ultimate satisfaction comes through when you're operating with a core sense of optimism, enthusiasm, hopefulness, and joy.

At your core, you're here to express yourself. You have a driving need to use your creativity through self-expression and to dig deep and get to know your own emotional life so that you can heal yourself and others—through counseling, entertainment or anything within the communication arts. You deeply understand the power of words and work to hone your communication skills.

Some of the qualities you bring to the table are youthful optimism, possible eccentricity, excitement, and potential fame. When you've tapped into your authentic sense of expression—and then inspire others to use and express theirs—you're fulfilling your heart's desire. If you give up on your dreams and don't use your talents creatively, you'll battle with depression and find yourself traveling down other unsatisfying or destructive pathways. You might feel the issues of the world so intensely that it's emotionally overwhelming, making optimism and your innate buoyancy an ongoing challenge.

Often the 3 brings so many talents and ideas with it, it's difficult to focus on just one—making procrastination or scattered focus a hurdle. On a core level, you'll be challenged with learning to identify and embrace your own emotional life and often will be most effective in helping yourself help others through your gift of words (both verbal and written), through your amazing sense of wit and humor, by being lighthearted, and a good communicator and listener.

Some of your internal struggles might include emotional ups and downs, depression, or being pessimistic and critical. Superficiality and gossip are defaults for you when you aren't in alignment with your heart's desire. Your 3 Soul Urge number calls you to express yourself and help others do the same in the most positive, funny, and emotionally connective way possible.

You can be challenged with the opposite of your calling—having trouble with emotions, resisting the spotlight, and having problems feeling joyful and optimistic.

With the 3 as your Soul Urge, this might be something only you can see or feel. Or alternately, you may communicate and entertain with a vengeance and show this more gregarious part of yourself more often than not. It ultimately depends on the other numbers in your chart and how those energies mix and match with your communicative and performative 3 Soul Urge.

4 Soul Urge: *You have a deep need to accomplish something tangible that people find beneficial in their day-to-day lives.*

When you look deep into your soul, you have an underlying and pressing need to build something of lasting value in the world. This can be a family of your own, a business or other enterprise.

Deep down you need to build a stable environment for yourself and you work hard to create this in your life. Some of the underlying key values are honestly, loyalty, and trustworthiness. Know that you have the potential to be a stellar marriage or business partner. Your heart's desire revolves around being practical, hardworking, and achieving goals using step-by-step processes.

Underneath it all, you desire to build a life where you feel anchored, rooted, and grounded. Family life often calls to you—a point of your ultimate soul's growth resides in your ability to create your family of choice where you feel secure, understood, and appreciated.

You're the systems-builder and keeper of order. You might lean toward rigidness, stubbornness, and blunt communication. Alternately, you could avoid putting down roots and reject hard work. Some of your internal struggles might include an aversion to coloring outside the lines and a fear of taking risks. The number 4 is all about coming to terms with limitations—working with them, understanding when you've created your own limitations, and working through and around whatever the perceived limitations might be in order to get where you want to go.

Down at your core, you desire outlets for managing, organizing, and creating a foundation from which to build your life or enterprise. Don't let fear of criticism or the trap of low-level work stop you from creating the foundation from which you build your life. Don't succumb to seeing work as a necessary evil—since work is a huge part of the energy of the 4—it's the number of concerted effort, after all! You might find that it takes you a while to settle in on a career that suits you.

Folks who have a 4 as the Soul Urge often either work really hard from early on in their lives *or* they take their sweet time before they realize that they feel much better when there's a focused plan and a commitment to the effort it takes to get the job done. Make a decision. Put down roots.

With the 4 as your Soul Urge, this might be something only you can see or feel. Or alternately, you may work with great tenacity, bask in checking off the goals on your punch-list, and revel in sharing your vast knowledge with others with great consistency and generosity. With the 4 Soul Urge, it's all about a sense of accomplishment. It ultimately depends on the other numbers in your chart and how those energies mix and match with your steady and hard-working 4 Soul Urge.

Master 22/4 Soul Urge: *You have a deep need to become a masterful teacher and manifest inspired practical ideas.*

When you look deep into your soul, you have an underlying and pressing need to build something of lasting value in the world—and to use your strong knowledge-base to teach and instruct others. With a 22/4 Soul Urge, the foundation of your deep desire resides with the energy of the number 4. You're the ultimate teacher, developer of systems, and purveyor of hard work while meeting clearly defined goals.

Then you must add on the double 2. The 2 is all about diplomacy, patience, love, and is highly emotionally sensitive, while the 4 is all about gathering knowledge, building and maintaining systems and foundations in life—and going about it all in a reliable and steady fashion. The energy of the 4 is related to limitation and feels most comfortable with rules and often sees things as black or white, while the energy of the 2 is related most directly with emotions and focuses first and foremost on the needs of others.

The ambition of the 4 is centered around accomplishment and tangible results while the ambition of the 2 is centered around relationships, emotional connections, and being of use to others.

Can you see how there might be a few issues along the way? It's a constant push/pull between wanting to play by the rules, color within the lines, and stay inside the box. Yet the Master number is asking you to *risk*—to step into the spotlight, into leadership positions, and trust in your ability to manifest and have positive effects in the larger scheme of things. It's a constant wrestle with letting go of micromanaging while taking the plunge and thinking bigger. You're perpetually riding the teeter-totter of "let's just stay home" and "let's work over-time, build this, and bring it to the world."

The 22/4 is the master builder and the master teacher. You can be the work-horse of the world and that attribute can often tip over into the realm of the work *martyr*—" If you want something done right you just have to do it yourself" attitude. Understand that most numerologists will say that the number 22 is the most powerful force in numerology.

This energy carries with it a potent ability to manifest great things—yet the requirements are focused goals, organization, and dogged step-by-step processes.

The trick is to understand that this isn't the energy of the slap and dash sort-of enterprise. It's the energy of slow and steady progress—of building something solid, tangible, and useful. The 22/4 comes to work early and goes to bed late (metaphorically speaking). You're at your optimal when recognizing and blazing through limitations—both external limitations and limitations that are self-imposed. You're here to create something that stands the test of time.

This Soul Urge number is a powerful one demanding that you learn how to focus and manifest in the practical world. You're in it for the long haul! When you're engaging with the challenging aspects of the 22/4, you can struggle with being hard-headed, bossy in a not-so-useful way, and inflexible.

If you work with the under-active elements of the 22/4, you'll veer toward an inability to set down roots, be incapable of making a decision or commitment about work, family or career—or simply opt out of anything requiring dedication.

Some of your internal struggles might include being discouraged or done in by the intense requirements of this demanding Soul Urge. You might find that you have trouble bringing forth any of your ideas into form in the material world because you suffer with a sense of confusion, overwhelm or lack the determination to dig into something and stay the course. Since you're learning all about the intricacies of setting goals and making it happen, you can struggle with giving up before you even begin or lack the fortitude to stick to something long enough to see it come to fruition.

Know that your 22/4 Soul Urge is a profound journey that offers you multifaceted opportunities to create a solid, steady, and stable home environment while also creating things of lasting value in the world—whether that's by using your teaching and knowledge skills or creating actual products that benefit people's everyday lives.

At your core, you're a spiritual guide who is highly intuitive and also immanently practical. With the 22/4 as your Soul Urge, this might be something only you can see or feel.

Or alternately, you may tap into your masterful teaching, embrace your heightened ability to work hard to achieve goals, and make positive use of your super-charged spirituality in a substantial way. It ultimately depends on the other numbers in your chart and how those energies mix and match with your inspired and spiritually focused 22/4 Soul Urge.

5 Soul Urge: *You have a deep need to effect change, embrace freedom, and show people how to live life to the maximum.*

When you look deep into your soul, you have an underlying and pressing need for freedom, change, and adventure. You're learning all about adaptability, progressive thought and action, freedom, and embracing the adventure of life. You're also learning how to do this productively! Therefore, some keys elements to your pathway include embracing responsibility, learning how to focus your energies and efforts, and living the dream by mastering the constructive use of freedom.

Underneath it all, freedom is your guiding force—therefore you might feel a consistent sense of restlessness and desire for new experiences at the expense of consistency or overall accountability. Your task is to develop a constructive and disciplined use of freedom so that you can focus on specific goals and have positive outcomes. You feel a yearning to embrace your adventurous spirit and follow your curiosity to explore the world around you.

Most often the 5 Soul Urge brings the characteristics of adventurousness, resilience, and spirituality to the table. Your heart's desire is one of liberation and self-determination. If you find yourself on the opposite end of the spectrum, you'll do battle with self-absorption, irresponsibility, and fearfulness.

One of the primary struggles might include paralyzing fear and feelings of restriction. You can move through intimate relationships like you're walking through a turnstile. And often you simply feel the need to have one foot in and one foot out with most things in your life, particularly with relationships. You might have a heightened self-centeredness or self-indulgence that places a wedge in your friendships and intimate relationships. You can swerve over into the high maintenance category with great ease.

Ultimately, your gift is showing others how to live fearlessly through your example. The key to your 5 Soul Urge is to work with boundaries and certain parameters or life can be chaotic, out of control, and ultimately ineffectual. The energy of the 5 is all about excess and escape, so you might wrestle with some addictive tendencies. The world is your ever-changing oyster. Experience awaits you!

You may have a tendency toward stirring up drama wherever you go or—on the other end of the spectrum—you might tend toward hunkering down into your own little world and fear even the most basic transition or change. Ultimately, your soul's gift is showing others how to live fearlessly and offering yourself a beautiful and expansive life lived by *doing*. For the 5 Soul Urge, every year is your year of saying "yes!"

Remember that there's a distinct difference between freedom and just wanting to escape or numb out. With the 5 as your Soul Urge, this might be something only you can see or feel.

Or alternately, you may bask in the excitement of life, embrace change, and act with a consistent and focused sense of freedom. It ultimately depends on the other numbers in your chart and how those energies mix and match with your freedom-loving and resilient 5 Soul Urge.

6 Soul Urge: *You have a deep need to provide loving service and a nurturing environment for yourself and your loved ones.*

When you look deep into your soul, you have an underlying and pressing need to nurture and serve. Whether it's your family and loved ones or your business or community, you're an expert at creating beauty, harmony, and balance—emotionally and aesthetically.

Down deep, you're a walking satellite dish of emotional receptivity and while that's a blessing, it can also be a curse. Your soul longs for a loving and comforting relationship partner and leans toward creating a family.

You're a natural counselor who can see past the obvious and often get miffed when others can't. You're an idealist—and a perfectionist. With a 6 Soul Urge, you may find yourself in positions of responsibility early on in life and a sense of heightened responsibility will continue as you mature.

Underneath it all, you need to feel indispensable to others and yet resent the fact that others rely on you too much or that your helping and supportive efforts are underappreciated.

You often have a polished presentation about you and denote an air of authority. Remember that your mission is to balance and modulate your sense of responsibility—not overly responsible (meddling, self-righteous, perfectionist) and not overly irresponsible (self-centered, judgmental, controlling). Some of your internal struggles might include self-righteousness, codependency or meddling martyr.

With the 6 Soul Urge, your true calling is in healthy nurturing, compassionate detachment, acceptance of others (get past that perfectionism!) and adding beauty and your beautiful vision to the world. When you extract yourself from your self-imposed world of *shoulds*, you're on the right track. You'll have a tendency to lose yourself and your identity because you're so busy taking care of others and taking over the responsibilities for others.

Or perhaps you default into the irresponsible side of the energy of the 6 and care only about yourself and what you want to do—and do it whenever you want to, despite the fact that you're shirking your duties and responsibilities to those around you.

You're in your element when you're the cosmic parent, expressing gratitude, acting with a generous spirit, accepting others even if you don't agree with their choices, and giving comfort to others in times of need. You express your soul's calling through loving relationships, nurturing, and service. You're in your element when you're taking accountability in a balanced way and by giving comfort to others in times of need.

With the 6 as your Soul Urge, this might be something only you can see or feel. Or alternately, you may act with loving compassion, use your creative visionary abilities to build a successful business and create beautiful surroundings, and be a supportive go-to person for friends and family. It ultimately depends on the other numbers in your chart and how those energies mix and match with your nurturing 6 Soul Urge.

Master 33/6 Soul Urge: *You have a deep need to nurture, heal, inspire, and bring a loving and healing presence to everything you do.*

When you look deep into your soul, you have an underlying and pressing need to nurture and serve—with joy and optimism. You're the nurturer—the magnetic visionary, justice seeker, and master or mistress of the domestic realm. Then add on the double 3. The 3 is all about creative self-expression, communication, optimism, and emotional sensitivity—

while the 6 is all about nurturing, love, duty, service, responsibility, and the creation of beauty.

The 33/6 is a rather enigmatic calling. It's as though your soul is asking you to elevate your thoughts and actions into the "Mother Teresa" realm while also being dynamic, creative, and joyful in the process. Try that on for size, right? Can you see how there might be a few issues along the way? It's a constant push-and-pull between wanting to be of service and help and heal others—and yet you might also find that your perfectionism and judgment of others gets in the way.

The Master number is asking you to *commit*—to step into the spotlight, into leadership positions, and trust in your ability to be joyful and helpful in whatever form you choose. It's a constant wrestle with letting go of self-righteousness and control while infusing love and service into all you do. You're perpetually riding the teeter-totter of "I want to heal the world" and "The world doesn't deserve what I have to give."

The 33/6 is the conduit of joyful, loving, and nurturing service. Yet you can easily tip into the martyr role. Rather than being helpful, you can opt for meddling. Rather than loving, you can judge harshly and critically. Understand that "Master" actually means "Teacher"—not someone who's superior, the boss, or a slave driver! With the 33/6 Soul Urge, your basic "Master 33/6 Soul Urge 101" Class is to master self-care. You must learn to know and love yourself first before you can extend your gift of love and service to others.

When you're engaging with the challenging aspects of the 33/6, you can struggle with being controlling, intolerant, and an unrealistic perfectionist. If you work with the under-active elements of the 33/6, you'll veer toward being taken advantage of to the point of resentment or ill health.

You'll be challenged with standing up for yourself with healthy physical and emotional boundaries. If you work with the overactive elements of the 33/6, you'll veer toward being a critical bulldozer or perhaps have issues with stepping into your higher calling by being addictive, irresponsible, and self-absorbed. It helps to know that that you're highly emotionally sensitive and energetically permeable. Boundaries, boundaries, and more boundaries are mandatory for the 33/6 Soul Urge.

Some of your internal struggles might include being discouraged or done in by the intense requirements of this demanding Soul Urge. You might find that you take on the weight of the world and can't see past its vast injustices and imperfections. You're an idealist and have the gift of seeing a bigger picture where others can't. This can lead to frustration and difficulty in seeing beauty in the smaller things. You're learning the perfection of the imperfection of everything. You're also learning to speak your truth in an authentic and compassionate manner.

Know that your 33/6 Soul Urge is a pathway offering multifaceted opportunities to inspire people with your joyful service and creativity—whether that's by acting, music, medicine, counseling, being a homemaker or any other creative endeavor. At your core, you're a spiritual guide who is highly intuitive and infinitely loving.

With the 33/6 as your Soul Urge, this might be something only you can see or feel. Or alternately, you may tap into your nurturing disposition, emotional self-expression and service, and make positive use of your super-charged spirituality in a substantial way. It ultimately depends on the other numbers in your chart and how those energies mix and match with your responsible and nurturing 33/6 Soul Urge.

7 Soul Urge: *You have a deep need to intellectualize and analyze, yet also a need to develop trust and faith while seeking your own answer to the meaning of life.*

When you look deep into your soul, you have an underlying and pressing need to seek out information and analyze it. Underneath it all, you have a burning need to seek out knowledge and dig into the depths of spiritual understanding. Your life-long task is to get to know the *true you*, inside and out. Your heart's desire leads you on a very internal journey. You need to dig deep and contemplate heavily.

You're the perfect researcher and everything always comes back to informing your own sense of inner wisdom. Your life is instructed by a powerful collision between practical, tangible data, and the analysis of it. Then on the other hand, you're highly intuitive and your gift—and your task—is to integrate the two (your intellect and your intuition) into a harmonious tag team. This is a deeply felt need.

You need a good deal of private solo time. If you find yourself isolated to the point of withdrawing from the outside world, you're straying from the constructive nature of your 7 Soul Urge.

You're someone people never really truly know because you're most often attempting to figure that out yourself. Some of your internal struggles might include your propensity for living in your head and intellectualizing everything.

You operate on a different wavelength than most and can easily be misread by others. Be careful with using sharp words, as you can hurt people without realizing it. You have exquisite observation skills and when you have a strong sense of spirituality (however that manifests for you), you're at your best. Otherwise, you can fall into superficiality, skepticism, cynicism or depression. You're innately intuitive and spiritually minded.

The highest and best use of your extraordinary talents are cultivating knowledge, processing it into new ideas or practical usage, and applying your advanced wisdom to the data. At your core, you're a gentle soul and your heart's desire is to truly know yourself and the mysteries of the planet and the invisible realms—and to share your hard-won wisdom with others.

With the 7 as your Soul Urge, this might be something only you can see or feel. Or alternately, you may be a masterful specialist in some area of expertise, the wise sage who people consult for advice and instruction, and someone who trusts the nature of their own existence fully and completely. It ultimately depends on the other numbers in your chart and how those energies mix and match with your probing and contemplative 7 Soul Urge.

8 Soul Urge: *You have a deep need to manifest financial security that allows you freedom and influence to make a difference in the world.*

When you look deep into your soul, you have an underlying and pressing need to gain self-mastery. Your heart's desire is to achieve and succeed in the material world. Deep down you need to master the elements of money, personal power, control, and authority. The 8 is a testing number and also an amplifier—it amplifies whatever it touches. When you realize that you're here to achieve power and abundance—and then act on that knowledge—your heart's desire will be fulfilled.

At your core, you need to achieve status and power. Wielding positive influence and being a respected authority in your field of expertise is your touchstone. It's important that you do well in the world and gain recognition for your accomplishments.

Having an 8 Soul Urge might explain your businesslike demeanor and deep desire for the finer things in life. It's your task to learn to be a confident and successful person without becoming corrupted or hardened by power and money—or beaten down and disempowered. Your path takes rigor and tenacity to manifest your soul's calling.

You have amazing potential for improving the lives of a lot of people. You're a masterful leader, manager, and organizer—a powerhouse made for material success. Remember that as you give, you receive. You're meant for positions of power and therefore often experience authority issues throughout your life. You can be easily misinterpreted because of a gruff, direct, and opinionated manner.

Or if you're working with the destructive tendencies of the number 8, you can feel disempowered and victimized. When you're thriving financially and giving generously, you're doing what your soul longs to do.

The first item of business that will open the gate for you to achieve your 8 Soul Urge is to dig deep and tap into your sense of personal empowerment. And believe me, you'll be handed a treasure-trove of opportunities to *step up* or be *stepped on*. The energy of the 8 demands that you dig into your power and move through obstacles—and there will be many obstacles. An 8 Soul Urge number means you have to step it up and make up your mind that you're in the world to make your mark.

Some of your internal struggles might include an over (or under) focus on money, becoming bullying or wallowing in self-pity. Or if you're working with the destructive tendencies of the number 8, you can be the ultimate doormat, self-destructive, and obstinate. When you're thriving financially and giving generously from your heart, you're doing what your soul was born to do.

With the 8 as your Soul Urge, this might be something only you can see or feel. Or alternately, you may be a masterful money manager, a giving philanthropist, a powerful and achievement-oriented organizer or other conduit for helping empower others. It ultimately depends on the other numbers in your chart and how those energies mix and match with your intense and power-focused 8 Soul Urge.

9 Soul Urge: *You have a deep need to achieve a higher state of consciousness, teach others how to give the highest and best of themselves, and learn the power of selfless-service.*

When you look deep into your soul, you have an underlying and pressing need to engage in some sort of humanitarian service. Underneath it all, yours is a spiritual path and you're here to love unconditionally and to be of service.

The number 9 is a sacred number. In numerology, it's the number of completions. It's the number of the old soul, of letting go, of releasing attachments, and of loss. You're at your optimal when you're tapping into your creativity, following your quirky creative pathway, and giving generously with your time, talents, energy or money.

At the end of the day, this Soul Urge number is a powerful one demanding that you learn to transform and heal (both yourself and others) while letting go of the past freely and without bitterness or attachment.

Ultimately, it's all about aligning with the higher spiritual pathway that teaches us that everything is temporary—the good, the bad, and everything in between. When the 9 is your Soul Urge, you may find yourself tripping over into the arena of bitterness, of intolerance, or gullibility. You may have to deal with enmeshment with your family of origin throughout your life. You often feel either resentment toward the family or feel overly responsible for them.

While the 9 is the path of universal wisdom, the road you travel can feel rocky and, at some times, thankless. You need to be aware that people respond much more favorably to you when you connect with them through being a compassionate active listener rather than a preacher, lecturer, or proselytizer. Understand that you can have an intimidating quality to you, despite your big heart.

Some of your internal struggles might include being perceived as arrogant or unapproachable. Realize that everyone thinks you have it all (or have it all together) and so you find it difficult to ask for help or support. It's not only okay to ask for help, it's very healing for you. You're truly connecting with your abilities to both give *and* receive—and usually the receiving part is much harder!

Know that your 9 Soul Urge is a powerful journey that offers you multifaceted opportunities to touch the lives of others and heal some of your own deepest wounds. At your core, you're a giving soul and your heart's desire is to serve others and leave the world a better place while you're here and when you're gone.

With the 9 as your Soul Urge, this might be something only you can see or feel. Or alternately, you may use your other-worldly creativity freely and passionately, act with compassion, and serve the higher good in a substantial way. It ultimately depends on the other numbers in your chart and how those energies mix and match with your compassionate and humanitarian-focused 9 Soul Urge.

Personality

This indicates HOW OTHER PEOPLE PERCEIVE YOU.

This is the way you present yourself to the outside world.

This is a counter-point to your Soul Urge.

THE PERSONALITY NUMBER

As a counter-point to your vowel-based Soul Urge number, the Personality number is derived by adding together the *consonants* in your name.

If you think about it, the vowels are more *internal* in terms of how they sound when spoken—and there are fewer of these letters in the alphabet. Vowels sound and feel softer.

On the other hand, the consonants are greater in number and also more *forward* or *active* in how they present themselves. When you add together the consonants, this indicates *the way the world sees you on an external level* as opposed to the Soul Urge, which reveals what you truly want (and who you truly are) on a deeply internal or soul level.

Since the Personality number reveals how others might see you—how you might be perceived by the outside world—think of it as the impression you make on a first date or when meeting people for the first time at a cocktail party. *This is how you present yourself.*

Go back to the chart outlining how to transcribe letters into numbers (in the section on the Expression/Destiny and Soul Urge) in order see how the consonants in your name break down. Here's an example of how to calculate the Personality number. *Notice that there's a "y" to contend with.* A decision must be made whether the "y" is used as a vowel or a consonant.

In writing out a calculation, most numerologists will place the number for the vowels above the name and place the number for the consonants below the name.

I feel it's interesting that the number for the vacillating letter "y" is the spiritually activated and elusive 7!

While some numerologists add "the long way," I have been taught that the proper way is to add each name separately and then add the one-digit number for each name together, much in the same way you add the month/day/year for the Life Path calculation.

Although I'm indicating both the vowels and the consonants using Beyoncé as an example, I'm doing so in order to give you a bit of practice and to see where you might be forced to use some critical thinking skills along the way!

Yet, right now we're illustrating how to formulate the Personality number by adding the consonants together.

B E Y O N C É   **G I S E L L E**   **K N O W L E S**
⬇   ⬇ ⬇   ⬇ ⬇ ⬇ ⬇ ⬇   ⬇ ⬇ ⬇
2   <u>7</u>   5 3   7   1   3 3   2 5   5 3   1

Beyoncé ("y" as a vowel):

$2 + 5 + 3 = 10$

$1 + 0 = 1$

Giselle:

$7 + 1 + 3 + 3 = 14$

$1 + 4 = 5$

Knowles:

$2 + 5 + 5 + 3 + 1 = 16$

$1 + 6 = 7$

$1 + 5 + 7 = 13/4$

13/4 is a Karmic number

We'll learn about Karmic Debt numbers in a following chapter.

With the "y" as a vowel, Beyoncé has a Karmic Debt 13/4 Personality

Beyoncé ("y" as a <u>consonant</u>):

2 + 7 + 5 + 3 = 17

1 + 7 = 8

Giselle:

7 + 1 + 3 + 3 = 14

1 + 4 = 5

Knowles:

2 + 5 + 5 + 3 + 1 = 16

1 + 6 = 7

8 + 5 + 7 = 20

2 + 0 = 2

With the "y" as a consonant, Beyoncé has a 2 Personality.

Which one seems right to you?

In this configuration, I feel the "y" in Beyoncé is calculated as a vowel because of the way it sounds.

Yet, once again, this is debatable. If we say the name *Beyoncé* out loud, the first "e" sounds like "ee" and the "y" sounds like "yuh."

Therefore, the "y" is silent or coupled up with the overall "ee" sound: "Be - ON - say" is how it might be pronounced.

If so, the "y" is a vowel because we can hear it being part of the pronunciation.

If it were pronounced: "Be - YON - say," then it would be considered a consonant, because it the "y" has the hard "yuh" sound.

It's also interesting to also look at Beyoncé's Personality number as it presents with her current name (stage name). As Beyoncé (rather than Beyoncé Giselle Knowles), she shows a number 1 Personality.

Again, this is a number that represents how people might perceive you. In numerology, the given name is always the foundational energetic matrix we've come to play out. Yet our current name becomes an overlay of energy that affects us. The longer we go by the current name, the stronger the energy related to that name becomes.

We can look at Beyoncé as a mixture of the 13/4 Karmic Personality number from her given name with the overlaying energies of a 1 Personality number, from her current stage name.

I'd give it the nickname: "The Hardworking Creative Performative Innovator." Or something like that. What would you call it?

PERSONALITY NUMBER DEFINITIONS

1 Personality: *You give the impression* that you're an innovator with tendencies to do things with independence and a unique spin. Self-motivated, competitive, and achievement driven, you appear to be at your best when you're in a leadership position. People notice that you need reinforcement and cheerleading to bolster you as you blaze your original trail. Others may find that your shadow side shows itself when you aren't acting with originality, independence, and vibrant creativity because you turn into the cynic, the rebel, or the depressive.

2 Personality: *You give the impression* that you get things accomplished through kindness, diplomacy, being accommodating, and through collaboration. You appear to have an easygoing manner and often display a sense of worry because you're so concerned about managing everyone's wants, needs, and emotions. Naturally intuitive and love-centered, people see that relationships are of the utmost importance to you. You're compassionate, rarely bored (because you're busy giving and serving others), and love to connect in a heart-centered way. Others may find that your shadow side shows itself when you take everything personally and are overly emotionally sensitive. They may find that you're caustic, childish or emotionally abrasive.

Master 11/2 Personality: Look at the traits of the number 2 and then look at the 1, and double it! You kick it up a notch and people notice that you're at your best when you're being an inspired creative in whatever capacity you choose. You give the impression that you're highly artistically creative, extremely intuitive, and over-the-top emotionally sensitive. You might read as a little flaky, dreamy, and anxious. You can present as somewhat self-absorbed with a rather fragile ego. You can come off as being loving and giving, with an edgy quality.

3 Personality: *You give the impression* that you're the entertainer and the creative genius. Funny, witty, smart, and social—people notice that you're also moody, can be scattered, and are often hard on yourself. Innately joyful, you have a happy effect on those around you. If you're feeling depressed, everyone feels the weight of your mood. People understand that friends are important to you and you have a gift of inspiring and uplifting others. Others may find that your shadow side shows itself when you opt for submerging or dumbing-down your aspirations for fear of being criticized or because emotional baggage gets the better of you and blocks your creative impulses.

4 Personality: *You give the impression* that you're at your highest and best when you key into your organization and management skills. You appear determined, honest, loyal, and reliable. People see you as the calendar maven, list keeper, and master of the punch-list. You like to get 'er done. Others notice that you're an innately gifted teacher and have many forms of expertise—from repair or construction to any other field of interest. You present as an artisan with a tenacious spirit and someone who'll come through with their promises. You're known as the best devil's advocate because you confront dishonesty or any other infraction having to do with something you feel strongly about. Others may find that your shadow side shows itself when you let inflexibility limit your success. Security and stability are important to you, yet others might observe that you can cut yourself off from success when you don't step outside of your own box.

Master 22/4 Personality: Look at the traits of the number 4 and then look at traits of the 2, and double it! The 22/4 is the most powerful number in numerology—yet it's also quite challenging to master the energies related to it. Others see you as a spiritual powerhouse and an empathetic soul, driven by a strong desire to help heal humanity in some down-to-earth way. While the Master 11/2 is often seen as a "dreamer rather than doer," the Master 22/4 is practical and driven by the need for accomplishment. You may give the impression that you're self-absorbed, a bit of a workaholic, and stubbornly self-limiting.

5 Personality: *You give the impression* that you achieve when you're adventurous, fearless, move with progressiveness, and adapt to change with grace and ease. People see that you have a tendency to succeed when you do things in a larger-than-life way. You come off as playful, fun, and usually love being the center of attention. Others notice that if you aren't living up to your high-octane standards, you'll be emotionally volatile or stir the drama pot. You're flirty, gregarious, and full of life. You're most likely well-traveled and adventurous. Others may find that your shadow side shows itself when you swing from extremes—either too free-wheeling and scattered *or* fearful and myopic. You tend to attract restrictive circumstances into your life in order to define your personal sense of freedom. You come across as self-indulgent and someone who has trouble prioritizing and following through. Often those with a 5 Personality have trouble showing up on time, committing to something after the fun wears off, or can be known as a party animal.

6 Personality: *You give the impression* that home, aesthetic beauty, and family are the locus for your endeavors. People see you as a self-proclaimed perfectionist whose focus often lands on taking care of everyone else. People see that you have natural nurturing tendencies and are usually great with children, the elderly, and animals. You appear to be a natural solopreneur who doesn't like being told what to do. Others notice that you're magnetic, a visionary, and a connoisseur of beauty. People may find that your shadow side shows itself when you revert to control freak mode and when you have trouble modulating your sense of responsibility—both with yourself and other people. Perfectionist tendencies have a dampening effect on your ability to be happy and accepting of yourself and others. People often see you as someone who's a bit too self-sacrificing or controlling.

Master 33/6 Personality: Look at the traits of the number 6 and then look at traits of the 3, and double it! The 33/6 is creative, expressive, and nurturing. People see you as someone who will come to the aid of those in need and who's always there to support those you love. Yet there's an odd mix here depending on how you embody the energies and characteristics of the 33/6. You may give the impression that you're caring and go out of your way to serve others. Or you may appear to be emotionally volatile, moody, judgmental, and scattered. Others see your powerful potential to use your creative expression to help and heal.

7 Personality: *You give the impression* that when you key into your innate skills with data analysis, strategic thinking, and intuitive genius, you're playing your best game. People see you as someone who's on a different wavelength than most. You can appear aloof and mysterious to others. People notice that you're always studying, asking questions, and analyzing the data. They're not sure how to read you because you're introverted and don't play the same game as everyone else. You're the ultimate observer, even though others may feel that you aren't paying attention to anything at all. Others might see you as a gifted intuitive and notice that you're at your best when you merge your refined scientific or rational thought-processes with your intuition. Others may find that your shadow side shows itself when you default into sharp communication, sarcasm (anger disguised as a joke), or skimming the surface of life superficially.

8 Personality: *You give the impression* that you're strong-willed, confident, and more powerful than most. People notice that you're often blunt, opinionated, and commanding and you have little patience for lolly-gaggers or time wasters. Others realize that for you, time is money and both are precious. You value money for all it can do for you in this life—it offers stability, security, freedom, power, and respect. Others see you as a person who values being an authoritative figure. You enjoy being a mover and shaker while using your influence and connections to bring powerful people together. People perceive you as being resilient and successful in the business world. Others may find that your shadow side shows itself when you're too dominating, controlling, and overly money-driven.

9 Personality: *You give the impression* that you're charismatic, creative, and a humanitarian. You've got tons of charisma and people naturally gravitate to you and think you're in charge. You're the expert at "fake it 'til you make it." People can see that you might you need to learn how to give *and* to receive—you often give too much of yourself. People envy your natural creativity. Others may find that your shadow side shows itself when you get drained emotionally when you don't establish good boundaries because you care deeply about the woes of the world. Others may think that you can lean toward fanaticism and have trouble being an active listener. Mostly, you're seen as a giver and a wonderful weirdo!

Birth Day

This indicates A SPECIAL GIFT YOU HAVE TO GIVE.

This is a point of identity & where you might feel most comfortable.

This is a gift you're meant to infuse into the power & purpose of your Life Path.

THE BIRTH DAY NUMBER

Your Birth Day number is derived from the day you were born. It's as easy as that. It's the one-digit number of the day you were born. If you were born on the 1st through the 9th day of the month, it's that same one-digit number. If you were born from the 10th onward, you simply must add together the two-digit number in order to get to the resulting one-digit number. Like so:

10 = 1 + 0 = 1
11 = 1 + 1 = 2 (11 is a Master Number)
12 = 1 + 2 = 3
13 = 1 + 3 = 4
14 = 1 + 4 = 5
15 = 1 + 5 = 6
16 = 1 + 6 = 7
17 = 1 + 7 = 8
18 = 1 + 8 = 9
19 = 1 + 9 = 10; 10 = 1 + 0 = 1
20 = 2 + 0 = 2
21 = 2 + 1 = 3
22 = 2 + 2 = 4 (22 is a Master number)
23 = 2 + 3 = 5
24 = 2 + 4 = 6
25 = 2 + 5 = 7
26 = 2 + 6 = 8
27 = 2 + 7 = 9
28 = 2 + 8 = 10; 10 = 1 + 0 = 1
29 = 2 + 9 = 11 (11 is a Master Number)
30 = 3 + 0 = 3
31 = 3 + 1 = 4

To avoid any confusion, it's like this:

Birthday: *December 29, 1986*

The only number we're looking at is the <u>DAY</u> OF BIRTH

In this example, the 29th

29 = 2 + 9 = 11 (11 is a Master Number)

In this example, you would have a Master 11/2 Birth Day Number.

Also understand that this is a *basic* look at the Birth Day number. You can dig deeper into the nuisances if you look at what *both numbers* in a double-digit Birth Day bring with them. You can also do this with the Life Path number and with all the numbers in your core numerology profile—*this is in the advanced realm.*

For instance, if you're born on the 12th or the 30th, your Birth Day number breaks down to a 3. Yet if you're born on the 12th, you can count on having aspects of both the 1 (leadership, individuality, creativity) mixed with the energy of the 2 (mediation, love, emotional sensitivity) that makes up the whole of your 3 Birth Day. If you're born on the 30th, the 0 intensifies the energy of the 3, so you get double the positives (creative self-expression, emotional sensitivity, performance) and double the challenges (self-doubt, emotional highs and lows, analysis paralysis) of the number 3.

Whenever a zero shows up, on the most basic level, it's amplifying the energy of whatever it touches or shows up next to. The 1-digit number is the same for all of these configurations, yet the nuisances in terms of the way you present with your Birth Day number can be greatly altered or enhanced by engaging with the double-digit number.

For our purposes, we're going to go with the basics. Yet if you want to begin to practice your numerology prowess, you might explore how the double-digit number comes to the table to inform the overall expression of the single-digit number.

The Birth Day number indicates a secondary lesson you're here to experience and master. Your Birth Day number is like a gift that you have to give—both to yourself and to the world. This number indicates a certain aspect of yourself and your personality that might be in synch with your other numbers or it could possibly explain why you feel you walk a delicate balance with the way you see yourself, your desires, and your actions.

Some numerologists place a lot of weight on the date of birth—so much so that they see the Birth Day number as taking precedence over the Life Path number in importance. Lloyd Strayhorn (author of *Numbers and You*) asserts that: "Your name is the 'teacher,' it tells you what you're here to teach, how you're to show others the way. Your birth date, on the other hand, sees you as the 'pupil,' and indicates what you're here to study, learn and master."

The more I work with people and their numerology charts, the more I view this number as an indicator of where you might feel the most *comfortable*—like that old comfy robe that you just can't bear to part with. It's often where you might find a stronger point of identity, whereas your Life Path is what you're developing and evolving into.

It's like the Life Path is the subject you signed up for that you hadn't a clue about. The Birth Day number feels like a class you already passed (and earned a good grade!) that you're now—*in this lifetime*—retaking. You're being called upon to take the gifts you bring with the Birth Day number and carry them forward into your Life Path purpose. You might envision this number like a birthday present, all wrapped up in festive paper, and topped with a fancy bow on top!

The energies contained with the Birth Day number are at their highest and best use when you're *integrating* them with your Life Path strengths and using it to enrich your Life Path purpose.

THE BIRTH DAY NUMBER DEFINITIONS

1 Birth Day

1 | 10 | 19 | 28

Your Gift: You're here to lead. You're ambitious and have a desire for success and achievement. You're most likely not the best at playing well with others! You can be an innovator, entrepreneur, risk-taker, and initiator. With the 1 Birth Day, you have a creative mind, great business instincts and—with the right training and initiative—can achieve great things in the material world. You have a broad vision and are able to get creative ideas up and running.

Off-Track: Prone to laziness and procrastination, you prefer to blame others for your ineffectiveness rather than pull up your bootstraps and take charge. Instead of working with others, you tend to plow through with blinders on without taking others into consideration. You might be rebellious for no productive reason. Or you sit on the sidelines and never risk taking the lead. If on the over-active end of the spectrum, you can resort to bullying behaviors and let self-centered desires control your course. With the 1 Birth Day, you can resort to angry outbursts and frustration instead of self-confidently blazing a pioneering trail. Ultimately, the gift resides in leadership, innovative and creative ideas, and healthy independence.

2 Birth Day

2 | 20

Your Gift: You're sensitive, intuitive, and diplomatic. Your talents reside in your harmonizing abilities, loving personal relations, and sensitivity to others. You bask in the beautiful environments you create. Wherever you end up, it feels like home! With a 2 Birth Day, you can be gifted artistically, musically, or have innate skills and talents with design. You're all about cooperation and work best in partnerships or in group settings—not off somewhere on your own. You're warm, affectionate, and you seek the same from others. You gravitate toward safety, security, and love. You seek and find reciprocal relationships where you're seen, heard, and valued. You feel most satisfied when you're not the one out front, rather you'd rather be the power behind the throne.

Off-Track: Succumbing to over-sensitivity, you're acutely aware of your surroundings and easily influenced by your environment and those with whom you come in contact. You're easily emotionally drained and are highly vulnerable to taking everything so personally that you become the walking wounded. With a 2 Birth Day, you can fall into immature patterns of giving and receiving love, attention, and praise—to the point of stunted personal growth and childishness. A deep lack of confidence and insecurity make you prone to withhold your wants and needs. Instead of expressing yourself directly, passive-aggressive communication becomes your wheelhouse. Ultimately, the gift resides in self-knowledge and the creation of loving connections.

11/2 Birth Day

11 | 29

Your Gift: As an inspired creative you're highly intuitive, sensitive, and possess visionary capabilities. Your head and heart are often in the clouds! Part of your nature is inventive, innovative, and psychically attuned. You thrive in peaceful environments where you can devote yourself to artistic or spiritual pursuits. Your presence is galvanizing, yet your highest and best use is to inspire others through your example. While you have leadership potential—as all the Master numbers push you into leadership roles—you're more a touchstone for healing and inspiration rather than being involved directly in the day-to-day hand-holding with people as they work through their struggles. You're at your best when you keep your feet on the ground and learn healthy emotional and energetic boundaries.

Off-Track: You experience nervous tension and an inability to shield yourself from the onslaught of negative emotional energy from those around you. When challenged with the energy of the Master 11/2 Birth Day, you tend to withdraw with resentment when you give too much and don't receive the appreciation or acknowledgment you feel you deserve. Other people's opinions about you matter a great deal and you lose yourself in your attempts to please or to punish. You'll do almost anything to receive praise and admiration from others. Your mind works intuitively—understand that your over-all sensitivity is your blessing and your curse. You're learning not to be so emotionally reactive and to soften your edge. Ultimately, the gift resides in creative leadership and intuitive awareness.

3 Birth Day

3 | 12 | 21 | 30

Your Gift: You have amazing creative talent and are a creative artist—at least at heart. You're a gifted communicator, writer, performer, entertainer—anything having to do with creative self-expression and overall communication is perfect for you. With a 3 Birth Day, you're high-energy, upbeat, witty, and charming. You're friendly, sociable, and loving—with a tendency to give freely to others of your time and talents. You're loaded with charisma, charm, and are naturally prone to being the Host or the Hostess-with-the-Mostess. In order to feel satisfied in your life, you need to engage in some sort of creative career, outlet or hobby. Remember: When you're laughing, you're learning!

Off-Track: Moody with roller-coaster emotional ups-and-downs, you can find yourself in the depths of despair and back again like a yo-yo. You find that your glass is half-empty and life feels emotionally debilitating and often hopeless. When struggling with the energies of the 3 Birth Day, you tend to gravitate toward gossipy talk and scatter your energies in so many directions that you're disappointed and frustrated that you can't set or meet long-term goals. You have a tendency to become the ultimate procrastinator. Passive-aggression or sarcasm becomes your emotional weapon of choice. Depression is a default mechanism that kicks in when you feel stuck, unable to express yourself emotionally, or unable to use your creativity in the way you would like to use it. You might present yourself as someone who has issues with substance abuse of some kind. Ultimately, the gift resides in creative self-expression and becoming a master communicator.

4 Birth Day

4 | 13 | 31

Your Gift: Hard work, reliability, honesty—you're the person others turn to when they need their proverbial Rock of Gibraltar or accountability buddy. You're highly disciplined, organized, and responsible. With a 4 Birth Day, you're at your best when you feel safe and secure and meet your responsibilities in a consistent, slow-and-steady manner. With the 4 Birth Day, you're in your element when you're taking care of practical matters. You're usually not a risk-taker or a big dreamer. Rather, you're the Master or Mistress of perseverance and you take your obligations super-seriously. If anyone can be counted on to get it done, it's anyone with a 4 Birth Day.

Off-Track: Prone to bouts of stubbornness and rigidity, you often miss opportunities because you're unable to step outside of your own self-imposed box. You tend to dig in, hover, and wait—cutting you off from opening yourself to other solutions or creative ideas. Since you struggle with inflexibility, you often experience repression, frustration, and feelings of insurmountable limitation. With a 4 Birth Day, you can teeter toward blunt and tactless communication—yet not understand when other people attempt to communicate on a creative or emotional realm, which sometimes feels foreign to you. You can become a workaholic and miss out on some of life's lighter pleasures. When challenged with the energies of the 4 Birth Day, if it isn't hard, punishing or grueling, you feel that something's wrong. The 4 benefits by attending to good health practices and by taking time for relaxing activities. Ultimately, the gift resides in creating stability and understanding your limitations.

22/4 Birth Day

22

Your Gift: Your potential is boundless as a leader, organizer, teacher or founder of a business or institution. This Master number yields great power, yet it's not a frolic. You have vision and the ability to manifest that higher vision, yet you'll be pulled down to the mundane by *fear of flying* into the vastness of your dream. With the Master 22/4 Birth Day, you're innately gifted with the ability to think on a vast scope, visualizing and organizing the details, and using your unique vision to methodically and systematically build something of lasting value. You're a natural artisan and feel an underlaying drive to accomplish something important. The 22/4 wants to heal humanity.

Off-Track: This Master energy is quite intense, so might not feel as though you're quite up to the task. You can be fearful of your ambitions and feel undeserving. Often people shy away from the potential of the Master number because it's definitely a marathon, not a sprint. You're off-track when dumbing down your goals, getting lost in the drudgery of the minutiae of work, and giving up on your visions because they veer off the course of sheer practicality. There will be blockages and limitations along the way, yet you're meant to stay the course. Ultimately, the gift resides in defining goals and dedicating yourself to the task.

5 Birth Day:

5 | 14 | 23

Your Gift: You're often itching to get out of town—to travel, have adventures, key into fun, and tap into your fearless need for excitement and change. You're adaptable, progressive, and thrive with variety. The 5 Birth Day often wears many hats in life and traverses off the beaten track. You're meant to experience the physical world in all of its glory, so you can be a bit of a rolling stone. Naturally curious, vivacious, and highly social, you have a quick mind and love shaking it up and exploring the world. If there's a party to attend, you're there—perhaps not exactly on time—but you'll be there! You attract people from all walks of life, love to experience the exotic, and long for variety.

Off-Track: Impatient, impulsive, and excessive, you lean toward over-indulgence and irresponsibility. You're the drama Queen or King, demanding constant activity and stimulation. You're easily bored, distracted, and restless—with a siren call of: "Don't fence me in!" The 5 Birth Day can be stubborn and headstrong, following your immediate impulses and desires, no matter what the repercussions. The key is to discipline your energies, contain your focus, and develop light routine and orderliness in your life. You can also experience the opposite pull of the 5 Birth Day, which offers heightened levels of fear, restriction, and self-sabotage. Ultimately, the gift resides in taking responsibility for yourself and creating vast levels of freedom in your life.

6 Birth Day:

6 | 15 | 24

Your Gift: Family-oriented, responsible, and nurturing are your trademarks. The 6 Birth Day is service-oriented and has a talent for settling disputes. You often have a knack for bringing out the best in those around you. You're a natural creative—artist or musician—and can also gravitate toward the healing arts. Your focus is on relationships and helping others. With a 6 Birth Day, your natural habitat places you in charge and responsible for the well-being of everyone. Children, the elderly, and animals are usually attracted to you and your loving energy. You have a great ability to see the long view and tend to be idealistic. The 6 is at your highest and best when you balance your responsibility to others with self-care and self-love.

Off-Track: Unable to strike a balance with your overweening sense of responsibility, you're overly stressed, worried, and on high vigilance about the wants and needs of those around you. With the 6 Birth Day, you feel as though you carry the world on your shoulders and set sky-high standards for your own performance and for those in your life. A perfectionist and a control freak, your disappointment in the world throws you into fits of self-righteous criticism where no one or nothing can meet your elevated standards. You give too much and then resent when people don't follow your advice or become too dependent on you. Ultimately, the gift resides in healthy boundaries and taking on responsibilities that feed you rather than deplete you.

7 Birth Day

7 | 16 | 25

Your Gift: The brainiac of all the Birth Day numbers, you contain a highly developed and analytical mind. Gifted with detached data analysis, research, and seeking answers to life's bigger questions, the 7 Birth Day does well when you specialize in one field and develop a deep level of expertise. You're also highly intuitive and should spend time and energy developing this aspect of yourself—it'll balance out your highly mental way of dealing with the world. You're a spiritual seeker—meaning, you're always searching for higher points of meaning and ultimately are meant to get to know *yourself*—truly, madly, deeply. When you connect with your spirituality—no matter how you personally define that—you'll finally feel content and as though you're in your element.

Off-Track: Heady, aloof, and judgmental, you can default into lofty intellect and look down on the masses. You're highly sensitive and feel deeply, yet expressing emotions feels dangerous and like speaking a foreign language. You must work at expressing yourself, trusting others, and communicating clearly. You're often misunderstood because you lack a way to communicate both rational thought *and* emotional feelings. You flourish when you have time alone and yet must beware of cutting yourself off from others and becoming too withdrawn. Guard against self-absorption and stubbornness. Understand you often feel as though you're on another wavelength than most people—yet don't punish others for thinking differently than you. Ultimately, the gift resides in the marriage of intuitive awareness and rational thought.

8 Birth Day

8 | 17 | 26

Your Gift: Ambitious, practical and business-focused, you need material abundance in order to feel satisfied in life. Money is a focus, although it doesn't necessarily come easily or smoothly. You're gifted with management and organization and thrive in leadership roles. The 8 Birth Day is ambitious, goal-oriented, and enjoys a challenge. Status is something to strive toward—respect from the world is important to you. You enjoy being a connector—a person who knows the manager, the celebrity or the owner. You're innately competitive, wanting and demanding power, control, and are often an authority figure. The freedom that financial abundance can bring you is a driving force in your life.

Off-Track: Over-focused on work, domineering, and controlling, it's hard for you to balance the intensity that achievement in the material world brings to the table. You have little patience for weakness—either yours or anyone else's. Yet when pushed again and again, you might find yourself blaming everyone and everything for a lack of success or achievement. Know that the 8 Birth Day number demands that you develop a tough skin. Perseverance, resilience, fortitude, tenacity, and proper positive attitude are key to success or failure. The 8 Birth Day demands that you define what you will and will not do for money, what value it holds for you, and how to empower yourself in every part of your life. Ultimately, the gift resides in empowering yourself on every level, with an emphasis on your financial life.

9 Birth Day

9 | 18 | 27

Your Gift: Creative, philanthropic, and compassionate, your gift is to be of greater service to humanity as a whole in whatever way your talent and desire takes you. You have an ability to connect with people from all walks of life. The 9 Birth Day often sees a grander vision of the world through your idealistic lens, yet also are capable of inciting change and transformation on both local and international platforms. You understand early on that you have charisma and can make anything happen when you focus on it. You'll learn to accept a certain amount of limited rewards for all you do, and yet you do what you do because you can't *not* do it. That's the true gift you have to give to the world. You use your quirky sense of creative expression to flavor your Life Path purpose with selfless-service.

Off-Track: You're charming and have leadership potential, yet if you default into bitterness, cynicism, and negative attachments, you can lose track of your primary gift—which is to serve humanity and make people's lives better. You can become a fanatic, standing on your soap box and telling everyone what to do and how to do it, rather than working with others and listening to more productive solutions for specific problems. If you're myopic and self-serving—with a splash of arrogance—you've lost your way. Ultimately, the gift resides in selfless-service and finding proper creative outlets.

KARMIC DEBT NUMBERS

When you see a 13, 14, 16 or 19 in your numerology chart, these are called Karmic Debt numbers. People usually cringe when they see one or more of these numbers—after they find out they're called Karmic *Debt,* after all!

The Karmic Debt can also be referred to as a Testing Number, Warning Number or Hidden Number.

Here is how you might look at it. Our numerology in general indicates *karma*. Yet the Karmic Debt numbers offer a *specific indicator* that there have been infractions in a past life, so if you know what these infractions were, this knowledge is amazingly powerful.

Right up front, please understand that if this shows up for you, it doesn't mean that you're bad and it doesn't mean that you're being punished!

It offers a focused way to pin-point and balance karma you've accumulated. Knowing how the Karmic Debt numbers might affect you offers a way to understand why you might have intensified issues in certain key areas.

This is also a way to appreciate even more so if you have "paid your debt" or balanced your karma in this area. Meaning, you're doing your work if you can say: "Wow, I used to have a lot of problems with this and yet I really don't anymore. I've really come to terms with that aspect of my life or my behavior."

Basically, the Karmic Debt number indicates that you have a debt to pay in this lifetime for the actions you performed in a former lifetime. Karma is not a punishment! It's a universal law of cause and effect. When you see one of these numbers show up as one of the core numbers in your chart, it's a message that you're working with specific issues or infractions from a past life.

When you see a Karmic Debt number, it's telling you that you'll experience significant challenges or difficulties with a particular topic in your life. It'll depend on where it lands in your chart as to what the over-all effect might be. While this can be seen as a harsh "uh-oh!" it's actually really good to know that the struggles you're most likely experiencing over and over again can be given a name and a reason for being.

I see the Karmic Debt numbers as indicative of heightened opportunities to learn, grow, and connect with your ultimate purpose.

It's rather like having credit card debt. You have to decide to forgo that vacation, eating out or buying that expensive car because instead you have to use that money to incrementally pay off your credit card. If you don't pay it off, the debt keeps accumulating, the interest rate goes up, and the debt consumes your life. The collections service starts calling. The Repo Man shows up. You get the picture.

When you see a Karmic Debt number, it simply indicates that you must balance the coffers. Luckily, knowing the nature of the debt you're paying is a bonus and a positive thing. When you can identify and name it, you can embrace it and do something about it.

I also find that when you look at your whole numerology profile, it's uncanny how many times the number in which you gained your infraction shows up as a key number in your profile. For instance, perhaps you have a 13/4 Life Path and a 3 Birth Day, giving added emphasis to the energy and calling of the 3, which is where you had problems last time.

Or perhaps you have a Main Challenge that is a 3 or you have more than one Pinnacle Cycle guided by the number 3. *There is always going to be an additional emphasis on the energy of the number that's next to the 1.*

For the 13/4, an emphasis in the energy of the 3. For the 14/5, an emphasis in the energy of the 4. For the 16/7, an emphasis in the energy of the 6. And the 19/1, an emphasis in the energy of the 9.

I can't emphasize this enough: You're not bad. You're not being punished. You're simply paying back a debt and working in an additional way to balance karma. The great thing about having basic knowledge about where your particular Karmic Debt is located gives you a great advantage as you make efforts to understand some of the difficulties you experience and also why you might have certain feelings and underlying issues with particular areas of your life.

The purpose of this is to empower and provide cheerleading for you as you work to understand what's required in order to do well on your Karmic Debt test!

In numerology, there are two types of Karmic numbers—Karmic Debts and Karmic Lessons. Karmic lessons indicate what you must learn in this lifetime because you didn't have the opportunity to experience or master the lessons before. Karmic Lessons are indicated by the numbers (derived from the letters) that are missing in your name. *We aren't delving into Karmic Lessons in this book.*

Karmic Debts are totally different from Karmic Lessons. If we just think about the different weight the concepts of *lessons* have as opposed to *debts*. Different levels of intensity for sure! Karmic Debts hold more weight overall, while Karmic Lessons are less intense. Karmic Lessons feel more like a part of your environment while the Karmic Debt is part of your personality and purpose.

While Karmic Debt numbers can show up in a variety of places in your numerology profile, we're focusing on how to understand them when they show up as one of your core numbers.

An entire book could be written about the Karmic Debt numbers.

The next section offers a brief description of how you might begin to work with them. Also understand that if this description just doesn't sound anything like you (or who you think you are), then potentially you're at a stage of development and maturity in your life—and have been working diligently on your own personal growth and evolution—where you're more in alignment with the constructive elements of the Karmic Debt. If that describes you, then hats off! You've been doing your work. It never hurts to give yourself a pat on the back for a job well done.

The gift you're given by knowing that you have a Karmic Debt to pay is this: Rather than feeling victimized, you can see that this is something that you brought on yourself—despite the fact that you can't remember it. Not in a shameful way, rather in a mindful way where you simply take responsibility for yourself. If you exert the energy and commitment to working in the positive realm of the Karmic Debt, then you'll reap the benefits. The Karmic Debt can feel like you're the Phoenix—you must go through an intense reconstruction or regeneration process in order to come to terms with—and clear—your karmic slate.

KARMIC DEBT 19/1

The Karmic Debt 19/1 indicates that in a past life wisdom, power, and spiritual knowledge was used and abused for selfish personal gain. If you have a 19/1 as one of your core numbers, you're now paying back for past infractions where lack of compassion and higher-level abuse of power were your behaviors. The abuses you acted upon were issues based in the number 9—meaning that compassion, integrity, and humanitarian concern were abused or distorted.

Remember that the number 1 (in 19) always indicates *selfishness*. There was a hefty abuse of *power* and the actions involved were extremely self-centered and the abuse wasn't based in ignorance—it was calculated and you understood what you were doing.

If you have the 19/1 as one of your core numbers, you'll most likely act upon the more challenging tendencies of the number 1 until the lessons have been understood, acknowledged, acted upon, and mastered. Understand that you're being tested to really, truly, deeply master and embody the positive aspects of the number 1! It's like you're being asked to become the poster child for the highest and best of the number 1—including empowered leadership, healthy independence, creative innovation, and resilient self-confidence.

The trick is that it won't be easy. No, not at all. You'll get a throw-down in the realm of the lessons of the number 1 and you'll be called upon to work it in a conscious and consistent manner. The path of the number 1 is the "school of hard knocks" anyway. Add the 19 on top of it and it might then become apparent why you might feel as though you don't get much of a break or that you get the short end of the stick in your life, no matter how much effort you exert.

The number 1 is all about #1. This is a lifetime where you're being called upon to step into the *self* in a very real way. It's a lifetime of individuation, individuality, independence, initiation, leadership, and innovation. When you have the added energy of the Karmic 19, you'll find more distinct challenges in controlling and modulating the ego and can continue to operate in the world with a very self-interested focus—without even realizing it. You may assert yourself to the point of intimidation—again, without realizing the extent to which you present this energy to others. Those with the excessive qualities related to the number 1 often find that 1 can be the loneliest number.

Part of the over-all challenge with the 1 is in a healthy balance of self-confidence that allows you to be the pioneer you're meant to be while not being a bully and dictator in the process. The 1 struggles with that "devil on the shoulder"—the negative tape that plays in your head over and over again. This can be a deafening roar when you add the 19 to the mix, causing behaviors based in a lack of self-esteem to take precedence. This can include aggressive behaviors and stubbornness to the point of not accepting help or support.

In relationship, this can manifest as a more substantial inability to choose equal and healthy relationships. Often the 19/1 struggles with co-dependent relationships or the strident need to be the boss in relationships. Or on the other end of the spectrum, can be the one who is dominated by a partner. The ultimate expression of the challenged elements of the number 1 is to be *alone*—to be unavailable for others to be in relationship with you because of the intensity of your own sense of self-importance and lack of empathy.

The oppositional pull presents itself with great strength when you're working with the Karmic 19/1. Therefore, you can be met with issues related to the opposite of your purpose. Rather than forging ahead with healthy independence, you can succumb to heightened levels of dependence in your life. Rather than being the leader and the initiator, you lack the confidence to step into yourself and opt instead for cynicism, judgment, and victimization. Instead of taking the path of the leader, you default into lacking ambition and in many ways just can't stand on your own two feet. You can lack initiative and follow-through and find it baffling and frustrating that you aren't feeling a sense of purpose and fulfillment. Often alcohol or other drugs can come into play as band-aids for your feelings of frustration or inadequacy.

If you're willing to meet your challenge, you can shift your perspective and look at your obstacles as detours—if you can see that your goal is actually to embody the most optimal and positive potential of the number 1, then you're operating at your highest and best. Just know at the get-go that you'll have to work harder to get there. You won't think it's fair. And it probably isn't fair—yet if the Karmic 19/1 is present, remember that you have this debt to pay and part of the payment resides in a rockier and more challenged path.

As we look at the Karmic Debt 19/1, it's valuable to investigate the primary qualities of the 9, because the infraction in the Karmic Debt is based in this number. I find that you're being asked to infuse a lot of 9 energy into your 1—which is sometimes tricky, yet not at all impossible!

At the same time, the role of the innovative and independent-minded 1 is the primary purpose, yet there is a large dose of selfless-service, concern for humanity, and learning to flow with loss as you go along. If you have a Karmic Debt 19/1, it's imperative to inform yourself of the attributes of the number 9. This is your missing link to fulfillment.

If you have the 19/1 in your numerology profile, I hope you're starting to see how the Karmic Debt shows up for you personally. It's confusing because there's an arm-wrestle with a desire for independence and leadership of the 1, and yet the 9 also demands that you truly step outside your own ego and serve a higher humanitarian function. Those with the 19/1 Karmic Debt will find themselves drawn to using their leadership capabilities and creative talents for a humanitarian cause.

The 1 demands that you become the master of *self* and refine your ability to trust the unique, innovative ideas bubbling inside of you. It's about assertion and standing up for yourself. Yet the demands of the 9 are always the "partner in crime," making sure you use your creative genius and leadership abilities *for the greater good*. The 9 also brings a level of limited rewards for your efforts, yet let's be clear about what that means. It means that you'll be amply rewarded when you're devoted to doing what you're passionate about doing because you can't *not* do it. Follow your heart, not your ego.

Many times, I find people with the 19/1 have difficulty finding a balance between the giving nature of the 9 and the more self-oriented 1. The common denominator between the two "bookends" of energy (1 = self and 9 = others) is the off-the-beaten track, quirky creativity that's the gift and driving force. As if that isn't enough, remember that the debt being balanced here revolves around the misuse and abuse of power. The 19/1 will always be challenged with people, circumstances, and situations where *others will attempt to control or overpower you*. You'll be required to have a thick skin and not be detracted by the opinions of others—while also being open to constructive criticism! Many numerologists observe the one of the primary issues with the 19/1 is a stubborn refusal to accept help or advice.

Working with the Karmic Debt 19/1 intensifies the issues that relate to the number 1. It's not easy. It requires concerted effort and focused commitment. It's testing you and requiring that you rewire the way you work with leadership, the *self*, ego, achievement, and independence. The destructive path might feel more familiar since you've been there, done that. This time, you're being asked to extract yourself from riding in that same rut in the road—you're required to create a new way of working with these themes that have positive results for you and everyone around you.

KARMIC DEBT 13/4

The number 3 in the Karmic Debt 13/4 represents creative energy, expression, and joyfulness that turned into superficiality, irresponsibility, and using words to hurt others during a previous manifestation. If you have a 13/4 as one of your core numbers, understand that you're now paying back for past abuses where carrying your share of the workload and your share of personal responsibility was seriously abused.

The Karmic Debt 13/4 indicates that in a past life you were lazy, superficial, and didn't take personal responsibility for your actions (or inactions).

As a Karmic Debt number, the 13 indicates that putting the petal-to-the-metal and digging in with some hard work and ongoing effort will be an ongoing requirement in this lifetime. The 13/4 tells you that you're being asked to monitor and master the *art of positive expression*—and you can understand that as thinking before you speak, not being critical and judgmental, and using your words to support and uplift others rather than to tear them down.

I also say that the key element to the 13/4 Karmic Debt is to learn to whistle while you work! You'll always be the one carrying a bit more of the workload, so why not make the most of it?

You're also required to develop a strong sense of discipline and use responsible action in all practical matters. Remember that there can be complexities here that stem from different methods of calculation of the number 4 itself. Often the 13/4 can also be calculated as the Master 22/4. It depends on your preferred method of calculation as to the final outcome.

What does that mean, really? I find that it means that it's a judgment call on your part. You're the only person whose living your life experience. It's best if you school yourself on the Master 22/4 and also the Karmic Debt 13/4 to see what feels right to you. Yet overall, my stance is this: *You came in to master the entirety of the essence and actionability of the number 4!*

As we look at the Karmic Debt 13/4, it's valuable to investigate the primary qualities of the 3, because the infraction in the Karmic Debt is based in this number. I find that you're being asked to infuse a lot of 3 energy into your 4, which is sometimes tricky, yet not at all impossible! Yet it helps to understand your basic job description before you head to work, if you know what I mean.

If you have the 13/4 in your numerology profile, I hope you can see how the Karmic Debt shows up for you personally. It's confusing, because there's an arm-wrestle with a desire for the playfulness of the 3 and yet the 4 demands that you buckle down and stabilize yourself. The 3 demands that you refine your levels of communication and bring a lighter spirit to everything you do. Yet the demands of the 4 are always at the control panel, putting you through tests of endurance and making sure you take responsibility for your thoughts, feelings, and actions.

Many times, I find people with the 13/4 have difficulty finding the lighter elements in life. Or alternately, find that settling in and planting their personal "root system" is next to impossible to achieve. Health concerns can sometimes be part of the mix, with a demand to use self-discipline to eat well, get proper exercise, and to tune your mind with meditation and other brain-balancing practices.

Many 4s wrangle with ongoing (or on-and-off) health issues, often with a focus on lower back weakness, thyroid imbalances, food sensitivities, autoimmune and adrenal issues, and skin sensitivities. As if that isn't enough, you'll need to focus on your chosen task and not give up on it, no matter what kinds of obstacles cross your path. Fatigue and exhaustion are often the trademark of the 4—and the 13/4 is certainly no exception.

While this might sound like "*What?*"—here's the ultimate message: Your life's work is all about committing for the long-haul. The 4 is absolutely gifted at manifesting great things on every level, whether it's your organic garden, incredible photography or volunteer work. It can also show up as building a successful business, becoming an indispensable employee, devoted parent or famous celebrity. Often the 13/4 finds ultimate expression in media or entertainment.

With an emphasis on the 3, the 13/4 finds its niche when expressing through art, writing, presenting, teaching or any other form of positive expression. You're being asked to whistle what you work and bring a playful and creative energy into everything you do. Positive expression is mandatory!

Where others would give up and throw in the towel, you carry forward, taking the necessary steps, dealing with the issues, and commandeering other people's personalities in order to get the job done.

Working with a Karmic Debt number intensifies the issues that relate to that number. It's not easy. It requires concerted effort and focused commitment. It's testing you and requiring that you rewire the way you work with communication, process, stability, knowledge, and hard work. The destructive path will feel more familiar since you've been there, done that. This time, you're being asked to extract yourself from riding in that same rut in the road—you're required to create a new way of working with these themes that have positive results for you and everyone around you.

KARMIC DEBT 14/5

If you have a Karmic Debt 14/5 as one of your core numbers, you're now paying back for past abuses where you acted upon your personal and selfish sense of freedom at the expense of others. The number 4 in the 14/5 represents the dodging of hard work and avoidance of responsibility from a previous lifetime. The 4 is all about stability, security, and using step-by-step processes to reach goals—achieved through concerted effort and by leaning into responsibility.

The 14/5 indicates that there was a hefty abuse of freedom through irresponsibility and shunning any sense of stepping up, being accountable, and following through with effort and hard work. It also points to issues relating to excessive or addictive behaviors. The number 5 is the teacher of the constructive use of freedom—or freedom through self-discipline. It demands a clear and delineated understanding of the difference between *freedom* and *escape*.

Understand that the person who has the 14/5 as one of their core numbers will most likely act upon the more destructive tendencies of the number 5 until the lessons have been understood, acknowledged, acted upon, and mastered.

Now you're being asked to tap into moderation—a healthy sense of discipline, commitment, organization, and routine while also embodying the *fearless flyer* that the number 5 asks of you. You must understand that committing to some sense of structure and order will actually offer the real freedom you crave. Only then can you create a plan, set attainable goals, and gain focus and clarity. You can expect to face experiences that test you by handing you some emotionally upsetting situations and even frustrating delays. Your test is in sticking to your commitments no matter what's thrown in your way.

You can't retract and limit yourself by becoming rigid and negative—or by *giving up*. Your success resides in your ability to remain flexible yet disciplined, focused yet open to change. You achieve best results with you remain determined to do the work and engage in the step-by-step processes that allow you to create personal freedom.

Speaking of goals—even determining how to create a goal and then focus on it in a productive way can elude the 14/5. You can't blame others, bad luck or that it's "just the way I am" on your inability to move forward with success. It takes concerted effort, focus, and determination—yet your tendency will most likely be to feel that it's all taking far too much work and far too much time.

If you have the 14/5 in your numerology profile, I hope you're starting to see how the Karmic Debt shows up for you personally. It's confusing, because there's an arm-wrestle with a desire for the adventurousness of the 5 and yet the 4 also demands that you buckle down and stabilize yourself. The 5 demands that you truly embody the optimal expression of the sensual, social, freedom-loving 5. I'll stress this is neon: *Your ultimate task is to—on a day-to-day basis—use freedom in the most productive and constructive ways.*

The demands of the 4 need to be ingested into the overall mission of the 5, putting you through tests of endurance and making sure you take responsibility for your thoughts, feelings, and actions. Understand, though, that this is the highest and best of the expression of the number 5!

Many times, I find people with the 14/5 have difficulty finding the lighter elements in life. Or find that embracing their wild side is more difficult. Sometimes these issues can flip-flop in life, with the 5 starting out wild and wooly and then digressing into succumbing to restrictive circumstances (or vice versa). I find that you're being asked to infuse a lot of 4 energy into your 5, which is sometimes tricky, yet not at all impossible.

As if that isn't enough, you'll need to focus on your chosen task and not give up on it, no matter what kinds of obstacles cross your path. While this might sound like "Oh *come on!*"—here's the ultimate message: Your life's work is all about operating in the highest octave of the 5—which is true freedom achieved with self-discipline. Having an adventurous spirit, embracing changing circumstances, and enjoying the sensual side of life are also mandatory with this Karmic Debt. And doing it all while showing up on time, having a plan and routine, not flitting from thing to thing, and taking responsibility for yourself on every level.

The 5 is absolutely gifted at evaluating new opportunities, learning through experience, and living life to the fullest. When in your element, the 5 is fascinating, fun, socially inclined, and predictably unpredictable. The Karmic Debt brings added intensity to the need to either settle in and calm down—or alternately to lean into your fearless and adventurous nature.

Working with a Karmic Debt number intensifies the issues related to that number. It's not easy. It requires concerted effort and focused commitment. It's testing you and requiring that you rewire the way you work with the constructive use of freedom, adventure, fearlessness, taking others into consideration, and taking responsibilities seriously. The destructive path might feel much more comfortable since you've been there, done that. This time, you're being asked to extract yourself from riding in that same rut in the road—you're required to create a new way of working with these themes that have positive results for you and everyone around you.

KARMIC DEBT 16/7

The Karmic Debt 16/7 indicates the misuse of *love* in a previous lifetime. Some numerologists suggest that this Karmic Debt number also indicates that you'll be challenged with leveling your ego in this lifetime.

The Karmic 16/7 is a spiritual actualizer. You'll be presented with experience after experience where life seems to crumble, where you embrace humility and your sense of higher purpose—and experience "death and rebirth" from a variety of vantage points. The infractions were based in the elements of the number 6—love, duty, service, relationships, responsibility, and home-life.

If you have a 16/7 as one of your core numbers, you're now paying back for past abuses where you were involved in illicit love affairs or perverse forms of sexual expression which resulted in suffering to others. The 16/7 tells you that there has been a hefty abuse of love through acts of self-centeredness, irresponsibility, and a distortion of loving feelings. The message here is that you're learning to get your ego in check.

As we look at the Karmic Debt 16/7, it's valuable to investigate the primary qualities of the 6, because the infraction in the Karmic Debt is based in this number. I find that you're being asked to infuse a lot of 6 energy into your 7, which is sometimes tricky, yet not at all impossible. At the same time, the role of the introspective and soul-seeking 7 is the primary purpose—yet there's a distinct focus on duty, family obligation, desire for relationship, and necessity for you to shoulder more responsibility as you go along.

I've found that most 16/7s have a much greater focus on family and relationships than "regular" 7s. This can be with intimate relationships and children, yet also with siblings, parents, and relatives. Since we're already talking about past lives, I would like to briefly discuss that aspect of the Karmic 16/7. Of all the Karmic Debt numbers, I find the 16/7 to be the most layered.

I'll make a professional observation (take it or leave it!) that many 16/7's experienced a traumatic death in a past life that comes up as a major point of processing and healing in this current lifetime. I credit my friend and colleague Kari Samuels with this observation that I have also found to have merit with the clients I've worked with who have a 16/7 in their numerology profile. I mention this in order to confirm or validate this possibility if you have a 16/7 and struggle with some inexplicable issues. Which is to say, the 16/7 receives tremendous benefits from doing past-life regression therapy, family constellations work or other forms of past-life clearing. This kind of therapeutic work would be a great place for any 16/7 to begin on their road to healing past-life trauma.

I've worked with 16/7s who are fearful that they're not paying back their Karmic Debt if they aren't married and living in a house with a white picket fence. I feel that the true issue is this: The Karmic Debt is not about having a traditional family and long-term marriage. It's about reaching a trust and comfort in yourself and your place in the spiritual and material world. How do you love? How do you take responsibility? How do you come to the table with family and relationship dynamics?

If you choose to be single, the Karmic Debt is being paid when you choose to nurture or mentor others, to offer your wisdom to help others, and when you feel comfortable in your own skin while also truly tapping into higher spiritual consciousness. I've worked with 16/7s who say that they try to be in relationships and yet it's a struggle to prioritize it. When met with a challenge, the 16/7 often reverts inward when their partner needs and wants them to reach out and open themselves to emotional support. This is often a point of great vulnerability and resistance. The 16/7 usually would much rather go it alone than to trust and rely on someone else to hold space for them, not to mention expose their painful emotions.

Many 16/7s experience heightened issues in the love and relationship department, including betrayal in some way, shape or form. This ranges from mild to dramatic, yet can show up as being in relationships where the 16/7 can't commit or ends up having sexual or emotional affairs. This can also come back to the 16/7 with their partner being unfaithful. Join the world, right? Yet this can be something that happens more commonly as the 16/7 works at balancing the Karmic Debt. It can also show up as losing friendships suddenly or unexpectedly, often because of the 16/7s inability to express themselves emotionally or because of a misunderstanding.

Remember, part of the process with the 16/7 is the *leveling of ego*, yet what does that really mean specifically? Sometimes it's a matter of being involved in a dysfunctional relationship for an extended period of time, with the experience offering you a plethora of opportunity to work on your ability to express, communicate, and make a clear decision about what you're willing to put up with (and not put up with) in a relationship.

Sometimes it's all about embracing the reality that you honestly don't want or need a traditional intimate partnership (or children) and to be settled and all right with that choice. The trouble comes in when you try to force a relationship when that isn't really what you desire, thinking you're somehow failing if you don't. I've known 16/7s who are truly connected with their intuition and spirituality who see their connections with people generally and with romantic partners specifically—as a working through of karma. This is a point of empowerment rather than a point of confusion or frustration.

I also want to emphasize that there is a huge and constant pull for the 16/7 to be involved in relationships and the 16/7 tends to take on more of the characteristics of the 6—with a propensity to prioritize home, family, and taking added responsibilities within those relationships.

A 16/7 friend of mine is a psychic, energy worker, and has gone in and out of relationships with the strong trust that each one of them is placed in her path (and she in theirs) to learn and heal. Of course, she didn't start out with such confidence in these matters. Which isn't to say that the 16/7 isn't allowed to have a traditional relationship or happy long-term relationship! It simply means that the key for the 16/7 is to trust and follow the inner calling, even when (or especially when) it makes no logical or rational sense.

Your life's work is all about following your inner voice and exploring the depths of the cosmos, while somehow being okay with having to do it in a human body on planet earth. The 16/7s trajectory is slow and process-oriented. It's a beautiful walk through the world where you get to poke and prod, find what piques your interest and passion, and become a wise expert in your field.

Can you have fun along the way rather than constantly feeling out of place, disjointed or off-track? You'll be met with many opportunities to start again, to revise yourself and your outlook on life, and reconfigure your identity as you learn and grow spiritually. The 16/7 has a quiet force, an underlaying intensity and an intuitive link to people, animals, and other elements.

The challenge is in coming to terms with impermanence and finding comfort in the times in your life in which you prefer solitude over social engagement. The key to balancing the Karmic Debt is in flowing with the process of destruction and rebirth. Opportunity presents itself for accelerated spiritual growth.

Working with a Karmic number intensifies the issues that relate to that number. It's not easy. It requires concerted effort and focused commitment. It's testing you and requiring that you rewire the way you work with trust, relationships, spirituality, intuition, and humility. The destructive path will feel more familiar since you've been there, done that. This time, you're being asked to extract yourself from riding in that same rut in the road—you're required to create a new way of working with these themes that have positive results for you and everyone around you.

Maturity

This indicates the CULMINATION OF YOUR LIFE PATH & DESTINY/EXPRESSION.

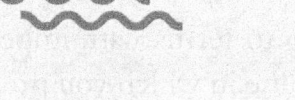

This is your ultimate destination.

This is the combination of your purpose & how you'll go about achieving that purpose.

THE MATURITY NUMBER

Getting older is inevitable. Numerologically speaking, we trust that gaining maturity is a beautiful and rich process that blends the power and potential of your Life Path number and brings it into alignment and balance with your Expression/Destiny number. The energy related to this number kicks in when we arrive into our 40s and beyond.

I find it somewhat humorous that with numerology, everything has a precise calculation—*except for the Maturity number*. The influence of this number appears to happen incrementally, segueing in more directly from the age of 35 – 50. This is when it begins to be felt and to gain traction.

As you traverse your life's path, your Maturity number provides you with a final point of destination. It's where you're headed, whether you know it or not. Usually, it comes as a *midlife message* which can feel like a crisis, changing/transformation point or a settling down.

In many ways, the Maturity number indicates the nature of your true self—an ultimate goal and encompassing mission. It distinctly guides and informs the second portion of your life.

Most numerologists agree that the impact of this number is in full force by the time you reach the age of 50 and continues to influence and guide you for the rest of your life. The gift of this additional energy is that suddenly you feel that you don't have the time nor patience to waste on things that aren't moving you toward this ultimate goal, whatever that may be for you individually.

You calculate the Maturity Number (also called the Reality or Realization Number) by adding your Life Path number and your Destiny/Expression number together.

If you have an 8 Life Path and a 2 Destiny or Expression, you'd add it like this:

8 + 2 = 10

10: 1 + 0 = 1

In this example, you'd show a 1 Maturity number.

What's also interesting about knowing your Maturity number is that sometimes it's in harmony with your numerology profile and sometimes—*not so much*. There can be *ease* or *friction* that you can experience if you have conflicting energies or if there's an overabundance of the energy presented by your Maturity number. Sometimes, it's not just hormones—*ha-ha!*

The Maturity number points to the *true you*—an amalgam of your Life Path and Expression/Destiny as a point of destination. I find that it has an underlying influence on our thoughts and actions as we reach into our 40s and beyond. It indicates your true power and your highest form of evolution.

Like always, as you become more seasoned and practiced with the numbers 1 - 9, you can begin to plug in the information whenever it shows up. The information for the Maturity number is no exception.

MATURITY NUMBER DEFINITIONS

1 Maturity

You're moving toward reevaluating what it means to be independent and stand on your own two feet. You're being called upon to take initiative, to be a leader, and to take creative risks toward achievement in any realm you feel passionate about. With this Maturity number, there's often a shift in life bringing issues related to *independence* onto center stage. Situations arise highlighting your sense of dependence or independence, your ability to connect and relate with others, and whether or not you behave in a dominating and controlling manner. This might look like a strong need to break free of dependent situations, evaluation of self-centered behaviors or a financial situation may change dramatically. Optimally, this is a stage of life where independence, innovation, and achievement can be experienced and enjoyed.

2 Maturity

You're moving toward reevaluating what it means use your sensitivity to the benefit of both yourself and others. You're being called upon to use diplomacy, to involve yourself with group dynamics, and to open yourself to healthy, balanced relationships. With this Maturity number, there's often a shift in life bringing issues related to *sensitivity* onto center stage. Situations arise highlighting your sense of yourself in relationship to others—meaning that you develop a strong sense of yourself without needing outside approval. This includes modulating over-sensitivity and contributing to healthy relationships. This might look like a need to understand the ways in which you've been *insensitive* to others—including an evaluation of self-centered behaviors. This can also present as a desire to contribute to something greater than yourself through group effort or the need to stop being taken advantage of by others. Optimally, this is a stage of life where friends, family, and group activity can be experienced and enjoyed.

Master 11/2 Maturity

The Master numbers always indicate a higher sense of spiritual purpose—no matter how you define it—plus more intense challenges. *You're moving toward* an extended period of spiritual evolution and illumination. You're being called upon to use diplomacy, to involve yourself with group dynamics, and to open yourself to relationships. *Plus* you'll spar with ego, being an introverted extrovert, and being called toward leadership. With this Maturity number, there's often a shift in life bringing issues related to sensitivity, artistic creativity, and overcoming obstacles to center stage. Challenges reside in the intensity in which you experience life, in the ways in which you'll be put to the test over and over again in the realms of personal challenges—along with physical and emotional sensitivity. Optimally, this is a stage of life where spiritually-based empowerment can be experienced and enjoyed.

3 Maturity

You're moving toward reevaluating what it means to be creative, expressive, and full of life. You're being called upon to step into your creativity, enjoy socializing, and express yourself with positive and artful communication. With this Maturity number, there's often a shift in life bringing issues related to *creativity and expression* onto center stage. Situations arise highlighting your sense of joy and enthusiasm, communication on all levels, and social interaction. This might look like breaking free of repression and expressing through artistic creativity—writing, performing, presenting, anything that uses creative self-expression. You have permission to *play* more! This can also present as an expansive sense of joy and purpose or debilitating emotional ups and downs. This Maturity number points to ease, luck, and abundance in your latter years when you're in alignment with your creative expression. Optimally, this is a stage of life where travel, inspired communication, and creative self-expression can be experienced and enjoyed.

4 Maturity

You're moving toward reevaluating what it means to work with limitation and yet garner deeply gratifying rewards for your efforts. You're being called upon to work diligently to reach practical goals, develop systems and processes that help you reach your desires outcomes, and to leave something of lasting value in the world. The power of organization and systematic thinking is key. With this Maturity number, there's a shift in life bringing issues related to *limitation and effort* to center stage. Situations arise highlighting your sense of adopting optimistic yet practical step-by-step processes to get where you want to be, understanding where you get in your own way by being rigid and dogmatic, and to understand the difference between managing and micromanaging. This can be a very satisfying time of life where you feel solid, secure, and settled. This may present itself where you experience events requiring that you examine the ways in which are overly responsible or irresponsible, as well as an evaluation of self-defeating behaviors based in feelings of restriction and limitation. This might also be a time where you take a look at the ways in which you have either been unable to commit to work or home life—which has led to undesirable outcomes—or the ways in which you have been a slave to work that has felt unsatisfying to you. Optimally, this is a stage of life where career or work, family, and knowledge-seeking can be experienced and enjoyed.

Master 22/4 Maturity

The Master numbers always indicate a higher sense of spiritual purpose no matter how you define it, plus more intense challenges. *You're moving toward* reevaluating what it means to make things happen on a grand scale. You're being called upon to be a manager and a leader, to root yourself in spiritual principles and practical know-how, and to help people live better lives on a practical, day-to-day basis. *Plus* you'll spar with stubbornness, being opinionated and sometimes rigidly dogmatic in your approach, and also engage as a high-level master builder or master teacher. With this Maturity number, there's often a shift in life bringing issues related to overcoming limitation, getting out of your own way (thinking outside the box), and striking a balance between work and self-care to center stage. Challenges reside in the intensity in which you experience life, in the ways in which you'll be put to the test over and over again in the realms of physical challenges, choosing security over taking a calculated risk, and opting for defeat over tenacious endurance. Optimally, this is a stage of life where pursuits leading to contributing practical knowledge to the world on a grand scale can be experienced and enjoyed.

5 Maturity

You're moving toward reevaluating what it means to gain multiple levels of freedom in your life. You're being called upon to work with the constructive creation of freedom, living a life filled with travel and adventure, and embracing a life of progressive change and flexibility—laced with some uncertainty. With this Maturity number, there's often a shift in life bringing issues related to the *disciplined use of freedom* onto center stage. Situations arise highlighting excessive behaviors and the ability to deal with changes productively. Versatility and vivacious and tactile living are highlighted. This might look like an abrupt change in life leading to an evaluation of your sense of freedom. This is a time where you'll evaluate the ways in which you have or have not used a focused approach to getting what you want in life. This can also present as a time where you display an inability to rein in excessive behaviors with food, alcohol, drugs, sex or other behaviors that control or distract you in a non-productive manner. Optimally, this is a stage of life where travel, change, and progress can be experienced and enjoyed.

6 Maturity

You're moving toward reevaluating what it means to nurture others—and family becomes an important focal point at this time. You're being called upon to work with love and service to others, to delight in home and family, and to develop deep compassion and affection. With this Maturity number, there's a shift in life bringing issues related to *modulating responsibility* to center stage. Situations arise highlighting self-righteousness or meddling behaviors, the strength of your intimate relationships and friendships, and in your ability and desire to provide compassionate service to others. This Maturity number points to financial freedom through marriage or inheritance, allowing for a comfortable and sometimes luxurious latter part of life. The focus during this time is on your involvement in home and family—with grandchildren, friends, and family of choice. This can hold opportunities for involvement in artistic creativity, counseling or any sort of mentoring, the healing arts, tutoring or other service to your community. Optimally, this is a stage of life where home, family, and a full-spectrum enjoyment of life can be experienced and enjoyed.

Master 33/6 Maturity

The Master numbers always indicate a higher sense of spiritual purpose—no matter how you define it, plus more intense challenges. The Master Maturity 33/6 is rare and only appears with the combination of an 11/2 and 22/4 Life Path and Destiny/Expression for a combined total of 33. *You're moving toward* reevaluating what it means use your extraordinary spiritual gifts to the benefit of humanity. You're being called upon to use compassionate service, duty and nurturing, and loving and joyful creativity. *Plus* you'll spar with ego, learn not to be hyper-responsible, and be called toward leadership. With this Maturity number, there's a shift in life bringing issues related to *co-dependence, balanced responsibility or severe emotional sensitivity* to center stage. Challenges reside in the intensity in which you experience life, in the ways in which you'll be put to the test over and over again in the realms of relationship challenges, stifling perfectionism, and carrying the weight of the world on your shoulders. Optimally, this is a stage of life where heart-felt service and high levels of creativity can be experienced and enjoyed.

7 Maturity

You're moving toward reevaluating what it means to live a life of introspection, study, and spiritual contemplation. You're being called upon to work with your deep need to *know thyself* through scientific study or philosophical thought, solitude, and spiritual growth. With this Maturity number, there's a shift in life bringing issues related to *truth-seeking* to center stage. Situations arise highlighting the need for isolated time to yourself, research or writing, and the search for inner peace and spiritual fulfillment. This can look like a personal crisis that demands a reevaluation of your beliefs. During this period, you might make a choice to be uncoupled or clearly define agreements around your need for solitude and contemplation. This can be a time where you share scientific breakthroughs, spiritual awareness or psychological insights with others. Optimally, this is a stage of life where spiritual study, contemplation, and wisdom can be cultivated, experienced, and enjoyed.

8 Maturity

You're moving toward reevaluating what it means to work with reward through accomplishment. You're being called upon to work with your talents with organization and management, to achieve financial success and recognition, and to use authority wisely and well. With this Maturity number, there's a shift in life bringing issues related to *achievement and empowerment* onto center stage. Situations arise highlighting the need to direct and lead, to pursue financial reward and abundance, and to work for the benefit of humanity—not just personal gain. This is a time where business takes precedence over relationships. Opportunities to engage in the larger realm of business or any arena where you're called upon to lead, manage, and organize. This can present as a dramatic change in career or vocation mixed with the desire to put aside personal relationships in order to focus on work and career. This doesn't mean you won't be involved in relationship or marriage, yet the business aspect is high priority. During this time, you'll evaluate the ways you have or haven't stepped into your power. Optimally, this is a stage of life where financial success, personal empowerment, and high-level achievement can be experienced and enjoyed.

9 Maturity

You're moving toward reevaluating what it means to work with selfless-service to humanity. You're being called upon to work with giving and contributing without thought of personal reward—letting go of *self* in order to learn to be of service to others—and to learn not to attach to particular outcomes. With this Maturity number, there's often a shift in life bringing issues related to *balance the needs of others with your own personal desires* to center stage. Situations arise highlighting your need to devote yourself to a higher need or purpose, to delve into a spiritual path in full force, and to use your extraordinary talents to heal, perform, write, teach or be a philanthropist. This may look like dealing with loss on many levels in order to surrender to your spiritual path. There can be a stripping away of identity, resulting in opportunities for deep personal transformation. There can be a realization that self-centeredness and lack of understanding others' perspectives feels dissatisfying and derailing. Forgiveness of self and others is a cornerstone of this Maturity number. Opportunities arise to be of service and use your compassion and creativity to make the world a better place. Optimally, this is a stage of life where selfless-service, deep levels of compassion, creativity, and international travel and relations can be experienced and enjoyed.

YOUR NUMEROLOGY PROFILE AS YOUR LIFE SCRIPT

In many ways, we can see our numerology chart as our Life Script. As we determine and outline how to map your path and purpose with numerology, it's clarifying to stop for a moment and create your Life Script from your core numbers. We can see the flow and overall plot-line through our cycles and other elements of time. We can understand our personality profile—or what I call your *purpose profile*—and basic character through our Life Path, Expression/Destiny, Soul Urge, Personality, Birth Day, Maturity, and so on.

Mapping your path and purpose is supported when you understand who's driving the vehicle! Since I have a theatre background, I find it illuminating to conceptualize it as your Life Script. You're the lead character in your story. As you traverse life, you're creating this incredible one-of-a-kind story that's an epic road trip!

While one can certainly just *kinda-sorta'* show up and bumble through their role within the story (life), certainly the chances for an engaging—if not award-winning—performance can be enhanced with research, study, analysis, and focus. Seeing how your Life Script can be mapped out and understood is an exceptional tool for verifying and charting your course.

One of the ways to analyze a role with a script is to break each line into actionable and active verbs—"I want *to hurt* this person. "I want *to earn* his trust." "I want *to prove* my love." That sort of thing.

Numerology allows you to define and hone in on the key elements and themes (actionable verbs) that are vital elements to your performance in life. Then you can dig deeper and make a decision about what you feel the character's through-line of action might be. This is the *one thing* that drives your character. It's the *one thing* that's the underlying motivation for everything you say and do with the world of the play or within the world that is your life.

And as Shakespeare observes: "Life is a stage and all the men and women merely players." There is great value in making decisions about the *through line of action* that becomes the guiding principle to your personal success and happiness.

The primary goal I have for you as you read this book is to walk away with simple, effective ways to begin to put all this barrage of numerology information together that makes some kind of cohesive sense!

People will often also say that they wish they'd known about numerology *a long time ago* because it would have made their lives a lot more productive and feel a lot more in alignment with their real purpose and passion. Then the question I get again and again is: "Now that I know my numbers and have learned a little bit about numerology, what do I do with it? What's next? How do I actually *use* the information?"

While it's challenging to come up with *one word* that's at the heart of each of the numbers 1-9, here's a way of distilling the core driver for each of the numbers. Remember that these mix-and-match given your unique chart.

THROUGH LINE OF ACTION... BY NUMBER

1: ACHIEVEMENT. The driving force for the number 1 is *"I want to achieve and I want to do it my own way."*

2: LOVE. The driving force for the number 2 is *"I want to love and to be loved in return."*

3: EXPRESSION: The driving force for the number 3 is *"I want to express myself, be heard, and understood."*

4: RESULTS. The driving force for the number 4 is *"I want results and a sense of accomplishment from everything I do."*

5: EXPERIENCE. The driving force for the number 5 is *"I want to experience everything in life with the fullest amount of freedom possible."*

6: TO BE OF USE. The driving force for the number 6 is *"I want to help, support, and nurture."*

7: MEANING. The driving force for the number 7 is *"I want to know why and how."*

8: POWER. The driving force for the number 8 is *"I want to be powerful, respected, and influential."*

9: COMPASSION. The driving force for the number 9 is *"I want the world to be a better place."*

Sometimes cutting to the chase and seeing the core to what drives us, triggers us, challenges us, and brings us happiness and satisfaction takes some concerted effort and a deep desire to perform your role in life to the best of your ability. Knowing what you're after—*exactly what you want*—is a powerful tool to actually getting it.

MAPPING YOUR NUMEROLOGY LIFE SCRIPT

You might write your own synopsis like this. Fill in the blanks with your corresponding number's keyword to see how your numerology script plays out.

My Life's Purpose is *insert Life Path number*.

The way in which I'll go about *insert Life Path* is with *insert Destiny/Expression number*.

My soul's calling is centered around *insert Soul Urge number*.

While I realize that others see me as primarily as *insert Personality number*, a secondary gift I have to give to the world is my *insert Birth Day number*.

As I evolve and mature, I'm heading toward *insert Maturity number*.

As an example, let's say this is your profile:

Life Path	4
Expression/Destiny	9
Soul Urge	2
Personality	8
Birth Day	3
Maturity	13/4

The way in which I'll go about <u>producing tangible results with whatever I do</u> *(4 Life Path)* is with <u>compassion by making the world a better place in whatever way I can</u> *(9 Destiny/Expression)*.

My soul's calling is centered around <u>giving and receiving unconditional love</u> *(2 Soul Urge)*.

<u>While I realize that others see me as primarily as an achiever</u> *(8 Personality)*, a secondary gift I have to give to the world is my sense of joyful self-expression *(3 Birth Day)*.

As I evolve and mature, I'm heading toward <u>basking in the results of my hard work while adding a dose of lightness and creativity to the mix</u> *(13/4 Maturity)*.

NUMEROLOGY & CYCLES OF TIME

Numerology offers a plethora of information about our lives. Along with our *purpose profile*, we can define and gauge cycles of time we'll experience during our lifetimes. This flows from the macrocosmic (Universal Year) to the microcosmic (our individual Personal Years, Pinnacles, and so forth).

While there's certainly no crystal ball, knowing the constitution of your cycles of time offers a powerful way to map out the building blocks of your life and to understand the environments in which you find yourself.

In this section, we'll discuss some of the key cycles of time numerology defines for us. Understand that we won't discuss some of what I consider to be the more advanced segments of time—like the Planes of Expression, Bridge numbers, Essence Cycle or Transits. While there's a whole world of information to be gleaned by knowing these cycles, this guide is purposefully directed at providing the basics in a way that hopefully won't be absolutely overwhelming.

Again, if your interest is piqued and you would like to explore advanced levels of numerology knowledge with these other cycles, please refer to the resource list at the end of this book.

THE UNIVERSAL YEAR

One of the reasons you simply can't resist making New Year's Resolutions is because you're feeling a very real, very profound shift in energy from one year to the next. By the numbers, it's undeniable.

The Universal Year is like the landscape or terrain you're driving through all year long and is calculated by adding the numbers of the current year together. You can think of the Universal Year as the state or country you're driving through on your yearly road trip.

A Universal Year means that *everyone on the planet* will be feeling the energy related to a particular number during the entire year.

You calculate the Universal Year by simply adding the numbers in the current year (let's use 2025 as an example) together like this:

$2025 = 2 + 0 + 2 + 5 = 9$

In this example, the Universal Year is 9.

All of us begin feeling this energy starting January 1 and it'll end on December 31 of the same year.

Here are the basic themes for the Universal Year Cycles. We can look at the definitions for the Personal Year Cycle and apply that information to understand the energies inherent in the Universal Year Cycles. They contain the same themes—the difference is that it applies to *everyone globally* as the over-all energy or climate we find ourselves navigating during the year.

The best way to conceptualize the energy of the Universal Year is to step back and look at the bigger global picture. What are the key political issues and how are they being addressed? How are international relations playing out and what current issues show up as a priority? What are the trends, incidents, and issues capturing media attention on a global level?

UNIVERSAL YEAR THEMES

1 Universal Year: *Everyone on the planet is immersed in energy related to* action, initiation, leadership, individuality, individuation, and finding a healthy and balanced level of independence.

Possible potholes: Self-absorption, narcissism, default to cynicism and judgment.

2 Universal Year: *Everyone on the planet is immersed in energy related to* patience, peace, diplomacy, mediation, interest in positive group outcomes, service to group dynamics, perfecting one-on-one relationships, authentic connection, and working together with a loving attitude.

Possible potholes: Impatience, emotional over-sensitivity, childish combativeness.

3 Universal Year: *Everyone on the planet is immersed in energy related to* self-improvement, creativity of all kinds, optimism, self-expression, authentic emotional communication, and travel. Performance and media take on new importance.

Possible potholes: Procrastination, depression, self-doubt, unchecked expression.

4 Universal Year: *Everyone on the planet is immersed in energy related to* hard work, goal setting, sharpening skill sets, knowledge building, systematizing, foundation setting, and teaching.

Possible potholes: Laziness, lack of focus, over-work, rigid viewpoints, disintegration of foundations in order to start anew.

5 Universal Year: *Everyone on the planet is immersed in energy related to* fun, fearlessness, adventure, travel, sensuality, self-indulgence, and change.

Possible potholes: Excess, escape or avoidance, fear, scattered focus, restriction.

6 Universal Year: *Everyone on the planet is immersed in energy related to* relationships, responsibility, home and family, justice, visionary pursuits, and a renewed commitment to beautifying surroundings.

Possible potholes: Heightened sense of judgment mixed with self-importance, non-productive perfectionism, irresponsible or overly responsible behavior.

7 Universal Year: *Everyone on the planet is immersed in energy related to* spiritual seeking, study, taking care of health, and spiritual growth. This is a time of internal contemplation, not a period to focus solely on financial concerns.

Possible potholes: Avoidance through superficial activities, over-analysis, feelings of frustration, and mistrust.

8 Universal Year: *Everyone on the planet is immersed in energy related to* money, finances, personal power, control, and authority.

Possible potholes: Financial loss or gain (or both), intense testing in the arenas of empowerment and money, feelings of victimization, aggressive reactions, and issues surrounding ethical behavior.

9 Universal Year: *Everyone on the planet is immersed in energy related to* surrender, loss, letting go, completions, transition, transformation, dreams coming true, focus on compassion and humanity as a whole.

Possible potholes: Hanging on to what needs to be released, overwhelm, emotional distress.

THE PERSONAL YEAR CYCLE

In numerology, we believe we experience nine-year periods of time called Personal Year Cycles. I call knowing your Personal Year number *knowing the theme to your party*. You don't want to show up at the wrong party in the wrong outfit for an entire year! *(seriously . . . !)*

We all feel this shift in energy, don't we? We get restless toward the end of the year, as the New Year's Resolution frenzy get underway. Numerologically speaking, there's a very real energetic transition that happens for each of us from year to year.

We feel this energy whether or not we understand numerology—or even believe in numerology. When you learn the theme to each Personal Year, you can align with the energy of the year rather than push against it. Know your theme and you'll find that you have much more success throughout the year. Or at least you'll be able to extract deeper meaning about why things are happening and how to make sense out of it.

Also note that the Personal Year Cycle runs from January 1 – December 31 (*not from birthday to birthday*), even though I find that the energy related to your Personal Year intensifies around your birthday. It also comes to a crescendo during the month of September.

Please be aware that some numerologists calculate the Personal Year to run from birthday to birthday.

It's up to you to decide which school of thought you feel is correct. When I refer to the Personal Year, I'm referring to a start of January 1 and an ending on December 31.

Remember also, when you're in a Personal Year that has the same number as your Life Path, you'll feel double indemnity from the slings and arrows of the year—you're going to feel all the positives doubly. This also means that you're going to be doubly challenged with the obstacles inherent in the year's theme.

When you experience a Personal Year that is the same as your Life Path number (or another of your core numbers), the year offers you many experiences and opportunities to bolster where you might have a weak link that needs strengthening within that particular theme. This simply might show up as more intensity or more dramatic occurrences or experiences that revolve around the key themes of your year.

For instance, say you have a 4 Life Path and you're in a 4 Personal Year. The key themes would be: getting serious about yourself and your life, creating and building foundations for yourself, clarifying and determining longer-range goals, working hard and smart, dealing with family issues, and moving through limitations. Depending on what's up for you personally as a 4 Life Path will determine the intensity and focus that comes at you during your 4 Personal Year. Let's say you're in your early 30s and you're struggling to decide on a career. The 4 Personal Year will bring this issue to the front of the line and demand that you step up and take control of this key element of your 4 Life Path purpose.

Let's say you're in your 20s. The 4 Personal Year for the 4 Life Path might bring you face to face with the need to snap out of it and get a reality check. Are you wandering aimlessly through life? Can't decide on a college major or a career path? Feeling frustrated because you work so hard for little gain? Or perhaps this is the time where you finally are forced to get your butt in gear, get off the couch, stop detouring around your responsibilities, and shape up or ship out!

The energies of the year manifest opportunities under the guise of challenges. Perhaps you get fired, which means you have to get real about deciding on another job that's more in alignment with your passions. Maybe you have a health crisis that makes you settle down and get real about what you're doing and how you're doing it. The experiences of the year offer a crash-course on a particular aspect within the thematic of the number.

I'm continuously fascinated by the accuracy numerology provides on every level. This section is designed to offer you some points of balance as you navigate your year. The exciting thing is that when we can frame our experience and anchor ourselves with the information, what could feel random and punitive pivots into *meaning and purpose.*

Calculate the Personal Year

EXAMPLE:

Take the date of birth:

November 11, 1990

Use only the MONTH and DAY

November is 11

11 is a Master number and isn't reduced.

Day is 11

11 is a Master number and isn't reduced

Then use the CURRENT YEAR

Let's use 2025 in this example as the current year.

2025 = 2 + 0 + 2 + 5 = 9

Now add the month, day, and current year together

11 + 11 + 9 = 31 and 3 + 1 = 4

In this example, you're experiencing a 4 Personal Year

PERSONAL YEAR 1

HIGH-POWERED YEAR MARKED BY YOUR DETERMINATION & INITIATIVE.

NEW BEGINNINGS & PLANTING SEEDS

WHAT DO I WANT TO SEE GROW AND BLOSSOM IN THE NEXT 9 YEARS?

THE GOAL: TO STAND ON YOUR OWN TWO FEET AS YOU BEGIN AN ENTIRELY NEW CHAPTER IN YOUR LIFE.

BRING IT ON	EXPECT
CREATIVITY	DOUBT
LEADERSHIP	TUNNEL VISION
INDEPENDENCE	DEPENDENCY
CONFIDENCE	STOPS-AND-STARTS
NEW STARTS	GOING SOLO
ALIGN WITH YOUR AMBITION	CO-CREATE!
STAND UP FOR YOURSELF	APPRECIATE OTHERS
TRUST & USE YOUR SKILLS	BANISH YOUR INNER VICTIM
OPENING TO HEALTHY EXPRESSIONS OF LOVE	BE ASSERTIVE, NOT AGGRESSIVE
SUPPORTING OTHERS	BALANCE THE EGO
KEEPING THE PEACE	CREATIVE PROBLEM SOLVING

1 PERSONAL YEAR

This is a year of new beginnings, independence, initiation and achievement. It holds more clarity than last year and serves as the start of a new nine-year cycle. The energy of the 1 Personal Year can be felt as a genesis—an absolutely new beginning if you're ready and willing to take the plunge. It's time to plant the seeds for what you want to see grow and mature over the next nine years. This is the final push of a three-year transition cycle (Personal Years 8-9-and now 1). You might be a bit fatigued at this point. But don't throw up your hands now! These next twelve months are very important, so don't waste them with frivolous activities or useless relationships.

The 1 can be a somewhat lonely year, where you feel that a lot rests on your shoulders and only you can get it done—without help from others. And while that's true, there's a huge difference between solitary pursuits based in healthy independence and being *alone*. Right now, *independence* is your mantra. This is the year to begin with as much of a clean slate as you possibly can. If any unfinished business is left over from your transitional 9 Personal Year, those loose ends need to be concluded (or at least acknowledged!) before you can fully engage in the magic of the initiating 1 energy.

A woman I know left a long-term relationship in her 9 Personal Year and wanted to have her hands washed of all involvement with her ex by her 1 Personal Year. Yet it didn't quite work out that way! They had some business-related entanglements that ended up extending well into the 1 Personal Year and beyond, much to her dismay. The important thing to observe from a numerology standpoint is that she *broke it off* during the 9 Personal Year (endings) and started a new cycle in her 1 Personal Year, with the intention to start anew.

She found herself standing at a threshold: a door closed behind her and a new vista laid out in front of her waiting to be explored. She did everything humanly possible to finalize the obligations with her ex while also focusing on creating her new life and applying a fresh commitment to her own business. Even though she wasn't fully and completely done with her ex until a few years later, that didn't negate the intent, energy, and action she initiated to get things moving in a different direction throughout the 1 Personal Year. That is the profound truth of a *new beginning*.

I use this story as an illustration, because often we frustrate ourselves when we look at this as a black and white scenario. She didn't *fail* at her 1 Personal Year because she still needed to deal with surprising leftovers from her break-up. She would surely have preferred a clean break—*and did everything in her power to create it*. Yet there were issues she couldn't predict.

During your 1 Personal Year you'll be challenged with stepping into your individuality and manifesting your independence. The more you can connect with the unique, off-the-beaten path aspects of yourself, the more successful you'll be. This year, the true you aches to come to the microphone and take center stage. Who *are* you? What's next?

There will be failures, according to your presumptions of how things should go, yet the year's designed to teach you some accelerated lessons in self-esteem, trusting yourself, and trusting your initiative and creativity. This is a time when you'll be required to stand strong and independently. The 1 Personal Year is a time when you'll be challenged to make substantial advances in the career-driven areas of your life. You'll be working intensely on getting your ducks in a row and following up with action, action, and more action.

This is a time where relationships can flourish—and yet often take a back seat to other matters—particularly career advancement. The key for you and relationships in a 1 Personal Year resides in finding your sense of independence and individuality within your relationships in a balanced and healthy way—*codependence no more*. It's a year where you'll be met with opportunities to define and create independence on all levels. You'll be tested with relationships that are enmeshed, co-dependent or where you are the *enabler* or the *enablee*.

You'll benefit from the initiating energy of the year when you focus with clarity on longer-range goals while also being nimble enough to take some calculated risks and tap into your pioneering spirit. This is the time to define and act upon long-range goals while taking the lead in your life. Understand that you won't land on your feet on January 1 with crystal-clear clarity about the direction you're headed. This is an entire 12-months devoted to formulating your new phase and bringing it into focus. This is truly the year to begin a new chapter. Bruce Springsteen (1 Life Path) says it this way—*life offers you clean white pages, daring you to write on them.*

HOW YOU MIGHT EXPERIENCE THE 1 PERSONAL YEAR – BY LIFE PATH NUMBER

1 LIFE PATH

The 1 Life Path experiences heightened benefits and challenges in the 1 Personal Year because the energy related to the year is exactly what you're here to master. You can expect some additional triggers and treasures coming your way in the realms of exploring your independence, galvanizing your initiative, stepping into your creativity and uniqueness, and taking bold steps into new beginnings. Since this is a double 1 energy, you'll potentially be offered some of your deeper shadows to be massaged, worked with, and called into the light. In a dependent situation? This is the year to extract from it. Have a strong desire to change your career situation or start a business? This is the year to do it and yet it likely won't be easy-breezy. Count on a need for additional levels of self-confidence.

2 or 11/2 LIFE PATH

The 2 or 11/2 Life Path in a 1 Personal Year can be a beautiful thing. You get to push the reset button and you also get to push yourself in the realms of stepping into your personal sense of independence and individuality. For a 2, this can be a weird process—but it's meant to support you in your 2 Life Path mission of self-individuation mixed with setting healthy emotional boundaries. Since this is a year to start a new chapter, often this can offer you a bit of anxiety as you're pushed to stand up for yourself in perhaps a more forceful way than you have in the past. The 1 Personal Year can be a year where you start a new relationship or when your career takes a different twist or turn. Often this is a time where you're tested with acting with courage and in stepping into yourself in a new and dynamic way. The oppositional energies of the 1 and 2 have one thing in common—that's the exploration and expression of the *self*. The 1 Personal Year demands that you become more outwardly assertive, while your 2 Life Path is constantly moving you to define yourself from the inside out. If you're a Master 11/2 Life Path, add to that the overall intensity your life holds for you every day and amplify the themes of independence, individuality, taking action, and taking calculated risks.

3 LIFE PATH

The 3 Life Path experiencing a 1 Personal Year can present in some interesting ways. The themes you'll experience include taking courageous steps forward in the realms of emotional expression, communication, and creativity. Any creative endeavors are very much supported this year. You can begin a new project, start a new job or relationship, and find new ways to express yourself in a positive and optimistic way. Since this is the beginning of a new chapter in your life, this may come with a review of how you speak your truth—or discovering whether or not you know what your truth is! If not, this is an optimal time for counseling, classes, or involving yourself in any process that opens your levels of self-expression to new heights. The 1 Personal Year challenges you to take the lead and grab onto courage in order to manifest your creative projects and reveal your emotional needs in relationships.

4 or 22/4 LIFE PATH

The 4 Life Path experiencing a 1 Personal Year is earmarked for new beginnings on whatever level you're working on that involves the continuous creation of stability and the cultivation of learning and knowledge. This can take the form of moving to a new home or completing the construction of your home or real estate project. You can amp up your business or change jobs into something you feel aligns with you and your current passions. This is the perfect year to return to school. The volatile energy of the 1 Personal Year might challenge you to color outside the lines a bit more than fits into your current comfort zone. It's your job to infuse this initiating energy in ways that expand all aspects of your life—from recommitting to good health to taking some additional training or classes to expand your career—or to simply expanding your horizons. If you're a Master 22/4 Life Path, add to that the overall intensity your life holds for you every day and amplify the themes of independence, individuality, taking action, and taking calculated risks.

5 LIFE PATH

The 5 Life Path experiencing a 1 Personal Year—this is definitely a time to step off the beaten path! This is a year where you're practicing your 5 Life Path skills and ability to embrace change and add your unique and individual spark to it as you go. Of course, you'll get to wrangle with your personal fear factor, whatever that may be. You'll once again be required to focus and reign things in even as you boldly go where no one has gone before. This initiating year can be marked with a geographical move, a new start with a relationship or business partnership, or any number of occurrences that rebuild your sense of fun, adventure, resilience, and change.

6 or 33/6 LIFE PATH

The 6 Life Path in a 1 Personal Year can offer a plethora of opportunities to continue an exploration of your deep sense of responsibility, duty, and service. The year can offer new advancements in your family dynamics, however that is defined for you at this moment. You can start new projects, start a family, or start an entirely new phase of life on any realm. This is a great year for initiating any kind of home-based project or building on your creative endeavors. Since you're always concerned with cultivating a nurturing environment, anything having to do with building and strengthening this area of your life and launching anything new in this area is favored this year. If you're a Master 33/6 Life Path, add to that the overall intensity your life holds for you every day and amplify the themes of independence, individuality, taking action, and taking calculated risks.

7 LIFE PATH

The 7 Life Path in a 1 Personal Year can be a beautiful opening for starting a new phase in any aspect of your life, especially if it involves a continuation of soul seeking and a deepening of your reservoir of wisdom. How does this look on a practical level? It can show up in your material world as a new job, a big relationship shift, a new training, or perhaps a big decision that becomes finalized. It can be a time where you embark on a higher level of personal and spiritual growth. It can also mark a huge *internal* shift that only you can qualify or quantify. Perhaps it's a move to a different city or a 180-degree turn in your career or in what drives you overall. Anything initiating a new start and a fresh perspective is favored for you this year.

8 LIFE PATH

The 8 Life Path in a 1 Personal Year can be an exhilarating, if not intense, time to get it together and get moving on your highest and best projects. Together, this combination can be amazingly powerful and productive as long as you're in positive alignment with these highly driven energies. As an 8, you're already mastering the art of manifesting in this material world. The new beginnings offered you this year serve as a springboard to launch the next highest and best version of yourself, period. For the 8, that has to do with personal empowerment and finances—and the career-focused energy of the 1 Personal Year will kick you into career-overdrive.

9 LIFE PATH

The 9 Life Path in a 1 Personal Year can be a weird cacophony of unexpected conditions and dreams coming to fruition! The numbers 1 and 9 are bookends—representative of beginnings and endings. As a 9 Life Path, you're always working with a certain level of letting go. The 1 Personal Year can be an exhilarating time where you start a new project, new relationship, or new train of thought. The 9 is always charismatic and creative and during the 1 Personal Year, you'll be called upon dip into your bag of past-life wisdom and step into a new phase of your life with a bold sense of curiosity and a desire to amp-up your levels of selfless-service. This is the time to lean into your creative genius and take the lead in your life.

PERSONAL YEAR 2

SLOWER YEAR FOCUSED ON TRUE RELATIONSHIP DEVELOPMENT

PATIENCE, LOVE & NETWORKING

HOW DO I WANT TO LOVE AND BE LOVED IN RETURN?

THE GOAL: TO CLARIFY YOUR EMOTIONAL BOUNDARIES & FOCUS ON LOVE AND RELATIONSHIPS.

BRING IT ON	EXPECT
SENSITIVITY	IMPATIENCE
RECEPTIVITY	REACTIVITY
TRUST-TIMING	INTUITIVE GUIDANCE
SLOW GROWTH	SELF-FOCUS
PATIENCE	INTOLERANCE
READY TO ATTRACT "THE ONE?"	EMOTIONAL INDULGENCE
ESTABLISHING BOUNDARIES	LESSONS IN NOT BEING TAKEN ADVANTAGE OF
GETTING TO KNOW YOU!	SITUATIONS TO STAND UP FOR YOURSELF
OPENING TO HEALTHY EXPRESSIONS OF LOVE	OVER-GIVING OR UNDER-GIVING
SUPPORTING OTHERS	DEPENDENCY
TAKE RESPONSIBILITY FOR YOURSELF	INTERFERING WITH OTHERS

2 PERSONAL YEAR

This year is all about slowing down and developing patience. Oh yes. Everyone's *favorite* thing to do! (*nervous laughter ensues…*) After your three-year period of intensity and transformation (the Personal Years 8-9-1) this is your hall pass to slow down, breathe, and focus on others. The last three years have been a self-focused period of time and full of weighty transitions and transformation.

This is a year earmarked for slower progress and is a time where you're watching and waiting as you tend to the "seeds" you planted last year. It's a time of percolation and designed as a year where relationships take front seat. It's an emotions-based year and great for networking, building intimacy on all levels, and a time where your sense of patience and diplomacy will be used, practiced, and tested. *Think of the 2 Personal Year as a time of gestation.*

Some of the challenges you may experience usually come in the form of frustration with what feels like a stand-still or a lack of over-all progress or forward momentum. Perhaps you're a Type-A personality and the hovering required this year is a *no-go*. If you continue to think it's business as usual and are unwilling to back off from pushing and advancing things *via* your own agenda, then this year can feel like a real kick in the pants. Just when you think things are in order and going your way, most likely it disintegrates right before your eyes as you frantically attempt to put it all back together the way you want it to be.

If emotions are a bit foreign or uncomfortable to you, then these twelve months can feel very confusing. Or alternately, if you're an emotional person by nature, you can get carried away inside the cacophony of emotions and have trouble maintaining balance or equilibrium.

One of the tricks of the 2 Personal Year is to follow up with right action while also being acutely aware of when you need to back off or let something develop. Yet—*oh-joy of joys!*—this can really be a great year for settling into yourself in an empowering and soulful way. When you work with others and involve yourself in activities that allow you to mix-and-mingle, then the beauty of the 2 Personal Year really shines.

It's not time to blaze forward solo. The most success is had when you connect with others and put yourself out there into your social circles. This is the perfect time to question who you allow into your life and who depletes you. Harmony is a key term and practice sport during your 2 Personal Year. It's a time to find harmony within yourself as you solidify who you are *now* and where you're going. Listening to constructive criticism is helpful this year, yet the trick will be to have healthy discernment about the source—where are the suggestions coming from? How valid are they? What can you learn about yourself and others by taking a look at what comments end up in the suggestion box, so to speak.

Of course, there can be discord this year. The reason? What better way to walk a mile in the shoes of others than to have a lot of shoes thrown at you at the same time? This isn't a time to be reactive. It's a time to be responsive, yes. But with measured contemplation rather than knee-jerk reactions.

It's a fabulous time for networking, finding *the one*, or reestablishing your connection with your intimate relationship. However, don't expect anything to transpire at a rapid pace. This is a year where you decide to marry or up-level your intimate relationship. Or perhaps it's the time to allow a relationship that isn't flourishing to fall away. If single, often you'll find a soul-centered mate and enjoy the additional time spent focusing on really getting to know each other.

This is a testing year in regards to setting strong yet supple emotional boundaries with friends, colleagues, and family. You'll be called upon to resign from being used as a doormat if that is something you find yourself succumbing to in your daily life. Or if you're challenged with connecting emotionally with others and follow more of Michael Scott (Steve Carrell's character) school of thought (from TV show *The Office*), then the lessons of the year will be more about gaining humility and developing a desire to actually open yourself to caring for and about other people.

Intuition can soar in a 2 Personal Year when you place perimeters around uncontrolled or undisciplined emotions. Your sense of style, design, and artistry of all kinds is also heightened during your 2 Personal Year. This is an optimal year to open and soften your heart, trust in divine timing, and develop strong and authentic relationships. Intuition is super-charged and feelings are amplified. *Patience* is a key theme.

PERSONAL YEAR 11/2

PATIENCE, LOVE & NETWORKING + SPIRITUAL ILLUMINATION

HOW DO I WANT TO LOVE AND BE LOVED IN RETURN & HOW DO I PUT HIGHER IDEALS INTO PRACTICE?

THINK OF THIS AS ONE-PART 2 & TWO-PARTS 1!

HURRY UP & WAIT! PATIENCE & LOVE MIXED WITH ACTION!

BRING IT ON	EXPECT
SENSITIVITY	IMPATIENCE
IMPORTANT PROJECTS	CREATIVITY
TRUST-TIMING	HIGH INTUITION
GROWTH SPURTS	SELF-FOCUS
PATIENCE	"FAME & FORTUNE"
READY TO ATTRACT "THE ONE?"	EMOTIONAL INDULGENCE
ESTABLISHING BOUNDARIES	LESSONS IN NOT BEING A "DOORMAT"
GETTING TO KNOW YOU!	SITUATIONS TO STAND UP FOR YOURSELF
OPENING TO HEALTHY EXPRESSIONS OF LOVE	OVER-GIVING OR UNDER-GIVING
SUPPORTING OTHERS	DEPENDENCY
KEEPING THE PEACE	INTERFERING

11/2 PERSONAL YEAR

In addition to the core elements of the number 2, you have the added intensity related to the Master number 11, offering additional challenges. Yet the potential benefits are enormous. Along with it being a slower, relationship-oriented and emotional year, you'll be presented with opportunities to learn profound spiritual lessons. This can manifest in every way imaginable—from coping with crisis to embracing massive success.

With an 11/2 Personal Year, you might not feel as though things aren't slower at all given you're also working with the double 1. Even if it's a hard driving year, you'll still experience more than your share of halts, delays, and issues requiring a heightened level of patience with demands that you relax into divine timing. The magnitude of the effect of the experiences you engage with this year can't be underestimated in the bigger scheme of your life, yet you won't understand the depth of the lessons until later.

Be aware that you can experience a higher level of nervous tension during an 11/2 Personal Year. This is a magical period of time and yet not immediately of the "sparkles and unicorns" variety! The Master number 11 is the number of spiritual illumination. If you're into astrology, you might think of this cycle of time as your Chiron year—a time where you get to take a look at the nature of your spiritual and emotional wounds. Then you get to meet up with them, acknowledge them, and do some deep work around healing them. An 11/2 Personal Year won't allow denial or avoidance.

And if that weren't enough, chances are that this isn't much of a slower year at all. In fact, it can feel even more hard driving and busier than last year! There's a lot to handle and a lot to process. Understand that this can be a time where you find yourself with surprising success, unexpected notoriety or even fame can come knocking at your door. The 11/2 Personal Year supports any artistic creativity. It's also a year where your intuition is highly activated and when you might feel called to heal and transform others through selfless-service and artistic creativity.

The year can feel more conflicted than usual. You might have a tendency to question your work, feeling as though you need to do more, something different or something more important. When you develop your intuitive guidance system, you'll have less difficulty discovering and acting on your true passion. When in doubt, place your feet firmly on the ground and make the effort to bring ideas into form.

On the flip-side, working with the intensity of the double 1's can bring challenges in not getting too carried away with your own self-importance. The 11 is the spiritual messenger, plain and simple. Yet there's really nothing "plain" or "simple" about it! This is a year to balance and embrace both yin and yang—doing and being.

How You Might Experience The 2 or 11/2 Personal Year – By Life Path Number

1 Life Path

The 1 Life Path experiences heightened frustrations and challenges in the 2 or 11/2 Personal Year because the energy related to the year is exactly the opposite of what you're all about. You can expect that you'll have some additional triggers and treasures coming your way in the realm of making friends with your softer side. This year tests you in your ability to slow down and take others into consideration. As a 1 Life Path, sometimes these are skills that require extra instruction as you turn your attention toward your relationship life and toward patiently cultivating whatever you placed in motion last year during your dynamic 1 Personal Year. Count on a need for bringing your attention outward and focusing on connecting in a heart-centered way. This is a year to watch things that you put into place last year develop and take shape. If this is your 11/2 Personal Year, then what I just said might fly right out the proverbial window! The double 1 of your 11/2 Personal Year pushes you to move boldly forward. Think of last year and then make it a double! The issue here is that there will be some built-in delays, derailing, and experiences that test your resolve and your ability to use diplomacy.

2 or 11/2 Life Path

The 2 Life Path in a 2 or 11/2 Personal Year can be a beautiful thing. You get to bask in your element, after all. The 2 Life Path experiences heightened benefits and challenges in the 2 Personal Year because the energy related to the year is exactly what you're here to master. You can expect that you'll have some additional opportunities coming your way in the realms of exploring your engagement with your relationship life, with peace-keeping, and with your emotional life. For a 2, this can be an intense process and it's meant to support you in your 2 Life Path mission of setting healthy emotional boundaries mixed with being the ultimate wingman or woman. If you're a Master 11/2 Life Path, add to that the overall intensity your life holds for you every day and amplify the themes of love, peacemaking (and peace-keeping), seeing others' points of view, and patiently being in the moment with the trust that all will unfold as it should. Don't forget that often this is the year to find your "one" that equals two!

3 Life Path

The 3 Life Path experiencing a 2 or 11/2 Personal Year can present in some intriguing ways. Count on your themes residing in cultivating patient steps forward in the realms of emotional expression, communication, and creativity. As always with the 3 Life Path, any creative endeavors are very much supported this year, yet the trick will be in navigating the timing—meaning it won't happen as quickly as planned. Moreover, the key player this year will be in the emotional realm. This is a year to cultivate your intimate and business relationships and also to slow down enough to dig into your emotional sensitivity and master a certain level of healthy and direct communication. In fact, your emotional life is highlighted in neon this year. Are you ready for a crash course in emotional acuity and setting solid emotional boundaries? This is a great year to up-level your intimate partnership or to attract a significant relationship.

4 or 22/4 Life Path

The 4 or 22/4 Life Path experiencing a 2 or 11/2 Personal Year can be a strange brew. This is a year where you're definitely defining your 4 Life Path ability to be a practical purveyor of all things emotions-based. Yet for the 4 Life Path, this isn't terribly intuitive. Let's face it, there's a lot of 2's floating around here (if you're a 22/4 in particular) and so you'll be equally blessed and somewhat cursed with heightened emotional sensitivity and required to step into a delicate balance of emotional connection that's framed with a pragmatic sense of getting things done in the material realm. The opportunities reside in building things at a slow and steady pace while taking the time to stop and engage in some socializing, team building, and relationship nurturing.

5 Life Path

The 5 Life Path experiencing a 2 or 11/2 Personal Year is in for an interesting ride. The 5 Life Path can be known for a certain sense of emotional volatility. This is a year where you're definitely practicing your 5 Life Path skills and ability to embrace change while mastering the art of emotional restraint. Of course, you'll get to wrangle with your personal fear factor, whatever that may be. This is a perfect year for getting your sales-hat on and networking like crazy. If you're a 5 Life Path looking for love, this is the time to go deep and feel into your desires and expectations for your love life. This slower-paced year can be marked with lessons in building strong authentic relationships. It's always a great time to travel or take some adventures with your current or new *plus one*.

6 or 33/6 Life Path

The 6 Life Path in a 2 or 11/2 Personal Year can offer a plethora of opportunities to continue an exploration of your deep sense of responsibility with a focus on home and relationships. The year offers new advancements in your family dynamics, however that's defined for you at this moment in your life. The energy of the 2 and the 6 are both very love and relationship-oriented vibes, so this will be the primary theme for you. How do you love and how do you want to be loved? Since you're always concerned with cultivating a nurturing environment, anything having to do with creating and strengthening home-related bonds is favored. This is definitely the year to tie the knot—or to untie the knot, if that's the direction your relationship is heading. Certainly, there's no avoiding the need to face your relationship dynamics and up your game. If you're a Master 33/6 Life Path, add to that the overall intensity your life holds for you every day and amplify the themes of love, peace-making (and peace-keeping), service to others, and focusing on family dynamics.

7 Life Path

The 7 Life Path in a 2 or 11/2 Personal Year can be a beautiful year for deepening your understanding of how you related to people on a core emotional level. One of the life-long lessons for the 7 Life Path is in getting out of the head and into the heart with more consistency. This is a perfect year to deepen your level of commitment to yourself—and love and understanding of yourself. It's also a great time to open your heart to a relationship, to heal old emotional wounds on every level, and to slow yourself down enough to continue to develop and understand your intuitive voice.

8 Life Path

The 8 Life Path in a 2 or 11/2 Personal Year can be an interesting time where you find the urge to merge. Relationship merger, anyone? As an 8, you're already mastering the art of manifesting in this material world. The patience-building time offered you right now serves as an opportunity to step into the *business of love and relationships* rather than a full-throttle focus on career and work. This can try your soul, as most often you're a no-nonsense guy or gal who is business-minded and driven to make things happen. Hold up there, oh-8 Life Path. You'll most likely get to meet up with delays, a few curve balls, and some other frustrations that can either make you crazy or alternately, you can devote some of the time you'll be hovering in limbo-land to other things, like a night at the comedy club or some romantic getaways.

9 Life Path

The 9 Life Path in a 2 or 11/2 Personal Year can be an engaging whirl of romance and slowing down to smell the roses, so to speak. The 9 is always giving and charitable. Yet most of the time, the 9 Life Path is a whirling dervish and is always doing, going, and us driven to get things accomplished. During the 2 or 11/2 Personal Year, you'll be called upon to dip into your relationship life in ways that build true intimacy. This can be a great time to cultivate whatever work-related projects you have going and yet the overall promise resides in strengthening and defining your relationships across the board—from family or origin to your significant other to work colleagues.

PERSONAL YEAR 3

SELF-IMPROVEMENT, COMMUNICATION & CREATIVITY

HOW CAN I IMPROVE MYSELF ON EVERY LEVEL?

THE GOAL: TO FIND YOUR VOICE, GIVE YOURSELF PERMISSION TO CREATE, AND ENJOY YOURSELF!

EXPRESS YOURSELF! FIND YOUR JOY!

BRING IT ON	EXPECT
PLEASURE	UPS & DOWNS
SEXUAL EXPRESSION	COMMUNICATION ISSUES
LAUGHTER	SCATTERED
CREATIVITY	OVER-THINKING
EMOTIONAL EXPRESSION	SKIMMING THE SURFACE
WORK ON YOUR PROJECTS!	PROCRASTINATION
INFUSE FUN INTO EVERYTHING YOU DO	EXTREME SELF-DOUBT
SPEAK YOUR TRUTH	OVER-INDULGENCE
GAIN NEW SKILLS & EXPERIENCE	AFRAID OF CRITICISM
LIVE A LITTLE!	EMOTIONAL TRIGGERS
EXPLORE	OVERWHELM

3 PERSONAL YEAR

This is a year for anything and everything self-improvement related. It's all about fun, creativity, and tapping into your expressive emotions. Take center stage. Enroll in a public speaking class or make over your image. This is your time to be out there, enhancing all aspects of your sense of yourself and stepping into the real, true, authentic *you*. As you think about it, it's less about self-improvement than it's about revealing and acknowledging the *self* that's already there—the original and authentic *you* that's potentially been buried or derailed because of what life has thrown at you.

This is also a year where you'll be challenged to work on expressing your emotions clearly and effectively, so you'll be offered plenty of opportunities to practice this feat. Ultimately, the lesson of the year resides in finding your joy, developing and acting upon your creative flow and creative urges—and speaking your truth. What do you enjoy doing? When do you feel that warm and vibrant sense of ease, playfulness, and *rightness* in your life? Do more of that.

Speaking your truth may sound well and good, yet this is a time where you'll be faced with the deeper quandaries surrounding this very question. What do you value? What do you believe? What is important to you? What are your deal-breakers? You also might wrestle with some unexpected emotional highs and lows. Often the 3 Personal Year points out where you have a weak-link in the way you engage with relationships and express your wants and needs. This is a time where you realize that you're asking people with whom you're in relationships with to come to the table and communicate with you in ways that you're not doing yourself! A spotlight can shine on your own need to be more emotionally vulnerable and more expressive.

This is a time where you can catapult into fame if you've been working in that direction. This is a red-letter year for anyone who's an artist or a creative. The energy of the 3 Personal Year infuses high-powered energy into your projects, so if you're on the fence about whether this is a good time to devote yourself to your creative projects, have no doubt that this is the year to *do it*. The energy of the 3 supports anything communication or performance related, from producing your album, to publishing your book, to launching your on-line course.

If you're an actor, musician, or any other performative artist, the energy of the year supports moving forward in a positive direction when you take yourself and your talents seriously. Focus on the nuts-and-bolts of expanding your project and you'll be supported with luck and opportunity. Keep in mind that this is the year to do all the creative work—get it all out there on paper, on the canvas, on camera, or wherever your medium belongs. Next year will be the time for implementation (launching, marketing, touring). This year supports the creative part.

If you're not an artist, this is the time to use any kind of creativity in your personal and work life. Tap into your creative problem-solving skills. You might be surprised at the positive results when you take a risk and bring to light some element of yourself—stepping outside the lines in the creative realm. How can you use your creativity and communication skills to transform into the next level in your life? What kind of self-improvement do you want and need? How can you express yourself and your emotions in a healthy and dynamic way? Be careful not to scatter your energies and spread yourself too thin.

Also watch your words. This is a time to be overly mindful of how and why you express yourself on all levels. Words have tremendous power and during a 3 Personal Year, words hold heightened impact. Use them wisely and well.

Also understand that this can be a challenging year where you can experience deep levels of emotional crisis points. You'll dredge up old issues until you can face them, name them, and resolve them. Often this is a year where you redefine your relationship when you or your partner aren't engaged in healthy emotional expression. You can feel a sense of malaise or depression if you aren't living the life you want to be living. This can be a time where procrastination can take the place of active self-improvement.

The 3 Personal Year is meant for fun, socializing, travel, and all lighter and joyful activities. It's a year where time with children is highlighted—and when you're encouraged to bring out the kid in you! You get a permission slip to explore and find enjoyment where and whenever you can. This is a time to be overly mindful of how and why you express yourself on all levels. When in doubt, lighten up! When you're laughing, you're learning.

How You Might Experience The 3 Personal Year – By Life Path Number

1 Life Path

The 1 Life Path can soar in a 3 Personal Year if you're truly in your 1 Life Path creative-zone. This energy expands and intensifies some of your creative projects and you benefit when you infuse some fun into whatever you're up to, either personally or professionally. The key to success resides in not going haywire and losing focus. You'll be offered some grand opportunities for your creative ideas to flourish. This is also a good time to take a look at self-improvement in whatever way your independent 1 Life Path is leaning toward right about now. Need a relationship upgrade? Time to take your business to the next level? Thinking about speaking or writing your book? As a 1 Life Path, the 3 Personal Year will put a spotlight on your creative impulses, emotional life, and style of communication. How's that workin' for you? Can it use a tweak? This is the year to learn more about how to communicate in the most effective way possible.

2 or 11/2 Life Path

The 2 or 11/2 Life Path in a 3 Personal Year can be an expansive and emotional year. The 2 Life Path experiences heightened benefits and challenges in one of the learning areas for the 2—in this case, developing and mastering your emotional life on a grand scale. This is a year to concentrate on how you do or don't practice healthy boundaries and how you engage yourself and others in the core lessons inherent with your 2 Life Path—including coming to terms with your emotional sensitivity and stepping into your authenticity. You can expect additional opportunities coming your way in the realms of exploring your engagement with your relationship life, levels of diplomacy, and the way you express yourself. If you're a Master 11/2 Life Path, add to that the overall intensity your life holds for you every day and amplify the themes of fun, optimism, creative self-expression, and emotional sensitivity. This is the year to tap into your joy and *express thyself!*

3 Life Path

The 3 Life Path experiencing a 3 Personal Year can present in some intense ways. You get double the pleasure and double the challenges with the high-frequency vibe of the 3. *Cha-cha-cha!* As always with the 3 Life Path, any creative endeavors are very much supported this year, yet the trick will be in focus, focus, and more focus. With the double 3 energy you'll really, truly, madly, and deeply be pushed to be inspired and bring that inspired energy into whatever you do. This is a fantastic year to take leaps and bounds in any and all creative endeavors, from finishing your book to getting hired for that acting job. Another key player for you this year will be in the emotional realm. The challenges reside in intense emotional ups and downs, a bit of analysis paralysis based in self-doubt, and getting clear about how you communicate. This is the perfect year to get support to move through past trauma by seeking out counseling or any modality that assists you in healing yourself.

4 or 22/4 Life Path

The 4 or 22/4 Life Path experiencing a 3 Personal Year can be a strange brew. This is a year where you're being pulled toward lightening up and living a little, which can be like pulling teeth to some of you 4's—*you know who you are!* The self-improvement vibe can't be underestimated this year and you can use this to your advantage. The 4 Life Path is all about following a plan and color-coding it on the calendar. Yet this is a year where you might open yourself to something new and different—whether it's a class, new hobby, or bringing a little zest back into your relationship life. This is a great year to infuse creative problem-solving into your work world and devote yourself to digging into your own reservoir of emotional flotsam and jetsam. Overall, you often opt for the serious side of things, and so this can be a great year to give yourself a permission slip to find humor where you can and enjoy things even when there's work to be done. If you're a Master 22/4 Life Path, add to that the overall intensity your life holds for you every day and amplify the themes of fun, optimism, creative self-expression, and emotional sensitivity.

5 Life Path

The 5 Life Path experiencing a 3 Personal Year is in for an extended roller coaster ride. The 5 Life Path can be known for a certain sense of emotional volatility. This is a year where you're definitely practicing your 5 Life Path skills and ability to embrace change while mastering the art of emotional self-expression—not emotional self-indulgence! Oh, I know there's a fine line there sometimes, dear 5 Life Path. This is a perfect year for strapping on your boogie shoes and livin' large in the *fun* realm. The challenges should be obvious and yet I'll lay it out for you. Both the 3 and the 5 are besties. They get each other and love a good laugh, a good party, and a late night on the dance floor. The partnering of the 5 and the 3 can make for some great stories and yet you'll need to use extra caution and mindfulness this year in order not to wake up next year with one big hangover (metaphorically, if not literally, speaking!). Focus on follow-through and not getting (too) distracted by the bright and shiny objects.

6 or 33/6 Life Path

The 6 or 33/6 Life Path in a 3 Personal Year offers a plethora of opportunities to continue an exploration of your deep sense of responsibility and duty. This is a year to really dig deep into the more fun, social, and expressive aspects of yourself and of life in general. The energy of the 3 and the 6 are both creative vibes and so this will be the primary theme for you this year. This is also a time where you can create new inroads to a home-based business or infuse some newfound creative juice into anything from your artistic pursuits to counseling to design. The synergy here is palpable. This can be a frenetic year that offers so much opportunity for immersion into how you communicate across the board. As a 6 Life Path, you're always focused on nurturing in some way, shape, or form. How do you express yourself within your relationships? This is a year where this theme is front and center. If you're a Master 33/6 Life Path, add to that the overall intensity your life holds for you every day and amplify the themes of fun, optimism, creative self-expression, and emotional sensitivity.

7 Life Path

The 7 Life Path in a 3 Personal Year can be a fascinating year for deepening your understanding of how you relate to people on a core emotional level. One of the life-long lessons for the 7 Life Path is in getting out of the head and into the heart with more consistency. It's also part of your life's trajectory to learn to express your deepest emotions. Guess what? The 3 Personal Year is your year, baby! On one hand, it's time to dig into the lighter side of things. On the other hand, it's also an opportunity to learn to locate your own emotional space and to make friends with that part of yourself on a deeper level. This is a perfect year to break out of your shell and find your fun, optimism, and just live a little. Where do you find enjoyment in life? When you infuse creativity into your work and personal life, the benefits are life-long. Let's face it, though, the 7 and the 3 are like awkward teenagers on a blind date. The 3 offers a buoyant and expressive vibe while the 7 Life Path is often a bit more introverted and cautious. This is a lovely year to focus on any kind of self-improvement and for you as a 7, that can often reside in your spiritual practice or in upping your expertise in whatever area you're focused on.

8 Life Path

The 8 Life Path in a 3 Personal Year can be an interesting time where you either take your creative pursuits into the big time or you infuse creative juice into whatever business project you're engaged in. As an 8, you're already mastering the art of manifesting in this material world. So how does that pan out during a 3 Personal Year? This is a time where self-improvement is at the helm and so for you as an 8, this starts with personal empowerment. Where do you feel a gap in your overall sense of empowerment? This is the time to focus on improving this part of your life. Already feeling pretty grounded and on the mark? Then this is your year to reap the benefits of your hard-driving 8 Life Path by taking a bit more time to travel, socialize, and have some fun. If you're an already creative 8 Life Path, this year can launch you into new heights with your creative endeavors when you tackle it with a businesslike focus mixed with playfulness. Success comes more easily and more robustly when you loosen up.

9 Life Path

The 9 Life Path in a 3 Personal Year can be an engaging whirl of creative projects. The 9 is always charismatic and incredibly creative—often artistically. During the 3 Personal Year, you'll be called up on dip into ways that you'd like to *improve thyself*. This is a dynamic period of time and a great moment to lean into your joyful sense of service on whatever level calls to you. If you're a creative 9 (which is usually the case), you get a golden ticket to embrace creative projects and to infuse your quirky sense of creativity into whatever you're involved with in both your personal and professional life. Communication is also highlighted and you'll get opportunities to practice direct and heart-felt communication. As a 9 Life Path, you're often working with honing your listening skills. This is a great year to tune into others and listen to what they have to say.

PERSONAL YEAR 4

HARD WORK, LIMITING CIRCUMSTANCES & LONGER-RANGE GOALS

WHAT ARE MY LONGER-RANGE GOALS AND HOW CAN I IMPLEMENT THEM?

THE GOAL:
TO GET ORGANIZED AND SET FIRM FOUNDATIONS THAT MAKE YOUR LIFE EASIER, SATISFYING, AND PRODUCTIVE.

SLOW AND STEADY WINS THE RACE. DEFINE GOALS AND SET UP SYSTEMS.

BRING IT ON	EXPECT
PRACTICALITY	UNFOCUSED
CONCERTED EFFORT	IMPULSIVE
MANAGEMENT	EXASPERATED
FINANCES	DISORGANIZED
FOUNDATIONS	LIMITED VIEWPOINTS
SUPER PRODUCTIVE!	CARELESSNESS
PERSERVERING	OVER-FOCUS ON DETAILS
SATISFYING RESULTS	IMPRACTICALITY
FOCUS ON SECURITY & STABILITY	APATHY
HEALING FAMILY ISSUES	STUBBORNNESS
FOCUS ON HEALTH	BURNED OUT

4 PERSONAL YEAR

Get ready to batten down the hatches and get serious about your future. It's time to work hard and sharpen your skill set. After your lighter and creative 3 Personal Year, it's time to time to slow down, steady your pace, and become more methodical about which goals you want to focus on. After last year, chances are you have some projects in the works that need to be tended to, nurtured, and implemented. This is a more serious year requiring hard work to set the foundation for whatever you're working on—job, relationships, health or family.

Often the first part of a 4 Personal Year feels good in the same way committing to a deep-cleaning of your house feels good. It's like the feeling of satisfaction you get when you clean out the closets and donate stuff that hasn't been used in years. Perhaps you also decide to replace the carpet and update the bathroom. Then you see how much nicer everything looks and feels and decide to reorganize the office and change the window coverings.

Oh—and now that you've done that, you realize you really need to get all your files into one place, color code them, and box them by year and category. And then . . . Get the picture? Understand that often there's a burst of energy and enthusiasm at the beginning of a 4 Personal Year and yet as the year wears on, it can start to feel rather arduous. Therefore, it's a good idea to understand at the get-go that a slow and steady pace will get you to the finish line with more of your sanity and good humor in tact than sprinting out of the starting gate in a mad frenzy to get it all done over a weekend.

Since the energy of the number 4 is all about foundations, often you'll find yourself building a house or moving to a new home. Home and your sense of security can take front seat. When you're experiencing a 4 cycle, you'll also work with limitation in various forms. How does this show up for you? A 4 Personal Year can challenge you with health, family, and career issues having to do with *limitation*. What limitations are to be worked with and negotiated through? What limitations do you actually create for yourself that aren't necessary? Don't let this concept scare you! Think of it as "proper care and maintenance" time.

This is a time where you'll be tempted to either over-work or under-work. Optimally, you'll need to forgo Happy Hour and stay a little later at the office to finish up that big report or file, complete the last part of the chapter you're writing, or think through the way you're wanting to systematize your project. While it may feel a bit thankless at times, you'll reap the rewards when you accomplish your goals step-by-step. Slow and steady wins the race.

It's a year to pay special attention to health maintenance. You'll have to consciously take time for self-care—plan it and prioritize it. Otherwise, burn-out is virtually guaranteed. A 4 cycle also tests you with some old family issues bubbling to the surface needing to be resolved or dealt with differently. Get ready for *that* little joyride. The relief, healing, and positive outcome from this family-oriented work is more than worth the effort. All in all, you'll glean the most satisfaction from the 4 Personal Year when you take the time to focus your longer-range vision, systematize your life in whatever way will make it much more effective in the years to come—whether that's by focusing on work, getting your house in order, reviving your health, or healing family issues.

PERSONAL YEAR

22/4

HARD WORK & LONGER RANGE GOALS + SPIRITUAL FOCUS & ADVANCEMENT

WHAT AM I BUILDING AND CREATING THAT HAS LONG RANGE POTENTIAL & IS REFLECTIVE OF MY SPIRITUAL MISSION?

THINK OF IT AS TWO-PARTS 2 AND ONE-PART 4!

DEFINE GOALS AND SET UP SYSTEMS. TIME TO TAKE ON YOUR BIGGER DREAMS!

BRING IT ON	EXPECT
PRACTICALITY	OVER-WHELMED
CONCERTED EFFORT	IMPULSIVE
THINKING BIG!	TIRED
FINANCES	DOUBTFUL
VISION	LIMITED - RESTRICTED
SUPER PRODUCTIVE!	NOT UP TO THE TASK
ENDURANCE	OVER-FOCUS ON DETAILS
LONG-TERM RESULTS	IMPRACTICAL
FOCUS ON SECURITY & STABILITY	FEARFUL
HEALING FAMILY ISSUES	STUBBORNNESS
FOCUS ON HEALTH	EXHAUSTION

22/4 PERSONAL YEAR

In addition to the core elements of the number 4, you have added intensity related to the Master number 22/4, offering you additional challenges. The potential benefits are enormous. Understand that the Master 22/4 is the most powerful number in numerology. It presents as The Master Builder and requires significant vision, focus, and tireless effort.

This Personal Year is quite intense and prods you to up the ante with your work and career goals. It often goes hand-in-hand with expanding your enterprises and thinking bigger. There are many challenges inherent in this energy, including devoting yourself to your work efforts at the expense of your personal relationships—or simply by placing emotional connections in the back-seat for now. When you experience a 22/4 Personal Year, understand that you're working with the foundational energies related to the number 4 and then with the double 2. You'll need a lot of patience and ability to "play well with others" and share the sandbox, so to speak.

You're being called upon to step up your enterprises and expand—take a risk and think bigger. This is just the nuts-and-bolts phase. The key element for the success and smoothness of the 22/4 Personal Year resides in a strong and clear focus on wider-ranging service to others. If you concentrate whole-heartedly on altruism, on serving the greater good in some significant way, shape, or form—that's when the magic happens. This is a butt-kicking year, truth be told. Understand that you're simply setting things up and getting them in line. Most often the work coming at you requires depth and is wider-ranging than usual. It can bring even the hardest worker into the fatigue-zone.

If there's ever a time to banish self-doubt and work at bringing your bigger ideas and aspirations into fruition, it's now. The point of focus will be on getting clear about what that is and what the long-range goal will be. *It's time to truly start with the end in mind.* Don't reinvent the wheel. This is a year that's set up for getting real. As Dr. Phil used to say: *"And how's that workin' for ya'?"*

The 4 or 22/4 Personal Year can get a bad rap. Or at least it can metaphorically be viewed as the "icky" vegetables you must eat before you're allowed to have dessert. It's all about formulating goals and aspirations in a clearly defined and actionable way. The 4 Personal Year is a marathon where slow and steady process is rewarded (eventually) over spontaneity and luck. If you're already an organized and achievement-oriented personality, the 4 Personal Year can be the time where you learn to roar.

Alternately, if organization, systems-building, and getting serious about your endeavors makes you either fall into a coma or drop everything and head out to extended Happy Hour—*well.* Then it'll feel off kilter and you'll befall a lot of grief in terms of feeling as though nothing is moving forward and everything takes much more effort than you think it should. It's as though everything you're doing is getting you nowhere. Even the simplest things turn into a huge cluster.

Sometimes it can feel difficult if you're traveling a lot or if there's a lot of activity since we think about "hard work" being like a ball-and-chain. Not necessarily so. You can make great strides in setting up foundations for your life and business by hustling. It'll all depend where you need the most bolstering—is your job okay yet your intimate relationship is a mess? Perhaps you need to commit to an actual home or geographical location. Maybe you're in a place in your life where it's all up in the air. The energy of the 4 forces you to bring it down to earth in a practical, no-nonsense way. If you're having a 22/4 Personal Year then all bets are off. This is a time for marked advancement with your enterprises and yet it won't be a casual walk in the park.

How You Might Experience The 4 or 22/4 Personal Year – By Life Path Number

1 Life Path

The 1 Life Path makes great strides during a 4 or 22/4 Personal Year. This is a testing time where you're required to have your creative projects already in place, because this is a foundations-setting time and the more you invest in getting the nuts-and-bolts in line, the better off you'll be. As a 1 Life Path, the 4 or 22/4 Personal Year puts a spotlight on taking care of your health in a concerted fashion. This can be a taxing time where there are deadlines, commitments, and other pressures that simultaneously demand your individual attention and input—while also asking you to let go of some of the micromanaging. A delicate balance. Overall, the 1 Life Path can optimally use the foundational energy of the 4 Personal Year to develop and manifest whatever longer-term endeavor you're focused on, whether that's a project, business enterprise, relationship or improvement of your health. If this is a 22/4 Personal Year, up the intensity on virtually everything you're putting into place. This is the time to think big and make those goals even farther reaching than you might otherwise dream about. A humanitarian and service-focus is a key element. This is a time where personal relationships take a back seat to your business enterprises.

2 or 11/2 Life Path

The 2 or 11/2 Life Path in a 4 or 22/4 Personal Year can be a grounding and foundational year, mixed with a little crazy! This is a year that doubles down on whether or not you feel safe, secure, and well-loved. This can be a time where home-related issues come up as a priority, including the surfacing of issues related to your upbringing. You can move into a new or different home. You might find yourself taking the plunge and move in with your intimate partner or put a ring on it. This is a year where your job or career might come up for review. Do you enjoy your job? Are you being valued in your work environment? If not, what are the practical steps you might consider taking in order to make this aspect of your life better and more satisfying? If you're a Master 11/2 Life Path, add to that the overall intensity your life holds for you every day and amplify the themes of longer-term goal setting, concerted effort, setting up systems of operation, and feeling secure. This is the year to get your plan in place and get 'er done. If this is a 22/4 Personal Year, up the intensity on virtually everything you're putting into place. Frustrations and limiting circumstances, anyone? This is the time to think big and make those goals even farther reaching than you might otherwise dream about. The chances for some spiritual growth—however you might define it—is in the mix this year.

3 Life Path

The 3 Life Path experiencing a 4 or 22/4 Personal Year can present in some fascinating ways. As always with the 3 Life Path, any creative endeavors are very much supported this year, yet the trick will be in bringing that creative energy into practical reality. For the 3 Life Path, the 4 Personal Year can feel rather grueling and relentless because the 3 loves the creative part and the 4 demands a plan, budget, accountability, and a sense of pragmatism. This is time to put it on the calendar and get real. This is a fantastic year to take one or more of the creative projects you developed last year (during your 3 Personal Year) and focus on making them a reality. Is your book ready to publish? Is your course ready to get finished and the marketing plan in place? Did you cultivate more clients or customers last year and now it's time to offer another product or service? Did you get a promotion at your job last year and now you're proving yourself in your new position? This is the time to get it all in place and running like clockwork. If this is a 22/4 Personal Year, up the intensity on virtually everything you're putting into place. This is the time to think big and make those goals even farther reaching than you might otherwise dream about.

4 or 22/4 Life Path

The 4 or 22/4 Life Path experiencing a 4 or 22/4 Personal Year is a real butt-kicker—potentially in the best possible way. It's not for slackers or for the faint of heart! The 4 or 22/4 Life Path experiences heightened benefits and challenges in the 4 or 22/4 Personal Year, because the energy related to the year is exactly what you're here to master. You can expect that you'll have some additional opportunities coming your way in the realms of exploring your engagement with setting and achieving goals, with putting forth proper effort, and with creating your personal sense of security. The red flags will be in the over-work (or under-work) department—and also in the realm of dealing with some old family wounding that might come up for a major review. You'll be tested by being presented with limitation after limitation this year. When you understand and expect that, you'll be ready to either take it in stride or not allow yourself to get demoralized. This year takes endurance and you'll need to take breaks consistently to avoid burn-out and overwhelm. If you're a Master 22/4 Life Path, add to that the overall intensity your life holds for you every day and amplify the themes of setting things in motion that will have lasting value, tenaciously working to make things happen, and working with (around and through) limitations. If this is a 22/4 Personal Year, up the intensity on virtually everything you're putting into place. This is the time to think big and make those goals even farther reaching than you might otherwise dream about.

5 Life Path

The 5 Life Path experiencing a 4 or 22/4 Personal Year is in for a rude awakening. The energy of the 4 and 5 couldn't be more oppositional. Yet when they can come to the table with a clear idea of the strengths and weaknesses of each, then they can assign each other tasks and work in tandem to make magic! The issue is that as a 5 Life Path, your mantra is "Don't fence me in!" while the 4 Personal Year demands that you show up on time to help construct—and then paint—the fence. The beauty of this year is that your focus needs to turn to the *self-discipline* part of your

5 Life Path mission of *freedom through self-discipline* or the constructive use of freedom. This is your time to call in all your reserves and come up with some clear goals, get a plan in place, and to take the actual steps to focus and follow through on a longer-term vision. You'll most likely arm-wrestle with any distractions, indulgences, or escape mechanisms that you rely on to pull you away from the task(s) at hand. Just remember that what you set up, systematize, and commit to this year sets the stage for more levels of freedom that you've ever known. It's worth the effort! If this is a 22/4 Personal Year, up the intensity on virtually everything you're putting into place. This is the time to think big and make those goals even farther reaching than you might otherwise dream about. Also know that this is a time where your personal relationships often take a back seat to your business enterprises.

6 or 33/6 Life Path

The 6 or 33/6 Life Path in a 4 or 22/4 Personal Year can offer some amazingly powerful opportunities for building and creating more stability in your life across the board, particularly within your home life. This is a time where the energy of the hard-working and goal-setting 4 assists you in taking yourself and your enterprises seriously. This can be a time where you build a house, move into a new living situation, or make a remodel or renovation a priority. It's a fabulous time to build your business—using incremental and well thought out processes rather than impulse. As a 6 Life Path, you're always focused on service and nurturing and this is a year where this is what you infuse into how you deal with all the work you'll be involved with in order to solidify whatever part of your life needs structure and stability. The challenges can reside in getting too ensconced inside of your own box. Meaning, you can become easily frustrated with others this year when they don't meet your expectations. If you're a Master 33/6 Life Path, add to that the overall intensity your life holds for you every day and amplify the themes of setting things in motion that will have lasting value, tenaciously working to make things happen, and working with (around and through) limitations. If this is a 22/4 Personal Year, up the intensity on virtually everything you're putting into place. This is the time to think big and make those goals even farther reaching than you might otherwise dream about.

7 Life Path

The 7 Life Path in a 4 or 22/4 Personal Year can be a powerful time for planning, organizing, knowledge seeking, and information gathering. Both the 7 and the 4 thrive with heady pursuits and the energy of the 4 or 22/4 Personal Year supports you in digging deeply into whatever facet of your life is coming up as a priority. This is a time for contemplation and for taking the steps to bring things into solid form. Do you want to strengthen your relationship life? How's your career? Are you rethinking your career path and wondering if a change would be realistic and if so, what would it take to get the training or get your foot in the door? Perhaps you started a job, project, or relationship last year and this is the year to build on it and take the step-by-step processes to solidify and strengthen it. The 7 Life Path is a natural analyst and this is a time to tap into your data gathering skills and set up an overall plan about how you would like these next five years (and beyond) to hash out for you. Always remember that a 4 or 22/4 Personal Year is a year of *endurance*. Take some breaks. Take time to reset and then get right back into it. Everything you get systematized and optimized this year allows you some never-before experienced levels of freedom next year. If this is a 22/4 Personal Year, up the intensity on virtually everything you're putting into place. This is the time to think big and make those goals even farther reaching than you might otherwise dream about. This is a learning-based year, no doubt about it.

8 Life Path

The 8 Life Path in a 4 or 22/4 Personal Year can be an intensely productive time. The 4 is like the younger sibling of the 8. When they show up together, they're often very much on the same page and speak the same language. It's all business this year—as if that's any news to you as an 8 Life Path. This is serious and the energy of the 4 Personal Year assists you in getting real, setting things up for success, and taking the step-by-step processes to lock it down. The issues? Can you say *burn out*? This is a year where pacing is key. This is a marathon year that demands pacing and so you'll need to be extra-vigilant about finding time and space for rest, relaxation, and rejuvenation. A key for you will be in softening your approach and your engagement with others. The energy of both the 4 and 8 can be like bulldozers blazing through a china shop. And together, you might be blowing everyone across the room just by walking into the room—and you don't even know it! Some tact and diplomacy will go a long way this year. Take time for physical exercise and some lighter activities as well. If this is a 22/4 Personal Year, up the intensity on virtually everything you're putting into place. This is the time to think big and make those goals even farther reaching than you might otherwise dream about.

9 Life Path

The 9 Life Path in a 4 or 22/4 Personal Year can present you with some amazing openings to bring order and organization into what you're doing. As a 9 Life Path, you're always infusing whatever you do with creativity, charisma, and heart-felt compassion. This is a year where you're encouraged to revamp and get things in order in whatever facet of your life needs it most. Are you engaging in a new project? This is the time to hammer out the details, get the crew in line, and take the steps to bring it all together. This can be a time where you get serious about a relationship, commit to a different living arrangement, or take your business to an entirely new level. Your challenges reside in making sure you're taking others into consideration as you blaze though it all. The 9 Life Path can have a tendency to do it all by themselves, even when it would be absolutely beneficial to tap into and trust the skills and talents that other people can bring to the table, whether that's in your intimate relationship or business life. There can be a strong sense of limitation this year that comes in for you to—in the way that only you can do it—infuse your creative problem-solving talents in order to blaze through it all. If this is a 22/4 Personal Year, up the intensity on virtually everything you're putting into place. This is the time to think big and make those goals even farther reaching than you might otherwise dream about.

PERSONAL YEAR 5

FREEDOM, CHANGE & FACING FEARS

WHAT DOES FREEDOM LOOK AND FEEL LIKE TO ME AND HOW DO I CREATE MORE OF IT IN MY LIFE?

THE GOAL: TO EXPLORE HOW TO FACE FEARS AND BE OPEN & RECEPTIVE TO DRAMATIC CHANGE.

FUN! FEARLESSNESS! ADVENTURE! A YEAR FOR SENSUAL EXPERIENCE.

BRING IT ON	EXPECT
TRAVEL	UNFOCUSED
CURIOSITY	ERRATIC
OUTSIDE-THE-BOX	MISDIRECTED
SEX	FEARFUL
NEW EXPERIENCES	STAGNANT
ADAPTABILITY	EMOTIONAL VOLATILITY
PLEASURE	EASILY DISTRACTED
EXCITEMENT	PROCRASTINATION
FREEDOM THROUGH SELF-DISCIPLINE	OVER-THINKING
MOVING THROUGH OBSTACLES	RECLUSIVE
GOING OUT OF YOUR COMFORT ZONE!	FEELINGS OF RESTRICTION

5 PERSONAL YEAR

What does freedom mean to you? More time? Money? A different job? Different marital situation? Getting your health back on track? *Freedom* and *change* are your themes for the year and it can feel like a whirlwind—so many pleasures (and challenges), so little time! There are lots of ups and downs, so the key for this year is flexibility, adaptability, and focus—otherwise drama and trauma may also be a recurring theme.

Lots of unexpected opportunities are bound to come your way, so be open to trying new things. It's time to travel and tap into your sense of fearless adventure—not necessarily a time to make a long-term commitment. The key to this year is establishing and acting on some semblance of self-discipline, otherwise you'll get to the next year feeling like this year has been one big hangover. If you don't stay the course, you'll end up with very little accomplishment to show for your time and energy at the close of the year.

It's set up as a transition point for change, new decisions, and new directions. It contains an energy that promotes opening up to something new and somehow infuses an imprint of sexiness to you—kind of like a pheromone. You think I'm kidding. Just wait and see! It's time for exploration, travel, and tapping into anything you feel offers a sense of adventure and of pushing your own boundaries.

This is a time where you benefit from having accomplished the foundational work last year, because now you have things in place that serve as a solid launching pad. How can the challenges show up? If you don't have things in place, the year can feel like a mental or physical tornado. Or alternately, you can hit your *denial* button and just force your way forward business as usual. Even though you know you're missing something, even if you haven't a clue what that something might be.

After the more practical energies of your 4 Personal Year, the energy of the 5 can feel intoxicating. The year starts out with a bang right out of the chute. You'll often be met with new people, new experiences, and new opportunities. Anytime you can opt to venture off your beaten track is favored in a 5 Personal Year.

This is a progressive time when you'll be pushed to explore the sensual side of life. This is a *pivotal year*—remember it's mid-way through your 9 Personal Year Cycle and it's a turning point for change and transition. Freedom is calling and you're required to throw your hat into the ring. *What's your answer?* There's nothing like defining your sense of freedom to bring up some long-held issues surrounding this very theme. Therefore, the 5 Personal Year offers a plethora of opportunity to face your fears, dismantle restrictions, and rekindle your adventurous spirit.

This can be a year where uncertainty rules the roost and oftentimes that can feel disconcerting, if not downright unacceptable. Some of the caveats include excessive behaviors—sex, drugs, alcohol, too much travel, and all the rest of it. Or excessive behaviors on the opposite pole—overwork, under-eating, too much exercise (yes, there is such a thing!). You might feel the siren call of escape and opt for numbing or zoning out rather than focusing and reining in all the high-level energies you have access to right now.

Given the energy of the 5 introduces issues related to freedom, you'll wrangle with issues and experiences related to *restriction*—this can show up anywhere you have trigger-points. Where do you feel tethered, stuck or smothered? In relationship. In family matters. With your health. Are you doing anything remotely satisfying with your job or career? If you're someone with "rolling stone gathers no moss" tendencies, the 5 can challenge you to not go off the chain and get lost in an ocean of self-indulgence. You're being called upon to stretch yourself, while also directing your energies in a way that's focused and productive. The catalytic energy of the 5 Personal Year can have you reeling with overwhelm.

One of the biggest misconceptions surrounding the fun, frenetic, and fast-paced 5 Personal Year has to do with fear. Oh yes, that. You'll be asked over and over again to reach out of your comfort zone and dip your feet into fear-filled waters. If that's too much for you, the 5 Personal Year can feel like a stagnant pool of water—complete with the stench and swarming insects. Or even more likely, you haven't opened the door and walked outside to even know that the pool of water actually exists. Instead, you stay well within the lines of comfort, safely, and familiarity—even if it's *uncomfortable* comfort, growth-stunting safely, and exasperating familiarly. This is your time to soar and see the world as your oyster! As Tina Fey observes: "Say 'yes' and you can figure it out later."

How You Might Experience The 5 Personal Year – By Life Path Number

1 Life Path

The 1 Life Path can rock the world in a 5 Personal Year if you're truly in your 1 Life Path creative-zone. This energy can expand and intensify your creative projects and you benefit when you infuse some fun and adventure into whatever you're up to, either personally or professionally. The key to success resides in not going off the rails and losing focus. You'll be offered some grand opportunities for your creative ideas to flourish and this is a year where new people, new opportunities, and new directions are the *expected unexpected!* This is also a good time to take a look at what your sense of freedom means to you in whatever way your independent 1 Life Path is leaning toward right about now. As a 1 Life Path, the 5 Personal Year places a spotlight on your sense of freedom and independence, on your ability to welcome constructive change, and on your ability to have a little fun along the way.

2 or 11/2 Life Path

The 2 Life Path in a 5 Personal Year can experience intensified experiences drawing your sense of yourself into the light. This can feel somewhat uncomfortable for the more introverted 2 Life Path. The energy supporting you this year is all about stretching your wings, facing your fears, and boldly going where you've never gone before. This is a time to step into your sensual nature and if you're a 2 Life Path who's single and ready to mingle, this is a red-letter year for sensual enjoyment on all levels. This is a great year to travel and step off the beaten path. All your relationships will benefit when you add a splash of 5 Personal Year fun into the mix. Be open to meeting new people and stepping out of your comfort zone. If you're a Master 11/2 Life Path, add to that the overall intensity your life holds for you every day and amplify the themes of freedom, adventure, fearlessness, and sensuality.

3 Life Path

The 3 Life Path experiencing a 5 Personal Year can present in some beautifully explosive ways. As always with the 3 Life Path, any creative endeavors are very much supported this year, yet the trick will be in focus, focus, and more focus. You'll also be met with the need to let things fall way if they don't hold promise—while following through on those things that *are* in alignment with you and need your time and energy to develop. This is a fantastic year to take leaps and bounds with any and all creative endeavors that you've been working on with vision and determination. The key will be lodged in your ability to open to a dramatic new opportunity (or two or three new opportunities!) and being able to flow with it rather than run from it. Another key player for you this year will be in the emotional realm. The challenges reside in some emotional ups and downs—with even more intense challenges than usual in not becoming too scattered and ineffective. Your sexual attraction is at an apex this year and this is a time to cultivate and enjoy the sensual side of life.

4 or 22/4 Life Path

The 4 or 22/4 Life Path experiencing a 5 Personal Year can be a strange brew. This is a year where you're being pulled toward lightening up and living a little, which can be like pulling teeth (without anesthesia) to some of you 4's—you know who you are! The "let freedom ring!" vibe can't be underestimated this year and you can use this to your advantage. This can feel really weird to the 4. The 5 and the 4 just don't understand each other, truth be told. The 4 Life Path is all about following a plan and having it on the calendar. Yet this is a year where you must open yourself to something new and different. You might have to operate with a bit more spontaneity—you won't have a choice. This is a great year to bring sexy back into your life and uncover what makes you feel vibrant and alive. Has life gotten way too serious lately? This is your year to bring in the fun, however that may manifest for you. You often opt for the serious and responsible side of things, so this can be a great year to give yourself a permission slip to find humor where you can and enjoy things even when there's work to be done. If you're a Master 22/4 Life Path, add to that the overall intensity your life holds for you every day and amplify the themes of freedom, adventure, fearlessness, and sensuality.

5 Life Path

The 5 Life Path experiencing a 5 Personal Year is in for an extended roller coaster ride. You get double the pleasure and double the challenges with the frenetic, high frequency vibe of the 5. The 5 Life Path can be known for a certain sense of emotional volatility. This is a year where you're definitely practicing your 5 Life Path ability to embrace change, enjoy your sensuality, see and be seen, and live large. You'll get to wrangle with your personal fear factor (make it a double!), whatever that may be. The challenges should be obvious and yet I'll lay it out for you. The double 5 can offer up a year that looks like a crazy romp on the wild side. Or alternately, this can be a year where whatever deep triggers you work with in the fear realm come up to be outed. What is the biggest fear that you've grappled with, well, *forever*? This can come into the arena to be worked through. You'll need to use extra caution and mindfulness in order not to wake up next year with zero accomplishments. Focus on follow-through, healthy discernment, and not getting (too) distracted by the bright and shiny objects.

6 or 33/6 Life Path

The 6 or 33/6 Life Path in a 5 Personal Year make interesting and yet somewhat strange bedfellows. This is a year to really dig deep into the more fun, adventurous, and sexy aspects of yourself and of life in general. This can be a frenetic year that offers so much opportunity for substantial immersion into issues related to freedom. What does freedom mean to you? What levels of freedom do you already have and then what do you dream about? As a 6 Life Path, you're always focused on nurturing in some way, shape, or form. How do issues related to *freedom* enter into your relationships? What does fun look and feel like to you? As a 6 Life Path, you're so busy taking care of everyone else that you end up losing sight of yourself and your own needs and desires. This is a year where that theme will be front and center. If you're a Master 33/6 Life Path, add to that the overall intensity your life holds for you every day and amplify the themes of freedom, adventure, fearlessness, and sensuality.

7 Life Path

The 7 Life Path in a 5 Personal Year can be a fascinating year for deepening your understanding of yourself—and the focal point for this inquiry will be in the realms of freedom, change, and sensuality. Honestly, the 7 and the 5 are an interesting combination. The 5's mantra is "Don't fence me in!" while your mantra as the 7 Life Path can be "Just leave me alone for a moment." This is a time where you'll jockey with your need to get out there and socialize, have fun, and ride the freedom train with your need to withdraw for a moment (or two) and regroup, reset, and refuel. The caution here will be in becoming mindful about what you put into your body. There can be a propensity to indulge on many levels, particularly with alcohol, sex, and drugs. This is a perfect year to focus on any kind of adventurous activities and for you as a 7, that can often reside in your spiritual practice or in upping your expertise in whatever area you're focused on. Maybe it's that yoga retreat in Bali. Skydiving lessons? The three-month backpacking trip in Europe? Let's go!

8 Life Path

The 8 Life Path in a 5 Personal Year can be a powerful time where you can infuse fearless adventure (either literally or metaphorically) into all elements of your life. As an 8, you're already mastering the art of manifesting in this material world. So how does that pan out during a 5 Personal Year? This is a time where constructive change and fearlessness are at the helm and so for you as an 8, this starts with personal empowerment. Where do you feel a gap in your overall sense of empowerment? What avenues of life do you avoid because you fear to tread those waters? This is the time to focus on stepping into—and coming to terms with—this aspect of your world. This is your year to reap the benefits of your hard-driving 8 Life Path by taking more time to travel, socialize, and have some fun. That tantric sex class just might sound good right about now! This year supports anything you do where you infuse your sense of fun and fearlessness into it. Of course, this requires some perimeters—yet as an 8 Life Path, you're good at organizing and prioritizing. Success comes more easily and more robustly when you loosen up. Be ready for some curve balls and hairpin turns. Take it as it comes and be open to new possibilities.

9 Life Path

The 9 Life Path in a 5 Personal Year can be an engaging whirl of travel and progressive projects. As a 9 Life Path, you're the ultimate world traveler—if not in practice, at least in theory. The 9 Life Path is known to be internationally curious and is often well-traveled. The 5 Personal Year is supportive of any and all travel plans you would like to act upon. This is a time to widen your lens and add some dimension to how you see yourself and place yourself in the world. The 9 is always charismatic and giving and during the 5 Personal Year, you'll be offered opportunities to expand your viewfinder on various levels. This is a dynamic period of time for you. If you're a creative 9 (which is often the case), you get a golden ticket to embrace progressive projects and to infuse your quirky sense of creativity into whatever you're involved with in both your personal and professional life. Sensuality is also highlighted and you'll get opportunities to bring romance into your life. As a 9 Life Path, this is a perfect year to face a few of your longstanding fears and lean into whatever you need to do in order to create a more expanded sense of freedom in your life.

PERSONAL YEAR 6

RESPONSIBILITY, RELATIONSHIPS & FEELING AT HOME

SHOULD I STAY OR
SHOULD I GO
OR
SHOULD IT STAY
OR SHOULD IT GO?

THE GOAL:
TO GET SERIOUS ABOUT HOW YOU LOVE AND HOW YOU WANT TO BE LOVED IN RETURN. DO YOU FEEL "AT HOME?"

EVALUATE YOUR RELATIONSHIPS & TAKE ON RESPONSIBILITY

BRING IT ON	EXPECT
RELATIONSHIPS	PERFECTIONISM
ROMANCE	CONTROLLING
RESPONSIBILITY	CRITICAL
SERVICE	JUDGMENTAL
MENTORING	SELF-RIGHTEOUS
FOCUS ON FAMILY	TOO IDEALISTIC
SPIFF UP YOUR HOME	HIGH EXPECTATIONS
SUPPORT OTHERS	"MARRIAGE OR DIVORCE"
FEED YOUR FRIENDSHIPS	OPPORTUNITIES TO GIVE
UPLEVEL YOUR INTIMATE RELATIONSHIP	CALLS TO COUNSEL OTHERS
PURSUE CREATIVE OR SERVICE-RELATED PROJECTS	FOCUS ON WHAT HOME MEANS TO YOU

6 PERSONAL YEAR

This year of responsibility and relationship evaluation offers a heightened sense of purpose and *warm and fuzzy* satisfaction in your home, family, and relationship life. It's magnetic for business and finances, yet not at the expense of your overall family obligations. This is a time to evaluate how you love, want to be loved, and how you relate to others.

The 6 Personal Year is a relationship evaluation year on all fronts. It depends on how willing you are to take a deeper look at yourself and how you actually engage in relationships. There can be frustration if you find yourself pointing the finger at everyone else. The energy of the 6 brings out levels of idealistic expectations about the world at large—and about yourself and others in your closer circle. If you operate with critical judgment as the default mechanism, then the year can go awry. You can experience serious bouts of miscommunication and misunderstandings with those you love, if not those in your professional life.

The 6 Personal Year can also feel off if you fall into the irresponsible route, shunning involvement in building intimacy with your relationships, and not paying attention to your home life—especially if you have children or other home-based responsibilities. Feeling exasperated and whiney is the first clue that you're not in the groove of the 6 Personal Year. How many eye-rolls will it take to step back and reevaluated your perceptions and your stance? It can also feel out of whack if you've got blinders on or are in denial about certain key relationships in your life and you're unwilling to step up to the plate, have some hard conversations, and commit to changing the dynamic. If you choose the *same-o same-o,* the 6 Personal Year will hit you like a wave at high tide.

After your freewheeling 5 Personal Year last year, it's time to buckle up and buckle down. There are heightened levels of family-based responsibility this year. *This is a time where all relationships are highlighted.* It's a good year to get married or engaged if you've been hovering around that decision. This is a perfect year to attract *the one* or to recommit and grow your current intimate relationship. It's also a time where you may seek divorce, a break-up or other relationship splits. This can be called the *marriage and divorce* year—and that can be seen both literally and metaphorically.

It's all about evaluating the relationships in your life, starting with your relationship with *you*. This is the year where you'll finally feel that click in knowing if a separation is necessary or you can also have the clarity you've been waiting for and officially say "I Do." Either way, these decision-making moments peak this year. The energy of the number 6 tests your sense of idealism, particularly when it comes to relationships. Do you give yourself away to your kids, spouse, parents, boss or friends? Or do you level judgment on those around you, impeding your—and their—happiness?

It's time to investigate how you feel empowered or disempowered in your domestic life. This is a year where you'll be asked to take on additional responsibilities with friends and family that may come in the form of a wedding, graduation, birth of a baby, military deployment, a loved one's health crisis, or any other family event. The trick is to participate in the way you want to participate. Take on the responsibility without resentment or over-commitment. Or step up and *take on* the responsibility if your tendency is to avoid it.

This is also a year where your home takes a front seat. Do you have a desire to move? Redesign the kitchen or bath? Revitalize your home with new landscaping design, water feature or planter? This is the perfect time to beautify your home on any level. On the career front, it's a make-or-break time for business. Your theme song for the year: "Should I Stay Or Should I Go?" Issues related to control and perfectionism are also under review. You'll be handed experiences that challenge you to let go of outgrown or counter-productive controlling tendencies. You'll also get to practice letting go of perfectionist tendencies and to lighten your demand that others adhere to your sometimes lofty or unrealistic expectations. Remember: If you do something out of duty it'll deplete you. If you do something out of love, it'll energize you. The 6 Personal Year is a beautiful time to enjoy the depth and power of deep connections and mutually nurturing relationships.

How You Might Experience The 6 Personal Year – By Life Path Number

1 Life Path

The 1 Life Path turns attention to your relationship life during the 6 Personal Year. This is a time to step back and focus on the key people in your life. It's beneficial when you take this time to focus on relating to and understanding those around you. Family life takes center stage in whatever configuration that's showing up for you right now. The magic comes when you can dig into the idea of co-creating rather than flying solo. This is your time to follow your urge to merge while also maintaining your healthy independence in the process. You'll be met with additional responsibilities this year, no matter how you slice it. This is a wonderful time to find your "person" or add to your level of commitment with your primary relationship. With work and career, a 6 Personal Year can ignite great success with anything service-related.

2 or 11/2 Life Path

The 2 or 11/2 Life Path in a 6 Personal Year can be an overflowing waterfall of all things love-centered! The energies of the 2 and the 6 speak the language of love and relationship—they just have different points of emphasis. Yet you can't escape this year that will pull your love life into the spotlight. This is across the board—with your significant other to your kids, pets, family, and colleagues. Understand that there are heightened emotions involved this year and you'll be met (once again) with the need to step into who you really are without losing yourself in the process. It's wonderful to be a pleaser on some level, yet you'll be challenged to find your strong yet supple boundaries this year as you traverse the terrain of family-based responsibilities. If you're a Master 11/2 Life Path, add to that the overall intensity your life holds for you every day and amplify the themes of responsibility, relationship evaluation, love, and service to others. Don't forget that often this is the year to find your *one* that equals two!

3 Life Path

The 3 Life Path experiencing a 6 Personal Year can present in some intriguing ways. Both the energies of the 3 and 6 are highly creative vibes and this is a year to step into those creative and artistic impulses. Moreover, this is a time where your vibrant 3 Life Path can shine in the relationship department. Get ready for your *plus one* and enjoy this year of relationship building. Of course, this requires you continue to refine your communication skills and you'll have ample opportunity for that during your year of heightened responsibilities with family, friends, and just across the board. As a 3 Life Path, you get to squeeze all the warm-and-fuzzy experiences out of the year that you possibly can. Given this is a time of relationship evaluation, this can be a make-or-break time for decisions about carrying forward with your relationship(s) or gently exfoliating some of them from your life. Take time to extract deep enjoyment from your relationships.

4 or 22/4 Life Path

The 4 or 22/4 Life Path experiencing a 6 Personal Year can be a solid time for battening down the hatches in the relationship realm. This year tests reserves where family dynamics are concerned. The opportunities reside in building things at a slow and steady pace—while taking the time to stop and engage in group dynamics differently. Emotional connection is a touchtone for the year. As a 4 Life Path, you're innately connected to your home, however you might personally define or create that for yourself. This is a time where *home*—and what that means to you both literally and figuratively—becomes a central theme. This can manifest in so many ways—moving or building a house, redeveloping the landscape design or interior, or redefining what home signifies to you. This can be a year where some deep-seated issues related to your sense of security and stability comes up for review. It's a powerful year for strengthening your connection to your home base. If you're a Master 22/4 Life Path, add to that the overall intensity your life holds for you every day and amplify the themes of responsibility, relationship evaluation, love, and service to others.

5 Life Path

The 5 Life Path experiencing a 6 Personal Year is in for an interesting arm wrestle. It's all going to depend on where you are in your 5 Life Path trajectory—meaning, how *old* are you? If you're old enough to have *been there, done that*, this is a time where you might consider settling in a bit. I actually despise the term *settling down* because it implies that you've been broken somehow—or that you've given up or given in. *Au contraire*, dear 5 Life Path. This can be a time where you find freedom by partnering. If you're an already-partnered 5 Life Path, this is a time to bask in the glow. Or if there's trouble in paradise, it's the year to make it or break it. If you're a 5 Life Path looking for love, this is the time to go deep and feel into your desires and expectations for your love life. You'll face your current biggest fear factor, whatever that may be. Know also that this is a time where you'll be called upon to step up to the responsibility plate and while some 5s are really good at this, some find it feels too constraining. Step into your responsibilities this year.

6 or 33/6 Life Path

The 6 or 33/6 Life Path in a 6 Personal Year offers double the pleasure and double the challenges related to the continued exploration of your deep sense of responsibility, relationship connections, and dutiful service. The year offers new advancements with family dynamics, however that's defined for you at this moment in your life. The double energy of the 6 brings out the very best in your naturally love-oriented vibe, and so this is the primary theme. How do you love and how do you want to be loved? Since you're always concerned with cultivating a nurturing environment, anything having to do with creating and strengthening home-related bonds is favored. Expect opportunities to enhance your relationship skills and to modulate your sense of responsibility. This is the time to up-level your style of nurturing and make some empowering decisions about what stays and what goes in your life. This is very much a time to learn more about co-dependence and about identifying and securing healthy emotional boundaries. Think about this as a time of deep nourishment—where you focus on nourishing yourself and also upon offering nourishment to others. If you're a Master 33/6 Life Path, add to that the overall intensity your life holds for you every day and amplify the themes of responsibility, relationship evaluation, love, and service to others.

7 Life Path

The 7 Life Path in a 6 Personal Year can be a beautiful year for deepening your understanding of how you relate to people on a core emotional level. One of the life-long lessons for the 7 Life Path is in getting out of the head and into the heart more consistently. This is a perfect year to deepen your level of commitment to yourself—and your love and understanding of yourself. It's also a great time to open your heart to a relationship, to heal old emotional wounds on every level, and to slow yourself down enough to continue to develop and understand your intuitive voice. Home and family are key elements this year and matters of the heart are front and center. This can be your time to call in *the one* or to carry forward with an existing relationship. You'll be called upon to step into the emotional fray a bit more than usual.

8 Life Path

The 8 Life Path in a 6 Personal Year can be an exciting time where you feel the urge to merge. Relationship merger, anyone? As an 8, you're already mastering the art of manifesting in this material world. This year supports all things relationship-oriented, particularly as it has to do with your home life. For the 8 Life Path, this can bleed over into your professional life as well, where you'll be offered opportunities to engage in a more nurturing way in your business, career, friendship, and private life.

Business itself can be magnetic during a 6 Personal Year, yet not at the expense of your home-based obligations. This year serves as an opportunity to step into the business of love and relationships rather than a full-throttle focus on career and work. You'll most likely get to meet up with a few relationship curve-balls along the way. Expect the unexpected and focus on developing greater intimacy or galvanizing the courage to say good-bye to any relationships that aren't serving your best interest.

9 Life Path

The 9 Life Path in a 6 Personal Year can be an intriguing whirl of romance with a focus on home, family, and stepping it up in the obligation department. The 9 is charismatic and giving and during the 6 Personal Year, you'll be called up on dip into your relationship life in ways that build true intimacy. This can be a great time for cultivating whatever work-related projects you have going and yet the overall promise is in strengthening and defining your relationships across the board—from family of origin to your significant other to work colleagues. This can be a time to revamp your home, freshen up the landscaping or to move to another residence. Overall, this is a beautiful time to cultivate your relationships on a different and more heart-connecting level.

PERSONAL YEAR 7

A YEAR TO PAUSE AND PROBE THE DEEPEST PARTS OF YOURSELF.

INNER WORK, KNOWLEDGE GATHERING & DIGGING DEEP

WOULD THE REAL ME PLEASE STAND UP?

THE GOAL: TO LOOK BELOW THE SURFACE AND REVEAL HOW TO STEP INTO YOUR NEXT LEVEL OF PERSONAL GROWTH.

BRING IT ON	EXPECT
LEARNING	LOWER ENERGY
ORGANIZING	DESIRE TO HIBERNATE
REFLECTION	FRUSTRATION
SOLITUDE	SHADOW WORK
ANALYSIS	GLORIOUS REVELATIONS
ENHANCED INTUITION!	DESIRE TO GAIN EXPERTISE IN A TOPIC
DELVING INTO THE MYSTICAL	REPRESSED EMOTIONS TO SURFACE
SPIRITUAL GROWTH	AVOIDANCE
PLANNING RATHER THAN DOING	NUMBING OR ZONING OUT
TIME TO CARE FOR THE PHYSCIAL BODY	QUESTIONING EVERYTHING
TRUST IN SELF & DIVINE TIMING	OVER-THINKING

7 PERSONAL YEAR

This year is all about delving inward. While you may see yourself functioning fairly normally, this is a time where you'll be heavily involved in deep inner work. It's a spiritually evolving year—meaning, you'll have many opportunities to test your sense of spirituality, however you define it. If you wonder how one might actually define *spirituality*, here is one way of looking at it. Brené Brown observes: "Spirituality is recognizing and celebrating that we are all inextricable connected to one another by a power greater than all of us, and that our connection to that power and to one another is grounded in love and belonging. Practicing spirituality brings a sense of perspective, meaning, and purpose to our lives." Spirituality is—in its most simple form—*self-awareness*.

This is your focus this year. How do you feel connected and how do you feel disconnected to life overall? How can you take steps to expand both your awareness and your experience with an expanded and powerful sense of purpose? This is a time where faith and trust are tested. You'll feel as though you want to retreat from the static of the outside world. Potentially this brings you into a space that's more quiet, detached, and introspective than usual, so don't let that surprise you. It's a year where you're gathering data, collecting knowledge, and probing your own inner depths. This can show up as being drawn toward travel or toward reading books, taking courses or engaging in workshops or seminars.

Don't push things—that can wait until next year when you start a three-year transition cycle. In her book *Numerology: The Romance in Your Name,* numerologist Dr. Juno Jordan observes that the 7 Personal Year depends upon "a right state of mind." She places the 7 Personal Year as a time for "mental house-cleaning"—when you're offered the opportunity to set your mental and spiritual house in order. This is the year for a retreat, sabbatical or just additional solo time. Your mission—should you choose to accept it—is to explore the depths of your soul's calling and be willing to recalibrate yourself so that you come into alignment with the you that you're excavating this year.

This is not the year to concern yourself with your material well-being or on financial growth. Leave that for next year. Needless to say (but I'll say it anyway), this doesn't imply that you abandon your earthly responsibilities! What is does imply is that this is not the year to focus on financial growth or push your career into over-drive. You're prepping for that, which launches into action next year.

This can be a valuable time to evaluate your sense of yourself and how you've chosen to position yourself in the world. *Nothing deep or heady about that, is there?* It's a time of deep contemplation or—if you're working with heavier tendencies in this cycle—big feelings of being a victim in your life. This is a time for introspection, meditation, and spiritual study. It's also a good moment for counseling or therapy, energy work, and anything else that allows you deep personal growth. There's a focus on embracing the inner depths. This is an *all about me* year in which the universe is giving you full permission to contemplate your own navel.

This may be a year where you're quiet and not as outwardly communicative as usual, so be clear when dealing with your relationships. Many numerologists refer to this year as a resting year or a year that serves as a vital pause before heading into a more active and transitional cycle of time. The 7 Personal Year can feel like a welcome respite from last year's focus on everyone and giving your *nurturing all*. This is a time of deep evaluation where core issues come up for review. Shadow work is unavoidable. It's a time for planning, thinking, researching, learning, and processing. Processing. And a bit more processing.

Maybe it's a year where you don't leave your partner, your partner leaves you. Where you need to take some extra time to deal with a mystery illness or issue. When some strange twist of fate lands on your doorstep. It can feel as though the world is taunting you and gives you the bait-and-switch—promising illumination and yet delivering confusion and curve balls. The occurrences and events of the 7 Personal Year demand that you trust the universal forces at work and flow with the inexplicable and intangible. If you're signed in for the deep dive, this can be a pivotal year for some beautifully life-changing internal shifts where you're the only one who can measure or know the significance—and trying to explain it to someone leaves you feeling even more like an extra-terrestrial.

If you're challenged with the internal work needing to be done, the year can feel frustrating and pull you into feeling victimized and getting stuck in the past or grinding gears that aren't quite in synch. If you refuse to involve yourself in self-realization on any level, you might instead opt for surface living—often showing up as involving yourself in as much emotional drama as possible. Or by gliding by with superficialities—small talk, insubstantial relationships or added time hanging out at the wine bar. Or it can feel off if you're unable to slow down, take in new information, and seek out new ideas and master new levels of data, in whatever way you might benefit.

Even though it's a year for planning rather than doing, if you haven't taken the initiative to research your next steps, you'll ultimately feel you've missed out on a valuable cosmic incubator for your own spiritual and personal evolution. The 7 Personal Year can rival the 9 Personal Year with an overall intense and demanding vibe. Open up and dig in. Slow down. Breathe. It will only lead you to a mystical magical place where you come to know yourself in a life-changing and profound way.

How You Might Experience The 7 Personal Year – By Life Path Number

1 Life Path

The 1 Life Path experiences interesting opportunities during the 7 Personal Year, because the energy related to the year is *somewhat* opposite of what you're all about. Expect additional triggers and treasures coming your way in the realm of slowing down and contemplating life in a more navel-gazing way. As a 1 Life Path, the 7 Personal Year offers a different level of opportunity for self-inquiry. Since the mission of the 1 Life Path is all about the *self*, this year can bring you up close and personal with some of the deeper, darker elements that could use some tending to. The oxymoronic thing about it is that as a 1 Life Path, you're hardwired to *do something active and tangible*. Not so fast, oh-1 Life Path achiever. This is the time to percolate—not to take action, action, and more action. Consider this your year of research and analysis. Take time to cater to your health needs. Quiet the mind. Slow down a bit.

2 or 11/2 Life Path

The 2 or 11/2 Life Path in a 7 Personal Year can be a funny mix. The 2 Life Path can take a deep emotional dive during the 7 Personal Year, since the year is earmarked as a time for deep internal personal growth. If you're a 2 or 11/2 Life Path, this is a fabulous year to perfect your art of energetic self-protection. A focus on meditation, learning more about your intuition or any other esoteric arts is favored now. You might also find yourself taking classes or learning about something that might take your work or career into the next phase. It's a great year to read a few books on healthy relationships and how to communicate effectively in relationships. Take time to tend to any health maintenance. Extract from being on high alert for everyone else's needs and point your attention inward. If you're a Master 11/2 Life Path, add to that the overall intensity your life holds for you every day and amplify the themes of introspection, knowledge gathering, and self-reflection.

3 Life Path

The 3 Life Path experiencing a 7 Personal Year can present in some interesting ways. Count on your themes residing in getting down-and-dirty with any emotional wounds you're harboring. As a 3 Life Path, you have plenty! A key element will be in slowing down and gearing down. Are you working on a writing or creative project? This is the year to take the time to complete it, tweak it or start it. Did you start or end a new relationship last year? This is a good time to review how you engage in relationships and sit with what comes up for you. This is a year where you benefit from engaging in the deeper elements of your psyche and focus on calling in your advanced-levels of personal and universal truth. As a 3 Life Path, you're being asked to speak your truth and yet it'll present with uncomfortable moments as you lean into it. This is a glorious time to open to your spiritual side and to learn more about anything you find healing, intriguing or inspiring.

4 or 22/4 Life Path

The 4 or 22/4 Life Path experiencing a 7 Personal Year shows up in ways that might challenge your 4 Life Path endurance skills. Since you're usually the slow-and-steady-wins-the-race person, the addition of the slower moving energy of the 7 Personal Year offers challenges in dealing with the personal depths involved this year. There are challenges and opportunities to work with old family stuff coming up and needing to be processed. This is a perfect time to take a class or enroll in the program that will take your career to the next level. Perhaps you dive into a new hobby or interest where you cultivate deeper knowledge that will last a lifetime. Any foray into the spiritual world is favored now—that can be deepening or starting a meditation practice, devoting yourself to hikes in nature or any other developmental tool for self-analysis. This year is designed to be your classroom, your library, and your psychic and intellectual research lab. If you're a Master 22/4 Life Path, add to that the overall intensity your life holds for you every day and amplify the themes of introspection, knowledge gathering, and self-reflection.

5 Life Path

The 5 Life Path experiencing a 7 Personal Year is in for an interesting ride. The 5 and the 7 share something in common—the need for space and control over your environment. This is a year where you'll double-down on your need for your room to roam—*and* unplug, detach, and ruminate on whatever issues are touching your mind, heart, and soul. You'll wrangle with your personal fear factor in a vast and deep manner. This introspective year can be marked with lessons in building your trust in change, personal growth, and in investigating how you're doing with the levels of freedom (or not) you've created in your life so far. It's a great time to travel for educational or spiritual purposes—or take some adventures that offer a learning focus. You can be challenged in choosing to escape from looking within in various ways, from using substances that dull and numb you out—to overwork, over-travel or alternately hunkering down and hiding out. This is a powerful year for some deep self-actualization.

6 or 33/6 Life Path

The 6 or 33/6 Life Path in a 7 Personal Year offers a plethora of opportunities to continue the exploration of your creative talents and visionary pursuits. The year offers contemplative moments regarding family dynamics—however that's defined for you at this moment. The energy of the 6 and the 7 don't necessarily *get* each other. The 7 Personal Year draws you inward—while your overall habit as a 6 Life Path is to direct your energies outward, while focusing on caring for others. This year feels somewhat foreign to you and you might struggle with developing and creating a balance. If you blaze forward business as usual, you'll pay a price. Self-care is highlighted right now. If you're a Master 33/6 Life Path, add to that the overall intensity your life holds for you every day and amplify the themes of introspection, knowledge gathering, and self-reflection.

7 Life Path

The 7 Life Path in a 7 Personal Year can be a beautifully intense year for deepening your understanding of yourself on every level. One of the life-long lessons for the 7 Life Path is in acknowledging and then developing both the analytical side of your nature while simultaneously acknowledging and developing your high-levels of intuition. This is *your year* that's earmarked for deepening your spiritual practice. This is also a time to delve into something new that intrigues you and opens yet another door into the development of your soul-based existence. You'll get double the pleasures and double the challenges related to the high vibe of the 7. As a 7 Life Path, the 7 Personal Year brings you up close and personal with whatever issue you're working with at the moment and magnifies it so that you can investigate it—and work with it in the in-depth way that only the 7 Life Path can. As you know, dear 7 Life Path, this doesn't necessarily translate into sparkles and unicorns. Enlightenment is an uncomfortable process and therefore you'll get a few of those experiences this year that challenge your sense of trust. It's a fabulous time for deep and transformational personal growth.

8 Life Path

The 8 Life Path in a 7 Personal Year is a bit of an alligator wrestle. The energy of the 7 and 8 live on different sides of the street. The 7's focused inward and is more interested in the intangible questions of life. As an 8, you're mastering the art of manifesting in the material world. The slower time offered you this year serves as an opportunity to step into the business of some deep soul-searching rather than a full-throttle focus on career and work. You'll most likely get to meet up with opportunities to slow it down and do some much needed planning and organizing. Pushing in your usual forceful manner just won't cut it this year. Take your foot off the accelerator and enjoy a year where you have a permission slip to back off and regroup, ponder, and learn something new. Pushing things forward with a focus on money or finances will only backfire. Take the year to rest, plan, and integrate new energies and new information.

9 Life Path

The 9 Life Path in a 7 Personal Year offers a powerful time for some *deep cleaning* on a soul level. The 9 works with the Buddhist principles of letting go of the past without bitterness and resentment, being in the present, and looking to the future with curiosity. It's part of your life's work as a 9 Life Path to focus on unconditional love and serve the greater good in whatever capacity you feel called to engage. This is a great time to dig deeply into your own psyche and to investigate what drives you. The 7 Personal Year calls you to slow down and *listen* to others more than you *speak* to others. It's a time where there will be experiences exposing levels of yourself you didn't even know existed. There's an overarching sense of loss (or grief or just deep levels of emotion)—and yet don't avoid this profound opportunity to open yourself more directly to your spiritual calling, however that comes into play right now. That can present as *spiritual* as in strengthening your mediation practice, taking esoteric courses or attending a spiritual retreat—preferably in another country since the 9 Life Path thrives with international travel. Or it can present as *spiritual* insofar as you have an opportunity to heal an old family wound, take steps to improve your relationships or take the time to work on a health issue.

PERSONAL YEAR 8

FINANCIAL GROWTH, PERSONAL EMPOWERMENT & ENDURANCE

HOW CAN I EMPOWER MYSELF ON EVERY LEVEL?

THE GOAL:
TO TAKE YOURSELF SERIOUSLY, GET YOUR FINANCIAL LIFE UNDER CONTROL, AND STEP INTO YOUR POWER.

START OF A 3-YEAR PUSH TIME! MONEY & EMPOWERMENT BOOT CAMP

BRING IT ON	EXPECT
FOCUS ON BUSINESS	UPS & DOWNS
INFLUENCE	ISSUES WITH MONEY
PROSPERITY	FEELING VICTIMIZED
CONFIDENCE	INTENSITY - PRESSURE
STEPPING UP	GRAND OPPORTUNITIES
STANDING UP FOR YOURSELF	OVER-FOCUS ON WORK
BEING BUSINESS MINDED	TESTING YOU IN STEPPING UP
FOCUSING & HAVING A PLAN	IDENTIFY YOUR AMBITION
EMBRACE SUCCESS!	BEING TOO CONTROLLING
CONFRONTING DISEMPOWERING SITUATIONS	ABUSING POWER
FEELING LARGE & IN CHARGE!	'REAP AS YOU SOW'

8 PERSONAL YEAR

It's a power year, baby! After a year of deep contemplation, knowledge building, and preparation—this is the time to focus on money, finances, and personal power. Just fair warning: This is the first year of a three-year *push* time. This is the start to a period of intensity focusing first on your financial health and personal sense of empowerment. Next year is the end of a cycle, and the year after is the start of a new cycle.

This year sets the groundwork. It's a testing year. You'll be tested first and foremost in the realm of *empowerment*. Meaning, you'll need to stand up for yourself in a strong, dynamic yet heart-centered way. Time to hit the ground running and focus your actions and energies on creating the financial abundance you want. A key theme resides in this question: *What does prosperity mean to me?* It's a year where you can experience big financial fluctuations, so be prepared to tap into your resilience. You'll be in work over-drive and also be handed opportunities testing your ability to assert yourself. Not once. Not twice. But over and over again all year long.

The energy of the 8 is an amplifier—super-charging whatever it comes into contact with, so take extra care to clean up your thoughts and follow up intentions with action. This is truly a time to get laser-focused about what you want and how you want to get there. Get ready to tap into your tenacity and endurance—because your 8 Personal Year presents itself as your strict personal trainer who has your best interest at heart, even though it might not feel like it! When you're done with the year, you'll be ripped, strong, and in the best shape of your life if you follow your trainer's program.

Remember to take breaks and pace yourself so your health doesn't suffer. Otherwise, you're bound to experience burnout. This energy is truly intense and brings up very real, deep-seated issues related to your sense of empowerment and your relationship with money—and demands that you deal with them. Right out of the chute, you'll benefit from understanding that this isn't going to be an easy-breezy year. It's demanding. Remember that the energy this year, next, and the year after is focused on stepping up, transformation, and then new beginnings.

This is often a career-focused time and yet relationships of all kinds come under scrutiny, with the highlight on where you're empowered and where you're disempowered. Is there an imbalance in your relationships—intimate, family or work-related? Are you a bully, enabler or too dominating? Or are you submissive, docile, and acquiescing? This is a time where healthy balance becomes priority. The energy of the 8 demands that you *step up or get stepped on*. It also challenges you to become the CEO of your life while also maintaining your compassion, humanity, and humility.

This powerful year is guided and supported by the number 8, the energy of manifestation. This is a starting point to some deep-level change and transformation. Rightly, this three-year transition cycle (the Personal Years 8-9-1) begins on a foundational level. This is your year for empowerment and for making things happen in the material world. Its focus is on money and finances—yet that's just the outward result of effort, organization, proper management, and follow-through.

The intensity of this year is undeniable. It's a twelve-month long test where you might pass the exam—and yet instead of getting a congratulatory break, the teacher piles more assignments on your desk. Let's face it—this year isn't for the faint of heart and it certainly is set up to flush out the slackers. The real work here is taking yourself seriously and taking on a business-like attitude—and the year offers experience after experience with this theme.

Whenever people think of the 8, they not only think money, they often think *easy money*. There can't be anything more misleading about the energy of the 8. Yes, it's a powerful force and can magically manifest whatever it places its focus on. Those with mastery over this kind of energy can make things happen miraculously and often make it look easy.

The 8 isn't set up as lucky or easy. It's the "reap what you sow" energy. It demands effort, consistency, and requires clarity of purpose. The challenges are many because it bombards you with tests that can feel harsh and somewhat insurmountable.

This can show up in all kinds of ways. Do you need to ask for a raise at work and yet the thought of it gives you an upset stomach? Are you in an abusive relationship and fear getting out of it? Is your father still telling you what to do even though you're an adult? You get the idea. The empowerment issues can be subliminal or dramatic. Homeless? Addicted to drugs, alcohol or sex? Do you want to speak up for yourself? Do you continue to blame your circumstances on other people?

This is a year where you must understand that the place where you feel the most powerless is where you'll be pushed. The 8 Personal Year is like a drill sergeant at boot camp—it's all up in your face. Also know, though, that the energy of the 8 supports you in an extremely powerful way when you step into yourself and pull yourself out of situations of victimhood. It rewards you for making things happen despite the fact that you don't think you can—or at least feel it's excruciatingly difficult. You can do it! You're strong and resilient. This is the year to prove it.

Optimally, this year is a year where you'll step into rewards and acknowledgment for your ongoing efforts. This is a time where you can gain recognition as an authority in your field and begin to use your power, influence, and connections to expand your own financial resources and also to branch out and give generously to others. When you're fully on-board with the dynamic and powerful energy of the 8 Personal Year, it's a huge turning-point for success in all avenues of your life. The manifestation energy of this year can't be under-estimated. There are countless opportunities to embrace and dig into your strength of character, business demeanor, and make dreams a reality. High levels of ethics—and clarity about your direction—is necessary. Get ready to take a quantum leap—with generous leaps and bounds!—when you're ready to roll with the high-demands of the dynamic and empowering 8 Personal Year.

How You Might Experience The 8 Personal Year – By Life Path Number

1 Life Path

The 1 Life Path experiences heightened opportunities for sky-rocketing success in the 8 Personal Year. Both the energy of the 1 and the 8 are achievement-oriented and thrive when the pressure is on. It won't necessarily be smooth sailing, yet the 8 Personal Year is a launching pad for your 1 Life Path visions, dreams, and projects to manifest and take flight. The caveat is that you can take a detour and get knocked down and choose not to get back up. The 1 Life Path has a Master's Degree from the School of Hard Knocks—and the energy of the 8 is relentless insofar as it's constantly pushing you to act with the utmost ethics and to guide, direct, and manage in the most effective and productive way possible. The power in this combination can't be underestimated. Both are business, achievement, and success-oriented vibes, so you have no choice but to step into your power this year and forge ahead with the bigger picture in mind. This is a year where projects you've been working on begin to produce results. Or this can be a year where you struggle with your self-esteem, confidence, and feelings you'll never catch a break.

2 or 11/2 Life Path

The 2 or 11/2 Life Path in an 8 Personal Year is a power year. Both the numbers 2 and 8 understand each other on a basic level. Both are business-centered vibes with the 2 in the business of caring for others, love, and relationships—while the business of the 8 resides in financial success, ethics, and self-empowerment. The 2 or 11/2 Life Path can be stretched outside of the comfort zone this year, when you'll face intense challenges with stepping into your own sense of personal power, which is a mutual theme with the energy of the 2 and the 8. The 2 Life Path often doesn't prioritize personal ambition, yet this year demands that you invite some moments where you step to the front of the line. The 2 Life Path is working on gaining empowerment by not giving themselves away to everyone else. The energy of the 8 is about being assertive and making things happen, which often offers a bit of a conflict for the peace-loving 2 Life Path. This is a power year, no way around it. If you're a Master 11/2 Life Path, add to that the overall intensity your life holds for you every day and amplify the themes of financial success, personal empowerment, proper use of authority, and effective management.

3 Life Path

The 3 Life Path experiencing an 8 Personal Year presents in some fascinating ways. This is the year for the 3 Life Path to get real about money and step into a sense of personal empowerment. With the 3 Life Path, most often this is focused on coming to terms with your emotional life on whatever realm is needed at the moment. You can count on it being of more substance—needing to leave an abusive relationship, benefiting from quitting your current job or perhaps there's a hard conversation to be had with a family member. You know—those things that hold more weight and volume. The 8 Personal Year is a perfect time for a creative project to sprout legs and produce positive financial results. It's a time for you to move into your sense of self-confidence and to take yourself seriously. It's time to take control over your financial life and get things in order. This is a year where you can reap great rewards when you've been putting in the work.

4 or 22/4 Life Path

The 4 or 22/4 Life Path experiencing an 8 Personal Year feels like you're running a marathon chased by hungry tigers. This is a year where you're definitely pulling out all your 4 Life Path reserves. The opportunities reside in building things at a slow and steady pace, while also stepping into the higher expectations and performance demanded by the 8 Personal Year. The energy of the 4 and 8 are highly compatible insofar as the 4 is the younger sibling of the 8. While the 4 Life Path thrives and strives toward financial security, the energy of the 8 Personal Year demands that you raise your sights and elevate your goals. This is a time where all your concerted effort, goal-setting, and tenacious work starts to royally pay off. This can feel like an intensely challenging time filled with many tests, hurdles, gains, and set-backs. Make sure to put some *time off* days in your calendar or this is a time where you can be engulfed by overwhelm and overwork. Stick with it and you'll reap some substantial benefits this year. If you're a Master 22/4 Life Path, add to that the overall intensity your life holds for you every day and amplify the themes of financial success, personal empowerment, proper use of authority, and effective management.

5 Life Path

The 5 Life Path experiencing an 8 Personal Year is in for an interesting and possibly dynamic ride. This is your year of empowerment, dear 5 Life Path, and so what's the focus for you right now? Do you need to deal with where you stand in a relationship? Are you struggling with income and need to get real about your finances? Perhaps a health concern is your first priority. Whatever is a key element for you will be in the spotlight. You'll be met with the need to step into yourself in a more powerful way than you ever have before. This is the time to take charge of yourself and take responsibility for yourself across the board. You'll find success when you focus intently on the *structure* the 8 Personal Year supports and demands—management, organization, clear goals, and concerted effort are your key tools this year. It's time to place any emotional indulgence on the sidelines and focus instead on practicality. Infuse your adventurous spirit into all that you do, of course, and yet it's the time where you'll be tested to get things on the calendar and show up to the table.

6 or 33/6 Life Path

The 6 Life Path in an 8 Personal Year offers a plethora of opportunities to continue the exploration of your relationship world and your business prospects. The energy of the 6 and the 8 are both quite *driven*, just in different ways. As a 6 Life Path, this year can hold out ample and substantial opportunities to build your business or career and take it to new heights. This can be the year for your business to take off and reap incredible financial rewards. On the family and relationship front, the energy of the year tests you to once again set healthy emotional boundaries, level your expectations, and empower yourself on whatever level needs it most. If you're a Master 33/6 Life Path, add to that the overall intensity your life holds for you every day and amplify the themes of financial success, personal empowerment, proper use of authority, and effective management.

7 Life Path

The 7 Life Path in an 8 Personal Year can be an invaluable time that brings opportunities to fine-tune—to get to know yourself, your true needs, and true nature in a deep way. This is a year where you can step into your personal empowerment and begin to merge your spirituality with your material, day-to-day life. Be prepared to face issues related to trusting yourself and your ability to make your way in the financial world that will ultimately be more in alignment with your core values. Money and your financial life take a front seat right now and play a major role in your involvement this year. Empowerment comes in many forms, so prepare to make choices and decisions about empowering yourself on whatever level you're engaged with at this time in your life. Yet your career, work, and financial health are key players and require your focused attention.

8 Life Path

The 8 Life Path in an 8 Personal Year has the potential to open the floodgates to prosperity, success, and empowerment. When you have the same Personal Year as your Life Path number, you experience double the pleasures and double the challenges related to the number 8. As an 8 Life Path, you know that the demands of the 8 are, *well*, really demanding! While this can be an explosively expansive year for you, it won't come to the door purring like a kitten. All that you are, all that you want to create and manifest, everything that you're striving toward in your life is playing like one powerful, long note on the sheet of music. This is the time to bask in your accomplishments and keep it all flowing, organized, and managed. This is also the year where resilience is tested and any weak links dismantled. The obvious energy for you this year has to do with money, career, and financial gain. Yet don't underestimate personal dynamics as well. Use your power, connections, and influence with generosity and wisdom.

9 Life Path

The 9 Life Path in an 8 Personal Year can be a year of abundance and prosperity. As a 9 Life Path, you're always working with a certain level of letting go of stuff on every level imaginable. Yet often your big and compassionate heart leads you to money in ways that appears to be somewhat effortless to other people. It's a result of doing what speaks to you without the focus being on the financial outcome. As a 9 Life Path, you'll be compelled to donate and give to others. This is truly a *reap as you've sown* year, dear 9 Life Path, where you'll be offered rewards for your efforts. This is a testing year and therefore you'll have the opportunity to wrangle with whatever you're working on in the personal power department. Relationships? Health? Finances? What's your primary issue at hand? Whatever that is, it's front and center right now. Remember that what you focus on expands exponentially during an 8 Personal Year, so be mindful of where you place your focus and attention. Make sure you're placing your intentions most directly on the here and now rather than in the past.

PERSONAL YEAR

THE END OF A 9-YEAR CYCLE!
TRANSITION & TRANSFORMATION

WRAPPING THINGS UP, LETTING GO, & MAKING ROOM FOR THE NEW

HOW CAN I LET GO OF EVERYTHING I NO LONGER NEED IN ORDER TO MAKE ROOM FOR POSITIVE CHANGES?

THE GOAL:
TO ALLOW THINGS TO FALL AWAY IN ORDER TO STEP INTO A NEW & EXCITING PHASE IN YOUR LIFE.

BRING IT ON	EXPECT
CONCLUSIONS	HIGH EMOTIONS
ASSESSMENT	CLOSURES
FORGIVENESS	FEELING IN LIMBO
COMPLETIONS	REFLECTING ON THE PAST
LETTING GO	A SENSE OF LOSS
DREAMS COMING TRUE!	FEAR OF THE UNKNOWN
PERSONAL & SPIRITUAL EXPANSION	LIFE-CHANGING EVENTS
SAYING GOOD-BYE TO WHAT NEEDS TO EXIT	OPPORTUNITIES TO BE ALTRUISTIC
RENEWED SENSE OF GRATITUDE	OPENINGS FOR CREATIVE WORK
CHANCE TO FORGIVE SELF & OTHERS	REDEFINING YOUR CORE VALUES
OPPORTUNITIES TO LET GO ON ALL LEVELS	EMOTIONAL PROCESSING

9 PERSONAL YEAR

This is the end of a nine-year cycle. It's a year of completion, unraveling, and letting go of the old to make space for the new. This change can be somewhat dramatic and tumultuous—affecting possessions, relationships, jobs, geographical location, spirituality, and health. It's all under review this year. This is the year that's inviting you (oh, let's be honest, it's forcing you) to move on to an even more expansive cycle in your life when you choose to let go and allow what's no longer serving you to fall away. Don't despair! This is a year where you can revel in the successful culmination of all that you've been working toward for the past eight years and beyond.

The 9 Personal Year struggles with a bad rap. People sometimes recoil with fear and trepidation at the thought of letting go of things in their lives. Facing the 9 Personal Year can send people into a panic. Don't buy into that! This is a beautiful year that's often an emotional roller coaster of change, transition, surrender, and sets the stage for transformation and new beginnings.

Think about it this way. What's so awful about the end of a party? Or saying good-bye to a co-worker who's leaving for a new and exciting job overseas? How about the graduation party celebrating the mastery of a specific course of study and you're marking the time where you're finished with your coursework, getting through final exams, and moving into a different phase of your life?

That's the basis for the 9 Personal Year. It's a natural function of life, evolution, and desire. It's always moving you into the next bigger and better phase yet—just like that graduation party—it can feel emotional if not a bit sad, confusing, and disorienting. There is a sense of grief involved with saying good-bye to the people, places, and routine you've engaged in during your studies. Yet staying there would be, well, *weird*.

The point of going to college is to graduate and move on. The same for life in general. *And this is a point of graduation. It's a year of commencement—endings marking the opening for new beginnings.*

If you're eagerly and happily going with the oftentimes strange flow of the year—open to letting it all go or letting it all be seriously re-calibrated—well then, you're the odd duck in the history of the 9 Personal Year! Just as a point of reference: I have known people who experience just that—they are *so ready* for everything to change and when it does, they welcome it with open arms. Yet that is rare. The usual response resides primarily in low-level fear (and an elevated sense of anxiety) mixed with a high level of hanging on for dear life. The unknown is not a place that's a natural habitat for most humans.

The energy of the 9 is about loss—and *loss* in a more profound and spiritual sense. It's like the Buddhist art of making a sand Mandala and then performing a ritual where it's dissolved and dismantled. The energetic imprint of the Mandala will always be present, albeit not in physical form. Similarly, the essence of the 9 is a highly-charged spiritual energy supporting us in letting go of the illusion of control and permanence—and offers us a liminal space from which to trust and engage in the present moment. Pretty high-minded, eh?

Ultimately the 9 Personal Year is a game changer all the way around. We're not optimizing this transformational energy when we wallow in our losses or obstinately avoid letting go of things we truly know need to be released. At the end of the day, this is a year to clear out what's no longer needed in order to make room for a new, exciting, and more evolved chapter ahead. What's the saying?—the definition of insanity is doing the same thing over and over again while expecting different results? That is the feeling the 9 Personal Year brings—up close and personal. The 9 holds a humanitarian focus. The more you can give selflessly this year, the smoother the process. Forgiveness is a key theme.

It's a time where your dreams can manifest almost instantly if you're ready to let go of everything that's no longer serving your best and highest interests. It's a matter of evaluating what's finished and no longer serving a positive function and then moving forward without a net. You know people who are in a marriage or a relationship that's over with and yet they won't get a divorce or break up with their partner until they have another love interest waiting in the wings? Well, metaphorically (and sometimes literally!) speaking, the 9 Personal Year won't allow you to do that. You must break it off and then manage and master that empty space of nothingness for a while.

Needless to say, even the best of us are scared silly when it comes to change. Then to change something without knowing exactly what's next? *What?!* That's what's required this year. Some of the punctuation marks that can be the centerpiece of a 9 Personal Year can be divorce, health crises, getting fired or let go from your job, career change, geographical move, death of a close friend or family member or other loss that holds a greater magnitude than usual. It's like your life is a sand castle and the ocean tides bring in stronger waves that continue to lap away at the sand, resulting in its dissolution.

This can be the time when a child is born or leaves home, when retirement becomes official, when you graduate or go back to school, get a job promotion leading to a geographical move or experience other life changers. This shift can find its locus in your connection to a spouse—perhaps they get fired, get a promotion or something of that nature. While it's not happening directly to you, indirectly it's shaping your world. This can also be a year where you experience a magical transformation that you've been waiting on for a very long time! Think of that graduation or the birth of the baby—and how these experiences are the epitome of new beginnings wrapped up in an "endings" wrapper. Every new beginning is some other beginnings end.

This is an absolutely necessary time for growth, yet it's like Fall or Winter. It's time to cut back the overgrowth, clean up and evaluate the soil, and let it lay fallow until Springtime. It's a time of reflection. It's a time to bring in the empowerment gleaned in your 8 Personal Year and put your money where your mouth is (so to speak). This isn't a year for implementation or starting something significant. This is time for closure—not time to rush into something new. It's a time for sorting, organizing, and reviewing all aspects of your life. The demand that you face and embrace your truth—and the truth of your current situation—is at a peak. When you're ready and open to make very real changes, that's when you soar during this transformational year.

This is the grand finalé that offers the final episode of your nine-year series that is your life. No spoiler alerts please! Staying with the TV or movie theme, if the 9 Personal Year were a character from a movie, I would say it's Mary Poppins. The 9 Personal Year (we'll call her Mary) swoops in to help you move through issues and "spit, spot," put them to bed. Remember that Mary comes in to help the children (and the parents) see what the problem is—and then offers ways to solve those problems. She offers support and yet isn't particularly warm-and-fuzzy. She's matter-of-fact and detached, yet loving.

Then as the wind changes direction, she pops open her umbrella and leaves the family to deal with their new dynamics on their own. Get ready to invite Mary Poppins into your home this year. You might not agree with her methods or her mode of discipline, yet Mary also offers openings for fun, not to mention a few catchy show tunes!

How You Might Experience The 9 Personal Year – By Life Path Number

1 Life Path

The 1 Life Path experiences an interesting dynamic during the 9 Personal Year. Why? Because the 1 Life Path is all about action, initiation, and new starts while the energy of the 9 is the bookend to the energy of the 1, offering the yin to the yang. Now is the time where things fall away and a new reinvention point is on the horizon. This year demands surrender and the 1 Life Path would rather *make* something happen than *allow* something to happen. Ah, there's the rub! Ready yourself for some discomfort and confusion as you work on walking from *here* to *there* this year. Yet never fear. You're readying yourself for more new beginnings—which are your forté. This is your time to tie things up, let things go, and open to new possibilities.

2 or 11/2 Life Path

The 2 or 11/2 Life Path in a 9 Personal Year can be a powerful and transitional time. The 2 Life Path experiences dramatic shifts in your relationship life during a 9 Personal Year. This can be anything from your intimate relationship, to family and children or even friends and colleagues. Since you're always working in the realms of emotions and loving relationships, this year allows you to let go of things within your relationship life that just aren't serving your best interests any longer. If you're a Master 11/2 Life Path, add to that the overall intensity your life holds for you every day and amplify the themes of surrender, letting go, completions, and dreams coming true.

3 Life Path

The 3 Life Path experiencing a 9 Personal Year presents in complex ways. Count on your themes residing in creative self-expression and emotional sensitivity. As always with the 3 Life Path, any creative endeavors are very much supported this year, yet the trick will be in navigating the timing—meaning this is the year to complete things, not to start them. The key player will be in the emotional realm. This is a year to review your intimate and business relationships and also to slow down enough to dig into your emotional sensitivity and master a certain level of healthy and direct communication. Overall, this is a hugely transformative year and a time to come face-to-face with how you want to dig even more into your authenticity, whether that's with your career or within your relationship life.

4 or 22/4 Life Path

The 4 or 22/4 Life Path experiencing a 9 Personal Year can be a somewhat stressful brew. This is a year where you're definitely practicing your 4 Life Path skills and ability to be a practical purveyor of virtually everything. Let's face it—it's all up for review right now. The opportunities reside in (on one hand) dealing with everything that comes your way with your utmost 4 Life Path practicality. On the other hand, it's a time where emotions rise to the surface to be claimed and honored. This poses a challenge for the otherwise emotionally pragmatic 4 Life Path. Overall, this is a year of transition where you're offered opportunities to step into a new and revised version of yourself. If you're a Master 22/4 Life Path, add to that the overall intensity your life holds for you every day and amplify the themes of surrender, letting, go, completions, and dreams coming true.

5 Life Path

The 5 Life Path experiencing a 9 Personal Year is in for an interesting ride. This is a year where you'll be reviewing the core elements of your

5 Life Path trajectory and feeling out what stays, what goes, and what can be integrated into the next nine-year cycle. This year presents you with seismic shifts and yet as a 5 Life Path, change is your gig! Or is it? This is a time demanding that you open to constructive change and don't go down the rabbit hole of fear, despair or total inaction. Whether you believe me or not, as a 5 Life Path, the world is your oyster and yet often you question that reality for yourself. The key is in grounding and centering yourself. The 9 Personal Year is the time for review, renewal, and ultimately, for reinvention.

6 or 33/6 Life Path

The 6 or 33/6 Life Path experiencing a 9 Personal Year is in for some recalibration across the board. As a 6 Life Path, the 9 Personal Year marks a significant turning point in your home and family life. That can play out as a job or career change, a move, a relationship addition (or subtraction) or a focus on a health concern. The 6 Life Path is a well-known control freak—I observe that lovingly, of course. Letting go and surrendering control is the hardest part of the transitional 9 Personal Year. This is a time where you can struggle with letting go of your perfect vision of the way things were supposed to turn out—or the way everything is *supposed to be*—and surrender to *what is*. The 9 Personal Year is the time for review, renewal, and ultimately, for reinvention. If you're a Master 33/6 Life Path, add to that the overall intensity your life holds for you every day and amplify the themes of surrender, letting, go, completions, and dreams coming true.

7 Life Path

The 7 Life Path in a 9 Personal Year can be a deeply moving and transformative year. The common denominator with the 7 and the 9 resides in the high spiritual vibe and when these two numbers coalesce, the outcome will be apparent on the outside—and yet what happens internally will have even more meaning and volume to you as a 7 Life Path. The beauty resides in experiencing a full mind/body/spirit transformation and if there's any year where that's on the docket, it's the 9 Personal Year. There's a great quote that speaks to how you might experience the unfolding of the year: "Sometimes your mind needs more time to accept what your heart already knows." The 9 Personal Year is the time to connect your heart with your head in a more expansive way than you have in the past and to open to emptying yourself of all that's no longer serving you.

8 Life Path

The 8 Life Path in a 9 Personal Year proves to be a powerful time for empowerment and reinvention. The caveat is that the 8 Life Path is always managing, organizing, and taking the action needed to manifest things and to make things happen. That's your *modus operandi*. During a 9 Personal Year, the demands of the 8 are thwarted. It won't matter how much muscle you use—you won't be able to successfully push your agenda. The 9 Personal Year has its own agenda! There's an emphasis is on releasing, letting go, and tests your ability to surrender to the flow. This isn't exactly comfortable terrain for the 8 Life Path. The demand is for you to forge an opening for the completions and closing out certain people, activities, and *stuff* that's expired and no longer serving a positive function in your life. This will show up in the places where you're working intently on building your sense of personal empowerment, whether that shows up in relationships, in your financial life or in any other category that is a priority at the moment. Yet this "priority" holds more weight, because it's likely to be something you've been creating or avoiding for the last eight years, if not longer. This can be a magical time to step into your power and make decisive changes.

9 Life Path

The 9 Life Path in a 9 Personal Year shows up as a symphony of the Buddhist concept of letting go of the past without bitterness or resentment, residing in the present moment, and looking to the future with curiosity. As a 9 Life Path, you're always working with a certain level of letting go of stuff on every level imaginable. This is a year where you get double the pleasures and double the challenges related to the wise and compassionate number 9. This is a wonderful year to step into a higher level of philanthropic or altruistic activities. Selfless-service has its rewards and benefits and if there's ever a year where you'll feel the pull to give more, this is it. Forgiveness is a key theme this year. You're not immune to the transition points, yet you're used to it by now, right?—you wise and creative 9 Life Path. It's time to let go (again) and begin a new sand Mandala!

HOW DO I USE MY PERSONAL YEAR CYCLES?

To reiterate: The way I'm formulating the Personal Year Cycle is from January 1 – December 31, *not from birthday to birthday*. I'm aware that some numerologists consider the Personal Year to run from birthday to birthday. Look again at how it is calculated and you'll see it's from the start of the year to the close of that same year. I feel that it runs from January 1 through the end of December of the same year, given that's how it is calculated (month/day/current year). However, you'll experience *intensity* in the energies of the calendar year directly before and after your birthday. It's truly up to you and how it feels to you as you traverse your year. The meaning of the Personal Year remains the same, yet when it shows up is up for debate—year to year or birthday to birthday? You decide for yourself. I feel it's year to year.

Applying the knowledge gleaned from your Personal Year number is a multifaceted process with many benefits. First, knowing that you're in a 9 Personal Year, for example, certainly takes some of the confusion and resistance out of a year of tumultuous transitions. It won't take the sting away. Yet knowing that a year is meant to be a transitional and transformative is worth the price of admission. That knowledge alone allows you to step back and view your life through a new lens and direct your focus on the tasks at hand. It also offers validation and direction that you might not have words for otherwise.

I'll call out this key concept. Numerology is great in terms of offering information in the way of *words*. This book is an interpretation of key themes, points of arrival, and points of departure for the numbers. What we often forget or overlook is that numerology is engaging and affecting us all the time, whether we know about it or believe in it. *More than words and concepts, numerology is encoded energy.* It's something we feel. It directs traffic by placing people, happenings, and experiences into our lives. The Personal Year is a great example of how this might show up. It's also an incredible opportunity to use this energy to live our lives in the most intentional way possible.

You might consider mapping out all of your Personal Years you've experienced until now—or at least look at the major transitional periods encapsulated by the Personal Years 8-9-1. Use this information to come up with a skeletal framework of what can be considered the punctuation marks or turning points in your life. You'll find many times, when you're telling someone about your life, these are the moments that frame your story.

Knowing about your Personal Year Cycles validates the ways you're feeling and helps support beneficial choices. The exciting thing when numerology resonates with us is that we can focus on the themes that are being supported and understand what it is that won't necessarily bring us what we want. Meaning, we won't have to spend a load of time on wondering if the issues we're facing during the year are just coincidental or throw away items.

For example, if someone knows they're in a 4 Personal Year (a time for working hard and sharpening skill sets) and yet they feel the tendency to frolic and scatter their attention, they'll learn fairly quickly that it won't be a satisfying or productive year. If they follow their impulses, instead of feeling good about all the rambling around they're doing, they'll end up feeling frustrated because they went against the energy and purpose of the year.

I have a friend who's a 5 Life Path and his last 4 Personal Year was a very difficult time for him because he was being nudged (okay, *pushed*) to get focused and get some systems down in order to stabilize his real estate career. Yet he chose to avoid that and travel for most of the year (*so 5!*)—and then wondered why he was so depressed during this time. He *knew* it was because he wasn't doing the grunt work that was necessary to get things organized in a successful way. Yet he kept accepting opportunities to gallivant and travel for extensive periods of time. The irony is that he *knew* doing the work that his 4 Personal Year was asking him to do would ultimately become the foundation to financial freedom, which is a huge priority for him as a 5 Life Path—the freedom seeker!

There are certain Personal Years that challenge us more than others. My 5 Life Path friend and his 4 Personal Year is a perfect example. The energies related to the 4 and the 5 aren't usually the best of friends. The 4 seeks structure, stability, and is hard-working while the 5 often is the anti-4—craving change, adventure, and living with more immediacy. It's no wonder he had issues, because he was being asked to devote himself to certain things that he doesn't find second nature, desirable or fun in any way. Yet when we know the primary components of our Personal Year, we can gain the resolve to be more in alignment with the optimal energies and work more effectively with the challenges.

My 5 Life Path friend screeched to a halt about mid-year and re-dedicated himself to focusing on structuring his business. The side-door to this feat was ignited by hiring a personal trainer! His indulgent behavior throughout the year had caught up with him as well. He'd gained weight and wasn't happy about that at all. He started following a wellness program that his personal trainer devised for him, including exercise and diet. Since he was paying for it, he followed through with his commitment.

After several weeks with the trainer, he dropped some weight, gained energy, and felt better all the way around. That compelled him to have the focus and follow-through to get his business in order. It took him a while, yet he felt that he hadn't optimized the energy of his 4 Personal Year and was daring and brave enough to want to change it. He ended the year feeling much more in alignment with where he felt he should be with his life, health, and business. He was then able to feel the synergy that the 5 Life Path is ultimately seeking—gaining freedom by reining in indulgence and by instituting structured discipline.

Knowing what Personal Year your friends and family are in the midst of is a powerful tool for developing a deeper awareness of them and understanding their lives. Knowing where your friends and family are in their own Personal Year Cycles allows you to key into the core issues they're experiencing so that you can support them the best way you can. It helps to communicate with them in a richer way.

In fact, I have a habit of checking the Personal Year numbers of my close circle of friends and family at the start of each year. Knowing the energy guiding friends and family during each year is a handy tool to see what's at play with them in both their professional and personal lives. The bonus reward you reap is the potential of forging deeper understanding between you and your loved ones. Whereas in the past you may have felt you just didn't get why your wife did this, your father did that, or your best friend was a mess, now you have the opportunity to step back and evaluate. See what energies their Personal Years are bringing to them so that you'll be better able to support them with their struggles and engage with them in sharing the good stuff.

Knowing the cycles of the people closest to you in your life not only can help you understand them better, it also can help *you* ready yourself for how they'll impact your life during the year. The bottom line is that when you're operating within the energies presented to you during your Personal Year Cycles, you'll have amazing support from the universe to create success and satisfaction—and to extract deeper meaning from the experiences and happenings during the year.

THE PINNACLE CYCLE

Along with the Universal Year Cycle and the Personal Year Cycle, the last cycle we'll discuss is the Pinnacle Cycle. Although there are other cycles, bridges, planes, and transits in numerology, we're focusing on these three key cycles—Universal Year, Personal Year, and now Pinnacle Cycles.

The Personal Year is the most immediate energy we feel each year, while the Universal Year feels like the umbrella energy that everyone experiences during any given year.

The Pinnacles are four distinct periods of time that each of us experience—with the longest cycles being at the beginning and at the end of our lives, with two nine-year cycles in the middle. Each Pinnacle is a time of personal development.

The Pinnacles can be seen as the degree programs you signed up for during your life—and you get to study that particular subject matter for an extended period of time. Consider them to be like a master plan compartmentalized into stages of development. They are the building blocks of your life—and you take the experiences and skills learned throughout each cycle and bridge them to inform the next.

Each Pinnacle number represents the energy and lessons that are emphasized during a period of several years. Understanding the elements presented to you during your Pinnacle Cycles offers invaluable information about the focus and lessons to be learned during certain chunks of time, and also provides a great format for understanding why certain things happen during these periods of time. This is the *environment* in which you find yourself, offering you a particular trajectory through life.

In numerology, Pinnacles are sometimes called The Four Pyramids. Calculating your four Pinnacle Cycle numbers is not so much a predictive tool—although it can be used to map out a clearer vision of your past, present, and future—as a tool that offers support and guidance for your life decisions and actions.

If you learn about the Pinnacles later in life, it's a wonderful tool for reflection and extracting meaning and value out of your experiences. While there's no crystal ball by any means, having knowledge of your Pinnacles is a platform upon which to understand the trajectory of your life in a more conscious and meaningful way. Everyone goes through four Pinnacle Cycles in their lives. Yet we go through them at different times, depending on our Life Path number.

When I interpret a numerology profile, I always look to see if any of the core numbers in a profile show up in a person's Pinnacle Cycles. If so, to me it indicates a period of time where that particular aspect or element of their personality (as defined by the core numbers) is being highlighted for growth. Alternately, if someone experiences one or more Pinnacle Cycles that *don't match* with any of their core numbers, it's as though they were visiting a foreign country for that period of time, where they had to learn a new language and get used to different customs. This is often a time where a person felt out of place and out of synch with their environment.

CALCULATING PINNACLES

You've gotten this far, so this news won't surprise you. *Of course* there's more than one way numerologists calculate the Pinnacle numbers. I'm sharing the way I feel the Pinnacles are calculated (below) and yet I'll illustrate another way so you can make the determination yourself.

This is the basic formula for finding your four Pinnacles.

Just like the way of calculating your Life Path number separately adding the month/day/year, you work with the Pinnacles the same way.

1st Pinnacle   = Month of Birth + Day of Birth
2nd Pinnacle   = Day of Birth + Year of Birth
3rd Pinnacle   = First Pinnacle + Second Pinnacle
4th Pinnacle   = Month of Birth + Year of Birth

Let's see how you could do it both ways, and how the results aren't necessarily the same.

November 22, 1985

With the first way of calculation, you would do the math using:

November = 11 and 1 + 1 = 2

Day = 22 and 2 + 2 = 4

1985 = 1 + 9 + 8 + 5 = 23
2 + 3 = 5

Then you calculate this way:

1st Pinnacle: (month) 2 + (day) 4 = 6
2nd Pinnacle: (day) 4 + (year) 5 = 9
3rd Pinnacle: (1st Pinnacle) 6 + (2nd Pinnacle) 9 = 15 and 1 + 5 = 6
4th Pinnacle: (month) 2 + (year) 5 = 7

Now let's see the other option. In this way of thinking, you use the full number without reducing it first. When you have a Master number, the Master number is *not* reduced.

November 22, 1985

November: 11
Day: 22
Year: 1985

1st Pinnacle = (month) 11 + (day) 22 = 33
Since 33 is a Master number it is not reduced. This is the final number for the 1st Pinnacle.

2nd Pinnacle = (day) 22 + (year) 1985 = 2,007 and 2 + 0 + 0 + 7 = 9

3rd Pinnacle = (1st Pinnacle) 33 + (2nd Pinnacle) 9 = 42 and 4 + 2 = 6

4th Pinnacle = (month) 11 + (year) 1985 = 1,996 and 1 + 9 + 9 + 6 = 25; 2 + 5 = 7

With the first way of calculating, the Pinnacles show as:

1st Pinnacle: 6
2nd Pinnacle: 9
3rd Pinnacle: 6
4th Pinnacle: 7

With the second way of calculating, the Pinnacles show as:

1st Pinnacle:	33/6
2nd Pinnacle:	9
3rd Pinnacle:	6
4th Pinnacle:	7

The biggest change with doing the calculation the first way or the second way is minimal when calculating Pinnacle Cycles and the difference often reveals a Master number.

CALCULATE YOUR AGE DURING YOUR DIFFERENT PINNACLES

Now you must calculate the age you are during your different Pinnacles.

The age in which you begin and conclude each Pinnacle Cycle depends on your Life Path number.

To calculate your age during your 1st Pinnacle, use the **number 36** and *subtract* your Life Path number from it.

Example:

If you're a 9 Life Path, subtract 9 from 36.

$36 - 9 = 27$

This means that your 1st Pinnacle transpires from the *time of your birth (0) until you're 27 years old.*

To calculate your age during your 2nd Pinnacle, **add** 9 to the ending age of your 1st Pinnacle.

Example: For the 9 Life Path whose First Pinnacle ended at age 27 we calculate:

$27 + 9 = 36$

Your 2nd Pinnacle lasts from age 27 to age 36.

To calculate your age during your 3rd Pinnacle, **add** 9 to the ending age of your 2nd Pinnacle.

Example: For the 9 Life Path, whose 2nd Pinnacle ended at age 36, we calculate:

36 + 9 = 45

Your 3rd Pinnacle lasts from age 36 to age 45.

Your 4th Pinnacle starts at the end of your 3rd Pinnacle. This age initiates the energy engaging you for the rest of your life.

Example: For the 9 Life Path, whose 3rd Pinnacle lasted until age 45, the 4th Pinnacle begins at age 45 and lasts until death.

PINNACLE TIME GRID

	1ST PINNACLE TIME FRAME	2ND PINNACLE TIME FRAME	3RD PINNACLE TIME FRAME	4TH PINNACLE TIME FRAME
Life Path 1	Age 0-35	Age 35-44	Age 44-53	Age 53 -
Life Path 2	Age 0-34	Age 34-43	Age 43-52	Age 52 -
Life Path 3	Age 0-33	Age 33-42	Age 42-51	Age 51 -
Life Path 4	Age 0-32	Age 32-41	Age 41-50	Age 50 -
Life Path 5	Age 0-31	Age 31-40	Age 40-49	Age 49 -
Life Path 6	Age 0-30	Age 30-39	Age 39-48	Age 48 -
Life Path 7	Age 0-29	Age 29-38	Age 38-47	Age 47 -
Life Path 8	Age 0-28	Age 28-37	Age 37-46	Age 46 -
Life Path 9	Age 0-27	Age 27-36	Age 36-45	Age 45 -
Life Path 11/2	Age 0-34	Age 34-43	Age 43-52	Age 52 -
Life Path 22/4	Age 0-32	Age 32-41	Age 41-50	Age 50 -
Life Path 33/6	Age 0-30	Age 30-39	Age 39-48	Age 48 -

Numerologist Hans Decoz defines the Pinnacles by identifying the key element of each in this manner: The 1st Pinnacle is a stage of attainment. The 2nd Pinnacle denotes a time of obligation. The 3rd Pinnacle becomes a period to lay a foundation, and the 4th Pinnacle is a time of retrospection. I also see the 4th Pinnacle as a time of *culmination* when everything you've experienced, all the environments you've explored and navigated, and all that you've developed in your life to this point is brought together to rich fulfillment during the 4th and final Pinnacle.

Also note that if you're already into your 4th Pinnacle, don't let that discourage or depress you! Life is far from over. I always say, unless you get run over by a trolley or eaten by a shark, chances are you have an entire lifetime to live during your 4th Pinnacle. If you've been doing your work and have a desire to play out your final years with meaning and purpose, this is a great way to understand how to fully align with your highest purpose and gain the most fulfillment.

Now that you have determined your four Pinnacles and the ages that they occur, here are the basic characteristics that can help you navigate through, over, and around your particular Pinnacle.

1 PINNACLE
INDEPENDENCE & SELF-RELIANCE

1 — TIME OF ATTAINMENT

You find yourself in an environment that you eventually learn to extract from & form your own sense of self. Often a time of either acquiescing or rebellion. Fertile time for development of creative talents, leadership & finding yourself developing independence.

2 — TIME OF OBLIGATION

This is a period where you're being called upon to stand up for yourself & lean into your offbeat ideas or personality. Often this is where you need to develop a thicker skin, fail forward, and learn to take calculated risk (with proper intel!)

3 — TIME OF FOUNDATION

Courage, resilience & forward-thinking rule this period of time. Learning to extract from co-dependence & understand how to co-create is a hallmark of this Pinnacle. Balancing the ego, standing on your own two feet & inspired leadership are key.

4 — TIME OF CULMINATION

Stand up & be counted! Time to step up & march to the beat of your own drum. Challenges reside in being able to engage with others without pushing your own agenda. When refusing input from others, 1 can be the loneliest number.

1 PINNACLE

During this Pinnacle, you're focused on developing *independence, self-reliance,* and *individuality*. The primary energy during this phase of life is to achieve mastery in these areas. This is a time spent developing your ability to express your individuality by cultivating original ideas, by leading and directing others, by attaining success and achievement in the material world, and by gaining recognition for those achievements. This is a time for self-determination and is action-oriented. This is a period of time demanding that you stand on your own two feet and assert yourself in a clear and healthy way.

1st Pinnacle: When you have this number for a 1st Pinnacle, chances are your youth is spent learning how to develop and use original ideas. This is a time where you'll confront feelings of dependency and learn to extract yourself from dependent situations. You're learning how to stand on your own two feet and individuate yourself. You're called to lead and to rely on yourself without resorting to the downside of ego, stubbornness, and being self-centered or dominating. It's not necessarily a settling time because it's governed by exponential learning, which includes all the hard knocks that go with it. Yet this is a glorious time to gain mastery over yourself and march to the beat of your own drum.

2nd or 3rd Pinnacle (Main Pinnacle): As a 2nd or 3rd Pinnacle, the 1's grooming you for—and challenging you with—embracing leadership and developing all that being an effective and inspirational leader entails. You're being called upon to focus intently on these aspects: courage, drive, vision, focus, determination, and integrity. You might experience a certain degree of aggressiveness in your demeanor at this time or alternately, you might be more submissive or uncertain about yourself and your abilities. Your ability to get ahead is limited only by your own initiative during a 1 Pinnacle.

4th Pinnacle: A 4th Pinnacle with a number 1 is marked by initiating and creative energy. Any thought of slowing down or retiring is most likely not in the cards. Challenges and changes accompany this last stage of life and your accomplishments can be deeply gratifying if you've mastered the art of leadership, direction, and expression of your own original ideas. It's unlikely that you'll magically be handed golden opportunities for success—and if you are, take them and run with them. This is a time demanding innovation and usually you'll have to construct your own opportunities through desire, focus, self-determination, and the ability to take a punch, get up, shake it off, and keep going. As a 4th Pinnacle, you're prone to have substantial success and achievement with balanced self-confidence and proper drive. You might find yourself going it alone or enjoy an increased level of independence. If you're challenged with balancing the ego, this can be a lonely time.

2 PINNACLE
HARMONY & PARTNERSHIP

1 TIME OF ATTAINMENT

This is a stage where you must work to assert yourself & to understand your sensitivity. Often this is a period where you feel submissive, somewhat timid & are challenged with expressing yourself. You often take on the role as a 'pleaser.'

2 TIME OF OBLIGATION

This is often a time where relationships take front seat — marriage, children or other obligations. Patience & putting "us" in front of "me" is a keystone. Details & being supportive are key elements to be developed. Personal ambition can be a secondary concern.

3 TIME OF FOUNDATION

Tact & co-operation are the foundation for this period. Peace-keeping & being supportive are at the helm. The challenge resides in forming & maintaining healthy boundaries & getting to know yourself from the inside out.

4 TIME OF CULMINATION

Relationships, group activity & feeling as though you're appreciated for your contributions is key. Feeling accepted & acknowledged is a driving force. Learning to discipline sensitive emotions & being supportive is advised.

2 PINNACLE

When this is your Pinnacle number, you're being beckoned to envelop yourself in the elements of learning to *cooperate, share, be considerate of others,* and *be at your best when you are in harmonious relationships without sacrificing yourself in the process.* That last item is the real obstacle. The number 2 is the number of partnerships, patience, balance, and diplomacy. Therefore a 2 Pinnacle can be a time where love takes front seat, whether it's through marriage or partnership, parenting, or other experiences that involve loving relationships.

This is a time where you'll be called upon to work on—and perfect—your subtle art of relating. The number 2 also has to do with gathering and relating facts or data, perfecting details, and being a team-player whose strength lies in being of service in a calm and balanced way. Where precision and details are valued, you'll be happiest with your contributions. You'll learn to discipline your emotions while also bringing your emotional life to the forefront.

A 2 Pinnacle asks you to practice patience and tact. It won't offer much recognition for all you do during this time, so you must turn to yourself for acknowledgment in order not to feel resentful. Learning to create and hold emotional boundaries is key. This is a time where being an integral part of a group or community is where you feel most satisfied, comfortable, and confident. This can be a warm and fuzzy period when you're focused on contributing your heart and soul to your relationships and to your enterprises.

1st Pinnacle: If you experience a 2 as a 1st Pinnacle, count on being an overly-sensitive child who's easily hurt and who takes on the emotions of those around you. Since you're young and developing emotionally, you won't realize that you're feeling both your own emotions, plus those of everyone in your environment. This includes sensitivity to your surroundings. You may have difficulties with both verbal and emotional expression since you are overloaded with feelings that you're not yet mature enough to recognize and filter out. Your mother is likely to be a strong influence on you during this time, for good or for ill. This is a time when you can feel timid and submissive and have to work at defining and expressing yourself. A low or high level of anxiety is not an uncommon factor during this time. Often you navigate this sensitive Pinnacle by people pleasing.

2nd or 3rd Pinnacle (Main Pinnacle): A 2nd or 3rd Pinnacle with a 2 influence surrounds you with energies associated with working in balance with other people. This is a time that isn't so much *me* focused as *us* focused. When you master your ability to promote harmony in all things, show patience and a willingness to forgo individual credit based on your contributions to the whole, you'll be operating optimally. The work you engage in during this time is likely to be detailed and demanding. This is most often a time where marriage and children are priority. If you've been a stay-at-home parent, as just one example, it wouldn't be surprising to see this number in your 2nd or 3rd Pinnacle.

4th Pinnacle: If you have the number 2 as your 4th Pinnacle, it's an opportunity to cultivate harmony in all things—home environment, work conditions, family, and relationships. You can retire or continue to work—yet the key to feeling satisfaction and fulfillment will be in your development of patience, tact, and cooperation. You'll need to control a tendency toward over-sensitivity. If you don't work with this energy mindfully, the tendency will be to get your feelings hurt often and deeply. If you take every little thing personally, instead of cultivating your ability to relate well with yourself and others, you'll experience a substantial amount of angst during this time. This is a Pinnacle set up for truly coming to terms with who you are from the inside out.

Master 11/2 Pinnacle

If you're working with the energy of the Master 11/2, you're developing an extraordinary connection with your intuition and experience a weighted level of sensitivity. The pressure to wear your psychic shield is at an all-time high under the 11/2 Pinnacle, since it creates quite a bit of volatility in the midst of enormous personal and spiritual growth. Optimally, the 11/2 Pinnacle allows you to catapult yourself into a creative, intuitive, service-oriented realm in whatever capacity you desire.

The 11/2 is an artistic, inventive, and creative vibe favoring outlets such as media work, music, art, dance, poetry or anything that involves creative endeavors with a visionary and future-leaning focus. Remember also that the influence felt with the 11/2 is somewhat esoteric in nature and ultimately connected with spiritual and metaphysical study and illumination.

This is a confusing time, marked with the distinct necessity to keep your feet firmly on the ground. It can prove difficult to find your bearings, yet you also feel as though you have a special gift that needs to be expressed and put into material form. You may also feel a bit detached from the day-to-day practicalities of the world. With the higher vibration presented by the number 11/2, you may feel a constant underlying sense of nervousness, tension or restlessness. Hypersensitivity and confusion about life's direction can be a challenge during this Pinnacle.

3 PINNACLE
CREATIVITY & EXPRESSION

1 — TIME OF ATTAINMENT

This is a time where you have the opportunity to develop artistically or creatively. The environment is often either supportive of creativity or (more likely) disallows emotions & expression. This time offers opportunity to develop an optimistic attitude & develop communication skills.

2 — TIME OF OBLIGATION

Success during this period depends on how you embrace your imagination & learn to speak your truth. Close friendships, relationships & the pleasure of life are supported. Activities where you can use expressive talents are favored.

3 — TIME OF FOUNDATION

During this period you might be drawn toward creative endeavors & be pulled toward encouraging & inspiring others. Fun, humor & lightness are cornerstones to this Pinnacle. Emotions need to be expressed or depression may be part of the picture.

4 — TIME OF CULMINATION

This time is marked as a lighter, social & freer period. Expression, creative pursuits, travel & a sense of ease are the hallmark. Challenges come with scattered focus or self-doubt. This is a beautiful opportunity to find enjoyment in every aspect of life.

3 PINNACLE

With a 3 Pinnacle, get ready to dig into your emotions and express yourself. The themes for this period of time are *communication, self-expression, creativity in all forms, joy, optimism,* and *locating and speaking your truth*. This is a time to get to know your inner life intimately, to identify and deal with your emotions, and to actively engage whatever creative urges you feel compelled to explore.

During this Pinnacle, you'll have no other choice except to dig deep in order to locate your underlying emotions and learn to communicate with clarity and purpose. If you attempt to hold your feelings and ideas inside yourself, you'll implode. Now's the time to allow yourself and others to see the true creative and emotional *you*. Honestly, this Pinnacle is set up for lightness—with a focus on enjoyable activities that support enjoyment, creativity, and expression. This energy is supportive of travel, social activities, friendships, and entertainment.

The foundation is being poured for growth and development of personal expression—particularly verbal (teaching, coaching, presenting), writing or performance. Even if you haven't felt particularly artistic or creative before, now you're likely to feel drawn toward participation in artistic creation of one kind or another—or at least infusing your particular form of creativity into whatever you do. The 3 is aligned with the joy of the present moment. Long-term plans made during this stage might not come to fruition exactly the way you planned. It's all about being with people, having fun, and taking on a youthful attitude. It can be an *easy come, easy go* stage, where variety and movement over-ride hunkering down and making things happen. Think. Dream. Imagine. Create. These are your key components for the 3 Pinnacle.

1st Pinnacle: While it sounds rather breezy, if the number 3 shows up during your 1st Pinnacle, it offers many challenges. While there may be lots of opportunities to develop and pursue artistic and creative potentials, chances are you won't recognize them or be willing to work at making them come to fruition this early in life. So instead, there's a tendency to scatter your energies or perhaps to work on fleeting ideas. Better yet, you may just be having too much fun to actually dig in and develop a level of expertise that goes beyond being a dilettante. The best spin—the 3 as a 1st Pinnacle encourages the development of a creative career. This is a Pinnacle where over-sensitivity to outside criticism can be debilitating and stand in the way of creative pursuits or of your ability to express emotions. Emotional highs and lows are common during a 3 Pinnacle. Experiencing blockages with expression and communication is expected during this Pinnacle.

2nd or 3rd Pinnacle (Main Pinnacle): If you're in a 2nd or 3rd Pinnacle, the 3 energy creates an environment composed of good friends and happy relationships, enjoyment, the pleasures of life, and creative self-expression. This is a time where your responsibilities and accomplishments are greatly dependent on your social demeanor and communication skills. You may be presented with opportunities to write, speak, design or take a job in the entertainment industry. This time is marked by imagination and expressive feelings. Great news! If you're nurturing the 3's healthy aspects during this Pinnacle, it has a natural attraction for money and an easier life full of creative pursuits, where you're drawn to encourage and inspire others. You could become interested in some aspect of the healing arts. Anything performance-related or communication focused is favored.

4th Pinnacle: If a 3 shows up for your 4th Pinnacle, there's a good possibility for travel, social activity, and an overall sense of lightness. Often this is accompanied with a freedom from financial worry. It can be a very comfortable final stage in life that's supportive of all creative endeavors, with a focus on fun and social engagement. The energy of the 3 is so curious, you'll want to learn something (or *experience* something) and then quickly move on to the next thing. You'll benefit by developing more focus and a sense of self-discipline in order to take full advantage of this creative, light, and happy period of time. You might easily get scattered, distracted, and drained. Stay disciplined and avoid superficiality and negative communication in the form of gossip, sarcasm, and pessimism.

4 PINNACLE
HARD WORK & ORGANIZATION

1 TIME OF ATTAINMENT

This is a stage where you learn the value of hard work & effort. This is a time when you desire stability & security yet it's rarely there for you. You learn to be dependable, reliable & conscientious. You can find yourself to be a dedicated student or alternately detour responsibility.

2 TIME OF OBLIGATION

Achievement & setting down roots are a keynote of this period. You learn to navigate limiting circumstances & make order out of chaos. Often you're drawn to start a family, build a house, move or simply set a stronger foundation in your life.

3 TIME OF FOUNDATION

Rising in the ranks with career, planning & setting realistic & attainable goals is a driving force. Being practical & frugal is at the forefront of this Pinnacle. This is a time of slow growth leading to substantial achievement. There are no boundaries as long as there is stability.

4 TIME OF CULMINATION

This is a time of harvest. There is a drive to work hard with clear goals that offer an incredible sense of satisfaction. Slow growth, perseverance & finding time to play, relax & lighten up is a requirement. This is a responsible time leading to much success.

4 PINNACLE

A 4 Pinnacle is a period where you're being called to build your life with solid, stable foundations that'll last. This is a time to focus on your root system and how to create security and stability. This is a Pinnacle where you're drawn toward creating security. This might show up as purchasing—or actually building—a home, concentrating your efforts on career advancement or starting and maintaining a family. This isn't a particularly light-hearted time because you're being tested by issues related to *hard work, organization, setting up effective systems, patience, endurance, working step-by-step,* and *moving ahead methodically.*

This stage is set-up for designing and pouring the proper foundation for your present and your future. It's a practical time where you're putting ideas into the material world and manifesting your vision with discipline and a serious attitude. Limiting circumstances are sure to be an integral part of your journey through a 4 Pinnacle. Frankly, it's not a time to mess around. You're being immersed in the energies that support a practical and realistic approach to life, therefore a demand for order, systems- building, and organization is key.

The 4 Pinnacle encourages you to be dependable, conscientious, realistic, and reliable. Determination and relentless effort are requirements and you may feel a strong compulsion and emotional need to immerse yourself in work and career during this Pinnacle. When you do, you'll thrive on that energy and feel satisfied with the tangible and lasting results you create.

1st Pinnacle: A 4 as a 1st Pinnacle sets you up for a demanding childhood and adolescence. You might find your economic circumstances demand more concerted effort and hard work on your part, pushing you into responsibilities that come to you too soon. During this Pinnacle, you crave stability, support, and security, yet often this doesn't exist in your world. This can also be a stage of life devoted to the pursuit of your education, where you take learning seriously, and your responsibilities are the center-point of life. In either event, it's unlikely you'll be involved in the normal frivolity of life because of the demands you face. Family dynamics—often, but not always, dysfunctional—command the energy of this 1st Pinnacle.

2nd or 3rd Pinnacle (Main Pinnacle): A 2nd or 3rd Pinnacle with a 4 emphasis fuels your ability to get ahead in the world and achieve—not so much because of innate talent as much as your drive and ability to out-work the competition. You might find some economic limitations during this Pinnacle placed in your path in order to test your commitment to building solid and steady foundations for your life—while not being beaten down by obstacles and limitations. Seeking security, working hard, and accomplishment are hallmarks of this Pinnacle. Family issues are to be worked through and healed as you devise your family of choice and establish your own stability.

4th Pinnacle: A 4th Pinnacle imbued with the 4 won't allow you to slow down or retire in the way you might desire or expect. The number 4 isn't a leisurely energy, so it doesn't even recognize the notion of *retire* or *slow down*. Moreover, you won't want to! A driving sense of purpose compels you during a 4 Pinnacle. The important factor is to do the work in front of you and to feel good about the sense of accomplishment. There's a possibility that economic conditions will control your ability to slow down or retire. Or alternately, you're building an empire and continue to put your heart, soul, and energy into this expansive enterprise. The 4 Pinnacle serves as a foundation to build something vital that has lasting value in the world. The 4 Pinnacle teaches you that effort is what counts. The upside: If you take this energy seriously and do the work, you'll reap the benefits for the rest of your life. As you're building your empire, you're setting up your positive relationship with money, your ability to meet deadlines, your ability to institute effective systems, and your positive way of dealing with limitations.

Master 22/4 Pinnacle

This Pinnacle is uncommon, coming into play only after you've experienced two preceding 11/2 Pinnacles. If you experience this Pinnacle, you've opted for an especially dramatic or traumatic pathway in life. Because of the prior 11/2 Pinnacles you've lived through, you've been challenged to engage in a profound way on a more evolved spiritual path. Most likely you'll have undergone radical changes along the way.

With the 22/4 Pinnacle, there's a chance to do something truly vital that affects people on a wide-ranging scale. You'll potentially build something of lasting value that benefits humankind in a way that keeps giving long after you're gone from this earth. The 22/4 is the number that opens the door to high levels of personal and financial success if you utilize your organizational and management skills to apply practical solutions to problems encountered in the everyday world.

This is a highly productive period of life, yet not light and easy. This Pinnacle is full of substantial tests. Focus and endurance are a must. Whether you like it or not, your actions set an example for others, so you must know that your actions speak louder than words during a 22/4 Pinnacle. It's a time where you're subject to extreme emotional and energetic sensitivity.

The ego must be balanced during this time. The propensity to take everything that happens personally and feel victimized. You'll need to establish a balance between your personal life and your work life, as there's a tendency for workaholism. Just remember that the 22/4 is a slow and steady process that isn't over until it's over. This is a period of time that demands that you take additional care of your physical body and practice diligent self-care.

5 PINNACLE
FREEDOM & CHANGE

1 TIME OF ATTAINMENT

This is a period where you're either given a lot of freedom in your youth or you instead feel restricted & smothered. Experience is the catalyst to growth & this is often a time where you're drawn to travel, seek adventure or dabble in escape mechanisms.

2 TIME OF OBLIGATION

Adaptability & healthy self-discipline are the cornerstones to this period. Commitment can be challenging & self-indulgence intoxicating! This is an amazing time to experience different cultures, people & to expand horizons on every level.

3 TIME OF FOUNDATION

This can be a "been there, done that" period where decisions about what you value, what stays & what goes & how you want to stabilze yourself comes into play. This can be a time where you seek freedom from confining situations. You're learning the productive use of freedom & to extract from feeling restricted.

4 TIME OF CULMINATION

Balance is key during this period. This is a fast-paced time with many changes, twists-and-turns. Travel can be a feature & you can find yourself either rambling around or enjoying the zest that comes with this buoyant & free-wheeling energy. Adventure awaits!

5 PINNACLE

When you have a 5 Pinnacle, get ready for what might be described as an "ADHD experience." This Pinnacle is a time for change and uncertainty—when it feels as though you're experiencing life without a filter. During this Pinnacle, you're immersed in frenetic energy and it's hard to know what direction to go or what to grasp onto. Ultimately, this is a time for loosening up patterns of restriction you have held on to in the past.

The 5 Pinnacle is all about developing a new sense of *freedom, liberation,* and *adventure.* Change is the mantra for this period of your life—and that means change in everything from career direction and business decisions, to spirituality and health, marriage and divorce. You name it. It's all up for review during this highly energized and catalytic portion of your life. If you're forward thinking and ready for a shakeup, this can be a brilliant time of transformation—yet not without the pain or discomfort associated with growth. This is not particularly a favored time to nest or settle down. Instead, you'll find yourself being drawn into the public world and feel an underlying need for adventure and freedom from constraints.

The major focus of a 5 Pinnacle is to learn to be adaptable and flexible. Don't resist this cataclysmic energy, yet also avoid impulsive decisions—including the strong urge to run away and avoid whatever you're experiencing. This can be a time of excess and tendencies to seek escape from the difficulties demanded by change and transformation. A hallmark of this Pinnacle resides in feeling restricted, tethered, and tied down—coupled with a strong and relentless desire to break free.

1st Pinnacle: A 5 as a 1st Pinnacle can be a tumultuous period because it's hard to find the stability to establish yourself, develop a sense of who you are, and set the foundation for what you want in adult life. Perhaps you end up moving geographically quite often during this 1st Pinnacle and it requires that you change schools and friends often. Maybe you have a strict family upbringing and feel hemmed in. Or perhaps you're brought up with ample freedom, permissive environment, and are allowed to forge your own way with more freedoms than most. Whatever the case, freedom is the central theme and experience, experimentation, and pushing boundaries is the name of the game. The 5 energy invites you to live by your own rules in many ways during this early time, which can be great if well managed. Yet most likely you'll find yourself going sideways! You're likely to experience a good amount of impulsiveness and a craving for unrestricted independence during this early stage. Alternately, this can be a period of time where you feel greatly restricted and face more than your share of fears.

2nd or 3rd Pinnacle (Main Pinnacle): If you find yourself in the 2nd or 3rd Pinnacle, the energy of the 5 supports your ability to progress and achieve in a fast-moving, highly fluctuating environment. Adaptability is critical to your healthy progress during this stage. Your desire for—and sense of—freedom is quite powerful and significant during this Pinnacle. You must be careful not to get too carried away and damage relationships or partnerships because of your unyielding urge for freedom, travel, adventure, and few restrictions. Special care must be taken to take personal responsibility for your actions and inactions. This is a time where you're magnetic and can have great success when you're flexible and forwarding-thinking—yet focused. Responsibility can be an issue during this period and commitment is often elusive during a 5 cycle.

4th Pinnacle: The 5 energy that guides a 4th Pinnacle results in a continuously fast-paced and ever-changing life. This won't be your road to a laconic retirement. Change and variety continue to present themselves and this can be an interesting and dynamic stage of life, potentially bringing freedom from overarching financial or domestic worries. Because the 5 Pinnacle is a time to expect the unexpected—and change is usually challenging for all of us—this period is exciting and possibly unsettling. It'll often prove to be a transformational time accented with restlessness and a distinct desire to get outside of your own box. There also may be tendencies to quit something before it's completed, to be promiscuous in your sexual life or to habitually overindulge in food, drugs, alcohol or other addictive outlets. There's a chance that this portion of your life will contain an abundance of travel. Maintaining balance is key and a test during this 5 Pinnacle.

6 PINNACLE
RESPONSIBILITY & FAMILY

1 TIME OF ATTAINMENT

This is a period with a focus on family, feelings of responsibility & nurturing. You often feel a strong identification or (dis)connection with family, with the possibility for a controlling parent or authority figure. Caring for others, service of some kind, with a feeling or pressure around your role in the family is key.

2 TIME OF OBLIGATION

Creating a family & your domestic life is a cornerstone to this period. Duty, self-sacrifice & love are highlighted. Creativity thrives, as well as business with a focus on service, relationships, children, animals or elderly. Challenges reside in creating healthy boundaries.

3 TIME OF FOUNDATION

This is a time where home & family are the focal point. Lessons in supporting & nurturing without controlling or crushing perfectionism is key element. Creativity, financial success & care-taking are major players during this time. Responsibility & self-care are necessary.

4 TIME OF CULMINATION

This is a time that can feel incredibly warm-and-fuzzy. Giving back & serving others are key elements during this rewarding & comforting time where you thrive in the joys of your relationships. You might be called to mentorship. Suspend judgment.

6 PINNACLE

Love, duty, responsibility, and *family* are the hallmarks of any 6 Pinnacle. This is a stage in life immersed in the energies of nurturing. You may choose to nurture your career or your family—or even your pets or employees—yet you can't avoid these years devoted to nurturing those around you, embracing your sense of responsibility, and modulating giving to others and giving to yourself in a balanced and fulfilling way. This is a time where *home* takes on new meaning. It can be a period focused on establishing and maintaining your nest, whatever that specifically means to you.

It's a prime time to marry or to settle in, appreciate home life, and up your commitment in your relationship world. If giving is lopsided and you give to everyone else and leave nothing for yourself, you'll certainly experience the difficult lessons that accompany that imbalance. Or if your behavior is lopsided in the opposite direction—where you're self-involved and self-absorbed at the expense of giving freely to others—you'll experience the difficult lessons that accompany *that* imbalance. You must achieve harmony within yourself and your chosen family.

This is the stage where there's an irresistible urge to establish or intensify your involvement with home, children (or your inner child!), with a focus on the beautification of your surroundings. The 6 also carries with it an energy associated with commitment to community and humanitarian service of some kind, so this might be a period of time propelling you toward involvement in some aspect of these services. There can be a call toward mentorship, involvement in the healing arts or any activity that offers your heart-felt talents to others.

Considerable money can be made during this Pinnacle when solidly focused on visionary contributions and service. This is a *love and marriage* stage with intense focus on children and the home. This can also be a significant time where you heal the child within. It can also be the *marriage and divorce* stage when a marriage as it stands can no longer be positively sustained or where you commit to an exclusive relationship or marriage. One of the influences of a 6 Pinnacle is experiencing an overwhelming sense of responsibility, bringing with it a feeling of restriction and being tied down. The bottom-line is that you're learning about responsibility and nurturing, plain and simple. You'll learn what's required and when enough is enough by setting and acting upon your personal boundaries, while also giving generously.

1st Pinnacle: As a younger person in the midst of a 6 Pinnacle, you're likely to find yourself knee-deep in duty and responsibility related to your home and family of origin. This may be because of the pressures you experience with parents and siblings—or you may find yourself entering into a marriage at an early age. Family, relationships, and *identification* with your family is a focal point for this 1st Pinnacle. This energy sets you up to experience controlling circumstances from a parent or another authority figure. Family is a key feature and either shows up as a place where you feel a strong sense of unity and identification—or where you struggle with dysfunction. You feel like the responsible party from an early age during this Pinnacle, where you parent your parents or have heightened responsibilities with siblings or other family-related dynamics.

2nd or 3rd Pinnacle (Main Pinnacle): If you have the 6 as your 2nd or 3rd Pinnacle, you find great achievement through accepting increasing levels of responsibility and interacting with a giving and nurturing attitude. Home and family take precedence over self-oriented endeavors. This can be the time when you marry, start a family or when you establish a home-based business or have a career centered around service in some way, shape or form. It's a time to attend primarily to the demands of *others*—family, friends, colleagues, community. The 6 Pinnacle provides ample creative energy and you can find a creative or artistic career flourish during this time. The 6 supports all justice-related pursuits and you might be drawn toward the law—or any career or volunteer effort with a focus on righting wrongs and promoting justice.

4th Pinnacle: If you have a 6 during a 4th Pinnacle, this period brings with it the rewards and pleasures of family, friends, and security. You'll feel the drive to settle and plant roots somewhere, have a home-base that feels nurturing and nesting, and where you're drawn to help, heal, and serve others. You'll most likely act on your feelings of philanthropy and feel compelled to place your time and energy on what you can do for the greater good, however that shows up for you. This is a stage where *giving back* is vital to your innate sense of well-being and purpose. When you experience this Pinnacle, you might tend to idealize the world, people, relationships, and even the *self*, resulting in stubbornness and being overly opinionated. By *idealize the world*, I mean that you find that you're continuously disappointed and disillusioned. Judgment needs to achieve balance during this Pinnacle and *acceptance* is an overriding theme. Overall, this Pinnacle is a time where home takes on a different meaning and focus than it has in the past, where you're called to take more responsibility upon your shoulders, and where a bit of self-sacrifice goes a long way. Your relationship life takes center stage and utmost satisfaction is gained within your home and relationship environment.

Master 33/6 Pinnacle

This Pinnacle is uncommon and demands that you operate with higher spiritual principles. This is an intense Pinnacle where you're consistently offered opportunities to master your emotions and learn to think expansively both in terms of spirit and matter. This Pinnacle requires self-sacrifice, yet the rewards are endless. Coupling the nurturing and visionary vibration of the 6 with the double expressive and communicative energy of the 3, you're a force for change, a teacher of teachers, and a person who shoulders great responsibility. Look at the energies related to the 3 Pinnacle (and double it!) and then consider the 6 Pinnacle as the foundational energy for the 33/6 Pinnacle.

7 PINNACLE
SPIRITUAL DEVELOPMENT & SPECIALIZATION

1 TIME OF ATTAINMENT

This is a period of intense & slow personal & spiritual growth with a focus on building trust (with yourself & others). A feeling of being misplaced is often a cornerstone to this period where life's bigger questions knock at your door. Denying a deeper dive results in feeling lost, frustrated & rudderless.

2 TIME OF OBLIGATION

Time to refine & specialize your skills. Both the intuitive or metaphysical world collides with the rational, logical aspects of life & demand to be valued & integrated. Soul-searching is guaranteed & you may find yourself in a teaching role or as an analyst of some kind.

3 TIME OF FOUNDATION

This period offers a plethora of opportunities to develop your spiritual nature. It's a time of intense yet slow growth. Relationships might not take precedence in this period yet if they do, you must work at communication & emotional connection. Developing openness & avoiding being critical help make this a balanced period.

4 TIME OF CULMINATION

Spiritual development & personal growth are the key elements to this period. Study, higher learning & contemplation offer many rewards. You find yourself uninterested in the more pragmatic aspects of life & get pleasure out of the wisdom & deeper levels of understanding you cultivate.

7 PINNACLE

Introspection and study are the key ingredients of the 7 Pinnacle. This is a segment of time where you're beckoned to *explore your inner world through study, research, intense introspection,* and *soul development* in whatever manner you choose to pursue it. You'll experience an unconscious desire to be somewhat reclusive, as your focus turns mainly toward advancing your experience and knowledge in your area of specialization. This is a time mixed with analysis, gaining knowledge, and huge leaps in your intuitive capabilities. This is a time of deep spiritual evolution, development of self-awareness, and personal growth.

It's during this Pinnacle that you'll experience a dramatic event that drives you to seek alternative information and knowledge through metaphysics and other spiritual methodologies. Or perhaps it's a Pinnacle that simply shows up as a deeply contemplative time insofar as your deep need to probe and ponder how you see yourself fitting into the scheme of life. If you have a 7 Pinnacle at the end of life, this is particularly relevant. Taking time to develop spiritually under the influence of the 7, you're setting yourself up for gaining substantial wisdom and skill, setting yourself apart from others in your ability to explain the unexplainable, and using your wisdom and knowledge to encourage others to seek and find their own inner-knowing. As you find yours, you'll then be prepared to assist others in finding theirs.

Intrinsic to this Pinnacle is a strict focus on learning, investigating, and gaining knowledge. You'll be pulled inward during the 7 Pinnacle, so chances are high that you'll become a bit of a loner during this time—as opposed to during other stages in your life when you'll feel more engaged with the outer world. Your comfort zone resides most distinctly in working alone or at least with few restraints. While marriage isn't out of the question, it'll take effort and clear communication for both partners to make it work during a 7 Pinnacle. You might even find yourself uninterested or unconcerned with material matters and shy away from involvement in practical affairs. Don't misunderstand this Pinnacle! Life blazes on around you and involvement is often, on the exterior, somewhat "normal." The real work during the 7 cycle is deeply internal and impossible to express in its full magnitude to others.

1st Pinnacle: If you experience a 7 as a 1st Pinnacle, it can be alienating, because it means you'll struggle with feeling alone and like you don't belong anywhere. Expect life experiences that serve as teaching tools for your journey in the development of faith, trust, and that open the door to truth-seeking. It's a time when you're often a serious student and—whether or not you can identify it as such—when you're motivated by inner yearnings. A 1st Pinnacle accompanied by the 7 can be a difficult and confusing time as it exposes deep questions about the nature of the world (and beyond) quite early in life. This exploration can come to pass thorough difficult experiences and emotional losses.

2nd or 3rd Pinnacle (Main Pinnacle): If you experience this energy in your 2nd or 3rd Pinnacle, you'll be offered an opportunity to refine and specialize your skills down to a fine art, if you so choose. You might find yourself directly involved with some sort of research—religious, spiritual or philosophical endeavors—during a 7 Pinnacle. Progress during this Pinnacle can feel painfully slow. The benefits won't be seen in your material or financial realm as much as in your spiritual life and internal world. Although financial success isn't out of the question during a 7 Pinnacle, it would most likely be the byproduct of study and analysis.

4th Pinnacle: With the 7 as a 4th Pinnacle, spiritual development is undeniable. You'll be called upon to teach others what you've learned within your area of specialization. Continued time for study, development, contemplation, and higher learning are keys to this final Pinnacle. The 7 at this point in life requires slight detachment from the practical realms and places renewed focus on philosophical or theoretical thinking and relating. You may find it difficult to connect with people on a superficial level during this time, so it's best to seek out like-minded souls with whom to share ideas and conversations. Be patient and open, though. People come to you to hear what you have to say because of the wisdom and knowledge you have cultivated and gained through your life experiences and through extensive study. It's part of this Pinnacle to become a teacher—perhaps in the traditional sense or maybe in a more inconspicuous manner.

Does this Pinnacle sound as if you must be a reclusive monk or the equal of Mother Teresa? Not so. Despite the concentration on personal growth, you still need to live in the physical world and you'll happily go out and dance the night away, enjoy passionate lovemaking with your sweetheart, and hold down a job. You can do those things, yet this Pinnacle requires that you allow yourself the time, energy, and space needed to focus and study all realms of experience with a special emphasis on self-awareness.

8 PINNACLE
EMPOWERMENT & FINANCIAL SUCCESS

1 — TIME OF ATTAINMENT

This is an intense period demanding that you step up or get stepped on! Right out of the chute you're asked to assert yourself, get a handle around what money means to you (& doesn't mean!) & empower yourself at all levels. Lessons can show up through difficult family dynamics, authority issues & ethics are required.

2 — TIME OF OBLIGATION

Time to tap into your business ability. This period is ripe for gaining traction with your career, partnering in marriage or business. Business acumen is rewarded & emotions are downplayed. Proper management is key, as well as balancing any controlling or dominating tendencies.

3 — TIME OF FOUNDATION

Power, financial success & influence are key features. Practical thinking, organization, long-term & bigger goals are favored. Taking your success & turning into giving back is a higher level of the expression of the 8, offering supportive energy for using power & influence to connect people & give back.

4 — TIME OF CULMINATION

Spiritual principles, wealth & power collide during this period. Establishing a lasting legacy is supported & this is often a time where success unfolds as long as your actions are balanced. Yet it doesn't mean it'll be easy! You'll continue to be tested. This is a time of great reward & recognition.

8 PINNACLE

The key elements to an 8 Pinnacle are *money, business, authority, ethics, personal power,* and *abundance*. This is a stage where you're bombarded with opportunities to embrace and define your personal relationship with *power, money,* and *achievement*. It has an intense focus on matters of responsibility, efficiency, power, authority, leadership, and management of financial affairs. Sounds exciting, right? Yet under the influence of the 8 Pinnacle, judgment is tested over and over again and your career becomes top priority.

This isn't a particularly easy walk in the park. This Pinnacle requires substantial shifts in your life and your relationships. While your opportunities for achievement, recognition, and financial success are heightened, it'll require a lot of strength, courage, and tenacity to do so. This isn't an easy Pinnacle. It'll demand a lot from you and won't let up—remember, the 8 is a testing number and an amplifier. The 8 Pinnacle is also tricky because—while it supports all things relating to money, power, and authority—it's unyielding in its demands that you get there through the use of the utmost ethics, honesty, integrity, solid leadership, and expressions of abundance.

The highest form of the number 8 has to do with giving as you're receiving, with no strings attached. This is a time where you're learning all about money—about what it means to you and doesn't mean to you. It's an extended period where you learn about what it takes to earn money and attract it—and also to spend it, possibly lose it, and gain it back again. It's a period of time fully focused on the establishment of your sense of empowerment with high-level focus on achievement, becoming an authority in your field, and using power and influence for the good of all.

Aspects of the 8 Pinnacle are status, success, recognition, business, and commercial activity. If you keep with it, this Pinnacle is set up to usher in improvements in your financial and personal power realms. The focus is on creative practicality with an emphasis on organizational and management skills and abilities. This is a time where you become a respected authority in your field and have the opportunity to use your influence for the greater good. Thinking and behaving in a business-like way is heightened and your powerful manifestation skills can't be contained when you're in alignment with the 8 Pinnacle.

1st Pinnacle: With the 8 as a 1st Pinnacle, you may become involved and interested in business or commercial activity at a young age. You may be the kid who mows lawns and starts her own business or perhaps you tap into a more aggressive 8 energy and find other moneymaking endeavors that surprise the adults around you. The focus and dedication to your entrepreneurial enterprise is unyielding. You'll face limitations and restrictions, which you'll find frustrating or downright debilitating. Or alternately, you find the challenge motivating and invigorating. The 8 loves a challenge. You excel at practical thinking. This is a time where personal power is tested and established. The 8 Pinnacle brings power struggles with authority figures—parents, teachers, bosses or others. It's an intense period teaching you how to step up or get stepped on. You're learning the benefits of power vs. force, self-control vs. control over others, and healthy empowerment vs. disempowerment.

2nd or 3rd Pinnacle (Main Pinnacle): If you encounter an 8 during your 2nd or 3rd Pinnacle, you're apt to find yourself immersed in the executive world or the world of finance—or you could be married to someone who is. You're required to rely more on rational judgments and less on emotional impulses. This is a time to think with longer-range goals with a focus on financial health and wealth. This is a period where career takes center stage and requires effort and energy. Personal ambition and success are in the driver's seat and the demands of this Pinnacle can't be underestimated. Your assertiveness and reserve are tested again and again, challenging you to become an empowered person who uses well-won influence and financial affluence to forge connections to those who can make things happen. Status, respect, and power all key players during this Pinnacle. The shadow-side of this Pinnacle presents as a harrowing environment that grinds you down and spits you out. That might look like battling addictions, rebelliousness that gets you into trouble or any other route detouring you from stepping into an empowered existence.

4th Pinnacle: With a 4th Pinnacle, you're not geared toward quiet retirement. The development and culmination of status, wealth, and power define this period—given that you act on both business principles *and* spiritual principles. This is your time to give back in substantial ways by using your gifts of money, power, and influence to help others. You're moved to leave a lasting legacy in some way, shape or form by becoming an authority in your chosen field. This can be a time of true abundance with both monetary and spiritual rewards when you come to the table willing to take control of your life on every level.

9 PINNACLE
COMPASSION & FOLLOWING YOUR HEART

1 — TIME OF ATTAINMENT

This is a period where you might feel extremely sensitive to the hurts of people & the world. There can be losses experienced during this time that lead you to be more compassionate & giving. Creativity is high & there can be over-giving or self-sacrifice. There can also be lessons learned about ego & arrogance.

2 — TIME OF OBLIGATION

This period can be a time for marriage & starting a family, yet it can also be a powerful time for progress with business or with creative work of all kinds. Involvement your community of choice or social causes show up here.

3 — TIME OF FOUNDATION

Travel & an interest in international affairs can come into play. Losses might challenge the desire for permanence or stability, yet you're learning the value of impermanence & letting go. A sense of selfless service can be an over-riding theme.

4 — TIME OF CULMINATION

This is truly a time to declutter your life. What brings you joy? You'll often be driven to simplify your life & focus on teaching, philanthropy or other forms of humanitarian service. Travel is favored & creative work is supported. Added emphasis on the Arts is common.

9 PINNACLE

If you have a 9 Pinnacle, you're expected to show the world what a true humanitarian looks and acts like on a day-to-day basis. You're developing the attributes of *compassion, love, ethics,* and *tolerance*—combined with a big dose of inspiring and uplifting others through compassionate giving. If this sounds like a big order to fill, it is! The 9 Pinnacle is marked by emotional crises because you're being asked to end and let go of all matters in your life no longer of service you and your higher purpose. This is a time of selfless-service in the purest sense.

This is a road toward wise maturity and involves healing emotional issues. This Pinnacle is a segment of life demanding the ultimate release of all the painful stories about your past that may haunt you or keep you from stepping into your fullest potential. The ultimate healing takes place during this Pinnacle when you surrender into transformation. There's plenty of potential for anything you want during this time when you're fully committed to playing your role in letting go and following your heart. Forgiveness is a key theme during a 9 Pinnacle.

When you surrender, all good things come to you. This is a time where you can literally create your own reality. Money, good fortune, loving relationships, vibrant health, purposeful living—these are all possible during a 9 Pinnacle when you're willing to let go, surrender, and reinvent. International travel, curiosity about other ways of thinking, living, and being are highlighted. Fame and fortune aren't out of the question with this Pinnacle, as long the foundation is based in love, giving, and service to the greater good.

1st Pinnacle: With a 9 Pinnacle at the beginning of life, the influence may be barely noticeable. Selflessness is an attribute that's developed over time and young children must first forge their identity for themselves before doing selfless-service in a healthy and productive manner.

When you experience a 9 as a 1st Pinnacle, you may be a child who is the friend to the underdog, who's a protector of the kids who get bullied, those who are handicapped or those who are ostracized in some way. You may be a bit of an outsider yourself as you attend to those on the margins. You can also be the bully and have experiences that enlighten you and demand that you exchange your *selfishness* for *selflessness*. The 9 Pinnacle in your early years can be a challenging period marked by losses, trials, and tribulations making you wise beyond your years.

2nd or 3rd Pinnacle (Main Pinnacle): A 2nd or 3rd Pinnacle directed by the 9 might set the stage for a life guided by humanitarian viewpoints, such as working humanitarian causes like climate change, human or animal rights—or with any other career or organization devoted to humanitarian causes. You may express such views through political action or social service, or in a variety of other venues. The thrust of your desires and actions rests in humanitarian action, whether it's through charitable contributions, volunteerism or direct employment within these realms of service. You might work for the Peace Corps or be an actor who is an activist for humanitarian causes. You might be a wealthy philanthropist who funds charitable organizations. Either way, your purpose is to effect positive change in the world and promote tolerance and compassion. The 9 Pinnacle is a time for integrating yourself with the higher principles of wisdom, selfless-service, and giving back to the world. Focusing directly on personal material gain during this Pinnacle will backfire. If you reject your higher calling, you'll also find difficulties. Following your heart and giving generously (while being led by the passion calling on your heart and soul) are the keys to this glorious Pinnacle.

4th Pinnacle: If the 4th Pinnacle is guided by the 9, work will tend to be more charitable in nature with plenty of opportunity to give much more of yourself. If you have done well financially, you might be drawn to using your assets to finance programs and support causes you believe in. This is a time where you've mellowed and have developed a more caring and heart-felt attitude about yourself and about others than in earlier periods of life. If you have a 9 as your 4th Pinnacle, you're required to rise above the fray and become a humanitarian in whatever capacity you choose. This is a period of time devoted to selfless-service, yet it's marked by an increase in creative desires and abilities. The arts can be a centerpiece during a 9 Pinnacle and a craving for international travel or with some kind of involvement in international affairs can play a major role.

PUTTING IT TOGETHER

When I look at a full numerology profile, I'm always attempting to gain a bird's eye view to see how to connect the dots. I look for where and when numbers repeat. I also look to see what numbers are missing and how that affects the profile. With Pinnacle Cycles, I look to see if any of the Pinnacle numbers match any of the core numbers in the profile. If so, these are periods of time where that particular aspect of yourself—showing up with specific characteristics within your personality or your purpose—is placed into an *environment* where the main subject to be studied is indicated by the themes inherent in the number. It's as though that aspect of yourself is placed within an incubator for a certain period of time.

Alternately, if one or more of the Pinnacles *doesn't* show up as one of the core numbers, it's as though you're being placed within an environment that is somewhat alien to you, yet you're being called upon to navigate the influences of that environment and integrate it into your life experience.

For instance, let's look at this layout of a possible profile and see how it might be interpreted.

Life Path	6
Expression/Destiny	3
Soul Urge	11/2
Birth Day	6
Personality	22/4
Maturity	9
1st Pinnacle	8
2nd Pinnacle	11/2
3rd Pinnacle (Main)	8
4th Pinnacle	3

Let's say this person's name is Theo.

In this example, Theo is traveling the 6 Life Path (nurturer, seeker of justice, idealistic, responsible, with focus on home and family). He expresses with witty and effective communication, is gifted with the ability to connect with people on an emotional level—and is driven to inspire, uplift, and motivate others (3 Expression/Destiny).

The desire underneath it all is to use his creative gifts to help, heal, and inspire (Master 11/2 Soul Urge), yet this causes some anxiety or nervous tension along the way because he wants to lead and be in charge, while also wanting to support and guide.

Theo is the super-6, given that both his Life Path and Birth Day are the same, which means that where he feels an innate point of connection (Birth Day) is the same as what he's checked in to learn, aspire toward, and master in this lifetime (Life Path)—the nurturing visionary. Theo really came in to master every level of the number 6. Cosmic parenthood, here he comes!

Other people see him as a workaholic who can sometimes be very self-limiting (22/4 Personality). Yet they also admire Theo's intelligence—both his emotional intelligence and his high IQ.

Now, if we then look at Theo's Pinnacles, we see that his 1st and 3rd Pinnacles are guided by the 8. *Theo doesn't have any 8's in his core numbers.*

His 2nd Pinnacle matches his Soul Urge, the Master 11/2. The Master 11/2 always presents a highly charged and volatile energy.

Theo's 4th and final Pinnacle is the 3, which is the same energy as his Expression/Destiny.

So how can we read or interpret this?

Here's an overview of Theo's life.

Theo was born into an affluent family—his father is a successful Hollywood producer and his mother, an actress. Even though he felt loved as a child, he spent a lot of time being cared for by various nannies while his parents were working. He often felt more mature than his parents, with a sense of responsibility to keep family dynamics in control when his father would drink too much or his mother would have one of her screaming tantrums.

Theo's parents divorced when he was ten years- old and both went on to remarry. Theo's father married younger women and had several other children with his various wives. Theo's mother never remarried, yet she had tumultuous relationships with many partners.

Of course, he was brought up in an environment inhabited by powerful and glamorous (and sometimes not so glamorous!) people in the entertainment industry. His parents encouraged him to use his creative talent and enrolled Theo in acting classes, music lessons, and any other subject where he showed interest. He became a rather good guitar player and songwriter.

At the end of his 1st Pinnacle, Theo crashed and burned. The 8 as a Pinnacle is a hard-driving cycle, offering experiences and opportunities to lean into ambition and rise in the ranks of power and money. Certainly, his family environment was the perfect set-up to figure out his place in the world of power and prestige.

As he bridged from his 8 Pinnacle into the 2nd Pinnacle, Theo's life literally collapsed. This fits with the Pinnacle shift from the power, money, and influence stage of the 1st Pinnacle (8), marking the segue into the spiritually illuminating Master 11/2. Theo had issues with drugs and alcohol and went into rehab. He started learning about meditation and got interested in astrology and energy work. He felt lost and as though his entire life lacked meaning and substance. Theo was at a distinct crossroads and needed absolute reinvention.

During his Master 11/2 Pinnacle, Theo felt a driving obsession toward personal growth and was drawn toward studying law. He got into law school and at the end of the 2nd Pinnacle (Master 11/2), Theo passed the Bar exam and started working as a lawyer.

At the beginning of his 3rd (and Main) Pinnacle—guided again by the 8!—he met the man of his dreams, got married, and he and his husband adopted a baby. And then adopted another. Given that he was brought up in the entertainment industry, Theo started out practicing entertainment law, yet soon realized that his heart and soul weren't in it. He slowly shifted his practice to specialize in family law with an emphasis in adoption for gay parents. He was able to use his connections and ties to high-powered people in the industry to support an organization he and his husband created to support and assist gay parents through the adoption process.

When a person repeats a number in the Pinnacle Cycles, I see this as an important indicator that they're here to dig into this subject matter and master this as their primary foundational environment. I see that people are prodded to up-level their expertise in the key components of the number they're repeating.

In Theo's case, he gets a repeated Pinnacle that's the rigorous 8. Interestingly, we can see that he had the full-spectrum 8 experience being born into a family of power, influence, money, and prestige. And while he enjoyed much that wealth can offer during that formative time, he also battled with the challenges related to the 8 Pinnacle—including over-indulging in drugs, alcohol, and lacked the personal drive to step into his own life. He rode his parents' coat tails and had to hit rock bottom before empowering himself to clean up his act and take his own life seriously.

During the 3rd Pinnacle (8), Theo used the spiritual growth he invested in during the 2nd Pinnacle and brought it in as his missing link to using the energy of the 8 Pinnacle in its highest and best formulation. During his 3rd Pinnacle, Theo came into his own, stepped into a powerful position as a lawyer, and began to follow his heart both in his personal life and his professional life.

As he begins his 4th Pinnacle (3), Theo is writing a book, is an expert who's called upon to speak at conferences, is often interviewed on podcasts, and enjoys playing guitar and writing songs with his two daughters.

The 3 Pinnacle promises a beautiful period of time supportive of all things creative and communication-focused.

As a 6 Life Path with a 6 Birth Day, Theo's life felt as though something was dormant if he wasn't in a committed, nurturing intimate relationship. When he married and had children, that aspect of his life's purpose was fulfilled. The 6 is also creative and justice-minded. Remember that Theo is a skilled musician and songwriter—as well as a lawyer! The 3 Expression/Destiny gives him performative and creative talent, and certainly it can't be overlooked that he spent a good portion of his life in the entertainment industry. Yet that wasn't enough to satisfy his ultimate longing to create a family.

Then he directed his legal specialty to help and guide gay parents in the adoption process, something that's completely in alignment with his 9 Maturity. With the 9 Maturity, there's a want and driving need to be of service to the greater good by using your skills and talents to assist, help, and heal on whatever level you're called toward.

In Theo's case, he has a heart-felt passion to use his power, knowledge, and influence to assist other gay parents successfully navigate the adoption process. This is a beautiful expression of everything he values and cares about.

By looking at Theo's example, you can see that there are countless ways to interpret and map a numerology profile. The more you practice with real people, the more fluent you'll get with how you process and apply the information.

CHALLENGE NUMBERS

Now that you know your Pinnacle Cycles, it's time to take a look at Challenge numbers. Knowing your Challenge numbers and understanding their meaning can open a window of understanding during each phase of your Pinnacles.

To know what you're up against is often half the battle of being able to fully embody your passionate purpose. Challenge numbers aren't meant to be *overcome*—rather they indicate what you must *become*.

The issue here is that when a number presents itself to you as a Challenge, it's bombarding you with the *destructive* aspects of that number while *simultaneously demanding that you operate in the constructive aspects of the number*.

We can also see the Challenge numbers as indicative of certain weaknesses we have that we're being asked to improve upon and turn into strengths.

Please keep in mind that this list is merely a glimpse of some of the *potential* extremes inherent to the Challenge number. The Challenge number by definition is confrontational. This number challenges you to overcome the opposing energies while becoming aligned with—and embodying—the constructive elements associated with a particular number. The Challenge numbers indicate specific areas where there are shortcomings in your character.

For instance, if you show a 4 Challenge number, you might not feel as though you want to get up early and seize the day, work hard, set up lasting systems for yourself, work through old family issues or concentrate on gaining as much knowledge as possible. You'll instead be challenged with the flip-side of the 4 energy and will more likely be compelled to sleep in late and go to bed late (with naps in between!), feel lazy mentally, physically, and spiritually—and refuse to see a bigger picture of your life.

That's why it's called your "Challenge," because the *challenging* energy entices you to stray from your more constructive purpose.

You can also opt for excess on the *other end* of the challenging aspects of the number 4, which might include overwork, feelings of limitation, exhaustion, and responding to life in a rigid manner.

When you know your Pinnacles and Challenges, you can become intimately knowledgeable about the particular themes you'll be working with during specific times in your life.

Some numerologists correlate the Pinnacle Cycles to occur simultaneously with the Challenge numbers, while other numerologists see the Pinnacles as separate cycles that aren't intimately connected with the Challenge numbers.

Again, you must trust your own judgment on this, yet for our purposes I'll connect the Pinnacles with the Challenges for ease and clarity. We'll also show the two different ways of calculating the numbers themselves, just like we did with the Pinnacles.

Notice how much difference there can be with when using subtraction rather than addition.

Numerologist Hans Decoz suggests that the Challenges are more fluid. Please reference *Numerology: A Complete Guide to Understanding and Using Your Numbers of Destiny* by Hans Decoz for a full explanation.

Otherwise, look at both the Pinnacles and the Challenges as running together in tandem. As you investigate your own Pinnacles and Challenges—and calculate the same for friends and family—you can make your own determination about how you feel the Challenges play into the time frame.

Also note that the 3rd Challenge is referred to as the Main Challenge.

This can be understood as a consistent energy infiltrating your existence throughout your life. This number is a key aspect to the world and environment in which you find yourself throughout your life. It's a central element and core subject matter in your life-school.

Here is how to calculate the Challenge numbers.

You must *subtract* numbers here rather than use addition.

Another funny thing you need to know is that there are no *negative* numbers in numerology, so you actually can subtract a larger number from a smaller number. If you subtract a 9 from a 2, for instance, what you end up with is a 7. If you subtract a 7 from a 3, what you end up with is a 4.

Also note that Master numbers are *reduced to their one-digit form* for the Challenge number calculation.

Here is the basic formula for finding your Challenge numbers.

1st Challenge	=	Day of Birth – Month of Birth
2nd Challenge	=	Year of Birth – Day of Birth
3rd Challenge	=	2nd Challenge – 1st Challenge
4th Challenge	=	Year of Birth – Month of Birth

Example:

November 22, 1985
November: 11; 1 + 1 = 2
Day: 22; 2 + 2 = 4
Year: 1985; 1 + 9 + 8 + 5 = 23; 2 + 3 = 5

1st Challenge:	(month) 2 – (day) 4 = 2
2nd Challenge:	(day) 4 – (year) 5 = 1
3rd Challenge:	(2nd Challenge) 1 – (1st Challenge) 2 = 1
4th Challenge:	(year) 5 – (month) 2 = 3

Here is the calculation if you use the second way to reveal the Challenge number. Remember, you're using the full value of the number instead of reducing it at the beginning.

1st Challenge: (month) 11 − (day) 22 = 11
Since 11 is a Master number, this is a final reduction.

2nd Challenge: (day) 22 − (year) 1985 = 1,963
1 + 9 + 6 + 3 = 19
1 + 9 = 10
1 + 0 = 1

3rd Challenge: (2nd Challenge) 11 − (First Challenge) 1 = 10
1 + 0 = 1

4th Challenge: (year) 1985 − (month) 11 = 1,974
1 + 9 + 7 + 4 = 21
2 + 1 = 3

Calculation when reducing first:

1st Challenge:	2
2nd Challenge:	1
3rd Challenge:	1
4th Challenge:	3

Calculation when using whole number:

1st Challenge:	11
2nd Challenge:	1
3rd Challenge:	1
4th Challenge:	3

Let's look at another example that might be more perplexing:

July 22, 1963
First way:
July: 7
Day: 22 (2 + 2 = 4)
Year: 1963 (1 + 9 + 6 + 3 = 19; 1 + 9 = 10; 1 + 0 = 1)

1st Challenge: (month) 7 − (day) 4 = 3
2nd Challenge: (day) 4 − (year) 1 = 3
3rd Challenge: (2nd Challenge) 3 − (1st Challenge) 3 = 0
4th Challenge: (year) 1 − (month) 7 = 6

Here's the calculation if you use the *second way* to reveal the Challenge number.

Remember you're using the full value of the number instead of reducing it down at the beginning. This is for the date July 22, 1963.

1st Challenge: (month) 7 − (day) 22 = 15
1 + 5 = 6

2nd Challenge: (day) 22 - (year) 1963 = 1,941
1 + 9 + 4 + 1 = 15
1 + 5 = 6

3rd Challenge: (2nd Challenge) 5 − (1st Challenge) 6 = 0

4th Challenge: (year) 1963 − (month) 7 = 1,965
1 + 9 + 5 + 6 = 21
2 + 1 = 3

This is just one example of how the result from the calculations can be completely different.

So, if July 22, 1963 were your birth date, you would need to choose the system of calculation that feels correct to you. If you're working with another person's chart, then you'll also need to be aware of the disparity that can happen with the different systems of reducing.

Always remember that you can choose the Master number if it shows up as an option no matter which system of calculation you choose.

Yet when you subtract with the original numbers (rather than the month/day/year already reduced) the results can be totally different from the first way of calculating.

In this example: July 22, 1963

Calculation when reducing first:

1st Challenge:	3
2nd Challenge:	3
3rd Challenge:	0
4th Challenge:	6

Calculation when using whole number:

1st Challenge:	6
2nd Challenge:	6
3rd Challenge:	0
4th Challenge:	3

You can see that the results for this person are quite different from each other! Again, this is where your own experience and feelings come into play. You must decide what system of calculation you prefer and feel is most accurate. *Personally, I use the first way of calculation.*

When you get different results, you'll be pressed to investigate why and how the results show up differently. I want you to be aware that your study of numerology is something that you gain mastery with over time—and that you also gain knowledge by practicing. Then you can truly determine your own beliefs and your personal way of working with this science and interpretive art.

CHALLENGE NUMBERS
REFERENCE GUIDE

1 — PRIMARY LESSON: INDEPENDENCE

CHALLENGES
You can experience situations demanding that you define and act upon your personal values, despite the overall consequences. You're required to stand on your own two feet.

OPPORTUNITIES
You'll learn to use your Will, step into self-confidence, and take the lead in your life in productive and assertive ways. This challenge offers many opportunities to step into leadership roles and act upon your unique ideas.

ISSUES
You might struggle with feeling intimidated by others, resulting in not standing up for yourself or alternatively, becoming too aggressive. Balance self-interest with the needs of others.

1 CHALLENGE

If the number 1 is a Challenge number, you're being called upon to *stand up for yourself, be true to yourself,* and *be self-reliant.* You're being called upon to step up to the plate and become a leader. This won't necessarily be a gift that falls into your lap. You'll need to cultivate leadership qualities, trust in your vision, and hone your people skills so you can be most effective in getting the job done. You'll be required to *embrace your weird* and capitalize on *quirky*.

During this time, you're likely to feel dominated by others in one way or another—professionally and in relationships. This feeling of being dominated might lead you to be competitive (and insecure), and you might experience an overwhelming sense of needing to achieve above all else. Your challenge lies in your ability to recognize when you're being pulled into this negative vortex and instead focus your energies on controlling the ego and keeping self-righteousness in check. You're learning about self-reliance and how to solve your own problems—and perhaps the problems of others—independently.

You need to cultivate your will power and intelligence, and cast tendencies toward argumentation and resentfulness aside. Cultivate confidence without defaulting to self-absorption or narcissism. This is a period where you'll come under fire by critics and detractors. The challenge is to securely stand on your own two feet. A default can be to be challenged with dependence, lack of ambition, fleeting initiative, and inability to take the lead.

CHALLENGE NUMBERS
REFERENCE GUIDE

2 — PRIMARY LESSON: SENSITIVITY

CHALLENGES
You can experience situations where you're overly concerned with the expectations of others. You try too hard to please and allow emotional sensitivity to overpower you.

OPPORTUNITIES
You'll learn to build your emotional and intuitive awareness in a way that has positive outcomes for you and for others. You develop depths of understanding and empathy for others.

ISSUES
You might struggle with repressing your own identity, thinking you're pleasing other people. You can default into fear, withdrawal, and lack of confidence in yourself. Too timid or too reactive.

2 CHALLENGE

This is one of the most common Challenge numbers because it revolves around *developing sensitivity to all human relations* and *developing a sense of seeing other peoples' points of view*. This is a lifelong challenge for all of us, yet when it's your Challenge number, it'll present with intense tests surrounding working with feelings of inadequacy, not standing up for yourself, and lack of self-confidence.

You'll be challenged with getting past basing your actions and decisions on what other people think or say about you. The challenge here is that you're being called to work with the energies of harmony, cooperation, and balance—and yet you're feeling none of this. Instead, you find it difficult to work with people because of your fear of criticism, or—*gasp*—of being ignored or under-valued.

You feel huge doses of self-doubt, lack of self-confidence, and there's always that nagging worry (sometimes tipping into paranoia) that other people are judging you. This would include cultivating your keen sensitivities as a strength, because you're so attuned to others and what they're feeling. You're faced with great difficulties in asserting yourself and making solid decisions. You might shy away from positions of responsibility and authority. You might lack ambition and feel innately insecure or unworthy. Your mantra for the 2 Challenge: *Don't take anything personally*. This is a time for slower, more deliberate growth, rather than seeking quick or immediate gain or results.

CHALLENGE NUMBERS
REFERENCE GUIDE

3 — PRIMARY LESSON: EXPRESSION

CHALLENGES
You can experience situations where you're debilitated by self-doubt and fear of criticism. The tendency can be to float by with superficial jokes, self-deprecation, and by denying your true emotions.

OPPORTUNITIES
You'll learn to trust yourself and your emotional life by using your energy to create - through art, writing, or any other creative outlet. You'll learn to speak your truth and allow others to do the same.

ISSUES
You might struggle with skimming the surface and lack the inner resources to express yourself. You may feel alone or caged within your own unexpressed inner world.

3 CHALLENGE

If you have a 3 Challenge, you're learning to identify your feelings and to communicate authentically. It's a time where you're learning and mastering one of the major teachings of the 3—your words have a profound impact on your life and on those around you. This is a period where you're deeply sensitive to criticism. The challenge resides in learning to take yourself and your feelings seriously. It may feel easier to use humor, pessimistic sarcasm or criticism to mask your feelings. Or perhaps your challenge will be in taking yourself *too* seriously.

Some of the tendencies that the number 3 brings with it are the propensities for superficiality, exaggeration, self-centeredness, moodiness, and scattered energy. What this Challenge is inviting you to do is use your creative energy to develop a positive, happy, loving, and inspirational spirit. Wasting 3 energy is like throwing away a priceless gift. It's the vibration of pure happiness.

You might feel the compulsion to do too many things at once during a 3 Challenge. Despite your heightened imagination and gift for words—both written and verbal—this challenge will knock you over with *blockages* when you want to express yourself effectively and honestly.

Instead of experiencing the optimistic energies the 3 has to offer, you'll instead be bombarded with the opposite. You'll struggle with feelings of negativity even to the point of becoming depressive, cynical, defensive, and reclusive. You may have a desire to practice your talents for writing, acting or speaking, yet you're reluctant to involve yourself with these activities because the thought of facing criticism is overwhelming. You turn to expressing yourself with a negative emphasis as cynicism or ruthless judgment, or you might hide your creative talents behind a façade of withdrawal and feelings of shyness. You're being called to develop and express yourself in a social and creative way.

CHALLENGE NUMBERS
REFERENCE GUIDE

4 — PRIMARY LESSON: ORGANIZATION

CHALLENGES

You can experience situations where the tendency is to be disorganized and lacking in drive and direction. You might feel you deserve things that you don't make a practical effort to create or earn.

OPPORTUNITIES

You'll learn to create attainable goals with a realistic view of life. Creating productive routines, order, and learning to be efficient are your golden opportunities for success.

ISSUES

You might struggle with having "pie in the sky" ideas that never come to fruition. It's your challenge to educate yourself, devise a solid plan, and move forward step-by-step. Results through effort bring rewards.

4 CHALLENGE

When you're met with a number 4 Challenge, you are *meant to learn about the value of discipline, organization, practicality, hard work,* and *frugality.* Take this to heart: This isn't an easy challenge. It's full of restrictions and limitations demanding that you learn how to succeed and work within these confines. It's also a time where you're challenged with learning to set your own personal boundaries with others, learning to temper impatience, stubbornness, narrow-mindedness, and self-righteousness.

With the 4 Challenge, you're being pulled to slow down, create a clear plan with obtainable goals, and then work tirelessly to achieve them. The 4 Challenge also suggests possible difficulty with work. Either you're challenged with not wanting to work, not liking the work you're "forced" to do or have problems completing tasks and working with efficiency. You may also exhibit tendencies to be careless and lack a sense of practicality.

With this number, it's difficult not only to focus on work and obligations, but equally as difficult even to see what the real issues surrounding work and obligations actually are. You might not feel that you're being lazy or undirected—you might feel you're just unlucky. Or make excuses about it. You get the idea.

With a 4 Challenge, it's vital to learn patience, understanding, and the practical and effective way to deal with what you might consider mundane responsibilities. You'll most likely also be challenged to learn the importance of working within the parameters of a time schedule, showing up on time and when you say you will, and managing downtime constructively.

CHALLENGE NUMBERS
REFERENCE GUIDE

5 — PRIMARY LESSON
STABILITY

CHALLENGES
You can experience situations where the tendency is to be impulsive and feel the need for personal freedom at any cost, leading to the inability to secure good outcomes. You'll do best not to run away when met with difficulties.

OPPORTUNITIES
You'll learn to create freedom through effort, focus, and follow-through. You'll seize opportunities by being flexible, adaptable, and forward-thinking. You can experience life to the fullest when you embrace change and exert self-discipline.

ISSUES
You might struggle with overindulgence and perhaps addictions that stand in your way. You can bounce from here to there, without positive output. Be more adventurous!

5 CHALLENGE

The challenge inherent in the 5 is that you'll feel highly charged. Think about how you've felt during the 5 Personal Years you've already lived through in your Personal Year Cycle. That's just a small glimpse of the feelings surrounding this longer segment of the challenging elements of the 5. Impatience, restlessness, and a relentless desire for personal freedom are at the core of this Challenge. This is *the* time to mindfully become free from limiting behaviors. The problem with that is that under this Challenge, being mindful is particularly hard.

With this Challenge, you'll find yourself being impulsive and unstable. You'll want to try everything at least once, so there's a chaotic and uncontrollable aspect to this energy. Change will be inevitable, yet it must be handled in a thoughtful, meaningful, and controlled manner. You'll be pulled toward evading responsibility rather than committing to healthy and constructive change.

All in all, this challenge requires that you learn, as early on as possible, to reign in reckless or irresponsible tendencies and to monitor your impulses. You can also be tested during this Challenge with inordinate amounts of fear, restriction or paranoia. The oppositional energy of the 5 can bring you a platter full of opportunities to break through fear by finding and establishing your (disciplined) freedom.

CHALLENGE NUMBERS
REFERENCE GUIDE

PRIMARY LESSON
ACCEPTANCE

CHALLENGES

You can experience situations where the tendency is to operate with a sense of crushing idealism. Often, nothing is good enough for you and you can't see the ways in which you stand in the way of your own satisfaction.

OPPORTUNITIES

You'll learn to understand the perfection of the imperfection of everything. You'll be able to feel appreciation for where people find themselves, while you can offer a helping hand or a kind word without judgment.

ISSUES

You might struggle with balancing a need for control with the reality of being of service, loving and giving, without making it dependent on your prescribed outcome. The call to service is part of this challenge.

6 CHALLENGE

When you experience a 6 Challenge, you'll feel burdened or overwhelmed by family obligations. You're learning to serve others and strike a balance between honoring your commitments to them with your commitments to yourself. This is no small task. Even if you're able to achieve some semblance of balanced self-care, you can't and shouldn't try to avoid caring for others under the influence of a 6 Challenge.

If you're operating with the destructive tendencies of the 6 Challenge, you may be myopically self-centered rather than generous and giving. This Challenge is often related to the energy of codependency, enmeshment, and giving for misguided reasons. You're prone to demanding extraordinarily high standards from other people and of yourself, which is in itself a setup for frustration and unhappiness. If leaning toward the challenges of the 6 energy, you're apt to come across as authoritarian, intolerant, and self-righteous. If you don't step back into the constructive aspects of the 6, your tendency during this time may be to get lodged in cynicism, criticism, and judgment.

Avoiding friction in relationships by emphasizing harmony, using diplomacy at every turn, and allowing others to set their own pace and live their own perfectly imperfect lives will be the key strategies for rising above the challenges of the 6. Ultimately, your challenge lies in learning, embracing, and practicing unconditional love and acceptance.

CHALLENGE NUMBERS
REFERENCE GUIDE

7 — PRIMARY LESSON
TRUST

CHALLENGES
You can experience situations that challenge your sense of belief and trust. You must overcome rejecting what can't be proven. There is skepticism about spiritual matters. You may cut off your connection with your intuition.

OPPORTUNITIES
You'll learn to move past the intellect and into the esoteric side of life. Faith in yourself and a higher sense of purpose is to be developed. There are chances to understand and practice humility and devote yourself to spiritual growth.

ISSUES
You struggle with repressing emotions and connection to spirit. You may isolate yourself or feel a vast sense of being alone in the world. Seeking a community where you explore your inner world is key.

7 CHALLENGE

The number 7 competes with the 4 in terms of the seriousness associated with its mission. While the 7 demands inner exploration, the chances of feeling alone and isolated are common. Contemplating the intricacies of life isn't mastered in a weekend seminar. Nor is it mastered in a lifetime. Yet that's the task you're being called to focus upon. Often there's a big test, serious repression or avoidance during a 7 Challenge.

The key lesson for a 7 Challenge is to understand that all your experiences—especially those that occur during this particular cycle—are fuel for your deep personal and spiritual growth. Develop trust in yourself. All that you experience during this period of life is meant to hone your powers of analysis and observation, intuition, and spirituality. You'll be asked to trust your analytic mind *and* your intuition.

During a period with a 7 Challenge, you'll be faced with difficulties brought on by your discomfort with your own inner thoughts and feelings. This could feel like detachment from people and situations or like tumultuous unexpressed and unresolved emotions. You might feel exasperated and helpless, as though you're a hapless victim of life who is unable to change or improve his or her situation or circumstances. There's also a strong tendency to chronically complain and criticize while offering no solutions to perceived problems.

The challenging aspects of the 7 Challenge might lead you to express in a negative manner. You may feel the impulse to avoid your feelings by putting up a wall of pride and aloofness. This is your opportunity to develop faith in your own abilities rather than to rely on the opinions of others or dwell on limitations.

CHALLENGE NUMBERS
REFERENCE GUIDE

8 | PRIMARY LESSON: EMPOWERMENT

CHALLENGES
You can experience situations that challenge your sense of personal and financial empowerment. Money is a priority, yet the tendency might be to make money the over-riding priority. Material desires need to be balanced.

OPPORTUNITIES
You'll learn to empower yourself on all levels. Using your influence, financial resources, and connections for the betterment of all is the golden opportunity. This is a powerful challenge opening doors to abundance, yet it takes effort.

ISSUES
You might struggle with money issues, legal issues, or other elements that test you to step up or get stepped on! Integrity, ethics, and giving back are the cornerstone to integrating this challenge successfully.

8 CHALLENGE

When the 8 is a Challenge, you're being called upon to think big, step up to the plate, and get it done. Achievement is expected during this period and so, of course, this will be the primary obstacle. People who experience an 8 Challenge either make it or break it—much in the same way that this happens with the 8 Life Path. It's a difficult Challenge, yet if you realize that you're supposed to be making money—*supposed to be successful*—perhaps you can shift out of the negative experiences and thoughts surrounding money and abundance. This could be the time of your life in which you experience your greatest financial success and highest levels of personal empowerment.

When in the groove, you're at the peak of both your financial and your spiritual abundance, because you'll be giving most generously. The destructive pull will be toward greed or self-absorption, and you'll believe that satisfaction can only be gained by accumulation and safeguarding. You might experience great difficulty and effort in your attempts to gain money, status and power—often to the exclusion of all else.

Family life and relationships suffer during this challenge since all your focus is on yourself and on your financial achievement (or lack thereof). You're being called to use your ability to earn money and acquire status and power with a sense of altruism and with a strict sense of ethics and philanthropy.

The caution here is to engage in all you do with authenticity—with ethics and honesty—and without greed and malice. If you lean toward the more destructive aspects of the 8, there will be a price to pay. The 8 Challenge also signals that you need to stop giving away your power. This can show up as severe levels of disempowerment overtaking you. Legal issues, addictive tendencies, and financial struggles can occur with an 8 Challenge. This is a period of development where you're being groomed to fully embrace your sense of personal empowerment and learn to empower others.

9 Challenge

There is no 9 Challenge.

CHALLENGE NUMBERS
REFERENCE GUIDE

 **PRIMARY LESSON: UNIVERSAL WISDOM**

CHALLENGES
You can experience situations that challenge the ability and desire to be of humanitarian service. This is the challenge of choice. It's all or nothing or all and nothing. There is a high level of responsibility with this challenge.

OPPORTUNITIES
You'll learn to devote yourself to selfless-service. You'll be given opportunities to clean up your thoughts and actions and focus on giving back with your individual gifts and talents. Extending yourself to something bigger than yourself is key.

ISSUES
You might struggle with resisting the call to share in the human experience and extend your empathy, compassion, and actions to be of service. Learning to be without prejudice or judgment is necessary.

0 CHALLENGE:

The Cipher Number

The 0 Challenge is called the Cipher Number. There is no 9 Challenge, therefore the 0 is representative of the 9. This number represents all or nothing—empty or full. You decide. This is the void. All or nothing or all *and* nothing. With this number, you are given a free pass, so to speak. Yet that free pass holds a heavier weight of responsibility. With great power comes even greater responsibility. You're being offered an enhanced dose of Free Will.

If you have a 0 Challenge, you can choose to amble idly along without a determined course or you can grab this profound opportunity to rise above your demons and achieve greatness. That is how powerful this energy can be. To meet the challenge of the 0, you must have some sense of mastery over the constructive aspects of all the other numbers.

The key is that you must keep humanitarian service front and center or this Challenge will derail you.

It's suggested that a person who has a 0 Challenge number on their journey is a well-traveled soul, so the 0 offers opportunities for the recipient to use his or her compilation of soul knowledge during his or her lifetime. There's great opportunity for expansion and growth under this Challenge. The obstacles faced during a 0 challenge may not be many or they may come at you from all directions. This is the "Challenge of Choice." Therefore, choice feels more confusing and difficult during this period.

The 0 challenges you to have the utmost faith in your own abilities to the extent that you can form a healthy sense of detachment with which you can analyze a situation, make a choice, and then act on that choice with ease and comfort—unconcerned and neutral in feeling regarding the outcome.

If you have a 0 Challenge in your life, it should not be taken lightly or cavalierly because with this Challenge, a decision must be made. We rarely make empowering choices by default. There is a lot of responsibility when you experience a 0 Challenge. Remember, this is the energy of the 9—selfless-service, humility, a humanitarian focus, and a giving heart are mandatory when working with the 0 Challenge. Use its energy wisely and fiercely.

NUMEROLOGY & RELATIONSHIPS

When we're incomplete, we're always searching for somebody to complete us. When, after a few years or a few months of a relationship, we find that we're still unfulfilled, we blame our partners and take up with somebody more promising. This can go on and on until we admit that while a partner can add sweet dimensions to our lives, we, each of us, are responsible for our own fulfillment. Nobody else can provide it for us, and to believe otherwise is to delude ourselves dangerously and to program for eventual failure every relationship we enter.

- Tom Robbins

When looking at relationships with numerology, it's vital to know the entire numerology profile and be familiar with the cycles each person is experiencing and has experienced in the past. We can look at the Life Path number as a starting point.

As you know by now, each number holds incredible potential. And each number holds challenges. The point is this: *There are both the upside and the downside to each of the numbers.* It all depends on how much you (or another person) are in alignment with the most healthy and expansive qualities of the Life Path mission. Or, how much you (or they) are acting on the more negative or destructive tendencies that come with the Life Path mission. Often, we are blocked in the key areas of our Life Path purpose!

Most people want to know why they aren't quite happy, why they find themselves in the same bad relationships again and again or why they do some of the same destructive things over and over again. When we look into the Life Path number, it'll let you know what your personal speed bumps look and feel like, what tendencies and obstacles you're bound to face over and over again until you acknowledge them and then begin to exert a certain mastery over them. Until we take ownership and responsibility for ourselves, we'll drive in the same rut in the road and continue to attract the same partnership dynamics.

It'll depend on your age, maturity, and how steadily you've been working on your personal evolution as to how you align with your Life Path information. It'll resonate differently when you're younger, when you're in middle age, and when you're older. Some issues you've worked through and mastered—some, *not so much!* Numerology teaches us that there are stages of development we all go through and we go through these stages for a reason—that reason is to challenge ourselves with circumstances that accelerate our ability to embrace and act upon our Life Path mission.

Given that relationship compatibility is something I'm asked about over and over again, I've decided to devote this section to how you might understand the Life Path numbers and basic propensities insofar as how they engage with other Life Path numbers in relationships. This can be intimate relationships or any other kind of relationship—friends, family, co-workers. This can be applied to business relationships and how you might operate within this important segment of your life.

I'm offering a brief profile for each Life Path in terms of how they might operate in relationships. Understand that this is a *basic guide* you can use to understand dynamics. As you learn to map all the core numbers in a numerology profile, you'll be able to extract even more depth and breadth of information with which to understand how you relate.

As we've discussed repeatedly, the full chart is the best way to get the full picture of a potential partner's complete profile, yet the Life Path is the obvious place to start.

Knowing numerology opens up the idea that we come to our lives to learn certain things and we have different levels of learning and different stages of development to traverse. People come in and out of our lives to assist us with our life's purpose—and we do the same for others.

I find it fascinating to work with couples and families. It's like we enter into family units like little dolphin pods. There are distinct dynamics that show up in families and we can begin to understand certain key themes that present within—and *represent*—the family as a whole. We can also often pin-point the "black sheep" of the family simply by comparing the numerology profiles of the family as a group.

When I read a person's numerology profile for intimate relationship compatibility, I focus on the Life Path and also on the Soul Urge to see how in alignment a couple might be. I also look at Pinnacle Cycles and the Maturity number to get a broader view on how a couple might grow and evolve together. Of course, the entire profile comes into play, yet I find these elements key to how I view possible compatibility.

RELEATIONSHIP COMPATIBILITY BY LIFE PATH

1 - If you are or are involved with a 1 Life Path: The 1 Life Path needs a cheerleader. They need praise and positive reinforcement. A 1 needs to be allowed plenty of processing/thinking time—just in general, yet also for dealing with relationship matters. The 1 Life Path is creative and needs to be encouraged to follow their unique vision. Since confidence is an ongoing issue for the 1, they need a relationship with someone who's in tune with their need for praise and supportive of their need for creative expression and calculated risk-taking.

Possible Red Flags: This person can have a temper. They're often in their head and tend to choose partners who aren't equals. A 1 Life Path is a natural leader, so (naturally) they need *followers*. On the downside, this person can be extremely self-focused and can develop a sense of dealing with people and situations with criticism and judgment. They can also have issues with co-dependency and addictive tendencies. This stems from a lack of self-confidence. This person needs to be #1.

WHY THE 1 LIFE PATH MIGHT PUSH LOVE AWAY

The 1 Life Path is here to get to *know yourself*. Really—from the ground up. You're the most self-focused of all the Life Path numbers because it's your mission in life to get to know yourself on every level. When it comes to love, the 1 often leans towards needing to be dominant and the one who's in charge in a relationship. While that might work for some, mostly it's a recipe for an unbalanced—and ultimately—unhealthy and rather immature dynamic.

You need someone who's your cheerleader, your support system, and who idolizes you. Yet because of this need, you often attract partners who are more like students and you take on more the role of the teacher. As soon as the student catches up with the teacher (and sometimes surpasses the teacher), well then, that's when the unraveling begins. The 1 is learning how to broaden the viewfinder and step outside of yourself and actually care about someone else in an unconditional way. The 1 can be fairly self-centered or self-focused.

The 1 Life Path can push love away simply by not having an awareness about other people's feelings and desires. Love can feel of secondary importance to you as you make your way in your work world and do what it takes to climb that ladder. You may distance yourself from love by doing the most oxymoronic thing—becoming the ultimate co-dependent.

Ultimately, your success in love resides in waking up to the fact that you need to partner with someone who's your equal financially, emotionally, spiritually, and in every other way. Only then will you understand how to co-create a thriving partnership. In relationship, it's not all about you all the time. You're such a dynamic presence and you can be an amazing partner when you step onto the playing field and toss the ball back and forth, so to speak. To continue with that metaphor, you're working at not hogging the ball all the time as the captain of the team! A reason why you might push love away? Insecurity mixed with self-focus.

And you might also step back and think of it this way. All the suggested ways you might push love away can also be how you feel on the receiving end of the relationships you've struggled with! Love might be pushed away by attracting people who want to control you, who prefer co-dependence or who have narcissistic tendencies.

The 1 Life Path's key to love? Put yourself in someone else's shoes, work at the give-and-take of partnership, and enjoy the pleasures and surprises that happen when you allow others to contribute their "stuff" to the relationship.

2 - If you are or are involved with a 2 Life Path: The 2 Life Path is someone you can count on! They're all about *love* and so being in a loving relationship is very important to them. They're super-emotionally sensitive, so be aware that they get their feelings hurt easily and they are also very much attuned to the emotions of others. They must have an arena to fully express themselves in their relationship with you or they'll shut down. They're givers who love to please. They're conflict-avoidant and can be great mediators. This person is often family and intimate partner-centered.

Possible Red Flags: This person can be co-dependent and a worrier. They also can be a champion micromanager. The 2 has a tendency to smother their partner. If working with the destructive aspects of their Life Path mission, they can be antagonistic and aggressive. They can over-give and then withdraw. They can hang on to old stuff with resentment, yet have trouble verbalizing their wants and needs. I've had many 2 Life Path's bemoan the fact that their own ambitions and desires have a tendency to fall away when they're in a relationship. The urge to merge is strong for the 2, yet needs individuation to be a healthy match.

WHY THE 2 LIFE PATH MIGHT PUSH LOVE AWAY

The 2 Life Path is the heart and soul of any partnership. *Two* is a couple, after all! You want and need a relationship to feel as though you're fulfilling your life's purpose. When it comes to love, here's the news for the 2. Since relationships are an integral part of your life's work, you'll get some test-runs in the love department.

The biggest obstacle for the 2 Life Path is an overweening sense of wanting to be what you think everyone wants you to be—whatever *that* might be. Most often, this is totally made up in your own head. You're the ultimate "I want you to want me" sorta' guy or gal. As a 2, you're *learning to define yourself*—not to rely on outside acknowledgement and approval from others. You can push love away by being emotionally hurt so early and so often that you project either a desperation or a tense aversion to entering into—and sustaining—a relationship.

The tendency is to immerse yourself in another person—to the point of smothering others or losing your own essence in the process. Ultimately, success in love resides in not mutating yourself to please others—yet rather by stepping into your own individual identity. Healthy emotional boundaries, anyone? Open and direct communication with a partner is crucial and yet often a very fearful path for the 2 Life Path to tread. A reason why the 2 might push love away? Wanting love to the point of desperation mixed with over-giving—then withdrawing with agitation.

And you might also step back and think of it this way. All the suggested ways you might push love away can also be how you feel on the receiving end of the relationships you've struggled with! Love might be pushed away by partnering with people who are childish and overly emotionally sensitive, who expect you to read their minds and then stonewall you (or who want to smother you), and who lack healthy boundaries.

The 2 Life Path's key to love? Enter into a relationship without wanting to fulfill your potential partners every need, just be yourself (warts and all!) and accept love and support—you don't have to be the one doing all the giving and sacrificing in a relationship.

Master 11/2 -
If you are or are involved with an 11/2 Life Path: Please read the descriptions for the 1 (and double it!) and then for the 2.

WHY THE 11/2 LIFE PATH MIGHT PUSH LOVE AWAY

When attempting to understand the Master 11/2, it's best to educate yourself on the 2 and also the 1—and double the energy of the 1. The 2 is the foundational energy you work with as an 11/2, yet you have a double dose of the opposing energy of the 1. What I will add here that is specific to the Master 11/2 as it pertains to pushing love away is this:

The Master 11/2 is a real handful! I say this lovingly, all you 11/2's out there.

As the pathway to spiritual illumination, yours is a constant striving for the perfect balance of yin and yang. Oftentimes, the 11/2 isn't the easiest to be in relationship with and here's why—the Master numbers feel conflicted and have an underlying anxiety that can bleed over into relationships.

The 11/2 is relationship-focused (the 2) and yet also wants independence, success, and glory in the outer world. There can be a real push/pull with the Master 11/2 that can, in simple terms, translate into being a supportive partner—which can include being a parent. Yet you often feel as though you've given up a large part of yourself by not going after bigger things in your career or creative life. Or alternately, you can devote yourself to career or creative projects while your relationship life eludes you. I realize this can be an issue for people on a grand scale, yet for the Master 11/2, it's often a crucial issue.

The 11/2 can push relationships away by being too emotionally needy or manipulative, leaving a potential partner drained and confused. The 11/2 can opt out of relationships because they find them too confining and limiting. You're on the fast-track to learning how not to take things personally and to balance a fragile ego. Harmonize the way you emotionally connect, give to others, and stand up for yourself firmly yet lovingly.

3 - If you are or are involved with a 3 Life Path: The 3 Life Path is quite passionate. They're full of humor, emotionally expressive, and can be great fun to have by your side. They're joyful and caring. They truly need to be *heard* in a relationship, so you must be a good listener and really care about their inner emotional life. They can be somewhat dramatic. These folks can usually handle a crisis like a pro. They want physical and emotional intimacy and want life to be fun. The 3 wants to laugh and be treated as though you only have eyes for them.

Possible Red Flags: This person can be married to their projects rather than another person. They can also battle depression. The 3 can be scattered and *live for today* without planning for tomorrow. Since the 3 Life Path is a creative, they can rival the 5 Life Path with promiscuity and addictive tendencies. If they're still learning about their emotions, it's impossible to know what they're feeling because they'll never express it. Even when asked they won't really know how to tell you the depth of their feelings.

WHY THE 3 LIFE PATH MIGHT PUSH LOVE AWAY

The 3 Life Path is a master or mistress of all things expressive. When it comes to love, the 3 is full of passion and need intense engagement with an intimate partner. What could possibly go wrong, oh-3 Life Path? The 3 often attracts *takers* in life—partners who are more like projects—even though you don't consciously seek that out. If there's one thing you would like in a partner, it's that you're emotionally supported and heard. Yet the problem is that somehow you attract those who are (not consciously, mind you!) intent on dimming your light. The 3 can attract narcissists and the emotionally unavailable like flies to fly paper.

The 3 Life Path can push love away by either being emotionally self-indulgent or alternately emotionally withholding. You might expect others to read your mind and fulfill every emotional corner of your existence, which isn't humanly possible. Ultimately, your success in love resides in *becoming one* with your emotional life to such a degree that you open yourself to a partner who can be your wing-person across the board, without needing to be your absolute emotional caretaker.

The 3 can be so devoted to their projects and creative life that they might push love away because it just isn't a priority, even if they're not consciously aware of that. On the other end of the 3 spectrum, if you're a 3 Life Path who is chronically depressed or if you're a sarcastic cynical pessimist, this pushes love away all by itself. There are few people in the world who would willingly sign-up to be subjected to that kind of relationship. So rather than attracting the taker, you're the taker. An overall reason why the 3 Life Path might push love away? Emotional volatility mixed with deep emotional wounding and trauma.

And you might also step back and think of it this way. All the ways we've suggested you might push love away can also be how you feel on the receiving end of the relationships you have struggled with! Love might be pushed away by attracting people who are emotionally unavailable, who are depressive, and communicate negatively—or who are scattered and lack the ability to follow through with things.

The 3 Life Path's key to love? Don't dwell in undisciplined emotions, get support to work through emotional trauma, and make room for creative outlets.

4 - If you are or are involved with a 4 Life Path: The 4 Life Path needs respect for taking care of you and their loved ones—and pets! This person needs organization and order in their lives, so if you're messy or unreliable, that usually won't float. They're very direct in their communication—there's not a lot of nuances with a 4 Life Path. This person needs total honesty or it's over. The 4 can give you security if that's what you're after. They need a partner who can encourage them—*gently*—to take risks in their lives. They're naturally curious and avid learners. If you want someone to center and ground you, this is the one.

Possible Red Flags: This person's a rule-follower—yet sometimes the only rules they follow are their own! They can provoke arguments even while they're saying they never argue. They can get lost in the drudgery of work. They can be bossy and become rigid in their thinking. The word "stubborn" was invented for the 4 Life Path! The 4 can have family/emotional issues that can guide many of their life choices. If you want a partner who has an adventurous or wild streak, this relationship might not be for you.

WHY THE 4 LIFE PATH MIGHT PUSH LOVE AWAY

The 4 Life Path is meant to be Practical Polly or Practical Paul. You're detail oriented and work to establish a strong sense of security. In some ways, the 4 can lean toward being *all work and no play*. When it comes to love, you're often not particularly gregarious or risk-taking. Now remember, there are different ways that each number will express, yet this is the core of the energy of the 4. Ultimately, you need routine, security, and stability—and yet sometimes it eludes you!

I feel the need to throw out a few examples of 4 Life Paths, because I find that people pigeonhole the 4 as boring or predictable, and that's just not the case! Think about 4 Life Path's Quentin Tarantino, Brad Pitt, Jimmy Fallon, and Keanu Reeves. And Chelsea Handler, Oprah Winfrey, Kate Hudson, and Nicole Kidman. Boring? Stodgy? Predictable? I think not. Yet underneath it all, the 4 Life Path prefers something tried-and-true, whether it's between the sheets or with the daily routine. When in your game, the 4 is honest, trustworthy and loyal, and demands the same from anyone with whom you might share your bed and your life. Whether male or female, most often you take a dominant role in your relationship. You're the one who takes charge and sets down the rules of engagement.

The 4 Life Path can push love away by being emotionally distant or emotionally unavailable. Often this is based in a history of being hurt, abandoned or abused—which can be something you know about yourself consciously—and often think you've totally moved beyond. Often the 4 doesn't reflect inward enough to be open to engaging themselves in the therapeutic work necessary to understand their overall patterns of relationship engagement. Or more likely, this is something you don't understand about yourself because it can be a somewhat unconscious element of your life. You may know that you had a difficult time of it growing up, yet you're unaware of *how much* that pain or trauma actually impacts your relationship life in present time.

I've found that those with the 4 Life Path are truly here to create the family of their choosing—where you feel a sense of ultimate care, comfort, support, and security. Since that's something you're here to accomplish, sometimes it can feel like *mission impossible* to actually accomplish it. Either you attract those who force you to do the caretaking and the lion's share of the heavy lifting in the relationship or on the other end of the spectrum, you're the 4 who evades responsibility and pushes love away by not understanding how good you'd feel if you'd actually put down some roots, invite responsibility, and choose to commit to someone for the long haul.

Love can elude you because you can be practical rather than romantic and pragmatic rather than open to experimentation and spontaneity. The 4 can also wrestle with being too controlling. Relationships can become something that's part of your daily punch-list rather than a symbiotic alchemy between you and your partner. The 4 Life Path can be the ultimate realist, which can either create a more workaday approach to your love life or make you shy away from investing yourself in a relationship at all.

And let's not forget your stubborn streak! The 4 is known for being incredibly stubborn and has difficulty changing course emotionally or being open to new ways of thinking, new routines or just doing things differently than it's always been done. In this way, you can be left behind in the realm of relationship, left to slavishly adhere to some outdated and outmoded way of relating that doesn't serve you or a relationship in a happy and dynamic way. Often the 4 will go to his or her grave *needing to be right*, so much so that the 4 won't budge one iota in order to make a relationship work. An overall reason why you might push love away? Unresolved emotional wounds mixed with a need for control.

And you might also step back and think of it this way. All the suggested ways you might push love away can also be how you feel on the receiving end of the relationships you have struggled with! Love might be pushed away by attracting people who are stubborn and bossy, who either adhere too much to routine or those who have a lot of trouble with routine and structure or who are self-limiting and rigid in their approach to life. More likely, though, the relationship patterns fall more toward coupling with those who aren't the most responsible people and you end up taking up that slack.

The 4 Life Path's key to love? Be more flexible, play a little more, and get support to work through emotional trauma.

Master 22/4 - If you are or are involved with a 22/4 Life Path: When attempting to understand the Master 22/4, it's best to educate yourself on the 4 and also the 2—and double the energy of the 2. The 4 is the foundational energy you work with as a 22/4, yet you have a double dose of the opposing energy of the 2.

WHY THE 22/4 LIFE PATH MIGHT PUSH LOVE AWAY

The Master 22/4 is built for relationships, yet they can be hard-won. Oftentimes, the 22/4 isn't the easiest to be in relationship with and here's why: The Master numbers feel conflicted and have an underlying anxiety that can bleed over into relationships. The 22/4 is very relationship-focused (the 2) and yet also wants and needs to achieve something substantial in the outer world (the 4).

Why the 22/4 might push love away? Because the 22/4 can be more devoted to their career or individual pursuits and that leaves little room for the cultivation of intimate partnership. The 22/4 can push relationships away by not being aware of the emotional issues that need to be confronted and healed before a healthy relationship can be created.

The 22/4 Life Path's key to love? Learn not to limit yourself. Balance work and play. Be open to a relationship where you aren't the only one setting the ground rules!

5 - If you are or are involved with a 5 Life Path: The 5 Life Path needs *freedom*! This person's Mantra is: *"Don't fence me in!"* A 5 is the life of the party, loves to travel, and is the ultimate adventurer. The 5 is a highly attractive and energetic person. They need encouragement to complete one thing at a time before moving on to the next. They love eating great food, traveling—anything tactile. They're often adventurous sex partners who're sensual, intelligent, and exciting.

Possible Red Flags: This person needs their space and freedom—however *they* might define it. The 5 isn't likely to commit to a relationship early in life—yet if they do, there are a few blips along the way. They can be fiercely loyal to a partner later in life, as long as they can continue to have their independence and freedom. The 5 can be scattered and also sway between total dependence *on* you and total independence *from* you. Addictions can sometimes come into play, because the 5 is the master of escape. Be prepared for lots of emotional high-intensity.

WHY THE 5 LIFE PATH MIGHT PUSH LOVE AWAY

The 5 is built for sexual and sensual experiences, yet not necessarily for long-term monogamous relationships—at least not usually at the get-go. Before you react defensively to that, please know that this is *suggestive of tendencies*. I know 5's who've been married for years, yet they'll also tell you that it hasn't been easy. Of course, relationships in general are never easy, right? But overall, the 5 Life Path is usually a wild-child in the sexuality department.

Or alternately, the 5 can feel extremely restricted in this arena, yet the underlying desire is to get out there and experience all that the world—and a variety of partners—has to offer. Whether the 5 Life Path *acts* on those desires is up for grabs. Yours is the most sensual and sensuous of the Life Paths. You're here to experience all the sensual world has to offer—within certain perimeters!

When it comes to love, you're often the *easy come/easy go* kinda' guy or gal. Experience is the name of your game and so you're drawn to the unusual, if not the dramatic. Often the 5 Life Path is more about *quantity* rather than quality—meaning, you're apt to engage with sexual partners who are *sexual* partners rather than *relationship* partners. Not that you won't try out the usual or the traditional, yet it often won't hold your attention for long. Sometimes (not always!), the 5 Life Path can live by rather unorthodox or at least non-traditional sexual or relationship morés—open marriage, no belief in traditional marriage (read that as *no belief in monogamy*) or a host of other more creative or non-committal approaches to relationships. The 5 Life Path can be a serial monogamist—or someone who just loves to play the field.

You can push love away in various ways, yet here are the two primary issues. The first: You don't fully grasp the way you indulge yourself and quickly move on to the next adventure. Again, you're seeking stimulation, experience, and of all the Life Path numbers, can have an addictive quality about the next "thing," the next escape, the next high. The second: You can become involved and then hang on far after the shelf life is expired in a relationship. Yet this really drags you down. I find that 5s often have *one foot in and one foot out* as they tread through relationships.

You're a person who'll needs space and freedom. That often comes about early on as immersing in a relationship and then (metaphorically speaking) running out the back door at 3 a.m. while pulling your pants up. The 5 Life Path can have a habit of leaving more than your share of emotional collateral damage in your wake, even when you think you're being crystal clear about your non-committal or wavering status. A partner wants and needs for you to be fully *in* with a relationship and take full responsibility for yourself and your actions. This is a bit tough for the 5 Life Path to achieve. You tend to feel trapped, confined, and stifled even under the best of circumstances.

Love can elude you when you're unable to cope with the day-to-day realities that a true partnership brings to the table, where every moment isn't intensely engaged with your high level of self-focused standards. A reason why you might push love away? The need for unabashed freedom mixed with self-indulgence.

And you might also step back and think of it this way. All the suggested ways you might push love away can also be how you feel on the receiving end of the relationships you have struggled with! Love might be pushed away by attracting people who are sexually promiscuous, ambivalent about commitment, and who are fearful and self-indulgent. You might also attract those with heightened levels of addictive or controlling behaviors.

The 5 Life Path's key to love? Be clear about your desire (or lack of desire) for commitment, enjoy your many exploits and adventures knowing that once you've experienced a variety of liaisons and really want a long-term relationship, you're an incredible partner—it's a matter of making the decision that's what you want.

6 - If you are or are involved with a 6 Life Path: The 6 Life Path is the ultimate nurturer and is highly responsible. If you want a marriage partner who would be a ready, willing, and able parent, this is usually the one. This person needs to be in control, so know that about them. They're great at continuously putting out fires and sometimes feel lost if they aren't the one who's responsible for everything. These folks don't take criticism or outside suggestions very well. Always use praise and constructive criticism with a 6 Life Path. In their optimal, the 6 is a responsible, heart-felt, compassionate nurturer who's in it for the long haul.

Possible Red Flags: This person can idealize their partner at first and then become disappointed when reality sets in. They can be a perfectionist and self-righteous. They can become a martyr if they gravitate toward the destructive tendencies of the 6. On the darker side, they can be super-critical of their loved ones and quite difficult to partner with because they can never be satisfied.

WHY THE 6 LIFE PATH MIGHT PUSH LOVE AWAY

Of all the Life Path numbers, the 6 Life Path is meant for a life built on love and relationship. You go together like love and marriage—horse and carriage! When it comes to love, you're the cosmic parent and natural nurturer. Yet since that is a focal point for you, the 6 Life Path has a few hoops to jump through on the way to lasting and healthy partnerships. The 6 Life Path feels a vast void when not actively engaged in a relationship and you can find yourself *otherwise spoken for* earlier rather than later in life. You derive a distinct level of satisfaction when you're deeply ensconced as a couple. The *last choice* for your theme song would be "Love the One You're With." You only want to be with the one you love, period.

You can push love away when your unrealistic expectations and ideals about your partner reach out to crush them and—as a result—your relationship. The 6 Life Path has a bar that's so high in the love department that it can be *mission impossible* to please or satisfy you. You find the smallest (or the largest) of your partner's infractions unacceptable and then default to scathing judgment and harsh criticism. Understand that this stems from your own exceedingly high levels of expectations for your own behavior. You're a perfectionist, after all. While that's part of your charm and overall effectiveness in life, it can prove to be a toxin within your love life.

As a 6, you might default into the other realm of the mission of the 6, which is to avoid responsibility and detour around true commitment—at the same time, wondering why you feel there is something dormant in your life that you just can't put a finger on. Ultimately, you're meant to thrive in relationship. Yet if you're always over-burdened and sacrificing, this doesn't create a healthy and mutually respectful partnership. If you avoid going all in and committing yourself to a relationship, then that's a hurdle as well. A reason why you might push love away? Perfectionism mixed with unrealistic idealism.

And you might also step back and think of it this way. All the suggested ways you might push love away can also be how you feel on the receiving end of the relationships you've struggled with! Love might be pushed away by attracting people who are either too meddling and take on too much responsibility (or who are just the opposite—who are aloof and irresponsible), those who are critical and judgmental or who are controlling perfectionists.

The 6 Life Path's key to love? Supporting and nurturing others in a healthy and dynamic way, taking on responsibility in a happy and productive manner, and taking care of yourself as well and diligently as you take care of others.

Master 33/6 - If you are or are involved with a 33/6 Life Path:

When attempting to understand the Master 33/6, it's best to educate yourself on the 6 and also the 3—and double the energy of the 3. The 6 is the foundational energy you work with as a 33/6, yet you have a double dose of the opposing energy of the 3.

WHY THE 33/6 LIFE PATH MIGHT PUSH LOVE AWAY

The Master 33/6 is built for relationships, yet they can be difficult to balance. Oftentimes, the 33/6 isn't the easiest to be in relationship with and here's why: The Master numbers feel conflicted and have an underlying anxiety that can bleed over into relationships. The 33/6 is very relationship-focused (the 6) and yet also wants and needs to bring their artistry and creativity into the outer world through the double energy of the 3.

Why the 33/6 might push love away? Because the 33/6 can be more devoted to their career or individual pursuits and that leaves little room for the cultivation of intimate partnership. The 33/6 can push relationships away by being overly emotionally sensitive and somewhat controlling. This person can have heightened levels of control and perfectionism that can erode the fabric of healthy relationships.

The 6 Life Path's key to love? Learn to express—yet discipline—your emotions. Modulate and balance your over-the-top sense of responsibility. Be open to caring for yourself as much as you care for others.

7 - If you are or are involved with a 7 Life Path: The 7 Life Path is always seeking *the truth*—about the world, about themselves, about *everything*. They're really attractive because they have an air of mystery about them, don't they? This person needs a spiritual base or they'll flounder. If they haven't found this base, they can be superficial and might have addictive tendencies—anything to avoid the real issues at hand. If they've found their base, they're loyal and loving. These people have trust issues, so make sure you're honest, trustworthy, and true to a 7 Life Path. This person thrives in nature and needs processing time by themselves.

Possible Red Flags: The 7 needs isolated time alone. It's nothing against you personally. As long as you allow them downtime without fear or nagging them about it, they'll come back to you refreshed. This person is intuitive and also highly analytical. They have issues with trust and are working on being vulnerable and open. Often a 7—on the one hand—wants a relationship. And on the other hand, sometimes they don't. They enjoy time by themselves.

WHY THE 7 LIFE PATH MIGHT PUSH LOVE AWAY

Ah, the enigma that is you, oh-7 Life Path! The Seeker. The Spiritualist. The Analyst. The Perfectionist. The Skeptic. The Hermit. You're a smoldering mystery to others—and sometimes to yourself! When it comes to love, you're often kinda' into it and—then again—kinda' not. Let's be clear: You need your alone time, your processing time, and your unplugged time. Yet, that doesn't preclude a beautiful love partnership! It does point to the fact that levels of communication about your need for space need to be heightened when you're in a relationship.

Let's not forget your perfectionism and your heady intellect. You'd rather concentrate effort on doing whatever it is that's capturing your imagination than to take your head out of that etheric/analytical world and devote yourself to a relationship on *terra firma*. You can push love away when your intellect blocks out or overrides your heart or your emotions on a consistent basis.

In many ways, love is something that you desire on a more theoretical level. You're the analyst after all! It's as though you keep yourself one-step away from the actual experience and instead end up being halfway in and halfway out—part active participant, part passive observer. While sex and intimacy can play a prominent role for 7s, often this aspect of life takes a secondary position on your list of priorities. A reason why you might push love away? Over-intellectualizing mixed with detached judgment.

And you might also step back and think of it this way. All the suggested ways you might push love away can also be how you feel on the receiving end of the relationships you've struggled with! Love might be pushed away by attracting people who are emotionally detached, who are untrusting or untrustworthy or are unsure they really want to be in a committed relationship—or who are superficial and just skim the surface.

The 7 Life Path's key to love? You're connected to yourself in a way that invites a trusting relationship, you offer a depth of both emotional and spiritual connection with a partner, and you trust the flow of your life while also actively participating in it.

8 - If you are or are involved with an 8 Life Path: The 8 Life Path is all about money, power, and authority. It's no wonder you're attracted to an 8! They're usually magnetic and outgoing. These people like to present well and they like for their partner to shine. The image they present is important to them. This person can be highly romantic and yet also a workaholic. The 8 is intense and also intensely charming. You need to be able to support them when they need you—and back off when they don't. The key to their heart: Unquestioned support and the ability to make them laugh.

Possible Red Flags: The 8 can be blunt and opinionated. They're all about achievement and can be singularly focused on their career. They might see their relationships more in business terms rather than intimate terms. On the other hand, an 8 Life Path who's not yet stepped into their Life Path mission can be the ultimate victim, financially impoverished or simply lacking initiative.

WHY THE 8 LIFE PATH MIGHT PUSH LOVE AWAY

Intensity, thy name is 8 Life Path. Overall, your optimal expression is being at ease with financial abundance, using power and authority wisely and for the good of others, not dwelling in the negative or becoming a victim to circumstances. Ultimately, you're at your best abundantly giving of time, money, and influence to make the world a better place. Your personal mission is to develop abundance and empowerment in every aspect of your life.

When it comes to love, you're a *time is money* kind-of person and you think in business-like terms. You look for a partner who fulfills the role of the other half of your power couple and you often value someone who's physically attractive and who looks good on your arm. Let's face it, you're focused on work and career, so much so that your significant other can tend to feel neglected and overlooked, even though you're simply attempting to be a stellar provider. You have a need to control and that extends to relationships. You can be generous and yet tend to feel that money (or status) can be used as a substitute for one-on-one emotional engagement.

You can push love away by being overly controlling and fixated on power or dominance. Emotional availability can be a challenge because emotions are a secondary feature as you forge a path to material success. You have zero tolerance for anyone who crosses you, either in love or in business. You seek a relationship that can support and help you fulfill your goals in life and while you can offer support to a partner, your needs come first.

If you're challenged with the material abundance that's at the core of the 8 Life Path, love can materialize in a more dire way—with you in the role of the abused (or alternately you can play the role as the abuser). When you're disempowered, your relationship life can embody and exemplify your deepest shadows. A reason why you might push love away? Emotionally distant mixed with an unyielding need for power.

And you might also step back and think of it this way. All the ways we've suggested you might push love away can also be how you feel on the receiving end of the relationships you have struggled with! Love might be pushed away by attracting people who are dominating and controlling, who are workaholics or who are victimized and lacking power and initiative.

The 8 Life Path's key to love? As an 8, you shine when you embrace your power and yet allow some softness to come through! You're at your best when you can create a relationship that doesn't feel like a business partnership, where you share control, and allow yourself to be emotionally vulnerable.

9 - If you are or are involved with a 9 Life Path: The 9 Life Path has tons of charisma. This person is so attractive on many levels. They're a natural humanitarian and have a giving heart. These people are highly romantic and in the relationship department, they really need to be told what you want, what you like, and what to do to please you. They thrive with positive instructions. This person never asks for help, so they can be experiencing lots of problems and you might not even know it. You need to dig deeper with a 9 Life Path to get to the bottom of their real feelings.

Possible Red Flags: The 9 has a hard time asking for help and can have some heavy family issues. They can be fanatics on some level and have a difficult time letting go of all kinds of things—from past relationships to personal possessions. The 9 can have difficulty being in the present moment, so you might not always feel as though they're truly listening to you. They can have family, abandonment, and worthiness issues. On the darker side, they can live in a world created by their own bitterness and resentment about the past.

WHY THE 9 LIFE PATH MIGHT PUSH LOVE AWAY

The 9 Life Path is full of compassion and brimming with love. When it comes to relationships, the 9 is often a hopeless romantic with high ideals about love and about how intimacy should play out in their own world. The 9 Life Path is the ultimate giver and yet learning how to give *and* to receive, without conditions and without control. The 9 is actually highly emotional and yet can have trouble navigating personal emotions and the emotions of others.

You're learning to extract yourself from co-dependent relationships across the board—from family of origin to your intimate partner. Some 9s can be emotional hoarders—hanging on to the past as if you're grasping at a lifeboat while drowning. You're certainly at your best when you're moving with the flow rather than ensconced in old stories about the past and replaying old hurtful experiences.

You can push love away when you default into doing things your way without taking your partners desires into consideration. The irony here is that you're often over-doing in your relationship, yet it can be more in line with control and a lack of interest in listening and truly hearing what your partner has to say about their wants and needs. You can be the ultimate enabler, doing for others until you realize that you've created co-dependent leeches in your life.

You must let your guard down and ask for what you need because your needs aren't easily read by others—you have to ask for help. This is a hard one for the 9. You're learning how to allow yourself to be vulnerable. In relationship you want to please and also would love to be adored by your partner. Yet often love is only acceptable to you on your own terms and your terms only. The 9 Life Path can have blocks with relationships due to unrealistic romanticism mixed with enabling.

And you might also step back and think of it this way. All the ways we've suggested you might push love away can also be how you feel on the receiving end of the relationships you have struggled with. Love might be pushed away by attracting people who are arrogant and self-serving, who are co-dependent or master enablers or who have difficulty with emotional connection.

The 9 Life Path's key to love? You're at your highest and best when you allow yourself to ask for support—while also giving the same. Relationships thrive when you embrace the ebb and flow of life with open arms.

Natural Match, Compatible or a Challenge?

While there are no absolutes with relationship compatibility, there are ways to understand what numbers flow more easily with each other and what numbers might cause friction or misunderstandings. Who do you just naturally *get?* Who are you naturally in synch with and share a similar energetic imprint?

I calculated the numbers for my group of best girlfriends from high school and there were two 3's, a 6, and a 9! All natural matches. Numerologists work with relationship compatibility in many different ways and there are lots of ways of looking at compatibility.

Glynis McCants groups the numbers in a way I find useful (see *Glynis Has Your Number*), so I'll use her basic guidelines here. Some numerologists call the challenging numbers "toxic." I prefer to say that they're just a bigger challenge to you, that's all. Once you understand the main components to each number, you can begin to see why it might be a waste of time pursuing an intimate relationship with people whose numbers don't match up with yours.

Once again, keep in mind that the Life Path number is just *one* number in your full chart. If you're a good match according to your Life Path number, you also need to know the other key numbers that influence each of us. Your Life Path number might not be a match to someone else's and yet your *other* numbers line up perfectly. Or vice-versa.

Also keep in mind that sometimes you can match perfectly with a partner and it just doesn't work out. Or alternately, your numbers on paper look like a train-wreck and yet you and your partner have a happy, healthy, long-term relationship.

1, 5, 7 are mind numbers – always thinking

3, 6, 9 are creative numbers – always creating things

2, 4, 8 are business numbers – always taking care of business

2 in the business of creating loving relationships

4 in the business of creating stability and security

8 in the business of creating financial abundance

Numerologist Dr. Jordan observes that the 1, 5, and 7 are the "go-getters." These are the people who initiate and push things forward according to their own ground-rules.

Then the 2, 4, and 8 are considered to be the "carry-outers." These are the personalities who manage activity, modulate it, and keep the group working toward a common goal. These are the people who know what it takes on a practical level to get things accomplished.

Dr. Jordan considers the 3, 6, and 9 the "easy-takers." These are the folks who enjoy the finer things in life and feel that it's their destiny to have what they want. She sees that this person has the capacity to easily create substantial financial abundance by allowing others to help and support their intentions, projects, and goals. The 3, 6, and 9s are the creatives who can see a bigger picture to ultimate success and are most often aren't afraid of taking the detours that will lead them to success. They're more apt to have more of a comfort zone with stepping outside the lines and taking a non-linear path.

I find the number 2 and 6 gravitate toward each other because they both value home, family, and relationships.

The 3 and 5 gravitate toward each other because they are both energetic, youthful, and free-spirited.

The 3 and 9 often gravitate toward each other because they're highly creative and charismatic.

The 1 and 2 sometimes gravitate toward each other because they seek the yin to their yang—the 1 takes the lead and the 2 likes to follow.

Oddly, the 4 and 5 are often found together as a couple—at least for a while. If opposites attract, then that is the odd couple! The 4 values stability and the 5 values personal freedom.

The 4 and 7 often end up together. They both enjoy their solitude and are voracious learners. Plus, they meet in the middle in terms of emotional (dis)engagement.

The 1 and the 8 will often form an alliance, yet always with power struggles.

So, you can see how not all couplings must be *by the book* and yet knowing the numbers can highlight certain issues with a particular clarity and insight. How can we apply this information? Let's use a few examples. Remember, these are brush-strokes and suggestive of basic values, attitudes, and possible personality traits.

1 Life Path: Let's go directly to your challenging numbers. For you, those are the 4, 6, and 8. Why? Well, the 4 and the 6 are equally stubborn and need to be top dog. As a 1 who wants to have a similar amount of control, this usually won't fly for you. The 4 has difficulty taking risks—something you thrive upon if you're in your game as a 1. The 6 often prefers home-and-hearth, something that might not connect with you at your core, even though I have seen successful couples with the 1 and 6. The 8 would be more of a competitor with you, so that might not be a good match either. The 1/8 couple would have to be extremely communicative about their power dynamics.

2 Life Path: Challenges here are with the numbers 5 and 7. Why? The 2 is all about one-on-one partnerships. You're all about taking care of people, of serving the group, of getting it all done behind the scenes. The 5 is the *out-there* freedom seeker and isn't necessarily a good match because they need freedom and space to roam. You want a relationship that you can count on and one that's more predictable—and certainly you want a relationship that's less volatile. You want someone whose ultimate desire is to hang out at home with you! You usually won't get that with a 5. The 7 is also a number needing isolated time away from you and might not be able to attach emotionally with you in the way you require. You prefer a match with similar needs and values. The 5 and the 7 pose challenges to you in these basic ways.

3 Life Path: The numbers 4, 7, and 8 pose particular challenges for you. Why? The 4 is also a slower and more deliberate thinker. You as the 3? You think with lightning speed and slowing down your communication style for the more literal-minded 4 might drive you bonkers. The 4 is the process-oriented number who feels safe when they have a game plan and a bit of money in the savings account—not something you really focus on. In fact, you often live in the present moment without much of a plan for the future. This won't work for a 4 Life Path partner. You just don't get the number 7 because they tend to be more aloof and have trouble trusting. If anything, you trust too much and so you'll find it hard to *get* that this might be a core issue for a 7 Life Path mate—even though I've seen many partnerships between the 3 and 7 Life Path. Yet

I don't see these couplings running particularly smoothly. And the 8. The 8 might be attractive at first for you as a 3 Life Path. They're usually commanding and they appreciate your energy and attractiveness. Yet at the end of the day, as a 3 Life Path, you need someone who's a listener—where you feel heard on a profound emotional level. The 8 Life Path often can't be bothered with that kind of emotional connection. The 3 wants to be the priority—not second fiddle to their partner's business life. The 3 is all emotion while the 8 is all business.

4 Life Path: Your challenging numbers include the 1, 3, 5 and 9. Why? The 1 won't give you the respect you need for your analytical and systematic processes. They operate with creativity and opt for risk over security. Not only will that drive a 4 nuts, it'll give the 4 bleeding ulcers. You operate with *some* creativity, trumped by your foundation-building skills. The 3 is too flaky for you. You can become annoyed with their happy-go-lucky attitude and emotional ups-and-downs. The 5 is the anti-4! And the 9 can be a bit much for you as well, since they operate out of their creative mind and can be risk-takers. And let's face it, both the 4 and the 9 have certain family issues and putting you both in the same house might be overwhelming in that area of your lives.

5 Life Path: Challenges here are with the numbers 2, 4, and 6. Why? Because the 2, 4, and 6 have oppositional core values to yours. You're attracted to a free-wheeling lifestyle and have great difficulties settling in for the long-haul during your early years—and sometimes life-long. This is *not* the white-picket fence that many number 2's, 4's and 6's are after from the get-go. All the numbers that challenge you need a solid, steady, committed partner who has more of a tendency to envelope themselves in the "we" that a committed relationship brings with it. The number 5 is the freedom seeker and basks in the glow of the sensual side of life. Your core need for independence clash with the 2's need for devoted love, the 4's need for stability and security, and the 6's need to build a solid nest and a family.

6 Life Path: You find your biggest relationship challenges with the numbers 1, 5, and 7. Why? The 1 needs to be the leader in their lives and *you* need to be in control. Can you say *train wreck waiting to happen?* The 5 is the anti-you—so irresponsible and self-absorbed. You need and value being solid and responsible. The 5 wants none of that (or struggles with these traits)—another case of clashing core values. And the 7 is a mystery to you. They're always seeking, asking questions, and have troubles with trust. The 7 absolutely needs some isolated time alone and that might not float with you. You'd end up taking it personally. You're the responsible, nurturing, magnetic visionary who needs the support of a partner and you also want to be in control of—well, of everything!

7 Life Path: You have the highest number of challenging numbers, yet don't let that discourage you. You're a spiritual being and you're here on a mission. The challenges in relationships reside in this basic idea: You really want to be in a relationship—and yet underneath it all, you kind of *don't want* to be in a relationship. It's almost as simple as that. You'll find yourself challenged by these numbers: The 2 leaves you feeling smothered. You need time to yourself and that's a hard one for a 2 Life Path—they'll take that as rejection. The 3 is so open that you might find they step on your emotional toes in ways you don't even understand, yet it feels threatening or exasperating to you. The 7 Life Path is *learning* how to understand and embrace emotions. The 3 can just be *too much* for you. The 6 wants a life-mate, something you may or may not value in the same way as the 6. The 8 is always attractive at first, then won't provide you with the understanding and attention you want on a soul-level. The 9 can rub you the wrong way with their rebellious attitude. I feel compelled to add something here for you, 7 Life Path. Some 7's will rejoice in hearing that they're not innately set up for partnership in the same way that other Life Path's might. It gives a sense of relief—validation that you're not just crazy. You just prefer a different lifestyle. Yet also know that I often find that some 7's—particularly Life Path 16/7's—find themselves intimately involved in relationships much of their lives. The 7 Life Path contemplates and processes more than the average person and often comes to the conclusion that the price to pay in relationships is too high.

8 Life Path: Your challenging numbers are 1, 3, 7, and 9. Since you're usually dynamic and often successful, you're initially quite attractive. Your challenges might go like this: The 1 needs to be in charge and so do you. Don't think that'll fly for long—or if so, lots of communication about your respective roles needs to be openly negotiated. The 3 might be swept off their feet by you, yet your opinionated and blunt communication style will damage their fragile emotional sensitivity. The 7 needs their isolated time and they're working on their sense of higher purpose and spirituality. The 8 is all about mastering the material world and the 7's all about mastering the spiritual and intellectual worlds. The 9 Life Path tests your patience with their quirky personality and they'll challenge you within your need for control.

9 Life Path: You're the number of universal wisdom. You're a humanitarian at your core. Your challenging numbers are the 4, 7, and 8. Since you're so creative and often travel at your own speed, so to speak, you are at odds with the "slow and steady" risk avoiding 4. The 7 may annoy you because you walk parallel to each other and just never quite connect. The 7 has a hard time trusting—you have a hard time listening and truly tuning into another person. The 8 is usually all about money (or the lack thereof). The 9 Life Path can come up against some core issues related to money, power, and humanity when they're involved with an 8 Life Path.

This is just a brush stroke to create a picture of the basic components operating when investigating relationships through Life Path numbers. I'm always fascinated how people mix and match, and I want to emphasize the importance of analyzing the full numerology chart.

Also know that different experts see relationship compatibility differently. For instance, this is how Master numerologist Hans Decoz addresses relationship compatibility:

1 Life Path: Most compatible with the 3 and 5

2 Life Path: Most compatible with the 8 and 9

3 Life Path: Most compatible with the 5 and 7

4 Life Path: Avoid the 3 and 5 (the need for lasting solid relationship is stronger than any other number)

5 Life Path: Wide choice of partners, choose who's not predictable or demanding

6 Life Path: Most compatible with all numbers because of self-sacrificing tendencies

7 Life Path: Least likely to get married

8 Life Path: Most compatible with the 2 and 6

9 Life Path: Most challenged of all numbers when it comes to romance

You can see how Mr. Decoz categorizes the wants, needs, and basic tendencies of the numbers with a different interpretive style. *Always remember that numerology is both a science and an art.* As you learn the science, you then develop your own interpretive art as to how you put it all together.

When you look at couples with Life Path numbers that might appear to clash, perhaps their Life Path numbers are challenges—yet the rest of their chart is in alignment. And overall, I'll put money on the fact that these couples have done some major compromising and learning along the way. I did a reading for a woman who asked me about her husband. She's a 5 and he's a 4. I said that she must drive him crazy! Her eyes welled up with tears. When I told her why she challenged her husband, it was a huge relief to her. She could finally see the core themes for them as a couple. They struggled with exactly their core issues *via* their Life Paths—she wants freedom and spontaneity and he wants predictability and security. Yet for her, to have the veil lifted was a way for her to enter into conversation and an enlightened sense of compromise or understanding with her husband.

The intriguing thing about numerology is that it points to a person's innate value system. Any relationship counselor will tell you that in order to sustain a happy and healthy relationship it's vital to have matching values. This will sustain through life crises, health issues, loss, transition, and all the ups and downs that a long-term relationship demands.

The only way you'll attract the right person into your life is when you feel good about yourself, love yourself, and feel purposeful and happy just as you are. Only then will you attract the perfect complement to your life. Remember: We attract what we think we deserve. As a practical reminder, no matter how perfectly your numbers might match, you won't have a true love relationship if you or your partner is currently struggling with substance abuse, serious addictions or with mental illness.

To be clear, I feel that you can engage with a relationship partner who's actively in recovery for addictions or mental illness. Yet if a partner has serious addiction problems and/or mental health concerns and is unwilling to seek help and support, that's when a true co-creative relationship isn't possible. This goes for relationships with friends and family as well as with intimate partnerships.

Also remind yourself that you and a potential partner can have perfectly matching charts and yet it just doesn't work. I've seen partnerships with couple's whose charts looked totally incompatible and yet they were in happily committed relationships. When both you and your partner are operating in basic alignment with your Life Path purpose—this is when your relationship thrives and become deep, soulful, and intimate.

Relationships show up for a purpose and even when it doesn't last forever, it doesn't mean that it wasn't meant to be. Culturally, we have an extremely limited view about how relationships function. Think of it this way: Rather than "I had a failed marriage/relationship." Revision: "I had a successful marriage/relationship that ended." Our relationships are here to serve our growth and evolution.

HOW TO CONTINUE TO USE NUMEROLOGY AS A TOOL IN YOUR EVERYDAY LIFE

Personally, I've found that diving into the art and science of numerology contains levels of development, processing, digestion, and development. Most of us just want to know the basics and use that information as we need it. It's like those of us who enjoy astrology—and yet only know about our Sun Sign and Mercury Retrograde!

It's the same with numerology. Sometimes just knowing the Life Path number and Personal Year cycle is enough for many people. Yet when you get fired up about it, soaking in how the numbers show up in all aspects of our lives becomes a fascinating hobby—if not a mild obsession. There's always more depth to delve into and it takes a lifetime to practice and continue to hone your knowledge and abilities.

This is to say, this book outlines the basic components of a numerology profile and there's a vast amount more to learn if you chose to do so. There are other periods and cycles to consider, transits, planes of expression, bridge numbers, and all kinds of other detailed ways to dissect and get very specific about your profile. Often, you'll find yourself expanding out and exploring different areas of numerology that pique your interest. If this is you, take a look at the list of resources at the end of the book for some suggested reading that can begin to take your numerology prowess to the next level.

Like learning a new language, becoming proficient with numerology requires the same sort of desire and dedication. To become fluent, you must first master the basics and then practice, practice, and practice! As you do this, you'll become more sophisticated in your ability to see and feel how a profile works and what it might offer to a particular person. You'll gain vocabulary that allows you to apply meaning into the flow of a chart. As you speak with people about their experiences in relation to their numerology, you'll be able to frame how the numbers actually show up for different people under different circumstances.

Getting up close and personal with your numerology offers you the over-arching answer to life's oldest and most burning question: Why am I here? What am I supposed to be doing? Even more vital is the knowledge that what we came here to do is always going to be the most difficult or challenging thing for us to do. Yet knowing the themes to where our purpose—and our issues—reside is a magnificent step toward giving ourselves permission to focus on how to align with and act upon that purpose.

Numerology offers a deep level of guidance to show us how each number carries particular and definable traits and characteristics. While everyone engages these characteristics in a unique way, numerology lays the groundwork so that we can understand the underlying "operating system" each of us works with depending on the configuration of our core numbers in our numerology profile. We can apply this to all of our relationships—the relationship with ourselves, intimate partners, family members, friends, and colleagues.

3 KEYS TO UNLOCK YOUR PATH & PURPOSE

Here's what I observe to be true. There are three basic forces or questions that people find universal and pressing. I find this over and over again when people engage in any kind of group forum where we define and discuss the Life Path number or any other facet of numerology.

These three points of inquiry become the triad that people explore as they traverse their pathway to define, refine, and attempt to understand what the purpose of their life is all about.

IDENTITY

The first compelling force is *identity*. When people watch a video or view a post about their Life Path, they'll first and foremost assertively identify themselves. "This is *me!*" There's an urgent need to use the Life Path as a point of identification. Often people will assert themselves: "11 Life Path Aquarius w/8 Expression!" or whatever configuration they choose to share.

The point being, *numerology provides a starting point for purpose in the form of identity.* People want to feel seen, heard, and appreciated for who they *really* are. We want to anchor ourselves in an immutable and timeless feeling of purpose in the form of personal identity. I find that most of us—*deep down*—simply want to be seen, loved, and valued for who we are on an unconditional basis and on a soul level. Have you ever seen kids playing at the park or swimming in a pool? Most often, there's a constant flow of: *"Mom, Mom, Mom, Mom, look at me! Look! Look! Look at me!"* We eventually grow out of this need for incessant acknowledgment from our caretakers, yet the primal need for recognition and unconditional love itself never goes away.

A SENSE OF BEING SPECIAL

The second compelling force is the desire to have confirmation that we are *special*. People want to assert their identity and then have a sense of validation that they are indeed unique, special, and are on an important mission in this lifetime. Often, we get really sensitive or have an underlying urgency about this! People want details and depth around who they are *specifically* and about their own personal experience that proves that they're being called upon for a vital and extraordinary cause—that there's a very *specific thing* that they're supposed to be doing in order for fulfill their contract in this lifetime.

This is a driving force for those on the path of self-inquiry and spiritual growth. Philosophers (and others) throughout time have devoted themselves to these deeply-rooted questions. Why am I here? What's my purpose? How can I *know* what it is and be *sure* about what it is? Mostly, people turn to numerology to verify and validate *who they are* and to have some sense of clarification that they're *on the right path*.

Every religion and spiritual belief system innately addresses this concept. In most traditions, the concept of I AM is central to self-awareness and enlightenment. The levels of identity in our human form as they merge with the I AM of the soul is a concept that's paramount and universal. "I AM not the body, I AM not the mind, I AM not the emotions, I AM the soul." Yet this meaning, purpose, and passion plays out in layers as we navigate our basic forms of identity and purpose *as a human being*.

Each Life Path number offers a conduit to spiritual growth and enlightenment, just through different terrain. Astrologer Susan Miller asserts that "astrology reveals the condition, but you decide the outcome." The same can be said for numerology. Your numbers allow you to map the conditions on your pathway through life, therefore allowing you to be prepared for the terrain. Yet it's up to you if you even want to gas up the car and get on the road!

A DESIRE FOR ACKNOWLEDGMENT FOR ENDURING DIFFICULITES

This is an interesting aspect and the third compelling force. The thought process might look like this: This is *who* I am, this is *why* I'm that way—and now do I get bonus points for making it through all the pain, suffering, and difficulties life has brought to me? Can someone award me a gold star? Can someone verify that I'm doing well, that I'm not dropping the ball, and that I'm perhaps doing better with my difficulties than someone else might?

It's a rarity when someone doesn't feel as though they've lived an extremely difficult or at least challenging life. There's a deep, underlying need to make sense of the difficulty—and also glean some acknowledgement and admiration for what they've been through. Yet, as Brené Brown observes, everyone has a story that will bring you to your knees.

We reach a state of spiritual and personal maturity—and serenity—when we see that while our difficulties are certainly our difficulties, our experiences aren't unique only to us. All of us experience the death of a loved one and losses in terms of jobs, dreams, and relationships. We all have our hearts broken, our feelings hurt, and feel misunderstood. There can be abuses (extreme and subtle) and catastrophic events that befall us. Yes, many people endure extraordinary circumstances, undeniably so. Yet somewhat ironically, I've noticed that those people are rarely the ones calling out for pity or recognition as being special. In fact, quite the contrary.

If we use numerology to map our path and purpose in life, we can see how we enrolled in the "liberal arts college of the earth," where we're all here as students and the curriculum's set up to offer us a nibble of each of the major subjects: (1) independence and leadership; (2) diplomacy and patience; (3) creation and expression; (4) stability and hard-work; (5)

freedom and sex; (6) responsibility and family; (7) analysis and intuition; (8) money and power; and (9) selfless-service and humanitarianism. Each of us are required to take coursework offering the fundamentals of each of the core courses of study. Yet we come in having already chosen our Major—our Life Path.

If you take the basic narrative of your Life Script (that you filled out earlier in this book), you can then place that narrative into context by knowing the Universal Year, Personal Year, Pinnacle Cycles and Challenges. At this point, you have a detailed map of who you are, why you're here, and how you'll go about doing what you're here to do.

The beautiful thing is that you can have the identical name and identical birthdate as someone else, and yet your life is absolutely unique and one-of-a-kind. There is no other *you*, no matter what. You choose how to proceed on your path—where you might take a few detours, where you might go off-road, and where you decide to take a flight instead of a car! You might run out of gas on the way and be stranded in some unknown terrain until you can make your way to a gas station. Maybe your transmission falls apart, you blow a gasket or get a flat tire. Maybe you don't even have a car and instead decide to walk, bike, hitchhike, take a taxi or public transportation. In many ways, the metaphor of your mode of transportation can be seen as how you choose to use your physical vessel—your body, mind, emotions, and spirit.

Knowing your cycles with numerology helps derive meaning out of the family you were born into, the country or state you live in (or have lived in), jobs you've had, friends and relationships that have come and gone, and every other facet of how your life has unfolded and continues to unfold.

One of the final observations I would like to make is this. Everyone I've encountered who's drawn to a path of self-awareness and spiritual awakening often does so because of something extraordinarily difficult that happens in their lives. The death of someone they love. An accident or health crisis. An ego-busting job loss. A soul-crushing rejection or betrayal. Or something intensely dramatic can change things in an instant.

I have a friend who experienced a Tsunami, where her toddler daughter was swept out to sea and never found. Another friend was literally struck by lightning—and that was what ignited her abilities as a healer. I've connected with people who have had near death experiences, survived rape and incest, and who have lost people they love in dramatic and traumatic ways. As surreal as it is, people undergo extraordinary events that catapult them into absolute soul-centered reinvention. Sometimes it's a story that makes us say: "I wouldn't have believed it if I saw it in a movie!" Yet it happened to a real person who never thought anything so traumatic or dramatic could ever happen to them. *Then it happened.*

The ignition onto the spiritual pathway can arrive as a spontaneous revelation—some people wake up one day with an altered consciousness. Yet that's rare. Mostly, we careen onto our soul-seeking path through what we consider to be pain, suffering, and the absolute disintegration of ourselves, our world, and our identity as we know it when we're forced to deal with a personal crisis—or series of crises.

We begin urgently searching for alternative answers when the questions we're beginning to ask fall outside of a "normal" mode of inquiry. At these times, I find that people feel an intense and desperate need to find their *it*. What is *it—the thing* that I'm supposed to be doing with my life? Why did this happen? What am I meant for? What is my ultimate purpose? This is the biggest detour or pothole we come up against and this is something that numerology offers to us in its fullest and most dynamic formulation.

Let's say you're a kid and all you've ever wanted to be is a football player in the NFL (National Football League). Ever since you can remember, this is *it*—you're calling, what you know you're born to do. Let's say that through some miracle and defiance of the law of averages, you achieve this monumental goal. You even win two Super Bowls! The point is this: When do you retire? At the age of 36? Maybe 38? Perhaps even 30-years old if you sustain an injury. Does that mean that you're *done*? Since your *it* was playing in the NFL—*and you accomplished it*—is your purpose now complete and you're just taking up space in the cosmos without anything left to contribute? Are you finished? *No, you're not.* Even though this is a common problem with this type of limited thinking and often athletes, child actors, and others devolve and disintegrate when it's time to move their *it* into some other avenue.

Numerology outlines the key aspects of your *it* by providing the key elements and emotional states that you're seeking to embody and experience. Perhaps the boy who's *it* was to be a player in the NFL is a 1 Life Path and he can bridge his leadership abilities, independence, and incredible drive into a career where he takes his football experience and opens a restaurant, training facility or camp or maybe has an innovative idea that ends up becoming a company he starts. He could be a 4 Life Path who takes his tenacity, endurance, and work-ethic and applies that to another business or charity. If he's a 3 Life Path, he'll certainly find his *it* with sports broadcasting, podcasting, writing a book or with speaking engagements. We can go through all the Life Path's, yet you get the general idea. When we can get past thinking that there is *only one thing we're meant to be doing*, we can begin to breathe into ourselves and trust the flow of it all.

There's a great relief and something absolutely freeing in the knowledge that you've opted in with a particular purpose and also with a way to get there. Free Will is always at play—we can choose a million different ways to actually achieve what we set out to do. *There's never just one route to get there.* Using numerology to verify, validate, define, and refine your pathway and purpose through life is always at your fingertips. You're allowed to take as many course-correctives that you need to take along the road. Just make sure you enjoy the scenery, take a few breaks, stop for a picnic, enjoy the sunrise and sunset, and appreciate the way you're navigating your life's adventure.

RECOMMENDED RESOURCES

Felicia Bender - The Practical Numerologist Programs, Products, and Services

FeliciaBender.com

Felicia Bender. *Redesign Your Life: Using Numerology To Create The Wildly Optimal You* (FAB Enterprises, 2012)

____. *Master Numbers 11, 22, 33: The Ultimate Guide* (FAB Enterprises, 2018)

Numerology

Alana Fairchild. *Messages in the Numbers: The Universe is Talking To You* (Blue Angel Publishing, 2015) AlanaFairchild.com

Alan Oken. *Numerology Demystified* (Freedom, CA.: The Crossing Press, 1996). AlanOken.com

Dan Millman. *The Life You Were Born to Live: A Guide to Finding Your Life Purpose* (Novato, CA.: New World Library, 1993). PeacefulWarrior.com.

David A. Phillips. *The Complete Book of Numerology: Discovering the Inner Self* (Carlsbad, CA.: Hay House, 1992)

Dusty Bunker. *Numerology and Your Future: The Predictive Power of Numbers* (Red Feather Publishing, 2020) dustybunker.com

Faith Javane. *Master Numbers: Cycles of Divine Order* (Atglen, PA.: Whilford Press, 1988)

Glynis McCants. *Glynis Has Your Number: Discover What Life Has in Store for You Through the Power of Numerology* (New York: Hyperion, 2005) Numberslady.com

———. *Love by the Numbers: How to Find Great Love or Reignite the Love You Have Through the Power of Numerology* (Naperville, IL: Sourcebooks Casablanca, 2009)

Hans Decoz. *Numerology: Key to Your Inner Self* (New York: Perigee, 1994) Decoz.com

Julia Line. *The Numerology Workbook: Understanding and Using the Power of Numbers* (New York: Sterling Publishing, 1985)

Juno Jordan. *Your Right Action Number* (DeVorss & Company, 1979)

Juno Jordan and Helen Houston. *Your Name, Your Number, Your Destiny* (Newcastle Publishing Co., Inc., 1982)

Kay Lagerquist, Ph.D., and Lisa Lenard. *The Complete Idiot's Guide to Numerology: Release the Power of Spiritual Numerology in Your Life* (New York: Alpha Books, 2009). Numerology-Insights.com

Kevin Quinn Avery, D.Ms. *The Numbers of Life: The Hidden Power in Numerology* (Girard & Stewart, 1977)

Lloyd Strayhorn. *Numbers and You: A Numerology Guide for Everyday Living* (New York: Ballantine Books, 1997) lloyd-strayhorn.com

Lynn Buess. *The Heart of Numerology* (Light Technology Publishing, 2012) forevernumerology.com

Matthew Oliver Goodwin. *Numerology: The Complete Guide* (New Page Books, 1981)

Michael Brill. *Numerology for Decoding Behavior: Your Personal Numbers at Work, with Family, and in Relationships* (Rochester, VT.: Destiny Books, 2011). Awakener.com

___. *Numerology for Healing: Your Personal Numbers as the Key to a Healthier Life* (Rochester, VT.: Destiny Books, 2009).

Patricia Kirkman and Katherine A. Gleason. *The Complete Idiot's Guide: Numerology Workbook* (New York: Alpha Books, 2004). PatriciaKirkman.com and KatherineGleason.com

ABOUT THE AUTHOR

Felicia Bender. Ph.D. - The Practical Numerologist is devoted to helping people uncover their life's purpose—*and so much more*—with Numerology.

She is the author of *Redesign Your Life: Using Numerology To Create The Wildly Optimal You* and *Master Numbers 11, 22, 33: The Ultimate Guide*.

Felicia is the resident numerologist for AstroStyle.com and is featured in many media outlets.

FeliciaBender.com

Made in the USA
Middletown, DE
13 February 2024